THE WORD OF GOD IN HISTORY

A Course in Basic Bible Study

By

LOYAL R. RINGENBERG, M.A., Th.M.

Published by

THE HIGLEY PRESS
Butler, Indiana

To the memory of

my father

PETER RINGENBERG

who used to search the Scriptures with
me into the wee hours of the night

THE BOOK OUR MOTHERS READ

We search the world for truth. We cull
The good, the true, the beautiful,
From graven stone and written scroll,
And all old flower-fields of the soul;
And, weary seekers of the best,
We come back laden from our quest,
To find that all the sages said
Is in the book our mothers read.

—John Greenleaf Whittier

PREFACE

THE WORD OF GOD IN HISTORY is intended for use wherever a course in basic Bible Study is needed—for colleges and seminaries, teacher training classes, for mission schools, or for private Bible study.

What Is Basic Bible Study?

Basic Bible study begins with source materials, that is, with the Bible text itself, not with the conclusions of someone else who may have studied the Bible.

Basic Bible study is not an attempt to arrive at a finished interpretation of the Bible. Nor is it an attempt to deal, finally, with critical problems. As the words suggest, basic Bible study aims primarily to let the Bible speak for itself, to let it say all that it has to say, and to lead the student to give it a full hearing. The student may well withhold conclusions as to the meaning of many passages until he has had the advantage of a full survey of the Scriptures. The Scriptures, studied as a whole, often clear up the difficulty of particular passages. It takes the viewpoint of all Scripture to discover the design of the whole which God has intended.

Basic Bible study requires humility of the student. It permits no short-cut. He who would reach the truly higher levels of spiritual understanding must labor well on the lower level of Biblical content. It is this that will give solidity and authority in the classroom and in the pulpit. Such grounding in the truth is the source of genuine eloquence in preaching and teaching. But it is more. It taps the Rock from which spring eternal waters, and opens the way to heights and depths of wisdom not otherwise known to man.

Aim in Basic Bible Study

In basic Bible study the student **should make observation his main business.** Get acquainted with God by observing what he

v

has done, and by hearing what he has spoken. You are challenged to search God's word until you have found in it the key to an understanding of human history.

Church Leadership Calls for Basic Bible Study

While one may become a Christian through the indirect testimony and instruction of a parent, a catechist, a teacher or a minister, one who is himself to be a teacher or a minister should have a mind furnished with "first impressions" of the Scriptures. It will not do for him to say, "I believe this because my parents taught it to me," or "I am telling you what I learned from the catechism," or "This is true because it is our church creed," or "This is the theology of the school which I attended," or "This is what is being taught nowadays." He should be able to say, "Thus saith the Lord," and he should be able to do so intelligently.

Authority in the class room, in the pulpit, and on the mission field must be more than the parroting of second hand impressions. The strength of convictions necessary to convince an unbelieving world depends upon the effective exposure of the mind of the preacher and teacher to that Word which God has revealed.

Enjoyment of Basic Bible Study

While basic Bible study is essential in the preparation of the teacher and the minister, it is in itself the really enjoyable study procedure. The Bible yields its beauty, its design, and its transcendent grandeur to those who study it as it is. No work of art, in stone or in print, can reproduce the full spirit and glory of the Word. David exclaimed, "O how love I thy law!"

Suggestions for Successful Study

The forty-eight chapters of THE WORD OF GOD IN HISTORY may or may not constitute forty-eight lessons. The time needed to do the work of each chapter will vary with students. The Scripture **Reading Assignment** should always be done first. It is estimated that the average person can read the whole Bible through in 100 hours. That means that the average time needed to read the Scripture assignment of each chapter in THE WORD OF GOD IN HISTORY is about two hours. It is suggested that two additional hours be given to study the supplementary topics of each chapter.

If this amount of time cannot be spent on each chapter it may be well to divide each chapter into two or more lessons.

The **Historical Outline** in each chapter is intended as an aid to the discovery of the contents of the Bible text. In some chapters this outline includes very full details as, for example, in the study of the book of Deuteronomy. A long outline does not make the study of a book longer. It is quite the opposite. It gives the student a quick perspective of the subject matter of the book. Remember, the purpose of basic Bible study is **to observe**; the outlines help the reader to do this. The best way to overcome piecemeal and superficial reading of a text is to outline it.

The student is advised to check his study by the **Discussion and Review** questions at the close of each chapter. The questions, or some of them, may be assigned to particular members of the class for report during the class hour. Or, if preferred, some questions may be selected for discussion by the teacher with the class. Time will probably not permit a discussion of all **Discussion and Review** questions.

It is suggested that the pupil be permitted to choose one verse, or as many as may be decided upon, from the **Select Memory Passages** listed in each of the forty-eight chapters. In this way at the end of the course he will have a fine treasury of representative Scriptures stored away in memory.

The **Character Review** may be consulted before the reading assignment is begun so that the reader can be on the alert to become acquainted with all personages listed. A check can then be made at the close of the study. Ability to recall the characters in these lists will greatly assist one's memory of the history to which they belong.

The **Bibliography** at the close of each chapter is not intended to include all of the important reference works relating to the Bible. It includes a very select list which place at the hands of teacher and student materials which have proved of most use to the author in teaching courses in Bible survey. By use of these the text may be stepped up for class work which will challenge students of a more mature level.

Acknowledgements of the Author

As the author of THE WORD OF GOD IN HISTORY, I am under a debt of gratitude to more persons than can here be mentioned. To the Fort Wayne Bible College, where much of the technique and contents which make up this book were forged on the anvil of classroom instruction, I feel deep appreciation. For inspiration in earlier years and for historical materials given, appreciation is due to the late Professor Herbert S. Miller. For encouragements, suggestions, and criticisms, thanks go to President Safara A. Witmer of the present staff.

For the principles of interpretation learned in the classroom of Professor Howard T. Kuist of Princeton Theological Seminary, and through certain of his writings,[1] I shall never cease to be indebted. His emphasis upon observational reading of the Bible in advance of critical reading greatly strengthened my conviction that the most important factor in true religious education is the Word of God itself. True Bible interpretation, as one will remember it from Dr. Kuist's emphasis, is not a matter of what we do to the Bible but of what we let the Bible do to us.

For much helpful counsel and encouragement I wish to thank Dr. J. A. Huffman, President of the Winona Lake School of Theology, at Winona Lake, Indiana. For valuable help bearing upon the period of the Exile I am indebted to Dr. Edward J. Young of Westminister Theological Seminary at Philadelphia, Pennsylvania. For important guiding principles of interpretation I wish to acknowledge help received from Dr. Arnold C. Schultz of Northern Baptist Theological Seminary at Chicago, Illinois.

For reading the proofs, or portions of them, and for corrections and valuable suggestions sincere thanks go to Reverend Wilma Davis of Saint Augustine, Florida; to Professor Harold Freligh of the Missionary Training Institute at Nyack, New York; to Dr. Stephen Paine, President of Houghton College at Houghton, New York; to Professor Alice J. McMillen, instructor of Bible survey at Houghton College; to Professor W. B. Shunk, instructor of Bible Survey at Wheaton College, Wheaton, Illinois; and to Editor C. F. Yake of the Mennonite Publishing House at Scottdale, Pennsylvania.

Illustrations and maps throughout the text are the original productions of the author, but were drawn by Ralph Smith. The art work for the jacket, including the idea, is the contribution of Phyllis Brannen.

---

[1] Howard T. Kuist, *The Training of Men in the Christian Tradition*, (Richmond, Va.: Union Seminary Review, 1941).

Howard T. Kuist, *How to Enjoy the Bible*, (Richmond, Va.: John Knox Press).

For many long hours of typing and intelligent handling of details I am deeply indebted to Rhoda, my wife.

For the faults which my critics have failed to find full responsibility is mine.

Finally, special respect goes to Mr. Robert D. Higley, who, as a publisher, has had the vision to believe that the THE WORD of GOD IN HISTORY is the kind of basic text that Bible teachers need.

LOYAL R. RINGENBERG

CONTENTS

CONTENTS

PART FOUR

THE THEOCRATIC NATION

Page

PART FIVE

THE UNITED KINGDOM OF ISRAEL

PART SIX

THE DIVIDED KINGDOM—ISRAEL AND JUDAH

CONTENTS

PART SEVEN

GENTILE SUPREMACY

Page

PART NINE

CHRIST'S WITNESSES IN A WORLD MISSION

CONTENTS

ILLUSTRATIONS

MAPS

PART ONE

GENERAL INTRODUCTION

Chap'er 1

GOD'S WORD AND OUR BIBLE

1. How the Bible Came to Us

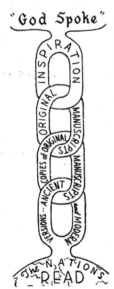

There was at the time of Christ a distinct body of literature known among the Jews as the Scriptures. Christ and the apostles rested their teachings upon the authority of these writings. They took great pains to demonstrate that the coming of the Christ and his Messianic ministry were according to the Scriptures. The literature to which they referred by the term Scriptures was essentially the same as our Old Testament. Classic New Testament passages establishing these Scriptures as the basis for Christian instruction are Luke 24:44-48; II Timothy 3:16-17; and Hebrews 1:1-3.

It is clear that the Bible is the record of what God has spoken through specially chosen human spokesmen. The Scriptures were written by prophets both to their own and to successive generations. The progressive forthspeakings of the prophets culminate in the Son. The New Testament Scriptures center in him; they are the report of qualified witnesses of what the Son said, did, and commanded to be taught. In their entirety, the Scriptures constitute a unified revelation; nothing essential is lacking and there is nothing superfluous. Perfect faith in God should result from such a revelation.

The full explanation as to when the Scriptures were written and as to how they came down to us in their present form would require a course in Biblical Introduction.[1] The main facts are so well established, however, that we are fully warranted in taking the Scriptures for what they claim to be. Without attempting a detailed account, it is of interest to follow the main facts in the chain of links which connect the Giver of the Scriptures with the present day reader.

Link One—Inspiration

Hebrews 1:1-3—"God, who at sundry times and in divers manners spake in time past unto the fathers by the prophets, Hath in these last days spoken unto us by his Son, whom he hath appointed heir of all things, by whom also he made the worlds; Who being the brightness of his glory, and the express image of his person, and upholding all things by the word of his power, when he had by himself purged our sins, sat down on the right hand of the Majesty on high."

II Timothy 3:16-17—"All scripture is given by inspiration of God, and is profitable for doctrine, for reproof, for correction, for instruction in righteousness: That the man of God may be perfect, throughly furnished unto all good works."

Link Two—Original Manuscripts

The Old Testament was written in Hebrew and Aramaic. The New Testament was written in Greek. All original manuscripts are lost. This has doubtless been best, else men might have attached a superstitious significance to them.

Link Three—Copies of the Original Manuscripts

These are sometimes called the "original text," but in reality they are copies of the originals. Several notable manuscripts (copies of originals) have been discovered. The growing science of archaeology opens up new possibilities of recovering more of these valuable documents.

Link Four—Versions

These are translations of ancient copies of originals, either from an older to a newer form of a language or into a different language. By way of the versions the word of God has come down to the peoples of our day.

---

[1] An excellent text, easily read, yet scholarly is: *General Introduction. From God to Us* by H. S. Miller. Word Bearer Press, Houghton, N. Y., Publisher.

GOD'S WRITTEN WORD

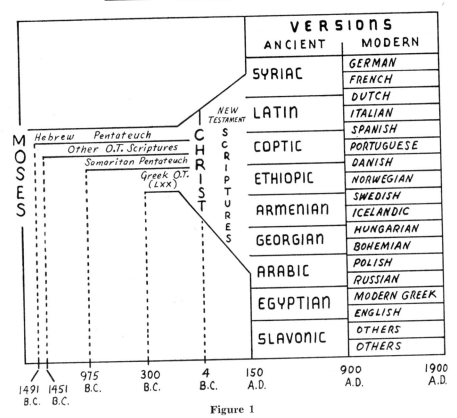

Figure 1

In 1790 A. D. less than a score of languages had the Bible. In 1804 the British and Foreign Bible Society was organized to promote the printing and translation of Bibles. At the end of a century The American Bible Society and other similar societies had been formed, and the number of languages with a Bible had grown to 446. In 1948 the American Bible Society reported that some part of the Bible had been published in 1108 languages. It is evident that we are now in the eventide of the Gospel day in which the word of God is to be given to all nations.[1]

[1] For a fascinating study of the history of the translation of the Bible into the main languages of the world, see *The Bible Throughout the World*, by R. Kilgour, published by the World Dominion Press, 156 Fifth Avenue, New York City. A similarly fascinating book is the title, *The Book of a Thousand*

2. The Time Perspective of Bible Writers

Figure 2 below shows the chronological view of things which the Bible, unaltered, is designed to impart to its readers. The Bible writers were men of this present world but they were also men of the eternal ages. Beginning where the Bible begins and closing where it closes, the human mind is given a satisfying perspective in reply to the questions which it raises, from the cradle to the

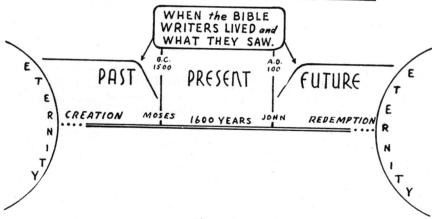

Figure 2

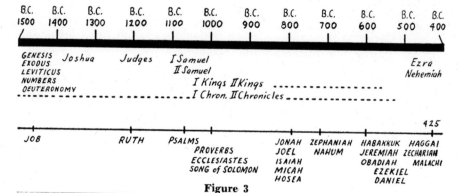

Figure 3

Tongues, by Eric C. North, published by the American Bible Society, 450 Park Ave., New York 22, New York.

TIME SETTING of NEW TESTAMENT WRITINGS

4 B.C.	30 A.D.	68 A.D.	100 A.D.
Matthew, Mark, Luke and the Acts			*John:* GOSPEL
	Paul's Letters (13)		
	Other Letters (6)		
			Letters (3)
			Revelation

Figure 4

grave. Apart from the testimony of the Bible, man in his limited view of history stands between two high walls—he cannot see backward and he cannot see forward. The Bible opens a window for him in each direction.

Figures 3 and 4 give the chronological basis for the study of Bible books. The general accuracy of these dates is all that needs to concern us. The diagram enables the student to see the point in history where he is studying. Reference to these figures as our study moves along from period to period will eventually develop a sense of time setting in connection with whatever Scripture is considered.

3. The World of Bible Times

It will pay the student well to get acquainted at the outset with the general features of the part of the world in which Bible scenes were set.[1] The way in which the Bible is tied up with actual geography is clear evidence of its historical character. Along with their view of the eternities the Bible writers constantly had their feet on some identifiable piece of earth.

Before any people inhabited the world the seas, mountain ranges, plains, and rivers were here. To a greater degree than is commonly realized these natural physical features determined the places where nations came to dwell, and the enterprises, habits and customs of these nations.

The important natural features to which attention should be given include the seas, mountains, rivers, and the lands. The Old

---

[1] A helpful work in Biblical geography will be found in *A Bible Atlas* by Jesse Lyman Hurlbut, published by Rand McNally and Company. In fulfilling the assignments of this topic see pages 1-6 and 13-16 of this atlas.

Testament World may be marked off on a world map by drawing a parallelogram with east and west boundaries at 30° and 54° east longitude and with north and south boundaries at 27° and 40° north latitude. Within this figure the student should be able to locate mentally the following seas:

1. The Caspian Sea
2. The Persian Gulf
3. The Red Sea (north part)
4. The   Mediterranean   (Great

Sea)
5. Dead Sea (Sea of the Plain)
6. Lake Van
7. Lake Urimiyeh

He should also form a mental picture of the location of the following mountain ranges:

1. The Ararat
2. The Caspian
3. The Zagros
4. The Lebanon
5. Mount Tauras

The following rivers are important:

1. The Araxes
2. The Tigris
3. The Euphrates
4. The Orontes
5. The Jordan
6. The Nile

The following lands are important:

1. Lands of the Mountain System: Armenia, Media, and Persia.

2. Lands of the Plain: Assyria, Elam, Mesopotamia, Chaldea, and Arabia.

3. Lands of the Mediterranean: Asia Minor, Syria, Palestine, The Wilderness (Shur, Paran, Sinai, and Sin), and Egypt.

Like a gem in the Old Testament world the land of Palestine is set. The interest of the Bible student will center in it from the twelfth chapter of Genesis to the last of Revelation.

4. The World's Textbook in Religion

The Creator in gracious providence has been the world's great teacher from earliest generations. He has not left himself without witness in the world. The eternal Word has been the "light which lighteth every man coming into the world" (John 1:9). In the created order the visible handiwork of God has never failed to speak of God's eternal power and godhead.[1] God sent his prophets in ages

---
[1] Rom. 1.

past through whom he made known special truth. Some of the utterances of the prophets have been recorded so that there is in our possession a knowledge of God's special revelation dating from the dawn of creation to the coming of the Son of God in the flesh.

No nation of history has been able, apart from the Bible, to produce the concept of a personal, spiritual God who is the absolute creator, sustainer, and redeemer of the world. Significantly, a pale copy of this concept may be seen in the backgrounds of all peoples; this speaks not of a source for present instruction, however, but of a smothered, flickering light, a light which is not presently expelling the darkness of men's minds.

The possession of such a text book as the Bible imposes upon one a certain obligation—an obligation to God, an obligation to oneself as the recipient of its knowledge, and an obligation to the race. It is an obligation to read intelligently, to yield to the truth learned, and to bear witness to the nations. Such an obligation is of course the occasion of delight for all who fulfill it.

5. Understanding the Word

The word of God is vital. It is living. When read and understood it is the greatest power that can enter the course of any nation's history. The original creation was produced by it. Men are made new by it. There is a sense in which God made all things in seven days; there is also a sense in which all things are being recreated by God. The Bible begins with creation and it ends with the new creation—new people, new heavens, and a new earth.

In the parable of the soils[1] the Lord pictured the varied power of the Word in human minds, depending upon their receptivity and their understanding of it. Evangelical Christianity depends for its spread in the world upon the intelligible presentation and the intelligent reception of the Word. Obviously, the purpose inherent in such an understanding is more than academic. Man should study to know God for God's sake, and he should learn his will in order to live by it. God's word in the life of man is intended to bring to fruition the highest purpose of the Creator.

As we noted in the early part of this chapter, the divine program of God's self-revelation is being extended to reach the nations. The spread of the knowledge of God and his kingdom as set forth

---

[1] Matt. 13.

in the Bible is vitally related to the new world order to be established at Christ's return. While now only individuals and scattered groups respond to the truth, the whole earth will then be lighted up. Said the prophet, "They shall not hurt nor destroy in all my holy mountain: for the earth shall be full of the knowledge of the LORD, as the waters cover the sea."[1]

6. Discussion and Review

1. Give the four steps by which the Bible has come from God to us.

2. Name the three versions of the Pentateuch which have come down from Old Testament Times.

3. Name the principal versions of the whole Bible up to 1000 A. D.

4. What do you observe that is hopeful in the history of Bible translations in modern times?

5. Over the span of how many years did the Bible writers live? What is the span of Old Testament writers? Of New Testament writers?

6. What three tenses were included in the perspective of Bible writers? What is the relation of time to eternity?

7. In how many minutes can you draw a map of the Old Testament world placing the seven prominent seas, the five important mountain ranges, and the six principal rivers?

8. In how many minutes can you draw a map of the Old Testament world placing the thirteen main lands?

9. What view of God belongs distinctly to the Bible? What three religions hold this view today?

10. Discuss the power of the word of God to create.

11. Show the relation between the Bible as God's word and the human faculty to understand.

12. Characterize basic Bible study.

13. Who should be concerned about basic Bible study?

14. Review: Trace the historical and prophetical aspects of revelation, showing how the Bible came down to us and pointing to the new world of prophecy.

7. Select Memory Passages

II Timothy 3:16-17; Hebrews 1:1-3; II Peter 1:21.

---
[1] Isa. 11:9.

8. Bibliography

Hurlbut, J. L. *Bible Atlas, Historical and Descriptive.* Chicago: Rand McNally
　& Co. pp. 1-6; 13-16.
Kenyon, Sir Frederick. *The Story of the Bible. A Popular Account of How It
　Came to Us.* New York: 1937.
Kuist, Howard T. *How to Enjoy the Bible.* Richmond, Va.: John Knox Press.
Kuist, Howard T. *The Training of Men in the Christian Tradition.* Richmond, Va.:
　Union Seminary Review, 1941.
Miller, H. S. *General Biblical Introduction, From God to Us,* Chap. I. Houghton,
　N. Y.: Word Bearer Press.
Orr, James. "The Bible," *The International Standard Bible Encyclopedia,* Vol.
　I, pp. 460-469.
Peloubet's Bible Dictionary. "Chronology" and Appendix.
Warfield, Benjamin J. "Revelation," *The International Bible Encyclopedia,* Vol.
　IV, pp. 2573-2582.

PART TWO

PRE-MOSAIC TIMES

PART TWO

PREMONSTRATENSES

Chapter 2

BIBLE LIGHT UPON THE
DAWN OF HUMAN HISTORY

The Antediluvian Era

1. Reading Assignment: Genesis 1-9.

(Read the Bible first)

2. Introduction—The Book of Origins

The first book of the Bible is called Genesis because it records the generations (beginnings) of things—of the worlds, of life on earth, of the human race, of sin, of religion, of the nations, and of redemption.

This book of beginnings covers the whole scope of what historians commonly call pre-historic times. It leads from those times into historic times. Strictly speaking, however, that which is pre-historic from the viewpoint of secular history is, from the viewpoint of the Bible, historic. Apart from the Bible, historians have been unable to trace a creditable history of things to their beginning. Because they have lacked the sources of information, they have had to leave us sorely unsatisfied. Genesis, however, is more than a human document. It has, under divine revelation, given us a chain of history from the beginning. While some skeptical historians have loudly denied this testimony, it has commended itself to the faith of millions of people in every generation. In recent times, moreover, scientists in the field of archaeology have

15

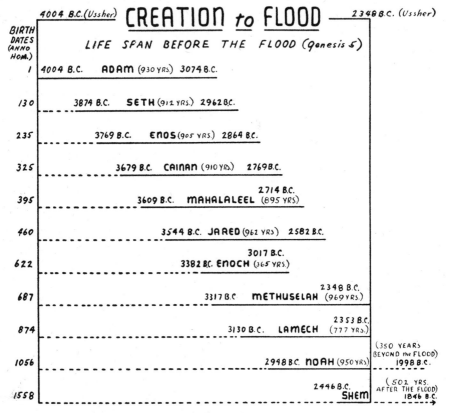

Figure 5

been digging up ancient sites so that even on the grounds of the secular historian, the Bible has been vindicated as to its historical reliability.

The difference between the Bible account of history and a secular account can be illustrated by a common experience. You enter a room where a motion-picture is showing a historical drama. You have missed the first half but you try to imagine what it was from what you see. There is very much of a jumble of characters and relationships. The plot of the whole can be only partly understood. You sit through, yet to the very end your mind is unrestful because you do not know the first half of the story. You are so concerned that you sit through a new showing of the film. Now you comprehend the plan of the drama and you are satisfied. Perhaps your guesses were partly true, yet you wanted them confirmed.

The history of the world is like a drama, less the element of fiction.   Apart from the Bible the important first half would have to be guesswork.   The Bible supplies the account of the world's beginnings and of the early history of man.   It unfolds a unifying purpose according to which history makes sense.   How thankful we should be that God saw to it that by special revelation the passing generations have had this unique account of the origin, the purpose, and the meaning of things.

3. Historical Outline

I. **How the Universe Came into Being (Gen. 1-2)**

1. Creation of the Heavens (A. R. V.) and the Earth (1:1)

2. Description of the Primordial Earth (1:2)

   (1) Void and without form (desolation and waste)

   (2) Darkness upon the face of the deep (abyss)

   (3) The Spirit of God moved (brooded) upon the face of the waters.

3. Days of Formation (1:3-31)

   (1) **The first day** (1:3-5)
   1) Light ordered; "it was good"
   2) Night and day ordained

   (2) **The second day** (1:6-8)
   1) A firmament (expanse, R. V.) ordered (vs. 6); made (vs. 7)
   2) The firmament c a l l e d "Heaven"

   (3) **The third day** (1:9-13)
   1) Separation of land and water ordered
   2) Water called seas: land called earth
   3) "It was good."
   4) Production ordered: grass, herb, fruit tree
   5) Principle of reproduction: "after his kind"
   6) "It was good."

   (4) **The fourth day** (1:14-19)
   1) Light holders ordered
   2) Their functions:
   a. To divide day from night
   b. For signs
   c. For seasons, days and years
   3) Three kinds of lights: sun, moon, stars
   4) "It was good."

   (5) **The fifth day** (1:20-23)
   1) Sea and air creatures ordered; created
   2) Principle of reproduction: "after his kind"
   3) "It was good."

   (6) **The sixth day** (1:24—2:1)
   1) Land creatures ordered (1:24); made (1:25)
   2) Principle of propagation: "after his kind"
   3) "It was good."
   4) Man ordered (1:26); created (1:27)
   5) Characteristics:
   a. Like God (1:27)
   b. God's earth ruler (1:26)
   c. A sexual being (1:27)
   6) God's mandate to man (1:28)
   a. Be fruitful
   b. Multiply
   c. Replenish and subdue the earth
   d. Rule the air, earth and sea creatures

4. How the Universe Came into Being

Three different answers are held regarding this question. The concept of evolution regards the present existing universe as the result of an eternal process of becoming. The concept of creation assumes the existence of an eternal God who at a given time brought the universe into being. Both of these concepts require faith, either in an eternal series of cause and effect or in an eternal creator. Unwilling to exercise faith, some hold another concept, which is that we cannot know (agnosticism) how the universe came into being.

The first concept has at least two illicit premises. First, it does not provide evidence for the belief in an eternal series; obviously such a series cannot be comprehended by the finite mind. Secondly, we have no links demonstrating that lower orders of being evolve into higher. There has been no case of dead matter becoming living matter. There has been no case of vegetable matter becoming animal matter. There has been no case of animals becoming human beings. In short, there is no historic demonstration of the evolution of species in the created order. In view of these deficiencies the concept of evolution has continued to be a very unsatisfactory answer to the question of the origin of the universe.

The second concept, that of creation, admittedly, cannot be fully demonstrated. Yet the basis for faith is perfect. The very created order—the heavens, the firmament, the marvelous harmony of things, the glory revealed by the manifestations of God through the prophets and through the Son—all of these are a convincing warrant for faith in a supreme Creator.

The concept of agnosticism has an element of truth in it. Of course what is created cannot fully comprehend the account of its creation any more than a babe can tell of its own birth. Yet when a babe matures in understanding it readily receives from its parents the knowledge of how it came into being. Agnosticism, while it seems to be very humble, is after all too dogmatic about its premise that nothing can be known about the origin of the universe. If the agnostic were more reasonable he would grant that the Creator might be expected to reveal the important facts of creation to men.

5. The Time of Creation

In modern times the theory of evolution has been stepped up to the status of accepted fact by many scholars. The concept has had an era of popularity during which it was customary to speak in terms of millions and billions of years in dealing with the antiquity of man. Obviously the dogmatic claims as to what took place in the universe during these millions of years is only guesswork. Yet guesswork offered as fact by men accredited as scientists can be powerful propaganda. Evolutionism has gone far to set aside the voice of God in history by placing its guesses in contradiction to the plain declarations of Scripture.

It is well to divide the question of the time of creation. When the universe was created was one thing (1:1-2). When the earth was set in order and furnished may have been another, so far as time is concerned. Notice that 1:1 speaks of the creation of the heavens (plural, A. R. V.) and the earth. Innumerable constellations were brought into being. Then the writer of Genesis reduces our focus to one little planet, the earth (1:2). It is described, not necessarily as chaotic, but as "desolate and waste," not having been adjusted to the light of other planets, and not having been developed according to any specific purpose. But the Spirit of God moved (brooded) upon it, awaiting the Creator's orders, by which it was to be made the inhabited cosmos that is pictured in the rest of the chapter. While all of these events are related as though they took place in prompt sequence, it is possible that great expanses of time may have been involved.

As to the time of the creation of man, however, we have more direct evidence. The ages of Adam and of his descendents are given in what clearly appears to be an unbroken lineage, from creation to the limits of historic times (Genesis 5, 10, 11). The margins of our Bibles record the date 4004 B. C. as the year of Adam's creation. This is what has commonly been called the "received" chronology,[1] and is the work of Archbishop Ussher. It is based upon the clear statements of the Hebrew text of the Pentateuch, and upon the assumption that there are no unrecorded generations. It should be recognized that the Septuagint and Samaritan versions lengthen the period to as much as 5411 B. C. The superior authority of the Hebrew text is generally recognized. Later chronologists have arrived at various dates for Adam's creation from these basic texts, ranging from 3500 B. C. to 7000 B. C. We know that Ussher's chronology is not entirely correct. It is convenient to use it, nevertheless, in the absence of any other commonly recognized system.

Though we consent to a division of the question of the time when the earth and man were created, there is no adequate easing of the tension between evolutionists and creationists by this division. Evolutionists have the habit of interpreting all natural processes on a uniform basis, and so long as this is the case they can not be expected to acknowledge the Genesis account of instantaneous creation, of either man or the earth, within the time allowable by any reasonable interpretation of Biblical language. The evolutionary geologist, for example, reasons that rock strata give us the calendar of the earth's existence. He proceeds upon the assumption that there has been a uniform ratio of development, making no allowance for unknown factors. The evolutionary astronomer reasons that the rate by which mass and energy in heavenly bodies

---

[1] *Note on the "Received Chronology."*

The Bible gives the only complete chronological data on the course of human history prior to the rise of the second Babylonian empire (Nebuchadnezzar, 7th century). It is futile to expect agreement among secular historians for the first three thousand years of human history because, apart from Biblical literature, they have no adequate source records. But it is in these early centuries that the Bible chronology is most specific and complete while the guesses of historians, depending upon non-Biblical sources, are the wildest. Whereas human histories of the world generally begin in a fog of mythological materials, the history of the Bible begins with declared facts of revelation.

Without neutralizing this positive appraisal of Biblical chronology, we would go on to disclaim complete accuracy for the set of dates which is known as the "received chronology" and which has found its way into the margins of our Bibles. While these dates are of value as a practical working basis they involve uncertainties and plain errors. The imperfections of the "received chronology" are traceable, not to the Biblical record but to the imperfections of such chronologists as Berosus of Babylon (4th century B. C.). It was Claudius Ptolemaeus (2nd century A. D.), whose works in astronomy provided

is observed to dissipate gives the key to the existence of heavenly bodies in past ages. In a similar way some anthropologists collect human skulls of various sizes and shapes, classify them, and assign the greatest age to the type most closely resembling manlike types of skull among present day apes. While such noted scientists as H. F. Osborn have declared the utter inadequacy of the evolutionary hypothesis as an explanation for the existence of things, the use of the hypothesis still continues widely.[1]

It will be well for the student of a basic course in Bible to do two things. 1. Let him recognize that science is very limited, that there are great gaps between facts, and that hypothesis is not fact. 2. On the other hand, the student should recognize that what God has revealed in Genesis is involved with mystery. God has not seen fit to fill in all the details nor to give all of the explanations. We do not know by what process, and by what time schedule, the worlds were brought into being. We do not know whether there were earlier orders of being on this earth than those which now inhabit it. We do not know all about the past

---

[1] H. F. Osborn, *The Origin and Evolution of Life,* (New York: Scribners, 1918).

the pattern for men of science until the time of Copernicus (16th century), who laid the foundations. mainly, for the "received chronology" of modern times. His "Canon of Persian Kings" has generally been relied upon to bridge the gap between New Testament times and the chronological chain of early human history as recorded in the Hebrew version of the Old Testament. Yet Ptolemy's canon has been disproved by Josephus of the first century A. D.; it has been contradicted by the Persian traditions preserved by Fidusi; and it has been disproved by the Jewish national traditions. Most significantly, Ptolemy's canons conflict with the Old Testament record itself. These facts should afford caution to Bible teachers who build intricate systems of prophecy based upon a time schedule. They should be sure that it is the Bible and not Ptolemy that they are building upon.

Dr. Martin Anstey, of England, in his extensive work in Biblical chronology, has demonstrated first of all the unreliable character of all dates given us by profane historians for the Persian period. He demonstrates, further, that modern systems of chronology based partly on the Bible and partly upon Ptolemy are bound to be more or less erroneous. He demonstrates further, however, that the prophet Daniel has given the distinctly Biblical continuation of Old Testament chronology. Daniel's seventy weeks (times or sevens), Dr. Anstey insists, are the only exact time chain connecting Old Testament chronology with the Messiah.

Our use of the "received chronology" should therefore proceed with reservations. We are sure, however, that the range of error is unimportant. Doubtless the chronology of human history lies somewhere in the approximate time compass of the "received chronology."

Students who wish to make a fuller study of Biblical chronology will find a fruitful source of help in *The Romance of Bible Chronology* by Martin Anstey published by Marshall Brothers, London. It is somewhat difficult to secure, but may be found in many of the larger theological libraries. The library of the University of Chicago has it.

history of the Tempter who appeared on the earth at the dawn of human history. We must refrain from making that which has been revealed to our limited understanding the measure of God's calendar in eternity.[2]

If God is to be reckoned with at all there will have to be faith. But if he is not reckoned with there is sure to be folly. Where he is fully reckoned with there is glory. Doubtless even in eternal ages, as God unfolds his wisdom to our developing faculties, our minds will continue to operate in a context of mystery. This is true simply because we will always be God's creatures and God will always be God.

6. How Sin Entered This World—Its Results

The first man, Adam, and his "helpmeet," Eve, stand at the beginning of human history with a clean slate. They were endowed with great prospects for good or evil. They lived in a perfect environment. Nevertheless, they were subject to the appeal and influence of evil. That they were subject to such appeal must not be understood as a defect in their original state; rather it was a necessary part of that liberty which qualified them for fellowship with God and for a place of honor and authority in the world. The historic origin of evil itself is involved with mystery, but it appears to have had its first inception in the mind of Lucifer (Ezek. 28; Isa. 14) who in the account of Genesis 3 is identified with the serpent. The real origin of evil, however, is a personal matter. Evil as it entered the lives of Adam and Eve, did so by their permission. It is true that they were deceived; but the deception was made possible only as they relinquished faith and obedience to God and espoused the appeal to selfish desire. Weighing the law of God against personal desire they chose the latter. This decision on the part of these first parents involved for them and their posterity separation from the ideal environment of Eden, and the curse of God upon the earth. Paul later said that God subjected man to vanity, with the purpose that man might be induced to find hope in the God whom he had set aside (Rom. 8:20). Prodigal man was to taste the beggarly diet of Satan's

---

[2] For a relevant and fascinating discussion of "carbon dating" as a method of establishing chronology see the article, *The New Deism*, by Edward J. Carrol in *His* magazine, December, 1951.

promises that he might be led to return to the sure word of the God of Paradise.

7. An Established Enmity

Genesis 3:15 contains the germ idea of Bible history. There are to be, said God, two seeds. The use of this figure is common to Scripture. "Seed" signifies progeny. The term is used also with reference to spiritual progeny. One may be born of God, or of the will of the flesh, or of the will of man, or of the will of the devil (John 1:12; 8:41-44). In a parable from Jesus, wheat signifies the children of the kingdom and tares signify the children of the wicked one (Matt. 13:36-43).

When Adam and Eve transferred their obedience from God to Satan they thereby became the children of Satan. Perhaps they were restored to the family of God through pardon and divine forgiveness. We are not told. It was made clear, however, that in their posterity there would be both children of Satan and devout children of God. These would be enemies. Ultimately the godly children of Eve would destroy the opposition, although the destruction would involve a wound upon the heel of the victorious deliverer.

It will be of much interest to trace the fulfillment of this promised righteous seed of the woman as we study the Bible further. Observe in 4:26 the distinction which came to be associated with the descendents of Seth. Observe also in 6:1-2 that the distinction had grown so that in the century before the Flood the godly seed were known as the Sons of God and these were distinguished from the "daughters of men." The intermixture of these was resisted ineffectually, by the Spirit of God. Eventually only one man and his family were free from the maelstrom of evil that had drawn away the Sons of God, and a righteous seed only was preserved from extinction. Observe that of the millions who lived in the antediluvian age the writer concerned himself with the genealogy of the line from Seth to Noah only.

8. The Moral History of the Antediluvian Era

Adam and Eve had three sons, Cain, Abel, and Seth, and "other sons and daughters." The writer of Genesis has recorded only a few of the names of the millions who must have lived during this

The MORAL HISTORY of MAN'S EARLIEST AGE
(GENESIS 4, 5, 6-9)

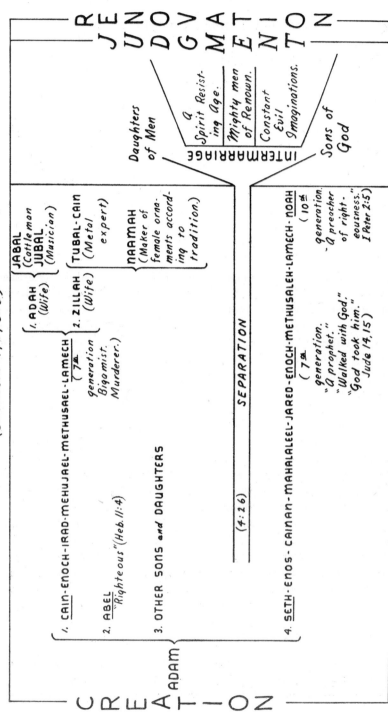

Figure 6

period of 1656 years (Ussher). Of the three older sons of the first family, Cain set the beginning of a course of evil, by spurious worship and by murder. Abel left the memory of a godly life; he was the first martyr. Seth, followed the godly example of Abel, and evidently passed to his posterity an inclination to serve God. In the time of Seth and his son Enos men began to call upon the name of the LORD (4:26), which led those who did so to be known eventually as the Sons of God (Chap. 6).

Lamech, the seventh descendant from Adam through Cain, was a bigamist and a murderer; his sons were magnates in their various earthly callings, while his daughter, according to tradition, was a promoter of female glamour. Lamech's family seems to have had a significant influence in the development of that age of renowned men and fair daughters.

Enoch, the seventh descendent from Adam through Seth, was a prophet of God (Jude 14, 15). He "walked with God," and God translated him without death. While men were generally becoming obsessed with worldly interests Enoch found his delight in God.

Noah preached righteousness (II Pet. 2:5) during a century in which lines of morality were all but faded out. Instead of seeing revival, he was destined to bear witness until apostasy had become nearly total in the world. As a preacher of righteousness he had the twofold message of judgment for the impenitent and salvation for those who would heed. The age closed in a dramatic climax of judgment and deliverance.

Noah's 370-Day Log Book

Year of Noah's Life	Month and Day		Events
600	2	17	The ark entered. Flood begins (7:11)
"	3	27	40 day rain. Ark floats (7:17)
"	7	17	150 days, including the 40; ark rests (8:3, 4)
"	10	1	Mountains visible (8:5)
"	11	11	Raven sent out (8:6, 7)
"	11	18	Dove sent out; returns (8:8, 9)
"	11	25	Dove sent out; returns with leaf (8:10, 11)
"	12	2	Dove sent out; returns no more (8:12)
601	1	1	Waters off the earth (8:13)
"	2	27	Earth is dry; Noah disembarks (8:14-19)

9. The Doctrine of Historical Uniformity

"All things continue as they were from the beginning" are the words of Peter in characterization of a latter-day delusion relating to the flood of Noah's day. This is known as the doctrine of uniformity which affirms, against all facts of history, that the cosmos as it is has resulted from a uniform development. Only such forces and processes which may now be found operating in nature are allowed as a basis of theorizing regarding the past.

It is of much interest that the doctrine of uniformity has in very recent times been amply contradicted on its own ground. Not only the Bible but the facts of history bear witness to the great flood.[1]

10.   Evidence of Racial Tradition

It may reasonably be expected that if there was a universal flood then those who survived would never forget the event, and every child would learn the story of it from his parents. Inasmuch as the book of Genesis was written possibly a thousand years later than the flood occurred we naturally inquire: Is there any record, outside of the Bible, of such an event? Ancient legends show that there is the account of this event in almost every national literature. To represent all of these accounts would expand this topic into a volume. Almost every one of the tribes of native Americans have well-authenticated myths of a universal deluge. In the mythologies of India, China, the Greeks, the Persians, the Egyptians, and the Chaldeans, the account of the flood is an integral part.

The following lines are Emerson's translation of a chant taken from an Indian myth:

"Long ago," they said, "came the powerful serpent when man had become evil.

The strong serpent was the foe of the beings, and they became embroiled, hating each other.

Then they fought and despoiled each other, and were not peaceful.

---

[1] The student will be rewarded by reading the recent works of Immanuel Velikovsky in which he gives a tremendous array of evidence gathered from a wide range of historical and traditional sources showing not only that there was a flood but also that the history of the cosmos has had many upheavals which have interrupted uniform development. His first work is *Worlds in Collision* and his second is *Ages in Chaos*. The second volume is to be followed by a third of the same title.

Then the strong serpent resolved all men and women to destroy
   immediately.
The black serpent monster brought the snake water rushing—
The wide waters rushing wide to the hills everywhere spread-
   ing, everywhere destroying.
At the island of the turtle was Manabozho, of men and beings
   the Grandfather.
Being born creeping, at turtle land he is ready to move and
   dwell.
Men and beings all go forth on the flood of waters, moving
   afloat everyway, seeking the back of the turtle.
The monsters of the sea were many, and destroyed some of
   them.
Then the daughter of a spirit helped them in a boat, and all joined
   saying, Come, help
Manabozho, of all beings, of men and turtles, the Grandfather.
All together, on the turtle, then, the men then altogether.
Much frightened, Manabozho prayed to the turtle that he would
   make all well again.
Then the waters ran off, it was dry on mountain and plain,
   and the great evil went elsewhere by the path of the cave."

The next lines are a portion of the Hindoo legend put to rhyme
by Dean Milman. Manu is represented as the mediator or representative between man and the gods. A great fish reveals to him
the impending judgment.

"When the awful time approaches—hear from me what thou
   must do:
In a little time, O blessed—all this firm and seated earth,
All that moves upon its surface—shall a deluge sweep away.
Near it comes, of all creation—the ablution day is near;
Therefore what I now fore-warn thee—may the highest weal
   secure.
All the fixed and all the moving—all that stirs, or stirreth not,
Lo, of all the time approaches—the tremendous time of doom.
Build thyself a ship, O Manu! strong with cables well prepared.
And thyself, the seven sages—mighty Manu, enter in.
All the living seeds of all things—by the Brahmas named of
   yore,

Place thou first within thy vessel—well secured, divided well,
From thy ship keep watch, O hermit—watch for me as I draw
    near;
On shall I swim before thee—by my horn thou'lt know me well.
This the word thou must well accomplish—I depart: fare thee
    well!
Over those tumultuous waters—none without mine aid can sail,
Doubt not thou, O lofty-minded—of my warning speech the
    truth.
To the fish thus, answered Manu—'all that thou requireth I
    will do.' "

We shall confine our quotations from these national legends to one more tradition, that of the Chaldeans. The quotation is from the narrative of Berossus.

"After the death of Ardates," says Berossus, "his son Xisuthrus succeeded, and reigned eighteen sari. In this time happened the great Deluge; the history of which is given in this manner. The Deity, Chronos, appeared to him in a vision and gave him notice that upon the fifteenth day of the month Daesius there would be a flood, by which mankind would be destroyed. He, therefore, enjoined him to commit to writing a history of the beginning procedure, and final conclusion of all things, down to the present term; and to bury these accounts securely at the city of the Sun at Sippara; and to build a vessel, and to take with him into it his friends and relations; and to convey on board everything necessary to sustain life, and to take in also all species of animals that either fly or rove upon the earth; and trust himself to the deep. Having asked the Deity, whither he was to sail, He was answered, "To the gods"; upon which he offered up a prayer for the good of mankind. And he obeyed the Divine admonition: and built a vessel five stadia (furlongs) in length, and in breadth two. Into this he put everything which he had got ready; and last of all conveyed into it his wife, children, and friends. After the flood had been upon the earth, and was in time abated, Xisuthrus sent out some birds from the vessel; which, not finding any food, nor any place to rest their feet, returned to him again. After an interval of some days, he sent them forth the second time; and they now returned with their feet tinged with mud. He made a trial a third time with these birds; but they returned to him no more; from whence he formed a judgment, that the surface of the earth was now above the waters. Having, therefore, made an opening in the vessel, and finding upon looking out, that the vessel was driven to the side of a mountain, he immediately quitted it, being attended by his wife, his daughter, and the pilot. Xisuthrus immediately paid his adoration to the earth; and having constructed an altar, offered sacrifices to the gods. These things being duly performed, both Xisuthrus and those who came out of the vessel with him disappeared. They, who remained in the vessel, finding that the others did not return, came out with many lamentations, and called continually on the name of Xisuthrus. Him they saw no more; but they could distinguish his voice in the air, and could hear him admonish them to pay due regard to the gods; and likewise inform them that it was upon account of his piety that he was translated to live with the gods; that his wife and daughter, with the pilot, had obtained the same honor. To this he added that he would have them make the best of their way to Babylonia, and search for the writings at Sippara, which were to be made known to all mankind; and that the place where they then were was the land of Armenia. The remainder, having heard these words, offered sacrifices to the gods; and taking a circuit, journeyed towards Babylonia.

"The vessel being thus stranded in Armenia, some part of it yet remains in the Corcryaen mountains in Armenia; and the people scrape off the bitumen, with which it had been outwardly coated, and make use of it by way of an alexipharmic and amulet. In this manner they returned to Babylon; and having found the writings at Sippara, they set about building cities, and erecting temples; and Babylon was thus inhabited again."

We would not attempt to harmonize the numerous traditions of the flood nor need we make an apology for the pagan coloring and the inaccuracies which are common to them. Our interest is to show that the flood is a fact of history for which there is a universal testimony.

The doctrine of uniformity is therefore, from the abundance of evidence available, seen to be a theory of the unlearned, of those who are willingly ignorant of a fact which they might know.

Further it is a doctrine that is calculated to lull into fatal slumber the generation of lust-loving people who are to live prior to the great universal judgment.

11. Discussion and Review

1. Give a suitable title for each of the first nine chapters of Genesis.

2. What are some things of which Genesis tells the beginning?

3. What may be said regarding the age of the universe? The age of the human race?

4. Enumerate the days of formation and tell what was accomplished on each day.

5. How did sin enter the world and with what results?

6. Characterize the descendants of Cain.

7. Characterize the descendents of Seth.

8. Name fourteen persons of this lesson about whom some fact of special interest is known.

9. Characterize the course of the moral history of the antediluvian race.

10. From your study of this lesson, state what is meant by the expression of our Lord, "As it was in the days of Noah" (Luke 17:26).

11. State the doctrine of uniformity and discuss it.

12. Discuss the significance of the evidences of a flood from racial tradition.

12. Vocabulary of Characters

Identify:

Abel	Lamech	Sons of God	Jabal
Adam	Enos	Noah	Tubal-cain
Adah	Cainan	Jared	Jubal
Cain	Enoch	Methusaleh	Zillah
Eve	Seth	Lamech	
	Daughters of Men	Naamah	

13. Select Memory Passages

Genesis 1:1; 1:2; 1:31; 3:15; 6:3.

14. Bibliography

Buswell, O. E. "Length of the Creative Days" in *Christian Faith and Life,* April 1935.

Flack. "God is not the Author of Confusion" in *Christian Faith and Life,* April 1933.

Free, Joseph P. *Archaeology and Bible History.* Chap. II, "Creation." Chap. III, "Early Civilization."

Green, William Henry. *The Unity of the Book of Genesis.* New York: 1910.

Huffman, Jasper A. *The Messianic Hope in Both Testaments.* Chap. I, "The Eclipse in Eden." Butler, Ind.: The Higley Press.

Huffman, Jasper A. *Voices from Rocks and Dust Heaps of Bible Lands.* Chap. IV, "Babylonian Stories of the Creation and the Fall." Chap. V, "The Babylonian Flood Story." Butler, Ind.: The Higley Press.

Kuyper, Abraham. *Women of the Old Testament.* Grand Rapids: Zondervan.
   1. "The Mother of Us All," pp. 5-8.
   2. "Ada and Zillah," pp. 9-12.

Mach, Edward. "Chronology of the Old Testament," *The International Standard Bible Encyclopedia,* Vol. I, 635-644b.

Marston, Sir Charles. *The Bible Comes Alive.* Chap. II "Archaeological Evidence for the Period from the Creation to Abraham." New York: Fleming H. Revell Co.

Miller, Dorothy Ruth. *A Handbook of Ancient History in Bible Light.* Chap. II, "The Origin and Antiquity of Man." New York: Fleming H. Revell Co.

Modern Science and the Christian Faith by Members of the American Scientific Affiliation. Chap. II, "Astronomy and the First Chapter of Genesis." Chap. III, "Geology and the Bible." Chap. IV, "Biology and Creation." Chicago: Van Kampen Press, 1948.

Nelson, Byron C. *After Its Kind.* Minneapolis: Augsburg Publishing House, 1948. (The first and last word regarding Evolution).

Nelson, Byron C. *Before Abraham.* Minneapolis: Augsburg Publishing House, 1948. (Prehistoric man in Bible light).

Ockenga, H. J. *"Have You Met These Women?"* Grand Rapids: Zondervan. Chapter VI. "The Woman who Turned Temptress."

Price, Ira M. "The Fallacy about the Time Values of the Fossils" in *Christian Faith and Life* magazine, April 1934.

Riley, W. B. *The Bible of the Expositor,* Vol. I. Chapt. II, "Do Genesis and Geology Agree?" pp. 27-48.

Sangster, Margaret E. *The Women of the Bible.* Chapt. II, "Adah and Zillah." New York: The Christian Herald.

Sangster, Margaret E. *The Women of the Bible.* Chapt. I, "Eve, the Mother of All Living." New York: The Christian Herald.

Tannehill. "The Chronology of Gen. V. and XI" in *Christian Faith and Life,* May, June, July, 1933.

Urquart. *New Biblical Guide,* Vol. I.
   1. "The Creation History," pp. 139-150.
   2. "The Chaldaean Genesis," pp. 152-166.

Young, Edward J. *An Introduction to the Old Testament.* Chap. II, "Genesis." Grand Rapids: Wm. B. Erdman. A study of the generations or beginnings of the book of Genesis with a scholarly treatment of special texts.

Wright, George Frederick. "The Deluge of Noah" *The International Standard Bible Encyclopedia.* Vol. II. 821-826.

Chapter 3

THE BEGINNINGS OF THE NATIONS

—From Noah to Abraham

1. Reading Assignment: Genesis 8:20—11:26

2. Collateral Reading: The Book of Job

(Read the Bible first)

3. Introduction

The importance of this chapter exceeds the length of the Scriptures with which it deals. The new beginning of the race after the Flood is marked by certain distinct features. God had revealed himself in judgment in such a way as to emphasize upon men's minds the peril of evil doing. On the other hand, this first family of the new world had received a most impressive experience of God's grace. Both of these aspects of God's nature entered into the covenant made with Noah. Noah, moreover, entered the new era in favor with God, and doubtless he passed on to his sons and to their families a sense of obligation to serve God. The fact of man's evil imagination, however, is not overlooked, and explains the widespread apostasy which eventually beset the new race and which left only occasional godly individuals, such as Abraham, who communed with God through faith.

Reference to the book of Job in this chapter is appropriate in view of the fact that this book has the marks of great antiquity. The setting of the book is clearly in the patriarchal age, there be-

32

ing no indications of such institutions as were established by Moses. Yet Job, in that early time, represents a disinterested piety which proves conclusively that godliness is not a matter of evolution, nor of advanced dispensations, but of personal faith and communion with God.

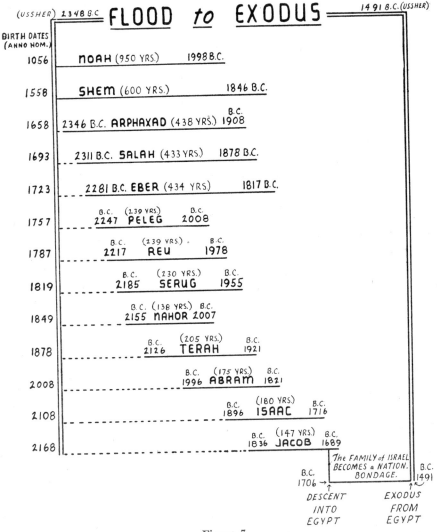

Figure 7

4. Historical Outline

I. **God's Covenant with Noah (Gen. 8:20—9:17)**
1. Favor with God through Sacrifice (8:20)
2. God's Pledge, Promise, Prohibition, and Token (8:20—9:17)

II. **A Prophetic Incident (Gen. 9:18-27)**
1. Regarding Canaan
2. Regarding Shem
3. Regarding Japheth

III. **The Progenitors of the New Race (Gen. 9:28—10:32)**
1. Noah the Racial Head (9:28—10:1)
2. The Sons of Japheth (10:2-5)
3. The Sons of Ham (10:6-20)
4. The Sons of Shem (10:21-31)

5. Summary Statement (10:32)

IV. **The Babel Incident — Dispersion (Gen. 11:1-9)**
1. Unity for Conspiracy
2. The Linguistic Deterrent
3. The Peoples Scattered

V. **Special Genealogy of Shem (11:10-26)**

VI. **Special Genealogy of Terah (11:27-32)**

Terah's Native City: Ur in Chaldea
Terah's Sons: Abram, Nahor, Haran
Haran's Son: Lot
Abram's Wife: Sarai
Nahor's Wife: Milcah

5. God's Covenant with the New Racial Head

The covenant of God with Noah is a document which belongs to the whole race. It was enacted as an expression of mercy on God's part in response to the true worship of Noah upon disembarking from the ark. Its first design was to free Noah's mind of the fear of another flood and to assure him that nature would thereafter be regular. In general, the covenant reaffirmed the status of headship over the creation to Noah, which had originally been assigned to Adam, and included the same divine purpose for the race to multiply, to be fruitful, and to replenish the earth. The rainbow was designated as God's perennial token of assurance to man.

Associated with the covenant is a negative feature. God did not overlook the potential existence of sin in the new world. He read the imaginations of the thoughts of men's hearts. He anticipated murder. In fact we may assume that he foreknew all of the bloody wars of history even to the World wars of our day. He therefore laid down a protective ordinance, authorizing men to penalize with death the person who would take the life of another. This particular ordinance may be understood to imply that God has vested in the social order the right to govern itself. Paul recognized this authority as applying to governments down to his day (Romans 13).

The Noahic covenant is thus in effect "while the earth remaineth." It is "an everlasting covenant between God and every living creature of all flesh that is upon the earth." As has been noted, however, the covenant itself provides for the punishment of evil doers, which doubtless includes the final overthrow, at Armageddon, of those who would destroy the earth.

6. What the New World Inherited from the Old

The race made a new beginning after the Flood. Yet it is important to recognize that through Noah and his sons an inheritance was transmitted which has left its traces upon all nations. There were matters of knowledge and there was a culture which enabled the new race to begin at a distinct advantage.

Figure 5 shows the chronological relationship of Noah and Shem to other persons before and after the Flood. Consider that Noah was contemporaneous with Methuselah for 600 years and that Methuselah had been contemporaneous with Adam for 246 years. Note also that Noah lived 350 years after the Flood, and that Shem, who had lived 98 years before the Flood lived 502 years after the Flood. Note that Noah died only two years before the birth of Abram. Shem was contemporaneous with Abram for 150 years and with Isaac for 50 years.

These facts make it abundantly clear that the new world was the heir by very direct links to all the knowledge of the antediluvian era. This is sufficient to explain the source of the various accounts of Creation and of Eden, which are found in the ancient writings of the peoples of the world. Though those accounts may be varied and inconsistent there is only one conclusion possible, which is that they point to historic facts regarding the origin and early history of the race such as the Bible clearly and consistently sets forth.

Industry and commerce had, evidently, greatly developed before the Flood. Already in the second generation of human history men began to specialize, Cain being a tiller of the soil and Abel a keeper of sheep. Later in the era, cattle raising, tent making, metal working, and the manufacture of musical instruments flourished. It is evident that the new world began in these skills at a hight point of advantage.

7. Noah's Prophecy of the Nations

In the incident of Noah's drunkenness we have something of a shock to our Christian standard. There is, however, nothing ex-

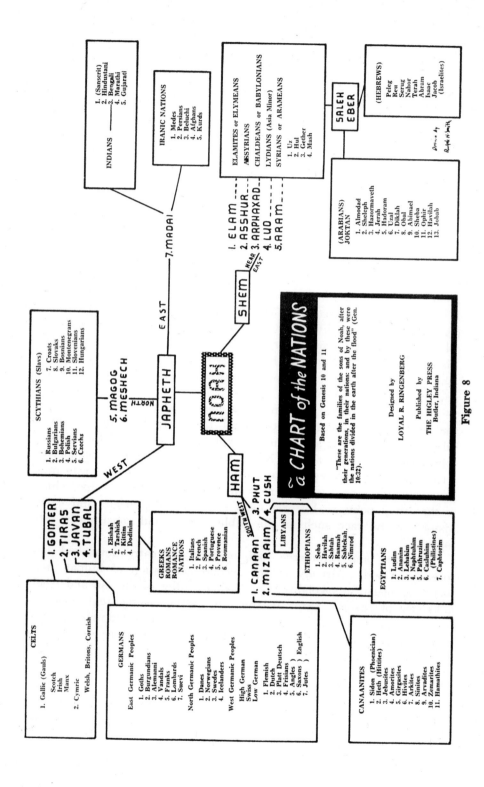

Figure 8

plicit in the Genesis account either in justification or in condemnation of Noah for this. The moral issue is not raised, yet we can easily observe that the affair led to what Noah by his own standards deemed to be immodesty.

Attention in the account is focused upon the unchaste attitude of Ham. Through prophetic gift Noah read from the character traits of his sons what the role of their descendants would be. Shem's descendants were to be blessed. God was to dwell in their tents, and the Canaanites (Hamites) were to be their servants. Enlargement was the trait which was to characterize Japheth.

Bishop Wm. G. Blaikie, speaking of the historic fulfillment of this prophecy, offers the following observation:

"In general terms, it may be said that most of Africa was peopled by the descendants of Ham; most of Central Asia by those of Shem; and most of Europe by those of Japheth. According to an Armenian tradition, Ham received the region of the blacks, Shem the region of the tawny, and Japheth the region of the ruddy. For a time some of Ham's descendants, particularly the Egyptians and Phoenicians, and the Cushite founders of Babylonia, were the foremost and most vigorous races of the world; but the period of their ascendency passed away: a great part of the Canaanites were subdued and destroyed by the Israelites; and even the Phoenicians, with their mighty daughter, Carthage, ultimately fell before their foes. Though the curse of Ham was formally pronounced on Canaan alone, it has been reflected more or less on other branches of his family; the black-skinned African became a synonym for weakness and degradation. The blessing of God rested very conspicuously upon Shem during the long period of Asiatic ascendency, and especially on the Jews—that branch of the Shemites that overpowered the Canaanites, and in whose tents God had his habitation, in the 'tabernacle of Mount Zion.' But the Shemites were a more stationary than a progressive race. In vigour, enterprise, and progressive power generally, the race of Japheth has excelled them all. For many an age the Japhethites were little known or heard of; they expended their energy in wild and warlike pursuits on the remote plains of Europe and Northern Asia. But for more than two thousand years they have been the dominant races of the world. Every year the race of Japheth spreads wider and wider over the globe; whole continents are peopled by him, and either as colonist or as trader, his foot rests upon every soil."[1]

8. The Tower of Babel

Genesis 11:1-9 records an incident which has had far reaching effects in history. Evidently Noah's descendants spoke the same language until this event took place. Some suppose that they spoke Hebrew, although there is very little evidence to prove it. It is conceded by linguistic experts, however, that common elements in the languages of the world point to a common parent language. The hand of God in this incident indicates that our present language barriers are not ideal, but yet a necessity arising out of the rebellious hearts of people. May it be supposed that when men cease their rebellion God will restore to them a common language?

It is very possible that the dispersion effected at Babel is referred to in Genesis 10:25. Eber was the ancestral head of Abraham and the descendants of the latter were accordingly known as Hebrews.

About six miles west of the modern town of Hillah, near the ancient site of Babylon, on the river Euphrates is a vast mound believed by a number of reputable scholars to be the actual Tower of Babel. Other scholars regard this mound as one of the **ziggurats** or staged towers of ancient Babylonia, probably of the same pattern as the Tower of Babel.

9. Ancient Empires of the Era

It is noteworthy that the history of imperialism began in the Hamite branch of the race (Genesis 10:6-12). Ham's grandson, Nimrod the son of Cush, is described as a "mighty one in the earth" who built a kingdom in the land of Shinar. He was the founder of Babel, Erech, Accad, and Calneh in Chaldea and of Ninevah, Rehoboth, Calah, and Resen in Assyria. Thus, in what are otherwise known as Semitic lands, the sons of Ham established the early Babylonian Empire.

The second great empire of the same period was promoted by Mizraim, another son of Ham. This empire centered in Egypt. Perhaps very soon after the dispersion at Babel the fertile banks of the Nile were discovered and the foundations of the early civilization

---

[1] Bible History, by William G. Blaikie. Thos. Nelson and Sons. Pp. 41-42.

of Egypt were laid. Manetho (250 B. C.) writes of thirty Egyptian dynasties. Much uncertainty still exists as to the early dynasties, as is also true of the early history of Babylonia. In both cases there are the indications of the greatest brilliance and of great strength in these pioneers of imperialism.

10. Religion in the New World

The history of the new race began with the clearest monotheism and with the purest worship, as is seen in the personal communion between Noah and God in connection with the Noahic covenant (Gen. 8:20-21). At the same time, however, we observe that sin existed potentially in the imaginations of men (8:21). Paul in writing to the Romans spoke of the time when the nations knew God, but followed in the same text to describe their departure from him (Romans 1). The history of the most ancient peoples gives us a picture of many gods whom men have made and whom they have invested with the attributes of deity; at the same time in all cases there is seen the existence also of the idea of a supreme being. Even the most benighted savages retain at the perimeter of their worship a certain regard for the supreme being who was known in the better times of their history.

Thus it was that when Abram came out of Ur of the Chaldees he separated himself from an idolatrous people (Joshua 24:2). Thus it was that when the nation Israel was formed it was the only nation that did not worship idols. It is clear that it was important for God to make a great manifestation of himself to them to draw their faith from idols to himself. To this end also, the first two commands of the Decalogue had to be specifically devoted to the abolition of polytheism and idolatry.

A positive example of true religion, coming from this early period is seen in Job the renowned man from Uz (Possibly Uzal, Genesis 10:27). In the first chapter of this book we observe that he was a just man, who feared God and hated evil. He assumed a priestly concern for the whole family. He believed in and worshiped only one God, Jehovah. He offered sacrifice for sin. He professed faith in a life after death. Most significantly, Job demonstrated a heart of true piety; he proved that he served and worshiped God for God's sake alone. Thus, it is exhibited that true religion is not a matter of evolutionary development, nor of later dispensations, but of personal devotion to God.

11. Discussion and Review

1. State in your own words the substance of the Noahic covenant.

2. Show of what importance this covenant is to the world today.

3. What did Noah predict concerning the descendants of his three sons?

4. On an outline map of the ancient world promptly locate geographically the general migrations of the sixteen grandsons of Noah.

5. Explain the manner in which knowledge was transmitted from the Old World to the New. What was the extent of such knowledge?

6. What is the Biblical explanation of the linguistic barrier between nations?

7. Report on Birs-Nimrud.

8. Give a brief account of the rise of the two great empires of antiquity.

9. Characterize religion in the New World from the time of Noah on to the days of Abraham.

10. What may be gathered from the book of Job as to the level of religious experience in general, and in special cases, during this early period?

11. Of what importance has this study been, thus far, for the student of Ancient History?

12. Select Memory Passages

Genesis 8:20

13. Character Review

Identify:

Noah	Sarai	Tiras	Arphaxed
Ham	Milcah	Cush	Lud
Shem	Gomer	Mizraim	Aram
Japheth	Magog	Phut	Eber
Abram	Madai	Canaan	Peleg
Nahor	Javan	Nimrod	Joktan
Haran	Tubal	Elam	Terah
Lot	Meshech	Asshur	

14. Bibliography

Free, Joseph P. *Archaeology and Bible History.* Topics: 1. The Noahic Covenant. 2. Noah's Drunkenness and the Question of Wine and the Bible. 3. The Table of Nations. 4. Failure of Man under the Noahic Covenant; the Tower of Babel. 5. Original Unity of Language. Chicago: Van Kampen Press, 1950.

Huffman, Jasper A. *Job, a World Example.* Butler, Ind.: The Higley Press.

Kuyper, Abraham. *Women of the Old Testament.* Grand Rapids: Zondervan. "Job's Wife," pp. 133-137.

MacCartney, Clarence E. *Trials of Great Men.* "The Trial of Job." Nashville: Abingdon-Cokesbury Press.

Miller, Dorothy Ruth. *A Handbook of Ancient History in Bible Light.* Chap. II, "The Origin and Antiquity of Man." Chapts. III and IV, "The Condition of Primitive Man." Chap. V. "The Post-diluvian Age." Chap. VI, "Light from the Book of Job." New York: Fleming H. Revell Co.

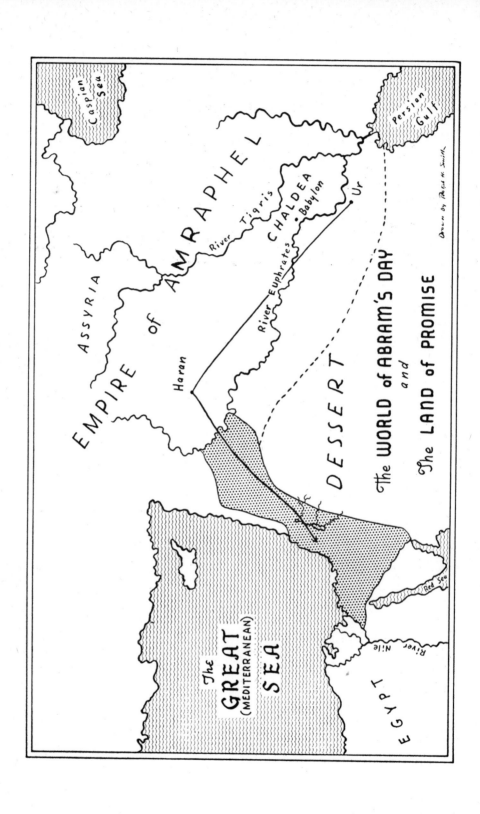

The WORLD of ABRAM'S DAY and The LAND of PROMISE

Caspian Sea

Persian Gulf

EMPIRE of AMRAPHEL

River Tigris

CHALDEA

Ur

Babylon

River Euphrates

ASSYRIA

Haran

DESSERT

The GREAT (MEDITERRANEAN) SEA

Red Sea

River Nile

EGYPT

Drawn by Ralph H. Smith

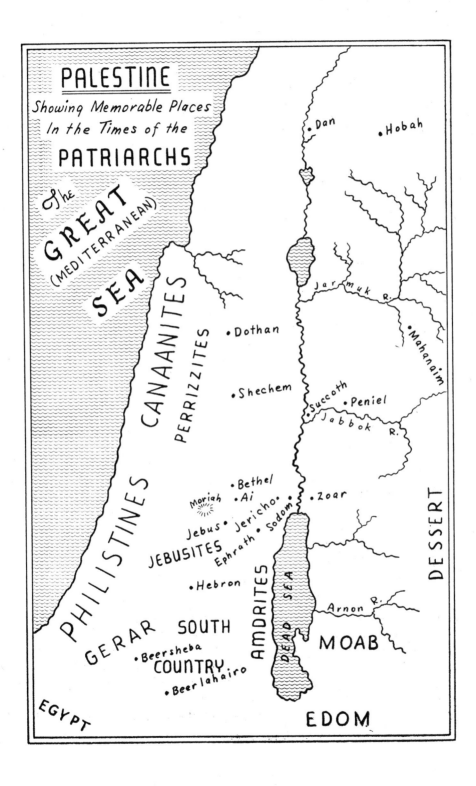

Chapter 4

THE PATRIARCHAL ERA

—Abraham and Isaac

1. **Reading Assignment:**   Genesis 11:27—27:46; 35:27-29; 36

2. Special Perspective in Bible History

The first eleven chapters of Genesis present a view of history which features the whole race. However, the author's spotlight rests upon the lineage of Shem as we come to chapter ten, and upon the family of Terah at the close of chapter eleven. Beginning with chapter twelve Abram and his family are central. It is not true, however, that by narrowing the perspective of Bible history to the Abrahamic race, the divine purpose becomes more limited. Rather, God began dealings with a special race, in view of his purpose to bring redeeming mercies to all races. The germ prophecy of Genesis 3:15 still furnishes the goal of history. This is clearly embodied in the call of Abraham and in the covenant which God gave to him and his seed (12:1-3).

Considering as we did in our last study that between Noah and Abraham all nations had degenerated from monotheism to polytheism and idolatry, we now observe that it became God's strategy to select a single man who believed, and to subject him and his descendants to such instruction and experiences as would enshrine before the world a knowledge of his attributes, of his law, of his glory, and of his redeeming purpose. This, of course, was to include the unfolding of a Messianic hope and the ultimate coming to the

44

world of the Son of God for the restoration of all believing persons
to the dominion of their Creator.

3. Historical Outline

The Career of Abraham (11:27—25:18)

I. In Ur of Chaldea (Gen. 11:27-30)

1. His Near Kin
   (1) Father: Terah
   (2) Brothers: Nahor, Haran
   (3) Haran's son: Lot
2. Death: Haran Died in Ur
3. Marriage: With Sarai (Terah's
   Daughter and Abram's Half-sister.
   Note: 20:12)
4. Offspring: None. Sarai was barren
5. His People's Religion—Idolatrous
   (Joshua 24:2)

II. In Haran (Gen. 11:31, 32; 12:1-5)

1. Departure of Terah's Family from
   Ur
   (1) The destination i n t e n d e d:
       Canaan (11:31)
   (2) The temporary abode: Haran
       (11:31)
   (3) Members of the group: Terah,
       Abram and Sarai, and Lot
       (11:31)
   (4) Terah's death at Haran (11:32)
2. God's Covenant with Abram (12:1-
   3)
   (1) Time and place: Probably
       while in Ur, but reaffirmed at
       Haran ("The LORD had said.")
   (2) God's command: "Get thee
       out . . . . unto a land that I
       will show thee."
   (3) God's promise: land, posterity,
       blessing
3. Abram's Obedience (12:4-5)
   (1) Departure from Haran for
       Canaan
       1) Age: 75 years
       2) Members of the group:
          Abram, Sarai, and Lot with
          their accumulated servants
          and possessions

III. In Canaan (Gen. 12:6-9)

1. **At Shechem**

   (1) The LORD appears to him,
       identifying this as the land of
       the covenant promise
   (2) Abram builds an altar
2. **At Bethel**
   (1) He pitches his tent
   (2) He builds an altar
   (3) He calls upon the LORD
3. Journey through the Land

IV. In Egypt (Gen. 12:10-20)

1. The Problem of Sustenance in
   Canaan
2. The Problem of Sarai's Beauty
   (1) Abram's faulty device
   (2) The LORD'S overruling hand
3. Abram's Return to Canaan

V. In Canaan (Gen. 12:20—25:18)

1. **At Bethel** (13:1-17)
   (1) Abram calls upon the LORD
       (13:1-4)
   (2) Abram and Lot separate agree-
       ably upon Lot's terms (13:5-
       13)
   (3) God copiously reaffirms his
       covenant promise to Abram
       (13:14-17)
2. **At Hebron** (13:18—14:12)
   (1) Tent site: plains (oaks) of
       Mamre (13:18)
   (2) Worship: He builds an altar
       (13:18)
   (3) Time: The days of Amraphel
       (14:1)
   (4) The deportation of Lot from
       Sodom (14:2-12)
3. **At Dan and Hobah** (14:13-24)
   (1) Hearing of Lot's capture,
       Abram arms 318 servants and
       retrieves Lot and the Sodom-
       ites and their goods (14:13-16)
   (2) Return meeting with Mel-
       chizedek (14:17-20)
   (3) Meeting with the king of
       Sodom (14:21-24)
4. **At Hebron** (Chapters 15-19)

(1) God again copiously reaffirms his covenant promise to Abram (chapter 15)

  1) God—Abram's "shield" and "reward" (15:1)

  2) Abram inquires about the promised seed (15:2-3)

  3) Not Eliezer, but a true son is meant (15:4)

  4) Abram's descendants are to be as the stars innumerable (15:5)

  5) Abram's belief . . . . and righteousness (15:6)

  6) God's original covenant promise will be kept (15:7)

  7) God's promise confirmed by a sign and a covenant (15:8-21)

  8) Time of inheriting the land (15:13-16)

    a. After Abram's people have been in servitude 400 years

    b. After their master (Egypt) has been judged

    c. After they have been delivered with great substance

    d. After Abram in "good old age" has been buried

    e. After the iniquity of the Amorites is full

(2) Ishmael a sorry substitute for the promised son (chapter 16)

  1) Sarai's suggestion: Hagar to bear a son for her

  2) Sarai's changed attitude after Hagar's conception

  3) Hagar's Flight

  4) Time of Ishmael's birth: Abram's 86th year

(3) God again reaffirms his covenant (chapter 17)

  1) Time: Abram's 99th year

  2) Abram's name changed to Abraham (father of a multitude)

  3) The rite of circumcision ordered

  4) Sarai's name changed to Sarah (princess, the mother of kings)

  5) The rite of circumcision carried out upon Abraham, Ishmael, and all the men of his house

(4) Three angels visit Abraham (chapter 18)

  1) Abraham shows great hospitality

  2) The birth of Sarah's son is specifically announced

  3) The destruction of Sodom and Gomorrah is announced

  4) Abraham intercedes for Lot and his family

(5) Two angels secure Lot from destruction (chapter 19)

  1) Lot's hospitality (19:1-3)

  2) Lot is protected by the angels (19:4-11)

  3) Lot is ordered to flee from Sodom (19:12-13)

  4) Response:
    Lot's sons-in-law mock
    Lot "lingered"
    Lot's wife "looked back"
    Lot and his two daughters escape to Zoar

  5) Lot's seed is perpetuated through his two daughters to whom are born Moab and Ammon.

5. **In the "South Country"** (Chapters 20 and 21)

  (1) The problem of Sarah's beauty (chapter 20)

  (2) The promised son is born (21:1-8)

  (3) Strife between the two mothers (21:9-21)

  (4) Covenant between Abraham and Abimelech (21:22-32)

  (5) Abraham establishes worship at Beer-sheba (21:33)

  (6) Abraham sojourns in Philistia "many days" (21:34)

6. **In the Land of Moriah** (22:1-19)

  (1) Time: "After these things" (22:1)

  (2) Distance: Three days of travel (22:3)

  (3) Purpose: To be tested (22:1)

  (4) Results: Abram's faith is proved; God's providence is proved (22:3-19)

7. **At Beer-sheba** (22:19—25:10)

(1) Notice of Abraham's kin in Chaldea (22:20-24)

(2) Sarah's death and burial (23:1-20)

　　1) Her age: 127 years

　　2) Place of death: Hebron

　　3) Place of burial: Cave of Machpelah
　　　　Note: This cave became the burial place for Abraham, Sarah, Isaac, Rebekah, Leah, and Jacob.

(3) Isaac's marriage to Rebekah (chapter 24)

　　1) Abraham's charge to his servant (24:1-9)

　　　　a. Isaac is not to marry a Canaanite

　　　　b. A wife is to be sought in Nahor's house (cf. 22:20-24)

　　　　c. God's angel is trusted for guidance (24:7, 12-14)

　　　　d. The test made good (24:15-28)

　　　　e. The servant m a k e s known his mission to Bethuel's house (24:29-48)

　　　　f. The proposal and its acceptance (24:49-58)

　　　　g. Departure for Canaan (24:59-60)

　　　　h. The meeting and marriage of Isaac and Rebekah (24:61-67)

(4) Abraham's children by Keturah (25:1-4)

(5) The death of Abraham (25:5-10)

　　1) His will: Isaac is sole heir

　　2) His gifts: To the sons of his concubines he gives gifts, and then sends them away, before his death, to the east country.

　　3) His age: 175 years

　　4) His burial:
　　　　By Isaac and Ishmael
　　　　In the cave of Machpelah

The Career of Isaac (Chapters 21-35)

I. Before Abraham's Death
　　Note: Isaac's life lies entwined with the biographies of his father and his sons. His birth, boyhood, and marriage are contained in the foregoing outline. The account of 25:19-26 is the record of events which took place while Abraham still lived. Accordingly Abraham had the satisfaction of seeing, after a time of protracted barrenness on Rebekah's part, the birth of twin grandsons. Upon the death of Abraham, Isaac resumed life with Rebekah and their fifteen year old sons, at Beerlahairoi in "the south country" (25:11).

II. After Abraham's Death (Gen. 25:27-35)
　　Note: Just as in Isaac's early life he was in the background while his father was in the limelight, so in his later life Isaac is in the quiet background while Jacob is featured conspicuously.

1. Aptitudes:
　　Esau a Cunning Hunter
　　Jacob a Plain Man of the Tents

2. Parental Favorites:
　　Isaac Loves Esau
　　Rebekah Loves Jacob

3. A Boyhood Deal: A Mess of Pottage for the Family Birthright (25:29-34)

4. Isaac Sojourns in Gerar (26:1-21)

　　(1) Occasion: Famine in Canaan (26:1)

　　(2) God's covenant reaffirmed to Isaac (26:2-5)

　　(3) Isaac's wife occasions envy (26:6-11)

　　(4) Isaac's prosperity occasions envy (26:12-14)

　　(5) Isaac's wells (26:15-33)

5. "A Grief of Mind" to Isaac and Rebekah (26:34)

　　(1) Esau's wives
　　　　1) Judith, a Hittite
　　　　2) Bashemath, a Hittite

6. Isaac's Blessings to His Sons (27:1-40)

　　(1) Jacob obtains the first blessing by deception (27:1-29)

　　(2) The deception discovered (27:30-38)

　　(3) Esau obtains a blessing also (27:39-40)

(4) Esau holds murder in his heart (27:41).

7. Rebekah Plans Jacob's Flight (27:42-46)

   (1) To escape the heat of Esau's wrath

   (2) To marry a wife of his kin

8. Isaac, Concurring, Sends Jacob to Secure a Wife of Laban's Daughters (28:1-5)

9. Esau, Observing His Parents' Displeasure with His Wives, Takes a Wife from Ishmael's Daughters (28:6-9)

10. The Death of Isaac (35:27-29)
Age: 180 years
Place: At Hebron
Burial: By Esau and Jacob, in the cave of Machpelah, where Abraham, Sarah, and Rebekah had been buried.

4. God's Covenant With Abraham

(Gen. 12:1-3)

It appears that God had made a covenant with Abraham while Abraham still lived at Ur of Chaldea. This is indicated by the King James Version of Genesis 12:1, although not by the American Revised Version. "The LORD had said unto Abram." What the LORD "had said" could hardly be the sequel to the death of Terah recorded in the last verse of chapter 11, for Abraham was called to leave "his father's house," and his "kindred." While in the migration of 11:27-32 Terah seems to have taken the leadership, yet it appears that Abraham rather than Terah had the divine purpose motivating him. Terah may have been an idol addict. At any rate it is made clear in Joshua 24:1-3 that the idolatry of Abraham's people was the occasion for a special covenant with Abraham. The covenant was simple but as comprehensive as the redemptive purpose of God for the nations. It consisted of a command and a promise. The command was twofold. He must leave home. He must go where God led. The promise was threefold. God would make of him a nation; he would give him a land; he would bless him and make him a blessing to all families of the earth.

In this covenant we are made conscious of the fact that there is a more significant person in Bible History than Abraham, Isaac, Jacob, or any other man. That person is God himself. God here reveals a purpose of love reaching to all nations. Consider it. In behalf of a world then given to idolatry, God planned the bestowal of universal blessing. This is to be accomplished, he said, through the agency of Abraham and his seed. Naturally, this purpose causes our minds to leap to the New Testament where such a purpose is revealed in the form of a definite program. But we must attempt to hold ourselves to Abraham's viewpoint and observe how he was led by faith even though he was removed by many years from the actual realization of the great outcome of God's purpose.

5. God's Covenants

ADAM (Gen. 2-3)	NOAH (Gen. 8:20—9:17)	ABRAM (Gen. 12:1-3; 13:14-17;
Starting Point— Fellowship	**Starting Point—** Fellowship	**Starting Point—** Fellowship
God's Endowment to Adam: (2:26-31) 1. Divine image 2. Dominion 3. Powers of procreation 4. Food	God's Promise: 1. Ground no more to be cursed 2. No more smiting of all creatures 3. Regular harvests	God's Promise: 1. A land 2. A posterity 3. Blessing
God's Assignment: 1. Be fruitful Multiply Replenish the earth 2. Subdue the earth 3. Have dominion over the living things	God's Assignment: 1. Be fruitful 2. Multiply 3. Replenish the earth	God's Command: 1. Leave 2. Go
God's Prohibition: 1. Tree of knowledge of good and evil	God's Prohibition: 1. Against murder	
Present Significance: 1. The curse 2. The promise	**Present Significance:** 1. Human government 2. Perpetual sign—the bow (17:8; 26:3; 28:13-14)	**Present Significance:** The covenant blessing: To all nations To all times

Figure 9

6. Sojourning with the Fathers

In order to become acquainted with the Jewish Fathers there is a simple course of study to be followed. Travel with them via the record. Know where they went and what events took place there. Know what can be learned of the time table of their sojourns. Know the main persons with whom they lived and associated. And most important of all, know of their distinctly religious experiences. Doubtless, after all, the most impressive character, in the end, will be, not any of the Fathers, but the Father God himself. To learn his self-revelation, his purposes, and his ways, is the important goal for study. To know God is the surest way of coming to an understanding of the world itself and of ourselves.

It is suggested that a red pencil be used to underscore in the

Historical Outline all main places where Abraham lived. Look these up on a map. With each place associate, mentally, the principal events and the approximate Bible references.

7. Discussion and Review

1. Determine the distance from Ur to Haran, and from Haran to Canaan.

2. Why did Terah not travel from Ur to Canaan?

3. After reading the assigned Bible text and mastering the historical outline, draw a map showing Abraham's travels and sojourns point by point. Form a mental picture of the main incidents belonging with each point.

4. Analyze the Abrahamic covenant as to its commands and its promises.

5. At the left side of a sheet of paper mark off lines by the chapter numbers 12, 13, 14, 15, 16, 17, 18, 19, 20, 21, 22, 23, 24, 25, 26, 27, 35, 36. Opposite each chapter number, list the principal persons featured. Underline the ten which you consider most important. Double score the person of first importance.

6. What reasons can you give for wanting to get acquainted with Bible characters?

7. What may be said as to the scope of perspective in Bible history?

8. Point out particular demonstrations of faith in the life of Abraham. Of Isaac. Were there any points at which faith wavered?

9. What incentive motivated Abraham's obedience? (Cf. Hebrews 11:8-10).

8. Select Memory Passages
Genesis 12:1-3; 15:1, 6

9. Character Review
Identify:

Terah	Sarah	Hagar	Esau
Nahor	Abraham	Moab	Jacob
Haran	Amraphel	Ammon	Judith
Lot	Melchizedek	Abimelech	Bashemath
Sarai	Eliezer	Rebekah	Laban
Abram	Ishmael	Isaac	Keturah

10. Bibliography

Guthrie, Thomas. *Studies of Character.* Chap. I, Abraham the Friend of God."

Kuyper, Abraham. *Women of the Old Testament.* Grand Rapids: Zondervan.
1. "Sarah," pp. 12-15.
2. "Hagar," pp. 15-19.
3. "Keturah," pp. 19-23.

MacCartney, Clarence E. *Trials of Great Men of the Bible.* Chap. II, "The Trial of Abraham." Nashville: Abingdon-Cokesbury Press.

Meyer, F. B. *Abraham and the Obedience of Faith.* New York: Fleming H. Revell.

Meyer, F. B. *Isaac and Jacob, Their Lives and Times.* New York: Fleming H. Revell.

Miller, Dorothy Ruth. *A Handbook of Ancient History in Bible Light.* Chap. IX, "The Babylonian Empire." Chap. X, "Early Egypt." New York: Fleming H. Revell Co.

Ockenga, Harold J. *Have You Met These Women?* Grand Rapids: Zondervan. Chapter III—"The Woman Who Laughed at God."

Sangster, Margaret E. *The Women of the Bible.* Chapt. III, "Sarah, a Princess." New York: The Christian Herald.

Sangster, Margaret E. *The Women of the Bible.* Chapt. IV, "Hagar a Bondwoman." New York: The Christian Herald.

Sangster, Margaret E. *The Women of the Bible.* Chapt. V, "A Monument and a Warning (Lot's Wife)." New York: The Christian Herald.

Sangster, Margaret E. *The Women of the Bible.* Chapt. VII, "Rebekah, the Bride of Destiny." New York: The Christian Herald.

Chapter 5

THE PATRIARCHAL ERA

—Jacob and His Family

1. Reading Assignment: Genesis 25:19—50:26

(Read the Bible first)

2. Introduction—Jacob's Homes

The life of Jacob falls into four major periods as to place. The first is his life at home with his parents in Canaan. The second is in the home, and in the employ of his uncle Laban in Padan-aram. The third is his own family life in Canaan. The fourth is the sunset period of his life spent in Goshen of Egypt.

3. Historical Outline

I. **Jacob in His Boyhood Home at Beer-sheba (25:19—28:9)**

Note: This period of Jacob's life is tied up with the life of Isaac, for which see the last part of the outline in chapter four.

II. **Jacob Journeying to Padan-aram (28:10-22)**

1. The Dream Ladder at Bethel (28:10-15)
    (1) Of angels descending and ascending
    (2) Of the voice above the ladder
    (3) Of the reaffirmation of the covenant

(4) Of the promise of God's presence

2. The Memorial Stone (28:16-19)
3. Jacob's Vow (28:20-22)
    (1) As a response to God's promise (28:20-21) ("If," in verse 20, has the sense of "considering that.")
    (2) The spot of this stone will be regarded as God's house
    (3) A tithe will be given upon return (28:22)

III. **Jacob in Padan-aram (29:1—31:16)**

1. Arrival at Laban's Well (29:1-8)
2. Meeting with Rachel (29:9-12)

52

3. Meeting with Laban (29:13-14)

4. Contract I with Laban (29:15-26)

5. Contract II with Laban (29:27-30)

6. Jacob's Children (29:31—30:24)

   (1) By Leah: Reuben, Simeon, Levi, Judah

   (2) By Bilhah (Rachel's maid): Dan and Naphtali

   (3) By Zilpah (Leah's maid): Gad and Asher

   (4) By Leah: Issachar, Zebulun, and Dinah

   (5) By Rachel: Joseph

7. Contract III with Laban (30:25-43)

8. Jacob contemplates leaving Haran (31:1-16)

   (1) Laban's countenance changes (31:1-2)

   (2) The LORD tells Jacob to return to Canaan (31:3)

   (3) Jacob confers with Rachel and Leah and they agree to leave (31:4-16)

IV. The Return Journey to Canaan (31:17—33:17)

1. Jacob separates his flocks, Rachel steals Laban's images, and they are off, unawares to Laban

2. Laban discovers their flight, pursues them, overtaking them at Gilead

3. Laban is warned of God to do no harm to Jacob

4. Laban's charge against Jacob: He left improperly, and stole his images

5. Jacob's charge against Laban: He pursued them too hotly and failed to appreciate faithful service. After serving for 20 years, and having had his wages changed 10 times, Jacob would have been sent away empty, had God not rebuked Laban

6. Laban and Jacob covenant together for peace (31:43-55)

7. Angels of God meet Jacob at Mahanaim (32:1-2)

8. Jacob sends a conciliatory message to Esau (32:3-5)

9. Messengers report Esau's coming (32:6)

10. Jacob, fearing Esau, devises measures of strategy:

   (1) The company is divided (32:7-8)

   (2) Jacob earnestly prays (32:9-12)

   (3) A peace token is sent to Esau (32:13-23)

11. Jacob's Peniel Experience (32:24-32)

   (1) He wrestles with a man (God)

   (2) He obtains God's blessing

   (3) His thigh is disjointed

   (4) His name is changed to Israel (a prince)

12. Jacob and Esau meet graciously; Esau returns to Seir (33:1-16)

V. Jacob in Canaan (33:17—45)

1. At Succoth temporary quarters are built (33:17). At Shalem (Shechem) Jacob purchases land, pitches his tent, and builds an altar to God (33:18-20)

2. Encounter with the Shechemites (chapter 34)

   (1) Wrong social relations of Dinah (34:1-3)

   (2) An agreement sought (34:4-19)

   (3) The Shechemites are circumcised (34:20-24)

   (4) Simeon and Levi, angered, destroy the Shechemites, secure Dinah and take the spoils (34:25-29)

   (5) Jacob protests, but is matched by a moral consideration (34:30-31)

3. Return to Bethel (35:1-15)

   (1) Preparations: Idols are put away, they cleanse themselves, and put on clean garments

   (2) Their status: The people fear them

   (3) God reaffirms his covenant

4. Gain and Loss at Ephrath (35:16-22)

   (1) Benjamin is born

   (2) Rachel dies in labour

   (3) Reuben has wrong relations with Bilhah

5. The Sons of Jacob (35:23-26)

6. Jacob and Esau bury their father (35:27-29)

7. Esau's Posterity from His Three Wives (Chapter 36)

8. The Home-life of Joseph and his Brethren (Chapters 37-38)

   (1) Joseph's place in the family at the age of 17

      1) Works with the sons of Bilhah and Zilpah

      2) The object of his father's special favour

      3) Hated by his brethren (37:1-4)

   (2) Joseph's dream of sheaves (37:5-8)

   (3) His dream of the sun, moon, and stars (37:9-11)

   (4) Joseph's brethren purpose to be rid of him (37:12-36)

      1) Joseph on an errand to his brethren at Dothan (37:12-18)

      2) The proposal to kill him (37:19-20)

      3) Reuben's alternative: to put him in a pit (37:21-24)

      4) Judah's alternative: to sell him to the Ishmeelites (37:25-28)

      5) The report to Jacob (37:29-35)

      6) Joseph's fate: sold to Potiphar, captain of Pharaoh's guard (37:36)

   (5) Judah's irregular family affairs (chapter 38)

      1) Marriage to a Canaanite (38:1-2)

      2) The three sons (38:3-11)

         a. Er, was wicked and God slew him

         b. Onan, displeased God and was slain

         c. Shelah, unjustly withheld by Judah from marrying Tamar, Er's widow

      3) Judah becomes the father of twins by Tamar (38:12-30)

9. Joseph's Advancement in Egypt (Chapters 39-41)

   (1) Joseph in Potiphar's house (39:1-20)

      1) He prospers and is made overseer of the house (39:1-6)

      2) He resists the appeal to commit adultery with Potiphar's wife (39:7-10)

      3) Potiphar's wife falsely accuses Joseph of unlawful approaches and has him sent to prison (39:11-20)

   (2) Joseph in prison (39:21—40:23)

      1) He prospers and is made overseer of the prison (39:21-23)

      2) Joseph, by God's wisdom interprets the dreams of the king's butler and baker (40:1-19)

      3) The butler is restored to his position but the baker is executed, according to Joseph's interpretation of their dreams (40:20-23) (Two full years elapse, 41:1)

      4) Pharaoh is troubled by two dreams; he can find no interpreter (41:1-8)

      5) The chief butler remembers Joseph and recommends him (41:9-13)

      6) Joseph, called before Pharaoh, declares the power of God to interpret dreams (41:14-16)

      7) The dreams and their interpretation (41:17 - 32): There will be seven years of plenty and then seven years of famine

      8) Joseph becomes second ruler of the land, to administer food supplies

10. Jacob's Sons Come to Egypt for Corn (chapter 42)

   (1) Jacob sends his ten sons, Benjamin excluded (42:1-4)

   (2) The sons appear to Joseph and do obeisance to him (42:5-6)

   (3) Joseph, recognizing his brethren, and withholding his own identity, charges them with espionage (42:7-14)

   (4) Joseph requires proof of their genuineness (42:15-28)

      1) First proof: They are all to be kept in prison while one brings from Canaan the younger brother whom they claim to have

2) Second proof: Out of godly consideration, Joseph
permits all but one to go
home and to return with
their younger brother

3) Joseph, hearing the brethren discuss their sin, is
moved to turn aside and
weep

4) The nine brethren journey
homeward, Simeon remain-
ing in view of their return
with Benjamin

5) They are amazed to find
their money in their sacks

(5) The brethren report to Jacob
(42:29-34)

(6) Jacob's reply (42:35-38)

1) You have robbed me of my
children, Joseph and Sim-
eon, and now ask for Ben-
jamin

2) "All these things are against
me"

3) "My son shall not go down
with you"

11. Jacob sends his sons to Egypt
again (chapters 43-45)

(1) Benjamin is reluctantly permitted to go (43:1-14)

(2) Joseph entertains the men at
dinner (43:15-34)

(3) Joseph devises a means of
further probing his brethren
(chapter 44)

(4) Joseph makes himself known
to his brethren, with weeping,
unrestrained affection, and
forgiveness. His brethren talk
with him

(5) Joseph's interpretation of the
sin of the brethren: "God sent
me before you to preserve you
a posterity on the earth, and
to save your lives by a great
deliverance" (45:7, 8)

(6) Joseph (45:9-11), then Pharaoh (45:16-24), give orders
to bring Jacob to Egypt

(7) The sons report to Jacob
(45:25-28)

1) He fainted and "believed
them not"

2) Seeing Pharaoh's wagons,
he revived, believed and
wished to see Joseph

VI. **Jacob In Egypt (Chapters 46-49)**

1. He takes all that he has with him

2. Offerings are made at Beersheba

3. God speaks to Jacob (46:3-4)

(1) "Fear not to go down into
Egypt"

(2) "I will there make of thee a
great nation"

(3) "I will go down with thee into
Egypt"

(4) "I will also bring thee up
again"

(5) "Joseph shall put his hand
upon thine eyes"

4. Personnel of the Company (46:5-
27)

5. Joseph meets Jacob in Goshen
(46:28-34)

(1) Their affections are satisfied

(2) Joseph plans for Jacob to live
in Goshen

6. Jacob and five sons are presented
to Pharaoh (47:1-10)

7. Joseph provides for his people a
land and nourishment (47:11-12)

8. Joseph institutes a policy for
famine days (47:13-26)

9. Jacob's Last Days (47:27—49:33)

(1) Jacob requests burial in Canaan
(47:27-31)

(2) Jacob blesses Joseph's sons
(chapter 48)

1) They are to be as Jacob's
sons, inheriting equally with
the brethren of Joseph

(3) Jacob blesses his sons (49:1-
28)

(4) Jacob charges them as to his
burial (49:29-32)

(5) Death of Jacob (49:33)
"He was gathered unto his
people"

10. The Remaining Years of Joseph
(Chapter 50)

(1) The burial of Jacob (50:1-14)

(2) Fears of Joseph's brethren
(50:15-18)

(3) Joseph's gracious viewpoint
(50:19-21)

1) "I am in the place of God"
(That is, in God's appointed
place)

2) "Ye thought evil against me," but "God meant it unto good"

3) Joseph covered the past with "comfort" and "kindness" and gave assurance that he would continue this attitude

(4) Joseph's last days (50:22-26)

1) His age at death, 110 years

2) He helped bring up his grandchildren

3) Canaan, the land of Joseph's hope

a. God will return the family of Israel to the land of Abraham, Isaac, and Jacob

b. Under oath the children of Israel are charged to bear Joseph's bones to his possession among the tribes in Canaan

c. Upon his death Joseph was embalmed and put in a coffin in Egypt, awaiting the removal of his bones to Canaan, and the resurrection

4. Why God Chose Jacob

It would be hard to make a case justifying the ethics of Jacob. Yet it is safe to say that he was a very human person. This, of course, means that God had a great deal of disciplining to do in his life in order to produce the graces of godliness. But Jacob had the kind of stuff in him that God can use; in this he stands in contrast with his brother Esau. Jacob had a prenatal aggressiveness which destined him to leadership of one kind or another. He was a shrewd bargainer for high values; and so far as Esau is concerned he bought, and did not steal, the family birthright. While the method followed in gaining the blessing involved dishonesty, the blessing secured was actually Jacob's. God could use Jacob as the father of the holy nation because he aspired to that place. On the other hand, a man who had no more regard for the covenant of God with the fathers than to barter it for a mess of pottage would not persevere to fulfill the purposes of God.

5. Jacob's Antagonists

Jacob's aspirations were rewarded by God's promises on the one hand, and they were relentlessly opposed by some person or persons throughout his active life. It appeared that his life would go down as a disappointment to himself and without any worthwhile fulfillment of his birthright blessing. He had finally surmounted the enmity of his brother. He had won his wives and great riches in spite of the miserliness of his father-in-law. And he finally returned to the promised land with his wives, his children, and his wealth. But no sooner had these barriers been hurdled than he began to lose the prizes which he had most cherished. His only daughter was defiled. His favorite wife was withdrawn by provi-

dence from his life. His sons were indulgent and wicked; by their
evil hands his favorite son was torn from his bosom. Jacob became a pessimist, almost a fatalist. When famine had brought him
to want, and when recourse to Egypt for corn involved him in

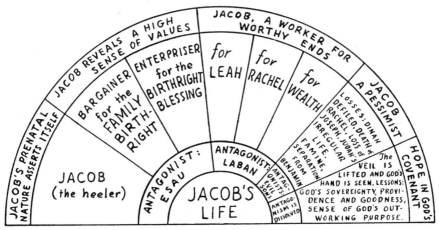

Figure 10

separation from Benjamin, the only remaining reminder of his most
loved Rachel, his despondency was complete. "All these things
are against me" are the words which express the utterly pessimistic,
yet wholly wrong view of his personal life which the years had
brought on.

6. The After-view of a Life of Struggle

Jacob's life closes with a period of most satisfying understanding against the background of personal discipline through which
providence had taken him. Jacob understood, in a day, what had
been the meaning of years of discipline. But the lesson was not
to him alone. His life and the life of his family displayed an historical object lesson of God's providence which grasping Jacob, his
envious sons, and all their posterity could not fail to see. When
two centuries later the children of Israel were born to national consciousness, the memory of the God of Jacob secured within them a
faith, a hope, and a sense of high destiny. The God who could bring
a happy end to such an unworthy and ill-fated family could do the
same for a nation in bondage. Viewed in the light of the experiences of Jacob's family, the covenant of Jehovah with Abraham's
posterity became a document of glorious hope.

7. Discussion and Review

1. What were the four places where Jacob's life was lived?

2. Form a mental picture of the main incidents, the associates, and the providential developments in each period.

3. Why did God choose Jacob?

4. Discuss Jacob's antagonists.

5. Characterize the view of life which Jacob came to express, and show the error of it.

6. Characterize the "after-view" of Jacob's family as they discovered Joseph in Egypt.

7. Of what importance were the experiences of Jacob's generation to his posterity in relation to the Abrahamic covenant?

8. Be able to relate the life story of Jacob. Of Joseph.

8. Select Memory Passages
Genesis 28:13-15; 45:4b-5

9. Character Review

Identify:

Isaac	Leah	Levi	Issachar	Potiphar
Jacob	Tamar	Judah	Zebulun	Pharaoh
Esau	Bilhah	Dan	Dinah	Er
Israel	Zilpah	Naphtali	Joseph	Onan
Laban	Reuben	Gad	Shechem	Shelah
Rachel	Simeon	Asher	Hamor	

10. Bibliography

Free, Joseph P. *Archaeology and Bible History.* Van Kampen Press. Chapt. VI, "Joseph in Egypt."

Kuyper, Abraham. *Women of the Old Testament.* Grand Rapids: Zondervan.
1. "Rebekah," pp. 23-26.
2. "Leah," pp. 30-33.
3. "Rachel," pp. 33-36.
4. "Dinah," pp. 40-43.
5. "Tamar," pp. 43-47.

MacCartney, Clarence E. *Trials of Great Men of the Bible.* Abingdon-Cokesbury Press, 1946. Chapt. III, "The Trial of Jacob." Chapt. IV, "The Trial of Joseph."

Meyer, F. B. *Israel a Prince with God.* London: Morgan and Scott.

Meyer, F. B. *Joseph—Beloved, Hated. Exalted.* New York: Fleming H. Revell.

Ockenga, Harold J. *Have You Met These Women?* Grand Rapids: Zondervan's Chapter II—"The Woman Who Commanded a Man's Love."

Phillips, Leroy. *Joseph the Dreamer.* Boston: W. A. Wilde Co.

Sangster, Margaret E. *The Women of the Bible.* Chapt. VI, "Leah the Tolerated, Rachel the Well-Beloved." New York: Fleming H. Revell.

PART THREE

THE TIMES OF MOSES
(1571-1451 B. C.)

Chapter 6

ISRAEL DELIVERED FROM EGYPT

(1491 B. C.)

1. Reading Assignment: Exodus 1-19

(Read the Bible first)

2. Introduction—Between Genesis and Exodus

Genesis closed with the family of Abraham enjoying favor and prosperity in Egypt. The revealing climax of that book directed the attention of every son of Jacob to the overruling providence which attended their family. They were made conscious of the fact that God was seeing to the fulfillment of the covenant made with Abraham. The manner in which God had preserved them from famine, even using human perversity to this end, must have given them a faith that he would not leave them to the caprices of the Pharaohs. What they knew of Jehovah as the God of Abraham, Isaac, and Jacob should have caused all eyes to turn to him. Abraham had been specifically told that before possession of the promised land could be realized, his descendants would be in servitude to a strange nation, and that after four hundred years they should be restored (Gen. 15:13-16). In the meantime God's clock of judgment would strike for the Amorites. Thus, the Israelites were not without an understanding of the fact that their existence in Egypt

61

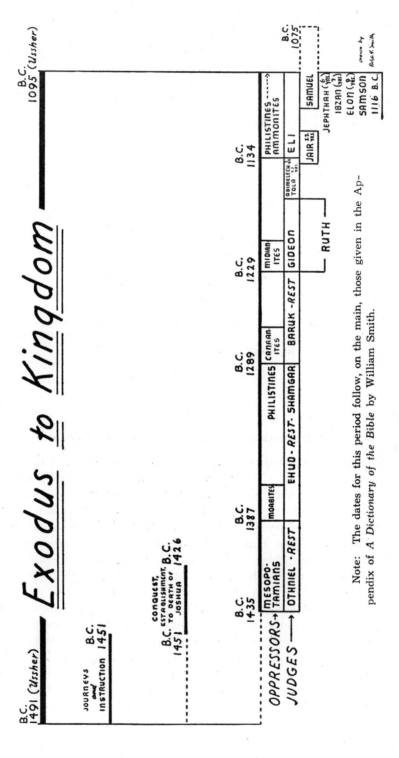

Exodus to Kingdom

B.C. 1491 (Ussher)

JOURNEYS *and* INSTRUCTION
B.C. 1451

CONQUEST,
B.C. ESTABLISHMENT, B.C.
1451 TO DEATH OF 1426
JOSHUA

	B.C. 1435	B.C. 1387	B.C. 1289	B.C. 1229	B.C. 1134	B.C. 1095 (Ussher)
OPPRESSORS→	MESOPO-TAMIANS	MOABITES	PHILISTINES	CANAANITES	MIDIANITES	PHILISTINES AMMONITES
JUDGES →	OTHNIEL-REST	EHUD-REST-SHAMGAR	BARUK-REST	GIDEON		

PHILISTINES ------→
B.C. 1075

SAMUEL

ELI
JAIR 22 YRS.

ABIMELECH 3U.
TOLA 23 YRS.

JEPHTHAH (6 YRS.)
IBZAN (7 YRS.)
ELON (YRS.)
SAMSON
1116 B.C.

RUTH

drawn by
Ralph H. Smith

Note: The dates for this period follow, on the main, those given in the Appendix of *A Dictionary of the Bible* by William Smith.

Figure 11

was related to a higher end than they had realized. Apparently, however, it was necessary for God to mightily demonstrate this power in order to renew hopes and quicken faith in the covenant which had been made with the fathers.

Exodus reveals the way in which God visits judgment upon those who are ripe for it and at the same time extends salvation to those who are called to be his people. Such a dove-tailing of the histories of different peoples is an unmistakable sign of God's over-ruling providence in the affairs of the world. Summarizing, we may observe the following distinct movings of God's sovereign hand up to the time of the Exodus:

The Four Hundred Year Period

Covenant	Deferment	Time Processes	
The Abrahamic Covenant (Gen. 12:1-3)	A 400 year interval (Gen. 15:13-17)	Israel taught God's providence Israel developed socially Israel forged in suffering Israel learning its need Iniquity of the Amorites (Canaanites) ripened Idolatry in Egypt ripened for judgment	E X O D U S

Figure 12

3. Historical Outline

I. **Israel in Egyptian Bondage (1:1—2:10)**

  1. Those Who Came into Egypt (1:1-6)

  2. Those Who Were Added (1:7)

  3. The New Dynasty and Its Policy (1:8-22)

    (1) The King's fear (1:9-10)

    (2) His unsuccessful device (1:11-12a)

    (3) Grief of the taskmasters (1:12b)

    (4) Intensified labors (1:3-14)

    (5) The second unsuccessful device (1:15-20)

    (6) The third device thwarted by God's providence in Moses' life (1:21-22; 2:1-10)

II. **God's Preparation of a Deliverer (2:1—4:28)**

  1. Moses' Ancestry (2:1)

  2. Childhood Providences (2:2-10)

  3. Moses at Forty (2:11-15)

  4. Moses in Midia (2:15—4:26)

  5. Increased Oppression in Egypt (2:23-25)

III. **Egypt's Judgment—Israel's Deliverance (4:29—12:36)**

  1. Moses and Aaron Gather Israel (4:21-31)

  2. Israel Believes, Bows, and Worships

  3. Preliminary Contests with Pharaoh (5:1—7:13)

  4. The Plagues (7:14—12:36)

    (1) Blood (7:14-25)

    (2) Frogs (8:1-15)

    (3) Lice (8:16-19)

    (4) Flies (8:20-32)

    (5) Murrain of beasts (9:1-12)

    (6) Boils (9:8-12)

    (7) Hail (9:13-35)

(8) Locusts (10:1-20)

(9) Darkness (10:21-26)

(10) Death of firstborn

1) Preparations (11:1—12:20)

2) The plague carried out (12:21-30)

3) It secures release (12:31-36)

IV. **Israel's Journey—from Egypt to Sinai (12:37—19:1)**

1. Rameses to Succoth (12:37—13:19)

2. Encampment at Etham (13:20-22)

3. Encampment at Pihahiroth (14:1-14)

4. The Red Sea—Victory (14:15—15:21)

5. Wilderness of Shur (15:22)

6. Marah (15:23-26)

7. Elim (15:27)

8. Wilderness of Sin (16:1-36)

9. Rephidim (17:1—18:27)

10. Sinai (19:1-25)

4. Israel's Rise in Ancient History

At the time of Abram's call the postdiluvian era was more than four centuries old. During this period, as we have learned, two great civilizations had developed, the Egyptian in the Nile valley, and the Chaldean in the Euphrates valley. Between these two great civilizations the national Israel arose as a tender plant.

It was called out of Chaldea (Babylonia). It was nourished to a national status in Egypt. It was then liberated to enter upon a unique history in the world.

Both of the two great civilizations from which Israel rose were

ISRAEL'S RISE in ANCIENT HISTORY

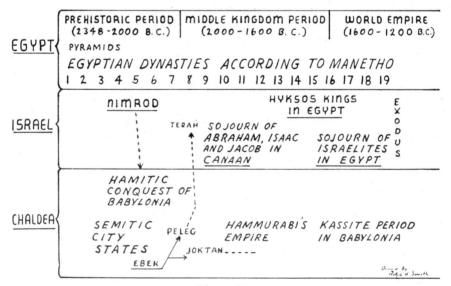

Figure 13

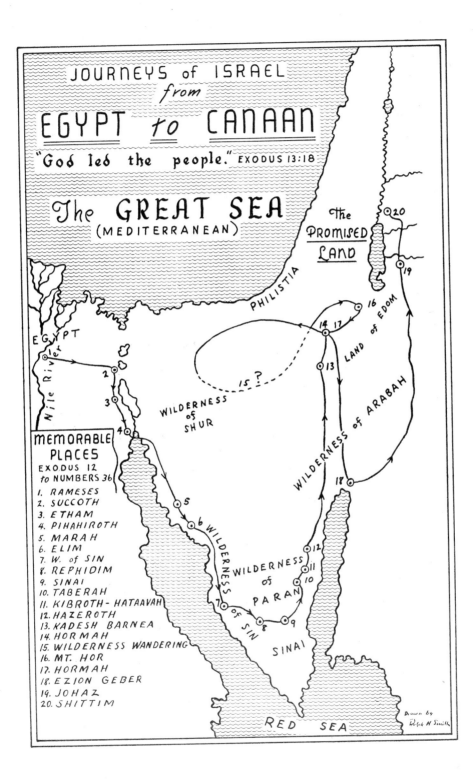

JOURNEYS of ISRAEL *from* EGYPT *to* CANAAN

"God led the people." EXODUS 13:18

The GREAT SEA (MEDITERRANEAN)

The PROMISED LAND

EGYPT

Nile River

PHILISTIA

WILDERNESS of SHUR

15 ?

LAND of EDOM

WILDERNESS of ARABAH

WILDERNESS of SIN

WILDERNESS of PARAN

SINAI

RED SEA

MEMORABLE PLACES

EXODUS 12 to NUMBERS 36

1. RAMESES
2. SUCCOTH
3. ETHAM
4. PIHAHIROTH
5. MARAH
6. ELIM
7. W. of SIN
8. REPHIDIM
9. SINAI
10. TABERAH
11. KIBROTH-HATAAVAH
12. HAZEROTH
13. KADESH BARNEA
14. HORMAH
15. WILDERNESS WANDERING
16. MT. HOR
17. HORMAH
18. EZION GEBER
19. JOHAZ
20. SHITTIM

Drawn by Ralph H. Smith

Hamitic, and were for the most part dominated by the pride of imperialists; they were idolatrous. One might wonder why God should have chosen to call Abram's people out of the idolatry of Chaldea and then decree that she should live under bondage to the Egyptians, who also were idolatrous. A possible answer to this is found in the fact that after Egypt's twelfth dynasty, Egypt fell into the hands of wandering tribes of Semitic nomads from Arabia and Syria. These nomads were probably ruling in Egypt at approximately the times of Jacob, Joseph, and the twelve tribal families which were being formed into the nation Israel. They are known as the Hyksos (shepherd) kings. If our supposition at this point is correct, then it is indeed remarkable of God's gracious providence that while Abraham's descendants were being nourished into a nation, dominion should have been transferred from Hamitic rulers to rulers of the more friendly Semitic race.

5. The Meaning of Exodus 12:40, 41

This passage has been taken by some interpreters to mean that the period of time from Jacob's descent into Egypt until the Exodus was 430 years. Such, by far the majority of interpreters agree, was not the case. In the first place, the text does not say so. It merely states that the Israelites **who dwelt in Egypt** sojourned 430 years; the text does not say where they sojourned. The Septuagint translators (about 280 B. C.) rendered this passage, "Now the sojourning of the children of Israel which they sojourned **in Egypt and in Canaan.**" The Samaritan version is the same. It is evident that the Septuagint and Samaritan versions are to be regarded as ex-

planatory emendations of the Hebrew text by the translators. These translators understood the actual meaning of the text to be that the general term "children of Israel" included also Abraham, Isaac, and Jacob, and that the sojourning was both in Canaan and Egypt. Strictly speaking, the fathers Abraham, Isaac, and Jacob were of course not the children of Israel, but Hebrew idiom made it natural for one living in Moses' time to speak of the existing generation on back to such a paternal ancestor as Abraham as the "children of Israel."

Genesis 15:13-17 is in harmony with this reckoning; in this passage a period of 400 years or four generations is allowed from the Abrahamic entrance into Canaan until the Exodus. Paul doubt-less understood that the period from the Abrahamic covenant until the Exodus was 430 years (Gal. 3:17).

Reckoning on the basis of this interpretation we arrive at the chronology in the accompanying table:

The Sojourn in Canaan and Egypt

		Yrs.	Yr. of world	B. C.	Authority
Abraham	Left Haran when he was	75	2023	1981	Gen. 12:4
Isaac	Was born	25 later	2048	1956	Gen. 21:5
Esau and Jacob	Were born	60 later	2108	1896	Gen. 25:26
Jacob	Horeb to Egypt	130 later	2238	1766	Gen. 47:9
Children of Israel	In Egypt	215	2453	1551	Ex. 12:40, 41
Total		430			

6. The Census of the Children of Israel

It has been contended by some that 215 years were too short a time to permit the growth of population reported in Exodus 12:37, namely 600,000 men. Let us figure it out. Jacob had 53 grandsons (Gen. 46:1-27). Two hundred fifteen years would be approximately six generations of 35 years. Assuming that each son had begat five sons (females are not being considered) we would have this equation: $53 \times 5^6 = 53 \times 15625$ or 828,125. This does not take into account the sons who over-lived their generations.

7. The Teaching Design of the Historic Exodus

The Exodus from Egypt was God's object lesson to the nations. Egypt had been raised as a peer of ancient times to make this demonstration. The record of it stands at the beginning of the life of that nation which has written the world's most widely read book. In the Bible the whole idol-worshiping world may see the historic combat which revealed the supremacy of the LORD God of Israel. A study of the quotations occurring in the accompanying diagram will make clear the fact that in the Exodus God was at work teaching the basic lessons of true religion.

God's Teaching Design in the Book of Exodus

Ref.	Speaker	Pertaining to	Occasion	What is Taught
6:7	God (Elohim)	Israel	The deliverance of Israel from Egypt	"Ye shall know that I am the LORD your God."
7:5	God	Egyptians	Speaking to Moses before the sign of "rods"	"The Egyptians shall know that I am the LORD when I stretch forth mine hand upon Egypt."
7:17	The LORD (Jahweh)	Pharaoh	The Plague of Blood	"In this thou shalt know that I am the LORD."
8:10	Moses	Pharaoh	The Plague of Frogs	"That thou mayest know that there is none like the LORD."
8:22	God	Pharaoh	The Plague of Flies	"That thou mayest know that I am the LORD in the midst of the earth."
9:14	God	Pharaoh	The Plagues	"That thou mayest know that there is none like me in all the earth."
9:29	Moses	Pharaoh	The Plague of Hail	"That thou mayest know that the earth is the LORD'S."
10:2	The LORD	Moses' Posterity	The Plague of Locusts	"That ye may know that I am the LORD."
11:7	Moses	Pharaoh	Death of First-born	"That ye may know that the LORD hath put a difference between Egypt and Israel."
14:1	The LORD	Egyptians	Announcement of the miracle at the Red Sea	"That the Egyptians may know that I am the LORD."
14:18	The LORD	Egyptians	Announcement of the miracle at the Red Sea	"That the Egyptians may know that I am the LORD."
16:4-6	The LORD	Israel	Wilderness of Sin —Giving of manna	"I will rain bread . . . . then shall ye know that I am the LORD."
18:11	Jethro	Jethro	Rephidim	"Now I know that the LORD is greater than all gods."

Figure 14

1. The chart reveals the Lord God (Elohim-Jahweh) as making himself known in such a way as to instruct: Israel, the Egyptians, Pharaoh, Moses' posterity, and Jethro.

2. In each case the purpose was to impress the people of Moses' time with a consciousness of the eternally existing One.

3. The demonstrations proved con-

clusively to these parties the fact of the LORD'S supremacy. **Israel** "saw that great work which the LORD did upon the Egyptians, and the people feared the LORD, and believed the LORD, and his servant Moses" (14:31). **The Egyptians** indicated their regard for the supremacy of the LORD in giving favor to the Israelites and urging them to leave (12:31-36). **Pharaoh** acknowledged the moral supremacy of the LORD (9:27). **Moses** extolled the LORD in his exclusive glory in the song of Exodus 15. **Jethro** most clearly shows the conviction of Jehovah's supremacy (18:11), saying "Now I know that the LORD is greater than all gods.

4. These demonstrations furnished the necessary and adequate groundwork of instruction for spiritual worship of the one true God. They were the preparation for instruction to follow, as set forth in the laws of righteousness and worship of the second half of Exodus, Leviticus, Numbers, and Deuteronomy. God is thus seen as the great teacher of men, unfolding at the outset such attributes of himself as to discipline this nation in his ways, in order to make them the teachers of the world. These great demonstrations of the LORD'S works in their behalf, the laws, statutes, and judgments which he gave, were to be the subject matter for instruction to their children (Deuteronomy 8).

8. How the Plagues Unseated Egypt's Gods

The Greek historian Herodotus says that the Egyptians were "religious to excess, far beyond any other race of men." Egyptian religion had come under the domination of a system of priests, and religion had become superficially esoteric (a hidden mystery). It was still acknowledged that there was one supreme God, but actual religious practice corresponded with the kind of degeneracy which the apostle Paul later described in the first chapter of Romans. Attributes, qualities, or functions of God such as his might, his wisdom, and his providence, were deified. The creation was stepped up to the status of these attributes; the sun, the moon, the stars, plants and animals, insects and birds, and even the dust of the field were worshiped. In all of this the one and only true God was given little regard, while religious practices were invested with elements which served the low desires of men, of priest and people alike.

The plagues were calculated to loose the minds of the people from their faith in Egyptian deities, on the one hand, and to create a basis for faith in the one true God instead. When the Nile was turned into blood it became the symbol of death instead of life. The plague of frogs was designed to raise disgust in the minds of the people against **Hecka** who was symbolized by the frog. The lice and flies were intolerable pests to the sacred beasts. The murrain of beasts struck further at the Egyptian veneration for beasts. Doubtless Apis, the sacred bull of Memphis was stricken. That the cattle of the Israelites were immune made it evident that the plague struck at Egyptian worship. The locusts devastated the verdure of the landscape and impoverished the granaries. The plague of darkness was a blackout of confidence in the Egyptian sun-god Ra. The final plague struck at the whole animal order, leaving no venerated animal unseated from its status of deity. It likewise struck at the pride of the Pharaohs. The death of the firstborn of men, in fact, was a rebuke directed squarely against human unbelief and rebellion. Faith in God to the extent of obeying his orders would have saved any family from grief. Thus, in a singular manner the principle of salvation was in operation in much the same way as when a few people had been saved in the ark, and the same as when men are now saved by obedience to the gospel of Christ.

When it is considered that Egypt was then a world peer, and when it is considered also that other ancient peoples had systems of nature worship similar to the Egyptian system, it can be seen that the Exodus was indeed a lesson from God to all men.

9. Responsibility for Pharaoh's Hardness of Heart

From the above observations it will be evident that God's demonstrations in the Exodus were calculated to lay the basis for a true faith. When it is said, therefore, that God hardened Pharaoh's heart the meaning is that Pharaoh so reacted to the truth as to be hardened. His pride was such that he had no place for truth. Pride is, essentially, a bias in favor of oneself, and an exaggerated idea of one's own importance which corrupts one's sense of values. Pride precludes right judgment. The facts reveal God as supreme. Pride has no regard for facts which do not reveal self as supreme. The result of repeatedly ignoring facts is that one becomes insensitive to the truth. That is hardness of heart. Hardness of heart in relation to God effects a final rejection of God's will and a forfeiture of the only suitable plan for human blessedness.

10. Pharaoh's Compromise Proposals

The role of Pharaoh in the history of this period is strongly suggestive of the bondage of humanity under Satan. Pharaoh fought to keep his slaves. When plagued, he gave in, but only temporarily and in no greater degree than necessary. The Israelites asked to be permitted to leave the land. Pharaoh resisted that request until four plagues had been enacted. Then he ordered a compromise proposal, namely: "Go ye sacrifice to God in the land" (8:25). Moses promptly rejected the proposal. Pharaoh proposed a second compromise: "I will let you go . . . . only ye shall not go very far away . . . ." (8:28). After the eighth plague he proposed a third compromise: "Go now ye that are men" (10:9-11). Before Moses and Aaron could reject his compromise he drove them out. In connection with the ninth plague he proposed a fourth compromise: "Go ye, serve Jehovah; only let your flocks and herds be stayed" (10:24).

It was only when the tenth plague had stricken the land, taking its favored son, that Pharaoh finally yielded (12:31-32). That his yielding was insincere, however, is proved by the fact that when he thought he saw an opportunity to get them back he feverishly pursued them. One may suppose that even when the drowning waters of the Red Sea gargled in his throat his proud heart had not changed its character.

If the suggestion is true that Pharaoh typifies Satan, then there is in this experience of Israel a clear object lesson of the relentless Satanic opposition that is arrayed against the children of God, and the necessity, on their part, for absolute resistance of all compromise of God's known will.

11.   Instruction Value of the Passover

It is significant that God took time, before the tenth plague was enacted, to give rather full instructions regarding the memorial which in years to come should keep the Israelites freshly conscious of their redemption from Egypt. This emphasizes the fact that God was at work building faith in the hearts of men. What he demonstrated in that night was his fundamental doctrine. The acceptance of redemption upon God's terms by implicit faith and obedience was a requirement to be impressed upon each coming generation. The meaning of the Passover Lamb in terms of atonement was not explained, nor was that necessary. One's theory of the atonement may not be perfect, yet one's appropriation of redemption may be complete. Even now, when the Lamb of God who takes away the sin of the world has been revealed, it is **receiving** the Savior as he has been offered that is fundamental. Faith and obedience are the first tests of orthodoxy.

12.   Instruction Value of Israel's First Journeys

God had already taught the Israelites the initial lessons of faith.

But deliverance from Egypt was only the beginning of his purpose for her. In the journey from Rameses to Sinai the lessons are so distinct that one may easily see God the great teacher at work.

Observe that at their first encampment at **Succoth**, when vengeful Pharaoh was still at hand, Moses took time to teach the people the significance of the Passover memorial and of the obligation to henceforth consecrate all their firstborn to God (12:43-13:10). Next, at **Etham** they were given the pillar and cloud to guide them. It is difficult to miss the suggestion that this has of the presence and guidance of the Holy Spirit in the lives of believers. At **Pihahiroth** Israel had a twofold lesson—the crisis of a hopeless situation, and the experience of seeing the full and final triumph over Egypt (14:4-14). At **Marah** again they experienced bitter waters only to prove the power of their God to sweeten them (15:23-26). In connection with this experience God gave the Jehovah-rapha (the LORD that healeth thee) ordinance which assured them of exemption from the diseases of Egypt. At **Elim** there were no bitter waters, but twelve springs and seventy palm trees, a spring for each tribe and a palm tree for each elder (15:27). At the encampment in the **Wilderness of Sin** God further demonstrated his providence by giving meat and manna (16:1-36). At **Rephidim** the need for water was the occasion for another miracle of providence (17:5-7). Here also God demonstrated that he was the source of Israel's power against their enemies (17:8-17), and was made known to Israel as Jehovah-nissi (Jehovah our banner). Important practical organizational changes were also considered. At Jethro's counsel Moses' load was distributed upon selected and competent subordinates.

By the time Israel reached Sinai they knew God to be not only their redeemer, but their guide, their provider, and their source of power. He had indeed borne them as on eagle's wings. They had every reason to receive his fuller instruction and to follow him.

13. Discussion and Review

1. How many Israelites came into Egypt? How many were there at the time of the Exodus (Exod. 12:37)?

2. What significant historical developments took place during the 400 years preceding the Exodus (Gen. 15:13-16; Exod. 12:40, 41)?

3. Explain the historical background of the statement that there was a new king in Egypt "who knew not Joseph."

4. Explain the new king's fear.

5. Indicate three main divisions in the life of Moses.

6. What took place in the contest with Pharaoh preliminary to the plagues?

7. Enumerate the plagues and show how they struck at Egyptian religion.

8. Tell the story of Israel's first journeys, relating the accounts which center about ten main geographic points.

14. Select Memory Passages

Exod. 14:13-15; 15-2, 26b

15. Character Review

Identify:

Moses	Miriam	Reuel	JEHOVAH	Eleazar
Aaron	Amram	Jethro	Nadab	Ithamar
Pharaoh	Jochebed	Zipporah	Abihu	

16. Bibliography

Blaikie, Wm. G. *A Manual of Bible History.* Chap. V. "Egypt." New York: Thomas Nelson and Sons.

Free, Joseph P. *Archaeology and Bible History.* Chap. VII, "Moses in Egypt." Chap. VIII, "Moses out of Egypt." Chicago, Van Kampen Press.

Huffman, Jasper A. *Voices from Rocks and Dust Heaps of Bible Lands.* Chap. VI, "The World's Oldest Code of Laws, the Code of Hammurabi." Chap. VII, "Tutankhamen and the Exodus." Butler, Ind.: The Higley Press.

Kuyper, Abraham. *Women of the Old Testament.* Grand Rapids: Zondervan.
1. "Jochebed," pp. 54-57.
2. "Pharaoh's Daughter," pp. 57-60.
3. "Miriam," pp. 60-63.
4. "Zipporah," pp. 64-66.

Kyle, Melvin Grove. *Moses and the Monuments.* Oberlin, 1920.

Lucas, A. *The Route of the Exodus of the Israelites from Egypt.* London, 1938.

MacCartney, Clarence Edward. *Trials of Great Men of the Bible.* Chap. V, "The Trial of Moses." Nashville: Abingdon-Cokesbury Press, 1946.

Meyer, F. B. *Moses, the Servant of God.* London: Morgan and Scott

Miller, Dorothy Ruth. *A Handbook of Ancient History in Bible Light.* Chap. XI, "Egypt in the Time of the Israelitish Patriarchs." New York: Fleming H. Revell Co.

Moorehead, W. G. *Studies in the Mosaic Institutions. The Tabernacle, The Priesthood, The Sacrifices, The Feasts of Israel.* Dayton, 1909.

Petrie, W. M. Flinders. *Egypt and Israel.* London, 1911.

Rawlinson, George. *Moses, His Life and Times.* New York: Fleming H. Revell.

Richardson, E. C. *The Documents of Exodus, Contemporary, Original, and Written.* Vol. 10, pp. 581-605.

Sangster, Margaret E. *The Women of the Bible.* Chapt. VIII, Jochebed, Miriam, and Pharaoh's Daughter. New York: The Christian Herald.

Young, Edward J. *An Introduction to the Old Testament.* Chap. III, Topic: "The Lord's Wonders in Egypt." Grand Rapids: Wm. B. Eerdman, 1950. Pp. 69-71.

Chapter 7

ISRAEL AT SINAI—
BASIC SOCIAL AND RELIGIOUS LAWS

1. Reading Assignment: Exodus 19-40
(Read the Bible first)

2. Pedagogical Order of God's Instruction

It is important to observe that God reserved the giving of law until he had first revealed himself in redemptive power. The night of the Passover deliverance was followed by two months of additional experience in which God especially revealed his providence in behalf of Israel. In those two months he demonstrated the adequacy of his care for his redeemed people. This was well calculated to get them to yield enthusiastically to his leadership. God's method has ever been the same. He first reveals his salvation, his good purpose, his providence, and his care. Then he reveals the way of life into which his redeemed people are to walk.

As Israel was assembled at the foot of Mount Sinai the people were impressed with this redemptive claim of God upon their obedience. They were challenged to consecrate themselves in view of the declarations of the law of holiness which were to be revealed. To this challenge the people responded with implicit commitment, saying, "All that the LORD hath spoken we will do." Then it is significantly reported that "Moses returned the words of the people unto the LORD" (19:1-8).

God knew, however, that to the appeal to loving obedience there needed to be added the full force of his sovereign authority and power. Some would consecrate themselves with due devotion, but others needed to know that God's law was a requirement backed up by fiery judgment. The fire and smoke, the thundering from the mount, and the roped-off area all warned the people that God is not to be regarded lightly.

Revelation and Life

REVELATION (Exod. 20:1-2)	Deliverance Guidance Providence Promises	Basic Law— The Ten Commandments (Exod. 20:3-17)	47 Ordinances and Precepts (Exod. 21:1—23:19)

Figure 15

3. Historical Outline

I. **Preparations for Hearing the Voice of God (Exod. 19)**

1. Time: Third Month, 14th Day (19:1-2)

2. Moses Ascends; Receives God's Message (19:3-8)

(1) Retrospect: goodness of God

(2) Condition of future blessing —obedience

(3) The covenant blessing: "Be mine own possession" "Be a kingdom of priests" "Be a holy nation"

(4) Ratification by the people

3. Moses' Authority to Be Established before the People (19:9)

4. Assembly of the People on the Third Day (19:16-25)

(1) Phenomena: Thunder and lightning A thick cloud Voice of a loud trumpet Smoke—fire as a furnace Quake of the mountain Increasing loudness of the trumpet

(2) Effect: The people trembled Note: Observe that it was while Moses conversed with Jehovah that the people were moved to fear. Note how God was thus establishing a re-

spect for Moses as their leader. Note also that this whole situation was calculated to secure respect for God and attention for what he was to say.

II. **The Giving of the Ten Commandments (20:1-17)**

1. Introduction (20:1-2)

2. Duties to God (20:3-11)

3. Duties to Man (20:12-17)

4. Effects upon the People (20:18-21):

(1) The people trembled

(2) Moses was requested to speak for God

III. **Twenty-three Special Laws with Stated Penalties (21:1—22:20)**

IV. **Twenty-four Precepts with Unstated Penalties (22:21—23:19)**

V. **Injunction against Compromise with Heathen Nations (23:21-33)**

VI. **Ratification of the Law (24:1-8)**

VII. **Moses, Aaron, Nadab, and Abihu Ascend the Mount and See the LORD (24:9-11)**

VIII. **Moses and Joshua Ascend the Mount for Forty Days (24:12-18)**

4. Moral Law in Israel's Economy

What is right? Ultimately, God only has the answer to this question. When human opinion alone is considered, righteousness breaks up into endless differences; each man makes a law suitable to himself or to his particular viewpoint. Fortunately, God has declared a law which expresses the idea of his all-wise mind for his human creatures and which affords the pattern for their highest good. This law, given to Israel in a tenfold form, provides a pattern of ideal social life for any people. This is true because all people are essentially alike in their relations. All need to be in right relation to God, to one another, and to themselves. These commandments as repeated in Deuteronomy and as interpreted by Christ were but the expression of the law of love. Love is the very essence of the nature of God, John said.[1] Man therefore fulfills the divine

_____
[1] I John 4:8.

likeness when love is the ruling principle of life. There can be no question about it, God intended that this fundamental law should govern his redeemed people Israel.

5. Applications of the Moral Law

It is believed that the Ten Commandments were spoken directly by God, but that subsequent laws were delivered by Moses. Moses, moreover, came to embody the power of legislation by virtue of his relationship to God. But no legislation was valid unless it gave expression to the basic Ten Commandments.

The laws which follow the Ten Commandments were not intended for the angels of heaven. Nor were they intended for resurrected and glorified beings in a future age. They were intended for people living in this world.

The twenty-three ordinances of Exodus 21:1—22:20 were intended to provide reparations in specific cases where the law of love would be violated. The list evidently included matters which most commonly required settlement. As time went on it would be necessary to establish applications of the law in many other matters. We must not judge this legislation by the standards of western Christendom. Laws were given, for example, for masters and slaves, not to abolish slavery. We are not inclined to impose the death sentence upon a youth who smites his parents, nor upon witches. Yet if we were wiser we would doubtless understand that this severe measure was intended to save life and to increase the well-being of the nation.

The twenty-four additional precepts (22:21—23:19) were intended to curb existing tendencies to evil without measuring the degree of guilt. Perhaps the penalties would vary with the circumstances of the case. It is impossible to completely catalog sins.

6. A Dwelling Place for God

We recall how God expelled Adam and his posterity from the garden of God because of sin. We now hear God speaking to his

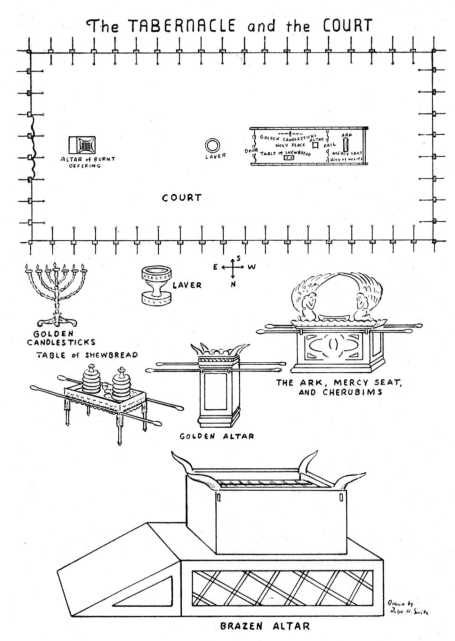

BRAZEN ALTAR

Figure 16

redeemed people, saying, "And let them make me a sanctuary that I may dwell among them" (25:8). The first commandment had required, "Thou shalt have no other gods before me." The positive aspect of that Commandment is now expressed—they are to prepare a central place for God in their midst.

Instructions were given in detail for the making and furnishing of this sanctuary. Doubtless the Israelites wondered about the meaning of many of the details in the building plans which God gave. Since Christ has come, we may now look back upon those plans in the light of the book of Hebrews (especially 9:24-28), and see how the plan prefigured the redemptive work of the Savior of men.

Though the Israelites may have understood little of the typical meaning of the tabernacle they built, it was nevertheless important for them to provide worship in the manner which God ordered. Obedience was an important element. Man lost his first communion with God because he would not obey God implicitly; the Israelites were now to regain that fellowship by yielding an implicit obedience.

7. Spiritual Principles in Israel's Worship

It is possible to over-estimate the degree of knowledge which the Israelites possessed as set forth by the symbolism of the Tabernacle. For example, they may not have fully comprehended the substitutionary death of Christ by their offering of the sacrificial lamb. On the other hand, the worship of the Tabernacle was real worship. The worshiper knew that sin must be forgiven. He knew what God required in the way of an offering, and he could obey or disobey God's order. While it is true, as the writer to Hebrews says, that the ancient sacrifice could not make the offerer perfect and that only the blood of Christ could do so, yet on the basis of faith and obedience, the righteous were justified, even in those days when instruction was by shadows. Had they spurned the Tabernacle law of offerings, that would have amounted to the rejection of the blood of the Lamb of God which taketh away the sin of the world.

Likewise in the use of the laver, and in the avoidance of that which God declared unclean, the worshiper was implicitly choosing good rather than evil, and that was significant morally and spiritually. It meant that he was trusting God and yielding obedience to his revealed will.

The use of strange fire in the sacrifices may not have been a serious evil in itself, but it was rebellion against God. It was setting aside his plan and his will, and how serious that is in the moral order only God himself can fully know.

Neglect of the Tabernacle and its calender of worship was spiritually wrong because it meant the neglect of God's presence in the midst of the nation.

8.   Discussion and Review

1.   Show how God prepared and conditioned the people for the giving of the Law.

2.   Why should people fear God?

3.   What do you understand by moral law? Is it arbitrary or necessary? Show why it is good.

4.   How are the laws of chapters 21-24 related to the Ten Commandments?

5.   What objective on God's part is sought in the instructions of chapters 25-40?

6.   Produce a free hand drawing of the Tabernacle and its principal items of furniture.

7.   Was Israel's worship real? Or did it merely anticipate real worship?

9.   Select Memory Passages

Exodus 20:1-17; 25:8

10.   Character Review

Identify:

Moses	Nadab	Bezaleel	Eleazar
Aaron	Abihu	Aholiab	Ithamar

11.   Bibliography

Dale, R. W. *The Ten Commandments*. London: Hodder & Stoughton.
Dykes, J. Oswald. *The Law of the Ten Words*. New York: George Doran Company.
Farrar, F. W. *The Voice of Sinai*. Thomas Whittaker. (It depicts the eternal basis of the moral law.)
Massee, J. C. *The Gospel in the Ten Commandments*. New York: Fleming H. Revell Co.

Masselink, Wm. *Sermons on the Ten Commandments.* (A pastor's presentation of the commandments to his congregation).

Miller, H. S. *The Gospel in the Hebrew Tabernacle Priesthood, and Offerings.* Houghton, N. Y.: The Word-Bearer Press. (A text fully documented with references to show the true symbolical significance of Israel's worship).

Moody, D. L. *Weighed in the Balances.* London: Marshall, Morgan and Scott Ltd. (Addresses on the Ten Commandments).

Morgan, G. Campbell. *The Ten Commandments.* New York: Fleming H. Revell Co. (An excellent work of 126 pages suitable for class use. One chapter is devoted to each commandment).

Sprunger, J. A. *The Gospel in Types.* Volumes I and II. Berne, Indiana: The Berne Witness.

Talbot, Louis T. *Christ in the Tabernacle.* Wheaton, Ill.: Van Kampen Press, 1942.

Chapter 8

ISRAEL AT SINAI—LAWS OF WORSHIP

1. Reading Assignment: Book of Leviticus
(Read the Bible first)

2. The Book of Leviticus

Exodus laid the foundations for redeemed Israel's social order in the bed-rock of the moral law. Jehovah had manifested his sovereignty in both the physical and moral realms. Yet all of this was not a sufficient basis for worship on the part of Israel. Accordingly, the last fifteen chapters of Exodus, we have observed, are concerned with preparations for a still further revelation of Jehovah from the Tabernacle. From it he was to speak, instructing the people in the laws of worship. This is the subject of Leviticus.

The book of Leviticus has many modern enemies. It has been stigmatized as a "bloody book," as antiquated, and as unhistorical. Others, while more sympathetic, regard it as having only typical significance, without having offered any real spiritual value to the people.

It should be borne in mind that this book comes to us in the very form in which it existed during the time of the Jewish economy including the time of Christ. Also, it is of significance that Hebrew boys were taught to read Leviticus as their first text. The book which we are to study deserves to be examined with much pains. Why was it considered of such importance?

The manifestations of God in Exodus disclosed the light of divine law against which the sins of the people were glaringly sil-

82

houetted. The nation was made conscious of a great lack. God called for holiness, and the thunders of Sinai sanctioned the demand. How could people approach such a God? Ah, this is the great question which gives Leviticus its significance. Its laws lead us from the fear that every sinner must feel, to a new relationship of confidence, faith, and worship. Leviticus was a gospel for Israel.

3. Historical Outline

I. **Law of the Five Offerings** (1:1—6:7)

1. The Burnt Offering (Ch. 1)
2. The Meal (Meat) Offering (Ch. 2)
3. The Peace Offering (Ch. 3)
4. The Sin Offering (Ch. 4)
5. The Trespass Offering (5:1—6:7)

II. **Law of the Offerings Supplemented** (6:8—7:38)

1. The Burnt Offering (6:8-13)
2. The Meal Offering (6:14-23)
3. The Sin Offering (6:24-30)
4. The Trespass Offering (7:1-10)
5. The Peace Offering (7:11-21)
6. Regarding Fats, Blood, and the Priests' Portion (7:22-38)

III. **Laws of the Consecration of the Priests** (Chapters 8-10)

1. Orders for Consecration (8:1-3)
2. Procedure (8:4-36)
   (1) Gathering of the congregation
   (2) Washing
   (3) Clothing
   (4) Anointing
   (5) Offerings
3. Eighth Day Offerings (9:1-21)
   (1) Aaron's Offerings
   (2) Peoples' Offerings
4. Climax: Blessing — Glory — Fire (9:22-24)
5. Judgment upon Priestly Unfaithfulness (10:1-10)

IV. **Laws of Purity (Chapters 11-15)**

1. Beasts (Chapter 11)
2. Woman (Chapter 12)

3. Leprosy (Chapter 13-14)
4. Personal Uncleanness (Chapter 15)

V. **Laws of the Great Day of Atonement (Chapter 16)**

VI. **Laws of Separation (Chapters 17-20)**

1. Where Blood Offerings Must Be Shed (17:1-10)
2. Offerings to Devils (17:7)
3. Eating of Blood (17:11-16)
4. Illicit Marriages and Customs (18:1-30)
5. Repetition of Many Laws and Regulations (Chapters 19-20)

VII. **Priestly Laws and Regulations (Chapters 21-22)**

VIII. **Laws of Sacred Seasons (Feasts) (Chapters 23-26)**

1. The Weekly Sabbath (23:3)
2. The Passover (23:5)
3. Unleavened Bread (23:6-8)
4. Sheaf (barley) Wave Offering (23:9-14)
5. Firstfruits (wheat loaves) (23:15-22)
6. Trumpets (23:23-25)
7. Atonement (23:26-32)
8. Tabernacle (23:33-44)
9. Sabbatic Year (25:1-7)
10. Jubilee (25:8-55)
11. Blessings and Curses to Follow Obedience or Neglect (Chapter 26)

IX. **Principles Regarding Vows, Firstlings, Devoted Things, and Tithes (Chapter 27)**

4. The Origin of Sacrifice

Sacrifices to God did not begin at Sinai. A law of sacrifice was already in effect in the family of Adam, and is seen in the true and false sacrifices made by Abel and Cain respectively. God's interest in sacrifices is evident in that special animals were reserved for sacrifice in the ark. Noah did not have to be taught how to make an acceptable sacrifice to God, as is seen in the pleasure which God had in the offering made immediately after the Flood. When Abraham came into Canaan the most conspicuous thing that he did was to set up altars at Sichem, at Bethel, and at Hebron. The very request which the Israelites made of Pharaoh was for permission to make a sacrifice to the LORD.

Religious sacrifice is an important religious practice among all peoples. Considering the fact that it existed in the first family we may properly assume that sacrifices in general have a common origin. In addition to this historic beginning there is also a very significant common psychological origin for sacrifice. Deep in the human consciousness there is a sense of need for sacrifice. The consciousness of sin calls for something to make that sin right. It did not take the commands of Sinai to make men conscious of the need for atonement. Missionaries do not need to teach the heathen the fact that they have this need.

5. Acceptable Sacrifice

Though sacrifices are made by all peoples, there is a difference in sacrifices. At the very beginning, one man's offering pleased God and another man's did not. It is not man's prerogative to say what shall constitute an atonement for sin. That right belongs to God. Sacrifice is not man's **right**; it is a God-given **privilege**. It is for man, therefore, to seek God and to offer the sacrifice which God requires. And when this is done it should be with no thought of personal merit, but in a spirit which fully recognizes God's grace and seeks his glory.

In the case of Cain and Abel, it is commonly supposed that the sacrifice of the former was rejected because it was bloodless. This may have been the case, although not all sacrifices commanded by God were blood sacrifices. The fact is stated, however, that Cain's offering was rejected because sin lay at the door. We are not told what this sin was, but this much is clear, the offering was made to suit Cain and not God. Whatever else was wrong the spirit of the offerer was unacceptable.

The instructions of Leviticus clearly bear the assumption that offerings are to be made according to God's specifications. This is

impressively set forth by the fact that when the law of the five offerings had been given and the priests had been consecrated (Lev.
1-9), God struck dead two of the priests who presumed to use "strange
fire" in their censers.

The offerings which Israel was taught to make embodied definite
principles of worship. As types they all pointed to spiritual realities
which centered in the one great offering to be made by the Lamb
of God. God had a clear pattern in mind which in the times of
the Messiah would become more fully obvious to human view.

6. The Levitical Law of Offerings

(Chapters 1-7)

Figure 17

Name of Offering	What Was Offered	What Was Done	Significance
Burnt	Cattle, sheep, or fowl	The offerer brought his offering to the door of the tent of meeting, laid his hands heavily upon its head which meant that it was his substitute, killed it, flayed (skinned) it, and cut it in pieces. Sheep were to be killed on the north side of the altar; fowls were killed by the priests. The priest sprinkled the blood of the sacrifice about the altar and on the fire, washed the carcass and inwards, cut them in pieces, prepared wood and fire, laid the pieces on the wood and burned it.	The offering was voluntary. It was intended as a sweet savor to God. The victim, wholly burned, signified the worshiper's entire self-consecration to God.
Meat (meal)	Fine flour with oil and incense	The offerer brought his offering to the priest in either of three forms. 1. If baked in the oven, it was to be either unleavened cakes or unleavened wafers mingled with oil. 2. If fried in a pan the same ingredients were to be used. Leaven was not to be used. Honey was not to be used. Salt was always to be used.	This offering was voluntary. It was a bloodless offering, hence never offered alone, but in relation to blood offerings; it usually followed the Burnt Offering. It signifies thanksgiving.

Name of Offering	What Was Offered	What Was Done	Significance
		3. If firstfruits were brought they were to be ear corn, parched with oil and frankincense.	
		The **priest** burned a handful of meal with oil and frankincense upon it as a memorial upon the altar. The remainder belonged to him. He likewise offered a portion of the cakes and kept the remainder. The same was true of the ear corn.	
Peace	Bullock, lamb, or goat	The **offerer** brought the offering as in the Burnt Offering.	This signifies the fellowship that has been effected between God and man.
		The **priest** sprinkled the blood on the altar. The caul, the liver, the kidneys, and the fat were burned upon the altar unto God. The priest's portion included the breast and the right thigh (7:31-34). The offerer might eat all that remained. Thus God, the mediator, and the offerer all partook of the same food (3:11).	
Sin	Bullock, for congregation; Ram or he-goat, for a ruler; Female kid, for a person; Two turtle doves or a young pigeon, for a poor person; or 1/10 ephah of fine flour without oil or incense, for a very poor person.	The **offerer** placed his hands upon the offering. The offering was slain and presented to the priest.	This offering was compulsory. It signified expiation for sins, especially sins of ignorance.
		The **priest** dipped his finger into the blood, sprinkled it before the veil of the sanctuary and the horns of the altar of incense, and poured the remainder at the base of the altar.	
		The fat was burned upon the brazen altar. Rest of carcass was burned in a clean place outside the camp. In the case of a ruler the blood was applied to the altar of burnt offering.	

Name of Offering	What Was Offered	What Was Done	Significance
Guilt or Trespass	Ram	A ram was selected and estimated, two shekels being the minimum. Procedure was probably as in the Sin Offering. Amends were made on the basis of estimated value plus one-fifth.	This offering was compulsory. It was a special kind of Sin Offering, expressing not only expiation but also restitution. It was always of a private character, six kinds of offense being listed (5:1-4).

7. Observations Regarding the Offerings

The offerings as they were practiced are in different order from that in which they are set forth in Leviticus 1-5. The practical order was Sin, Trespass, Burnt, Meal, and Peace. The first two in this order were compulsory. They provided expiation (forgiveness), without which the three voluntary offerings would have been meaningless. The five offerings afforded a balanced representation of the elements which make up true religion. Forgiveness through atonement is set forth first in the Sin Offering. The Trespass Offering involved not only divine forgiveness but the correction of human relations by restitution. The Burnt Offering signified the consecration of the offerer, including all of his body, and very fitly followed restoration to fellowship as signified in the Sin and Trespass Offerings. The Meal Offering provided the grace of thanksgiving as an accompaniment to the other offerings. The Peace Offering was a fellowship meal. It comes closest, perhaps, to approximating the significance of the Lord's Supper of our time. It points to that peace passing all understanding which characterizes the fellowship of the Church of Christ.

The required character of the offerings was stressed repeatedly in these instructions. It must be perfect and without blemish. In the case of the peace offering the meal must be "fine." This signifies two important things. First, worship of God is not true worship if it does not give that which is best. Secondly, God was designing a type of the perfect sacrifice which he would make as the actual atonement for sin (I Peter 1:18-19; Heb. 10:1-18).

The variety of things which might be offered was in gracious consideration of the means of the worshiper. The one-tenth ephah of fine flour offered by the extremely poor suggests the "widow's mite" of the New Testament of which Jesus said that it was more than any others had given.

8. Consecration of Priests

The conspicuous features of the ceremony by which the Aaronic priests were set apart are of interest. They were first washed, then clothed, and then anointed. These features are suggestive of the spiritual elements which qualify Christian believers as priests unto their God. In the New Testament these elements are the washing of regeneration by the word, the putting on of a new nature which constitutes our robe of righteousness, and the anointing of the Holy Spirit which is Christ's peculiar gift to his own. The offerings of the first and eighth days were then climaxed by a twofold manifestation of blessing upon the whole congregation and the appearance of God's glory at the tabernacle. That glory had appeared before when the Tabernacle was erected. At the close of this ceremony it again appeared to put into practical operation the redemptive work of the Tabernacle. From God's presence came forth fire which consumed the offering upon the altar. The effect was electric. The people shouted and fell upon their faces in worship. Such was the dramatic beginning of God's manifest presence in the midst of the camp of Israel.

9. Laws of Purity and Separation

The tenth chapter of Leviticus is a red light flashed at the establishment of Tabernacle worship to emphasize the difference between what God accepts and what he does not accept; between what is holy (consecrated) and what is not holy. The reasons for the distinctions made are not altogether understood. This does not mean that the distinctions were arbitrary. It does mean that true worship had to be exercised by faith in God rather than by complete understanding of his instructions. There are, however, plausible explanations, accounting perhaps in part at least for the distinctions required.

The distinction between clean and unclean beasts was recognized in the period before the Flood (Gen. 7:2), and was merely made into law at Sinai. It is evident that this distinction was abrogated for New Testament believers (Mark 7:19; Acts 10:12-15).

From these passages it appears that dietary distinctions as well as others were imposed upon Israel to keep them separate from the Gentiles. The gospel being intended to have universal acceptance, there was no longer the former need of racial separation, hence the dietary laws were abolished.

While it is admitted that some of the laws of chapters 11-15 and 17-20 have to us an obscure significance, it is evident that they were intended to promote cleanliness and health, and to hedge off the immoral customs of the day before they could be adopted and practiced in Israel. Considering the wickedness of the Canaanites and neighboring peoples, and the moral infancy of the Israelites, and considering the high destiny set for Israel as a channel of blessing to the world, there was ample justification for the separated life imposed upon the new nation.

10.   Israel's Calendar of Sacred Seasons

God's provision of a set calendar for Israel's year was calculated to keep the nation occupied with God. It is obvious that by the time all observances were kept there would be little time left for the people to attend the carnivals of foreigners. But the calendar had more than a negative purpose. These events were a constant reminder of religious truth and of God's providences in Israel's history. They were designed to keep her conscious of her high destiny in the world. The system of sabbaths—weekly, yearly, and every fiftieth year—had bound up in it a provision for a normal balance of work and rest, and of secular and holy. These sabbaths served as periodic breaks in undesirable trends toward worldliness, monopoly, and slavery. The history of nations reveals that something is needed periodically to keep the social order from being taken over by certain persons and classes who were born to places of advantage, and to provide release for others whose very lives are threatened with slavery.

There were three great feast seasons of the year. In the first month of Israel's year came the celebration of deliverance from Egypt. This occurred on the 14th day. It was followed by the feast of unleavened bread which lasted from the 15th to the 22nd days. In the **third month**, corresponding to Israel's arrival at Sinai and the giving of the Law, was the feast of first fruits. This was Israel's occasion to respond to the redemptive mercies signified by the Passover, and she did so with offerings of the first ripe wheat. In the **seventh month,** when heathen peoples would be distracting the Israelites with their New Year celebrations, God provided and required nearly a whole month of religion festivities. On the first day was the Feast of the blowing of Trumpets. The tenth day was the Day of Atonement (see chapter 16), the most solemn day of all the year. On this day the high priest entered the Holy of Holies to make an atonement for the sins of the nation. The fifteenth day marked the beginning of the Feast of Tabernacles, a week of celebration commemorating the wanderings of the Israelites in the wilderness. The people celebrated by living in booths and by daily sacrifices.

Every Jew faced the penalty of being cut off from Israel if he refused to attend these three annual feasts. The importance of the feasts is obvious. By them the people were to be kept conscious of their call as a nation, and of the marvelous working of God in their behalf. These memories were necessary as the foundation of a normal Israelitish faith in each generation.

11. Discussion and Review

1. Show that the laws of Leviticus are a continuation of those of Exodus.

2. Of what importance was this book to the Israelites? What question did it answer? What spiritual values did it provide?

3. Discuss the origin of sacrifice.

4. Discuss what distinguishes acceptable sacrifice. Who sets the standard for it?

5. Name, characterize, and indicate the significance of the five offerings.

6. Discuss the order of the offerings.

7. Discuss the required character of the offerings.

8. Show God's gracious consideration in the variety of things which might be offered.

9. Describe the ceremony which consecrated the priests.

10. Are the distinctions between clean and unclean fully understood? Are they arbitrary? Discuss.

11. List and briefly characterize Israel's sacred seasons.

12. Characterize Israel's predicted future in case of failure to observe God's laws, according to Leviticus 26.

12. Select Memory Passages

Leviticus 20:7, 8

13. Character Review

Identify:

Moses	Nadab	Eleazar
Aaron	Abihu	Ithamar

14. Bibliography

Fairbairn, Patrick. *The Typology of Scripture.* Vol. II. Edinburgh, 1864, pp. 317-460.

Gray, George Buchanan. *Sacrifice in the Old Testament.* Oxford, 1925.

Miller, H. S. *The Gospel in the Hebrew Tabernacle, Priesthood, and Offerings,* Houghton, N. Y.: The Word-Bearer Press.

Moule, Walter Stephen. *The Offerings Made Like unto the Son of God.* London, 1915.

Oesterley, W. O. E. *Sacrifices in Ancient Israel.* London, 1937.

Reeve, J. J. "Sacrifice in the Old Testament," *The International Standard Bible Encyclopedia,* Vol. IV, pp. 2638-2651.

Slemming, C. W. *These Are the Garments.* Grand Rapids: Zondervan Publishing House.

Slemming, C. W. *Made According to the Pattern.* Grand Rapids: Zondervan Publishing House.

Stewart, Alex. *The Mosaic Sacrifices.* Edinburgh, 1883.

Williams, C. B. "Sacrifice in the New Testament," *The International Standard Bible Encyclopedia,* Vol. IV, pp. 2651-2658.

Chapter 9

THE MARCH RESUMED

—From Sinai to the Plains of Moab

1. **Reading Assignment:** Book of Numbers.
(Read the Bible first)

2. Introduction—Relation of Numbers to Exodus and Leviticus

Numbers resumes the journey of the Israelites from the point where it was discontinued in Exodus 18. The last half of Exodus and the whole of Leviticus find them at Sinai. If the law was a schoolmaster to the new nation, then the period of Exodus 19 to Leviticus 27 constituted the academic years while in Numbers we have the record of their practical experience in applying lessons which Sinai had taught them.

At Sinai God had established the important institutions of the chosen people. The covenant had been made, laws for all phases of life had been given, a priesthood had been ordained, God's sanctuary had been erected and consecrated, and Jehovah himself had made known his presence in the center of their camp.

In Numbers we have the beginning of the course of history in which Israel was to be disciplined in the Law of their Redeemer and fitted for the central place in the outworking of world Redemption which they were chosen to fill.

The time notices of the text enable us to formulate the following diagram of Israel's new life:

92

Sinai Chronology

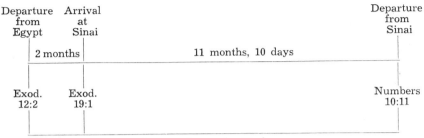

1 year, 1 month, 10 days

Figure 18

The book of Numbers covers a period of nearly thirty-nine years (1:1; Deut. 1:3). The historical facts of the book cover only a minor part of this time, leaving a long barren and silent period of wilderness wandering to which only mention is made.

3. Historical Outline

I. **The Last Days at Sinai—Preparations for March (1:1—10:10)**

1. Numbering and Arrangement of the Camp (1:1—2:34)
2. Appointments to the Levites (3:1—4:49)
3. Laws of Sanitation and Chastity for Camp Life (5:1-31)
4. Law of the Nazarites (6:1-21)
5. The Priestly Benediction (6:22-27)
6. Offerings of the Tribes for Tabernacle Worship (7:1-89)
7. The Candlestick and the Lamps (8:1-4)
8. Consecration of the Levites (8:5-26)
9. The Law of the Passover (9:1-14)
10. The Guiding Cloud (9:15-23)
11. The Trumpets and Their Uses (10:1-10)

II. **From Sinai to the Plains of Moab (10:11—25:19)**

1. Sinai to Hormah (10:11—14:45)
   (1) The order of march (10:11-28)
   (2) Hobab asked to be guide (10:29-32)
   (3) Travel signals: ark and cloud (10:33-36)
   (4) Lusting at **Taberah**; at **Kibroth-hattaavah** (11:1-34)
   (5) Sedition at **Hazeroth** (11:35—12:16)
   (6) Spies selected and sent (13:1-20) (at **Kadesh-barnea**)
   (7) Results; report; mutiny (13:21—14:10)
   (8) God's threat; Moses' intercession; God's penalty; Israel's remorse (14:11-39)
   (9) Israel's presumption and defeat (14:40-45) (at **Hormah**)
2. Instructions and Disciplines of the Wandering Period (Chapters 15-25)
   (1) Laws anticipating life in Canaan (15:1-29)
   (2) Cases of presumption (15:30-31)
   (3) A case of presumption (15:32-36)
   (4) Reminders (15:37-41)
   (5) Rebellion of Korah and his associates and the result (16:1-50)

(6) Aaron's rod (17:1-13)

(7) The Levites—responsibilities of and to them (18:1-32)

(8) Water of separation (19:1-22)

(9) Death of Miriam (20:1)

(10) Moses' sin—its occasion

(11) Excluded from passing through Edom (20:14-21)

(12) At Mt. Hor—Aaron's death and successor (20:22-29)

(13) Israel's vow and victory at Hormah (21:1-3)

(14) Fiery serpents and brazen serpent (21:4-9)

(15) Israel's journey northward: Oboth, Ijeabarim, Zared, the wilderness "on the other side of Arnon," Beer, Mattanah, Bamoth, Pisgah (21:10-20)

(16) Sihon defeated; land of Amorites possessed (21:21-32)

(17) Og defeated; land of Bashan possessed (21:33-35)

(18) Account of Encounter with Balaam and Balak (Chapters 22-24)

(19) Abode at Shittim—idolatry; whoredom; penalty; the Midianitish woman (25:1-18; cfr. Chapter 31)

III. **On the Border of the Land—Final Instructions (Chapters 26-36)**

1. The Second Numbering in View of Settlement in the Land (26:1-65)

2. Law of Inheritance Regarding Daughters (27:1-11)

3. Preparations for Change of Leadership (27:12-23)

4. Law of Offering on Stated Occasions (Chapters 28-29)

   (1) The continual burnt offering (28:3-8)

   (2) The Sabbath Day (28:9-10)

   (3) Beginning of months (28:11-15)

   (4) The Feast of Passover (28:16-25)

   (5) The Feast of Firstfruits (28:26-31)

   (6) The Feast of Trumpets (29:1-6)

   (7) Day of Atonement (29:7-11)

   (8) The Feast of Tabernacles (29:12-40)

5. Vows—Valid and Invalid (30:1-16)

6. Vengeance upon the Midianites (Chapter 31; cf. Chapter 25)

7. Assignment of Inheritance to Two and One-Half Tribes (Chapter 32)

8. Journeys Reviewed; God's Charge Regarding the Canaanites (Chapter 33)

9. The Limits of the Promised Land (34:1-12)

10. Inheritance of the Tribes (34:13-15)

11. Administrators Named (34:16-29)

12. Levitical Cities and Cities of Refuge Designated (35:1-34)

13. Inheritance of Zelophehad's Daughters; Marriage Instructions (36:1-13)

4. The Order of the Camp

The need for order and arrangement in leading two and a half million people is obvious. There was to be an order of encampment and there was to be an order of march. The order of camp was theocentric. The encampment of the twelve tribes constituted an enclosure. Next within this circle were the three Levitical families of the Merarites on the north, the Gershonites on the west, the Kohathites on the south, and the Levitical families, including Moses, Aaron and the priests, on the east. Within this enclosure was the court. Within the court was the tabernacle, and within the tabernacle was God who manifested himself in word and by his glory. Moses, Aaron, and the priests were situated on the en-

The CAMP of ISRAEL

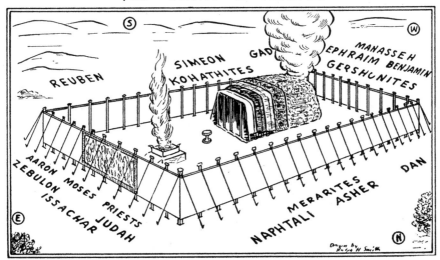

Figure 19

trance of the Tabernacle and stood between God and the people. When the camp was set the glory of the LORD was manifest above the Tabernacle, and when the camp moved the glory of the LORD arose and led the procession. It was seen as a pillar of fire by day and as a cloud by night. The use of trumpets was employed to secure the immediate action of the company.

5. The Order of the March

The standard bearers for the tribes were Judah on the east side, Reuben on the south, Ephraim on the west, and Dan on the north. When the signal to break up camp and march was given the standard bearer led the three tribes of his division.

Judah marched first, followed by Issachar, and Zebulun.

Then followed the Gershonites and Merarites bearing the Tabernacle (the heavier framework and coverings).

The second division, led by Reuben, fell in line next.

Behind Reuben came the Kohathites bearing the sanctuary.

Then came the third division of tribes led by Ephraim, and the fourth division led by Dan.

It is of interest to note that the first and rear divisions were the strongest, numerically.   The bearers of the tabernacle and of the sanctuary furniture were in the place of best protection. The positions were such that the bearers of the tabernacle had time to set it up "against" the time the Kohathites "came" (10:21) with the sanctuary.

It is clear that the ark was taken from the rest of the furniture and placed at the head of the procession (verse 33). The pillar and cloud above the ark indicated when, where, and how long the march was to continue. The consent of Hobab, Moses' brother-in-law, to accompany them, provided a familiar human eye to supplement the guidance of the pillar and cloud (10:29-32).

6. Lust, Pessimism, and Sedition

The complaints at Taberah (11:1-3), the lusting at Kibroth Hataavah (11:4-34), and the sedition fostered by Miriam and Aaron (11:35—12:16) indicated that the Israelites were determined to be poor pilgrims. In the course of these experiences it appears that even Moses' own kin not only yielded to the carnal desires of the people, but sided in with the dissenting element. The Israelites, complained about little things such as diet, but Aaron and Miriam, who were top leaders, broke out with censoriousness and jealousy against the leadership of Moses. God's prompt rebuke against them should have spoken loudly against the spirit of dissent. But the same rebellion continued to be manifest as is seen in the uprising of Korah, Dathan, and Abiram (chapter 16). The memorial plates made on this occasion and Aaron's rod which budded became permanent symbols in Israel against disrespect for God's constituted leader (chapters 16 and 17). Chapter 18 appropriately follows these lessons against dissenters by declaring responsibilities of and to the Levites.

It appears that no hope was extended for a person who sinned presumptuously (15:30-31). A test case of presumption is recorded in the same chapter (15:32-36).

It is evident that drastic measures were needed against any manifest spirit of disrespect for God, his word, and his leader. Had that spirit been condoned in any degree it is easy to understand how soon such a large company might have been demoralized, disorganized, and destroyed in the wilderness. On the positive side, their undertaking such a feat as the conquest of Canaan required an undivided nation. There was no place for personal ambition on any level. Had Moses been a self-established dictator the matter would have been different. But he was the meekest of men. He had not asked for leadership. It is always a serious matter to take issue with a leader who is really commissioned and anointed of God.

7. Forfeiture of an Open Door

Kadesh-barnea stands for opportunity. In Israel's case it came to stand for "fumbled opportunity." An overwhelming majority decision ruled against the way of faith in God, and planned to set up leaders who would take the whole nation back to bondage in Egypt. In Israel, however, there was a higher authority than the people's majority. The door of opportunity was by God declared closed, and those who had cherished leeks, onions, garlick, and Egypt above God's providence and promise would die in the wilderness.

The awakening of that unbelieving majority to their loss produced a frenzied, but futile and pathetic effort to enter the door that had been open. Sorry failure was the crown of their unbelief. The Amalekites swooped down and drove them to Hormah, and in the course of years their bones bleached upon the wilderness sands.

8. A New Generation Begins to Score Victory

Against the background of thirty-seven years of futile wandering in the Arabian desert, we see the beginnings of new advance in Numbers 21. It is significant that the new generation won its first victory on the same ground as had been the scene of their fathers' defeat at Hormah (11:40-45; 21:1-3).

Under a spell of discouragement, however, the new generation yielded to the same complaint and low desire which was voiced by the fathers a generation before. One wonders whether a few of those unbelievers may not still have been alive. If so, they probably were the source of this complaint. The deathly serpents sent among the people and the brazen serpent erected as God's provision for believers became an abiding memorial of the fact that a way of hope remained open for all believing persons (21:4-9).

9. Moses' Sin—What It Teaches

Moses' sin (20:7-13) disappoints us. We do not like to see

our "hero" forfeit the land of promise. Moses' failure, however, is much the same as that of anyone else who fails. He failed to have grace. His disgust for the people implied that he himself was above the need for God's mercies. He ceased to have the spirit of intercession for sinners.

On the other hand, we learn an encouraging fact from Moses, which is that his defection did not sever his relationship with God. This is clearly proved by the place which Moses had along with Elijah upon the mount of transfiguration (Matt. 17). His case suggests to us the possibility that others of that rebellious generation, who because they failed God forfeited the specific promise of the land of Canaan, yet through repentance and faith might be heirs of God's grace in eternity.

10.　The Israelites and Their National Relatives

ABRAHAM	Ishmael .... Ishmaelites
	Isaac—Jacob .... Israelites
	Esau .... Edomites
	Six sons of Keturah ....
	...... Midianites and other Arabian tribes
LOT	Ammon .... Ammonites
	Moab .... Moabites

Figure 20

Developments from the days of Abraham, Isaac, and Jacob became significant as Israel entered upon her national life. Not only the Canaanitish nations resisted her, but the offspring of Israel's carnal relatives manifested their old-time antagonism. Edom, settled at Mount Seir, forbad passage through her land. The Moabites and Midianites, though not strong enough to venture military power against Israel, sought to curse her, and by appeals to carnal desire to subvert her. These nations had become completely paganized. They continued an existence until after the Babylonian captivity when they eventually lost their identity. Their remnant was doubtless absorbed in the heterogeneous populace of Arabia.

11. The March of Triumph

Beginning with the victory at Hormah (21:1-3), the Israelites started upon the path of triumph. The resistance of the Edomites had occasioned temporary fear and some inconveniences, but after taking the way of the Red Sea and then moving northward along the east side of the Dead Sea, Israel gained victories of definite military importance. East of the Jordan, Sihon, king of the Amorites, had been recognized as the power of first military importance. Against his opposition Israel set her forces with complete victory. Next, Og, king of Bashan fell. These victories brought to naught all significant military resistance east of the Jordan, and sent an arrow of fear to the hearts of the kings of Canaan.

The book of Numbers has been called an ugly duckling. It is only in the closing year of its wilderness drab that the pearly white plumage of Israel's growth begins to appear. Situated on the plains of Moab, east of the Jordan, it manifested its real power, and the glory of conquest in the promised land appeared as a challenging halo above its head. Its destiny was too certain for Balaam to be able to curse her. Instead he could only proclaim prophetic tribute to her glorious Messianic future: "I shall see him," he said, "but not now: I shall behold him but not nigh: there shall come a Star out of Jacob, and a Sceptre shall rise out of Israel, and shall smite the corners of Moab, and destroy all the children of Sheth."

The vision of Balaam penetrated Israel's future, predicting her supremacy over Moab, Edom, and Amalek, and speaking with comfort of the Kenites (descendants of Jethro). It depicted the rise of Assyria and her fall at the hands of a power coming from the west (Macedonia). All of this demonstrated the high destiny which God had designed for the people of the Abrahamic covenant.

Nor could the lure to idolatry and adultery effectively degrade this beautiful swan. Though individuals yielded to the enticements of Moab and Midian, when the matter was known the swan cleansed herself with hot vengeance upon her seducers (Numbers 22-24, 31)

The book of Deuteronomy follows in the time and place setting to which Numbers has brought us, and has as its burden the concern that Israel shall respond to her high calling with undivided, sincere consecration to God.

12. Census of Israel
Before and after the Period of Wanderings
(Numbers 1 and 2, and 26)

	Before the Wanderings	After the Wanderings	Difference
Reuben	46,500	43,730	—2,770
Simeon	59,300	22,200	—37,100
Gad	45,650	40,500	—5,150
Judah	74,600	76,500	+1,900
Issachar	54,400	64,300	+9,900
Zebulun	57,400	60,500	+3,100
Ephraim	40,500	32,500	—8,000
Manasseh	32,200	52,700	+20,500
Benjamin	35,400	45,600	+10,200
Dan	62,700	64,400	+1,700
Asher	41,500	53,400	+11,900
Naphtali	53,400	45,400	—8,000
	603,550	601,730	—1,820

Figure 21

13. Discussion and Review

1. Draw from memory a diagram showing the order of the camp of Israel.

2. Describe the order of march.

3. How did God deal with insubordination as seen in Numbers 11-18? Cite the particular cases.

4. How do you justify the stringency with which God dealt with presumption (chapter 15)?

5. What is the significance of Kadesh-barnea in Israel's history?

6. What two significant experiences did Israel have at Hormah?

7. What lessons are taught by Moses' sin (20:7-13)?

8. What is the lesson from the brazen serpent (21:4-9)?

9. Show the ancestral relation of Israel to the Ishmaelites, Edomites, Ammonites, and Moabites.

10. Relate the victories of the Israelites after the battle at Hormah by which they established their supremacy east of the Jordan.

11. Of what military significance was the defeat of Sihon and Og?

12. How do you explain Balaam?

13. Explain why Numbers has been called an ugly duckling.

H4061

14. Select Memory Passages

Numbers 6:24-26; 14:8

15. Character Review

Identify:

Moses	Eleazar	Balaam	Zelophehad	Abiram
Aaron	Ithamar	Joshua	Anakims	Ishmaelites
Nadab	Kohath	Eldad	Amalekites	Edomites
Abihu	Merari	Medad	Canaanites	Midianites
Og	Gershon	Miriam	Korah	Ammonites
Sihon	Balak	Caleb	Dathan	Moabites

16. Bibliography

Albright, W. A. "The Oracles of Balaam," *The Journal of Biblical Literature.*
    Vol. LXIII. 1944, pp. 207-233.
Blaikie, Wm. G. *Bible History.* Section V, "Conquest of East Side of Jordan,"
    pp. 144-151. Section VI, "Moab and Midian," pp. 151-156. New York: Thomas
    Nelson and Sons.
Cox, Samuel. *Balaam.* London, 1884.
Free, Joseph P. *Archaeology and Bible History.* Topic: "The Book of Numbers."
    Wheaton, Ill.: Van Kampen Press. Pp. 112-117.

Chapter 10

DRAMATIC APPEAL TO ISRAEL
ON THE VERGE OF THE PROMISED LAND

1. **Reading Assignment:** Book of Deuteronomy
(Read the Bible first)

2. **Introduction: The Book of Deuteronomy**

Title and Purpose

The title of this book reveals its purpose but partially. It signifies the Second Law or the Law repeated. But Deuteronomy is not merely a repetition of the history and law set forth in the books which we have previously studied. Rather it is a repetition with particular emphasis in view of the new life upon which the Israelites were about to enter. It sums up the mercies of Jehovah toward Israel in the past and exhorts the new nation to obedience, henceforth, that God may do even greater things for them. It is filled from beginning to close with solicitude for the loving obedience of the redeemed people. The book emphasizes, especially, the **spirit** of the law, calling not for mere formal obedience, but for love to Jehovah with all the heart, soul and mind.

Occasion for the Book

The book has its occasion in the fact that Israel faced a turn in her national life. The years of wilderness wandering were about to give place to residence in the promised land. The new nation was to settle in cities, villages, farms, and vineyards. The numerous laws given at Sinai were now to be applied in the formation of her institutions. The seductive influences of Canaanitish life, including its gross idolatry and glaring immortality, would need to be withstood by regulations requiring the most stringent separation.

Authorship

The book of Deuteronomy is no exception to the unity of the Pentateuch. Some modern critics have assumed that it is of later origin than the other four books, coming into being possibly as late as the fourth century B. C. The simple fact is however, that not only the book itself affirms the Mosaic authorship (31:19), but in the New Testament also, it is directly ascribed to Moses (Matt. 19:7-8; Mk. 8:3; Acts 3:22; 7:37). The fact that the account of Moses' death occurs in the last chapter is no argument against the Mosaic authorship of the book. Naturally this account was added by an associate of Moses or by his successor.

3. Historical Outline

I. **The First Discourse (1:1—4:40)**

1. Introduction (1:1-5)
   (1) Subject: Words of Moses
   (2) Time: 40/11/1
   (3) Place: Plains of Moab, east of Jordan
2. Retrospect: Horeb to Kadesh-barnea (1:6-46)
   (1) Orders to Take the Promised Land (1:6-8)
   (2) Provision for subordinate rulers (1:9-18)
   (3) At Kadesh-barnea (1:19-46)
      1) The Mount of the Amorites to be taken promptly (1:19-21)
      2) Provision for subordinate rulers (1:9-18)
      3) Findings; reports; discouragement; unbelief; penalty; remorse; presumption; defeat; Joshua and Caleb commended (1:24-46)
3. Retrospect Continued: Kadesh to Beth-peor (2:1—3:29)

   (1) Long time spent encompassing Seir (2:1)
   (2) Policy regarding Land of Edom (2:2-7)
   (3) Policy regarding Land of Moab (2:8-9)
   (4) Mention of ancient races (2:10-12)
   (5) Time of Wandering—38 years (2:13-15)
   (6) Policy regarding Land of Ammon (2:16-19)
   (7) Mention of ancient races (2:20-23)
   (8) Victory over King Sihon (2:24-37)
   (9) The conquest of King Og (3:1-17)
   (10) Conquest to precede possession (3:18-20)
   (11) Moses' request; the satisfaction accorded him (3:21-29)
4. Exhortation to Go on to Complete Occupation of the Promised Land (4:1-40)

(1) Warning regarding forgetting God's law (4:1-13)

(2) Warning regarding idols (4:14-24)

(3) Evil anticipated as a disqualification for possessing the Land (4:25-28)

(4) God anticipating Israel's expulsion urges terms of restoration (4:29-31)

(5) God's peculiar favor perpetual upon conditions (4:32-40)

5. Cities of Refuge Appointed (4:41-43)

II. **The Second Discourse** (4:44—26:19)

1. Introduction (4:44-49)

2. The Giving of the Decalogue Recalled; Law Restated and Its Observance Pleaded (Chapters 5-6)

3. Instructions Regarding the Canaanitish Nations (Chapter 7)

(1) The nations named (7:1)

(2) They are to be destroyed, utterly (7:2) but gradually (7:22)

(3) A covenant with them forbidden (7:2)

(4) Marriage with them forbidden (7:3-4)

(5) Pagan worship to be demolished (7:5)

(6) Israel's call to a superior covenant (7:6-11)

4. Blessings Flowing from God's Covenant (7:12-16)

5. Israel Assured of Victory through Her God (7:17-26)

6. God's Purpose in the Wilderness Chastisements (8:1-9)

7. The Peril of Prosperity Anticipated —A Solemn Warning (8:10-20)

8. Why God Gave the Land to Israel (9:1-29)

(1) Because of the wickedness of the Canaanitish nations (10:3-4)

(2) Because of His Word to the Fathers (v. 5)

*(3) Not because of Israel's righteousness (9:5-29)

1) Her wilderness rebellions (9:7)

2) Her sin at Horeb (9:8-21)

3) Murmurings at Taberah, Massah, and Kibroth-hattaavah (9:22)

4) Unbelief at Kadesh-barnea (9:23)

5) Rebellion throughout Moses' life (9:24)

(4) God's honor must be preserved (9:25-29)

(5) God's manifest mercy (10:1-11)

1) In restoring the two tables (10:1-5)

2) In appointing a successor to Aaron—Eleazar (10:6-7)

3) In appointing the Levites to minister (10:8-9)

4) In answering Moses' intercession (10:10-11)

9. God's Requirements of Israel (10:12 —11:25)

(1) Fear God (10:12)

(2) Walk in His Ways (10:12)

(3) Love God (10:12)

(4) Serve God with all the heart and soul (10:12)

(5) Keep his commandments and statutes to procure their own good (10:13)

(6) Circumcise . . . . the heart (10:16)

(7) Love the stranger (10:19)

(8) Fear the Lord (10:20)

(9) Serve the Lord (10:20)

(10) Cleave to the Lord (10:20)

(11) Swear by **his** name (10:20)

(12) Love the Lord (11:1)

(13) Keep his charge, statutes, and judgments alway (11:1)

(14) Keep all the Commandments (11:8)

(15) Lay up God's word "in thine hearts" (11:18)

10. Covenant Memorials—Gerizim and Ebal (11:26-32)

11. Laws Concerning Religion (12:1—16:17)

(1) Paraphernalia of idolatry to be demolished (12:1-4)

(2) The designated place of divine service to be kept exclusively (12:5-28)

1) Exception — when distance is great meat may be eaten as desired if not for holy use (12:15, 20-22)

2) Warning: Blood not to be eaten (12:16, 23-25)

(3) Worship of other gods prohibited (12:29-32)

(4) The moral test to be applied to false prophets (13:1-4)

(5) Punishment of enticers to idolatry (13:5-11)

(6) Punishment of idolatrous cities (13:12-18)

(7) Pagan mourning forbidden (13:1-2)

(8) Clean and unclean beasts (14:3-8)

(9) Clean and unclean fish (14:9-10)

(10) Clean and unclean birds (14:12-20)

(11) Dead animals forbidden (14:21)

(12) Tithe for worship and Levites (14:22-27)

(13) Tithe for the Levites, strangers, fatherless and widows every three years (14:28-29)

(14) Rulings regarding the Sabbatic Year (15:1-18)
1) The Lord's release (15:1-2)
2) The foreigner an exception (15:3)
3) To be no poor (15:4-5) (cfr. 15:11)
4) Israel to be lenders (15:6)
5) Proper attitude to the poor (15:7-11)
6) Release of Hebrew slave (15:12-18)

(15) Firstling males to be sanctified (15:19-23)

(16) Feast of Passover and Unleavened Bread (16:1-8)

(17) Feast of Weeks (16:9-12)

(18) Feast of Tabernacles (17:13-15)

(19) Three feasts with required attendance and offerings (17:16-17)

12. Laws Concerning Civil Life (16:18 —21:9)

(1) Judges and officers ordered (16:18-20)

(2) Graves near altar and images prohibited (16:21-22)

(3) Blemished offerings unlawful (17:1)

(4) Idolaters to be tried and slain (17:2-7)

(5) Procedure in hard cases (17:8-13) (anticipating Judges Period)

(6) Instructions for kings (17:14-20) (anticipating Kings Period)

(7) What is due the Levites (18:1-8)

(8) Magical arts to be unlawful (18:9-14)

(9) The false prophet discerned (18:15-22)

(10) Instructions regarding Cities of Refuge (19:1-13)

(11) Regard for ancient landmarks (19:14)

(12) Number of witnesses required (19:15)

(13) Dealing with a false witness (19:16-21)

(14) Preparations for battle (20:1-20)
1) God's presence to expel fear of man (20:1-4)
2) Soldier to be qualified (20:5-9)
3) Taking foreign cities (20:10-15)
4) Taking cities of Canaan (20:16-18)
5) Regard for trees (20:19-20)

(15) Expiation of uncertain murder (21:1-9)

13. Laws Concerning Domestic and Social Relations (21:10—26:19)

(1) A captive woman for wife (21:10-14)

(2) The inheritance of a man with two wives (21:15-17)

(3) Dealing with an incorrigible son (21:18-21)

(4) Hanging—removal of body before night (21:22-23)

(5) Neighborly concern for another's property (22:1-4)

(6) Distinct apparel of sexes (22:5)

(7) Regard for a bird and its young (22:6-7)

(8) Bannisters for houses (22:8)

(9) Mixed seed prohibited (22:9)

(10) Ox and ass team prohibited (22:10)

(11) Garment of wool and linen (22:11)

(12) Fringes upon vesture (22:12)

(13) Regarding a bride's virginity (22:13-21)

(14) Regarding sexual relations with a married woman (22:22)

(15) Enticement—three cases cited (22:23-29)

(16) Those who may not enter the camp (23:1-8)

    1) One wounded in private organs (23:1)

    2) A bastard to the tenth generation (23:2)

    3) An Ammonite or Moabite to the tenth generation (23:3-6)

    4) An Edomite to the third generation (23:7-8)

    5) An Egyptian to the third generation (23:8)

(17) Warning against wicked army life (23:9)

(18) A man's personal uncleanness (23:10-11)

(19) Disposal of bodily waste (23:12-14)

(20) Sheltering a fugitive (23:15-16)

(21) Whores and sodomites forbidden. Their price unholy money (23:17-18)

(22) Usury from a brother unlawful (23:19-20)

(23) Inviolability of vows (23:21-23)

(24) Eating a neighbor's food within limit (23:24-25)

(25) Divorce regulations (24:1-4)

(26) A year's furlough after marriage (24:5)

(27) A man's millstone a forbidden pledge (24:6)

(28) Slave traffic of brethren condemned (24:7)

(29) Ruling regarding leprosy (24:8-9)

(30) Considerations regarding a man's pledge (24:10-13)

(31) Prompt payment of a poor servant (24:14-15)

(32) Personal responsibility of fathers and children (24:16)

(33) Impartiality in judging stranger, fatherless and widows (24:17-18)

(34) Gleanings to be left for the poor (24:19-22)

(35) Maximum stripes—forty (25:1-3)

(36) Ox treading corn to be unmuzzled (25:4)

(37) Law of the kinsman redeemer (25:5-10)

(38) Woman interfering in fight of husband (25:11-12)

(39) Unjust weights unlawful (25:13-16)

(40) Amalek to be blotted out (25:17-19)

(41) The confession offered in bringing the firstfruits (26:1-11)

(42) The confession offered in bringing the third year tithe (26:12-15)

(43) God and Israel vow to keep covenant (26:16-19)

III. **The Third Discourse—A Future of Blessedness in Contrast to Curses Set before Israel (Chapters 27-30)**

1. The Law to be Written upon Two Stones and an Altar Prepared in the Land (27:1-8)

2. Israel Espoused for a Special Relationship Which Should be Reason for Obedience (27:9-10)

3. The Tribes Divided to Stand on Two Mounts (27:11-13)

    (1) On Gerizim to bless: Simeon, Levi, Judah, Issachar, Joseph, Benjamin

    (2) On Ebal to curse: Reuben, Gad, Asher, Zebulun, Dan, Naphtali

4. Curses to Proceed from Ebal (27:14-26)

    (1) For image manufacture and worship

    (2) For disrespect for parents

    (3) For removing the neighbor's landmark

    (4) For misleading the blind

(5) For preventing judgment against strangers, orphans, and widows

(6) For adultery with father's wife

(7) For beastiality

(8) For adultery with a sister

(9) For adultery with mother-in-law

(10) For smiting a brother secretly

(11) For hiring to slay an innocent person

(12) For failing to confirm all of this law

5. Blessings for Obedience (28:1-14)

(1) Blessed in the city and field

(2) Blessed with fruition: of the body, of the ground, of cattle, of kine, of sheep

(3) Blessing upon the basket
Blessing upon the store (kneading trough)

(4) Blessing in coming in
Blessing in going out

(5) Blessed with victory over enemies (28:7)

(6) Blessing upon the storehouses (28:8)

(7) Blessing in all undertakings (28:8)

(8) Blessing in the Land (28:8)

(9) Blessing of a permanent special relationship with God (28:9)

(10) Blessing of respect by the nations (28:10)

(11) Blessing of plenty in the Land (28:11-12)

(12) Blessing of financial lending to many nations (28:12)

(13) Blessing of being head instead of tail (28:13)

(14) Blessing of being on top (28:13)

6. Curses (Penalties) for Disobedience (28:15-68)

(1) Cursed in city and field (28:16)

(2) Cursed basket and store (kneading trough) (28:17)

(3) Cursed fruit (28:18) of body, land, kine, flocks, and sheep

(4) Cursed in coming in and going out (28:19)

(5) Cursed in all doings—to destruction (28:20)
With cursing, vexation, and rebuke

(6) Cursed with pestilence—until consumed (28:21)

(7) Cursed with consumption

(8) Cursed with fever

(9) Cursed with inflamation

(10) Cursed with extreme burning (28:2) Until ye perish

(11) Cursed with the sword

(12) Cursed with blasting

(13) Cursed with mildew

(14) Cursed with brazen heavens (28:23)

(15) Cursed with iron earth (28:23)

(16) Rain to be changed to dust (28:24)

(17) To be defeated by enemies (28:25)

(18) To be tossed to and fro among nations (28:25)

(19) Carcases to feed birds and beasts (28:26)

(20) To be smitten with boils, emerods, scab, and itch (28:27)

(21) To be smitten with a heart of madness, blindness, and astonishment (28:28)

(22) To grope blindly, never prosper, and ultimately to be spoiled (28:29)

(23) No satisfaction to be received from possessions (28:30-34)
From wife, house, vineyard, ox, ass, sheep, sons and daughters, fruit of land and labors

(24) To be smitten in knees, legs, and with boils all over (28:35)

(25) Israel and her king (anticipated) to be carried captive (28:36-37)

(26) Locusts to spoil crops and worms the vines (28:38-39)

(27) Olive trees to cast their fruit (28:40)

(28) Sons and daughters to go into captivity (28:41)

(29) Locusts to consume trees and fruit (28:42)

(30) Stranger to rise above Israel (28:43)

(31) Stranger shall lend to Israel (28:43)

(32) Stranger to be head, Israel the tail (28:44)

(33) All these curses to come upon, pursue, overthrow, and destroy the disobedient (28:45-48)

7. Description of the Final Captivity and Dispersion among the Nations (28:49-68)

(1) The captor to be
   1) From far
   2) Swift as an eagle
   3) A strange nation
   4) A fierce and ruthless nation (28:49-51)

(2) Israel to be spoiled and besieged (28:52)
   1) Defenses to fail (28:52)
   2) Parents to eat their children (28:53-57)
   3) Endearment turned to an evil eye (28:53-57)

(3) Innumerable plagues to pursue her continually until only a few remain (28:58-63)

(4) Israel to be scattered to all nations (28:64)

(5) Pagan gods to be worshiped (28:64)

(6) There will be
   1) Ceaseless unrest
   2) A trembling heart
   3) Failing of eyes
   4) Pining of soul
   5) Uncertainty of life
   6) Futility of living (28:65-67)

(7) Israel to Be Reduced to Hopeless Bondage Again (28:68)

8. Espousal of the Covenant Pleaded
   (1) In view of Jehovah's past benefits (29:1-17)
   (2) In view of God's wrath to remove them from the Land (29:18-29)

9. Anticipation of Future Captivity
   (1) Promise of mercies upon conditions
      1) Jehovah will restore them to the Land from all nations, will circumcise their hearts, remove curses, and bless them abundantly

2) Jehovah's blessing to be contingent upon their return unto the Lord (30:2) and their whole-hearted observance of the covenant (30:10)

10. Israel Has Two Alternatives and She Is Fully Responsible (30:11-20)
   (1) The objection of inability answered (30:11-14)
   (2) Life or death are the destinies (30:15-20)

IV. **The Last Days of Moses (31-34)**

1. Moses' Encouragement of the People (31:1-6)
   (1) Moses explains his resignation
   (2) Joshua will lead them
   (3) Jehovah their God will be with them

2. Moses' Charge to Joshua before the People (31:7-8)

3. Moses' Charge to the Levites and Elders (31:9-13)
   (1) The law (Deuteronomy) delivered to them
   (2) It is to be read at the Feast of Tabernacles every Sabbatic Year

4. God's Charge to Joshua (31:14-15) (With Moses in the Tabernacle)

5. The Law Deposited in the Sides of the Ark (31:24-27)

6. The Song of Moses
   (1) Its occasion—the fact of future rebellion (31:16-30)
   (2) The song proper (32:1-43)
   (3) Hearers are begged to set their hearts upon it (32:44-47)
   (4) Moses instructed to go up on Nebo (32:48-52)
      1) To view the Promised Land
      2) To die
   (5) Moses' blessing upon the tribes (chapter 33)
      1) Introduction — Jehovah's great manifestations (33:1-5)
      2) The blessings (33:6-25)
      3) A tribute extolling the God of Jeshurun and his people (33:26-29)

7. Moses Shown the Land from Mt. Pisgah (34:1-4)

8. Moses' Death (34:5-6)
    (1) Burial in a valley of Moab near Beth-peor by God
    (2) The sepulchre known only to God
    (3) Moses' Age—120 years (34:7)
    (4) His health—unspent (34:7)
    (5) Thirty days of weeping in Israel (34:8)

9. Joshua Succeeds Moses (34:9)
    (1) His qualifications:
        1) Full of the Spirit of Wisdom
        2) Ordained by Moses' hands
        3) Israel respected him
        4) He obeyed God

10. Moses the Greatest of the Prophets (34:10-12)

4. Moses' Final Messages: Their Burden and Strategy

Having read the discourses of Deuteronomy, the reader is made conscious of an intense purpose and of dramatic strategy on the part of Israel's leader. In the first address the speaker reviews the whole miraculous background of the new nation with its climax of triumph over Sihon and Og, and then, by the inspiration of past achievement, urges upon the people the challenge of perpetual triumph (1—4:40).

The second discourse (4:44—26:19), which is the longest, includes a repetition of the law. The Ten Commandments are again given, but now the thunders of Sinai have been replaced by an appealing spiritual logic. Two principles are continuous. The first is that the LORD who gave the commandments is good. His holiness as expressed in his law has its source in his great love. Past promises, providences, and chastenings were to be understood as expressing that love. The second principle is that the essence of the obedience which God's law requires consists of love. This love is to be undivided, coming from the whole heart, and soul, and might. God's words were to be in the **hearts** of his people; to this end the reminders, instruction, reasonings, and warnings of chapters 5-11 were diligently pressed upon the consciousness of the people of the new nation.

The laws of the remainder of the second discourse, falling into three main categories of life, may seem to be too loaded with details to be a part of an appeal to the spirit of love. Someone may object that in these we have an emphasis upon the letter rather than the spirit of the law. To this we must reply that if love is to be genuine it cannot be excluded from any area of life. The wonder of this discourse is that it pictures God as condescending to take an interest in the particulars of human life—of religious life (12:1—16:17), of civil life (16:18—21:9), and of domestic and social life (21:10—26:19).

The abiding value of these many laws is not in their complete applicability to modern life. They were given to a stated people for a stated time and place, and with regard to a particular purpose. They have value for our study, however. They show, first of all that spirituality is to find appropriate expression in all areas of life. They show that government should concern itself with the proper application of principles. It appears that these laws were not proclaimed in a complete and systematic code which covered all matters conceivable; some of them were given as issues arose; others anticipated issues. It was the Pharisees who later attempted to prescribe a specific law for every conceivable human act. Another value of these laws, important to the student, is the insight which they afford into human life. There was no such supposition as the idea that virtue consists of following the dictates of nature. Nature was not thwarted, but it was ever made subject to law. Nor were the people left to their **concensus gentium** as though the vote of the majority could make a thing right or wrong. In Israel's economy all laws were the expression of the nature and wisdom of God in relation to the lives of his people.

Israel's response to God's law would determine her future. This was impressively expressed in a litany to be observed on the mounts Ebal and Gerizim. It consisted of a division of the tribes upon the two mounts, those upon Gerizim proclaiming blessings for obedience and those on Ebal proclaiming curses for disobedience. This exercise, which is announced briefly in the second discourse (11:26-28), is given in detail in the third discourse (chapters 27-30). The curses in the latter passage involve a prophetic description of Israel's final captivity and dispersion among the nations. The prophecy is accompanied with an appeal to Israel to return, even in captivity, to the mercies of God's covenant (chapter 29). Ultimately, however, the people were themselves declared to be fully responsible for their final destiny, which must be either life or death (chapter 30)

5. The Spurious Complaint of Inability

In Moses' third discourse he anticipated the human complaint that man is unable to keep God's commandments (30:11-14). The same complaint has been put into theoretical form by present day teachers who insist that man cannot and was not intended to obey God. In church history this teaching is called antinomianism (against law) which says that saving faith is of such a nature as to remove the obligation of obedience to God's law.

Moses' reply leaves no question about the matter. The Israelites were intended to obey God, and this intention implies the ability to do so.

Said Moses: "For this commandment which I command thee this day, is not hidden from (too hard for, A. R. V.) thee . . . . But the word is very nigh unto thee, in thy mouth, and in thy heart, that thou mayest do it."

The whole problem of fulfilling God's law lies in two things: God's revelation to the human heart on the one side, and man's appropriate response to that revelation on the other side. God's love manifest begets love in the reasoning heart. If this result fails, it must be, not a matter of ability but of unwillingness and rebellion on man's part. This is where the case must rest. It is not inability, primarily, but ill will that ails men.

6. How Could a God of Love Destroy the Canaanites?

The question may be raised, "If the LORD is really a being of love, how could he give such an order as is found in Deuteronomy 7:1-5, requiring the destruction of the Canaanites?

This question may be settled reasonably by reference to a principle of divine government and by considering the facts in the case. The principle is this: That it is God's right and his responsibility to determine the time of existence for the peoples of the earth in keeping with his love, holiness, and wisdom (study Acts 17:24-31). The facts are that the Canaanitish nations had become so wicked that they were a menace not only to others but to themselves. Sin had become so heartless and extreme that it was a mercy to unborn generations that they should no longer be perpetuated. Says Professor J. P. Free: "The archaeological discoveries . . . . have shown that the Canaanites sacrificed their children, that their temples were places of vice, and that their morals were so low that they would inevitably corrupt the people of God if they remained in the land."[1]

Not only was it not wrong for the Israelites to kill the Canaanites, as would be the case ordinarily, but God made it mandatory

[1] J. P. Free, *Archaeology and Bible History*, Van Kampen Press. Page 122.

that they should do so. Let no Christian look back upon Israel's conquests as representing a lower moral standard than that of the Christian era. God must be the judge of that. There is no higher ethic for a given person than implicit obedience to God's command. The later history of Israel gives the sorry result of Israel's failure to wholly obey God's command in this matter.

7. The Last Days of Moses

Moses' major addresses to Israel having been given, he proceeded to speak to the people more especially with regard to his personal departure. He explained why he could not enter the land, but made no complaint. Rather, his whole concern centered in those who would be entering. Here is a mark of his greatness, of his unselfishness, and of his true shepherd heart.

Moses did for Joshua, what every true leader should do. In withdrawing from leadership he was careful to build up the confidence of the people in the leadership of his successor. Of course he was wise enough to remind them that God would continue to be the leader in first command (31:1-6). In view of this, Moses gave a solemn charge to all of the human leaders, to Joshua, the Levites, and to the elders (31:7-13). He gave them the Law (presumably, the book of Deuteronomy), commanded that it be read publicly each Sabbatic year, and had it deposited "in the sides of the ark" (31:14-27).

The Song of Moses (chapter 32) has a double theme. The first theme is expressed in the candid words which close chapter 31. It is Israel's bent to sin and corruption. The other theme is the LORD'S goodness to Israel. The two themes are significantly brought together in the figure of 32:15: "Jeshurun (the righteous and favored one, Israel) waxed fat, and kicked . . . . then he forsook God which made him, and lightly esteemed the Rock of his salvation." Moses earnestly entreated all Israel to set their hearts upon the meaning of this song, the meaning intended being that by wisely heeding it God's blessing would remain upon them in the new land. On the same day (32:48-52; 34:1-4), Moses was ordered to ascend Mount Pisgah. From its lofty height he was permitted to view the land which Israel was about to enter. Before ascending he blessed the tribes (chapter 33).

8. The Death of Moses

The objection is commonly raised, against the Mosaic authorship of Deuteronomy, that Moses could not have written the
account of his own death (34:5-12). Naturally, Moses' successor
or someone under his authority added this account to the record.
It must be remembered that these records were the records of the
nation, not of the particular leader in authority. The successor for
such a service was fully provided for.

9.   A Tribute To Moses

On this subject one thing is important. The hero of the history
we have been studying is not Moses, nor any other man, but God.
The writer of Moses' obituary skilfully reserved first honor for
Moses' God and gave to Moses a related and subordinate honor.
Moses was distinguished as the "servant of the LORD." Human
categories of greatness are puny in comparison with such a distinction. Moses had indeed performed a feat of leadership which pales
the Alexanders and the Caesars, but honesty requires the world
to know that all he did was done as the servant of the final and
eternal sovereign of the universe. A faithful subordinate authority
under the LORD is a greater distinction of honor than to head a
world government which the LORD has not founded.

Moses' obituary also distinguishes him as "full of the spirit of
wisdom" (34:9) and as the "prophet" most intimately related to God
(34:10). Here again his greatness is a matter of his relationship
with God. That man is the wisest who has God's gift of wisdom.
That man is the greatest prophet to whom God most intimately reveals himself. Moses had at an earlier time been characterized as
the "meekest" of men (Numbers 12:3). We may observe from
Moses' life how God can impart his glory to those who are truly
meek. We may be encouraged by Christ's own words that the meek
are "blessed," that they shall "inherit the earth."

Moses was a man of high altitudes. We associate him with
Sinai and with Pisgah. But, while a moment of defection is given
as the reason for his being barred from dwelling in the Land, we
later see him upon a Mount still more favored, namely Mount Hermon (Matt. 17). Here with Elijah, he is received into the counsels
of the Son of God. We may well assume that Moses, the servant

of the LORD, will share with all who serve God, the full inheritance of the covenants of God in His eternal dominion over new heavens and a new earth.

10.   Retrospect: From the Border of Eden to the Border of the Promised Land

Looking back over the books of the Pentateuch it is remarkable that a distinct lineage is recorded. Why, every reader must ask, should a few names be lifted from the many who lived and died over the millenniums of time covered by the Pentateuch? Surely, in this particular we have one of the indisputable marks of the supernatural character of the Bible. These books were written in view of the coming of God's Son to identify himself with the race. This line of descent involves a number of steps of development up to the point of our present study. These steps should be well fixed in our thinking as we leave the study of the Pentateuch:

1. The Promise of the Triumphant Seed (Gen. 3:15)
2. Seth the Head of the Godly Line (Gen. 4:25—5:22)
3. Noah the Preserver of the Line (Gen. 6-10)
4. Shem, Blessed Because of His God (Gen. 9)
   (Arphaxad to Terah Lifted Out)
5. Abraham Chosen the Father of the Messianic Nation (Gen. 12)
6. Isaac the Supernatural Link—Heir to the Covenant
7. Jacob—Israel, the Father of the Tribal Heads
8. Judah—Head of the Messianic Tribe (Gen. 49:10)
9. Moses—The Type of the Great Prophet and Deliverer (Deut. 18)
10. The Messianic Nation Formed—Sinai (Exod. 12—Numbers 10; cf. Gen. 12:1-3)
11. The New Nation at the Border of the Promised Land (Deut. 34)

11.   Discussion and Review

1.   Deuteronomy is the repetition of the Law. Is this the full truth? Discuss.

2.   Describe in your own words the contents of each of Moses' three discourses. What pattern of logic do you discover in his appeal?

3. What is the abiding value of the many laws given to Israel?

4. Describe the ceremony at Ebal and Gerizim.

5. How did Moses answer Israel's spurious complaint of inability?

6. How do you justify God's command to destroy the Canaanites?

7. What do Moses' last days show of his unselfishness, of his foresight, and of his concern? What is the double theme of the Song of Moses (chapter 32)?

8. Who is the real hero of the book of Deuteronomy? What epitaph is given Moses?

9. Who wrote the Pentateuch? Who was its master-author?

10. Show by successive notices the unfolding of the prophecy of a Messiah in the Pentateuch.

12. Select Memory Passages

Deut. 6:4-12

13. Bibliography

Cameron, George G. "The Laws Peculiar to Deuteronomy," *Princeton Theological Review.* Vol. I. 1903, pp. 434-456.

Huffman, Jasper A. *Progressive Unfolding of the Messianic Hope.* Butler, Ind.: The Higley Press. Pages 1-34.

Morgan, G. Campbell. *Living Messages of the Books of the Bible.* Vol. I, "The Message of Deuteronomy." New York: Fleming H. Revell Co. Pp. 83-97.

Robinson, George L. "Deuteronomy," *The International Standard Bible Encyclopedia.* Vol. II. pp. 835-840.

PART FOUR

THE THEOCRATIC NATION
(1451-1095 B. C.)

Chapter 11

ISRAEL'S CONQUEST AND SETTLEMENT OF CANAAN

(1451-1426 B. C.)

1. Reading Assignment: Book of Joshua

(Read the Bible first)

2. Introduction—Relation of Joshua to Deuteronomy

The book of Joshua resumes the history of the Israelites at the point where Deuteronomy left it without any real break. Moses as Israel's leader wrote the Pentateuch. The same responsibility of atuhorship was a part of the duties of Joshua his successor (24:20). That Joshua is the author of the book bearing his name is evident from several facts. The book was written during the life time of Rahab (6:25). In the book there are numerous mentions of changes which had taken place since the times of the Pentateuch. Compare Numbers 34:13-14 with Joshua 14:1-4; Numbers 32:37 with Joshua 13:17; and Numbers 35 with Joshua 21. Joshua was one of the two associates of Moses, and that it was he who made these comparisons is therefore most plausible. As in Exodus the outstanding theme of Joshua is "redemption." The difference is that in Exodus stress is placed upon deliverance, whereas in Joshua, the stress is on possession. In the first there is redemption from bondage; in the second there is redemption to a new life.

119

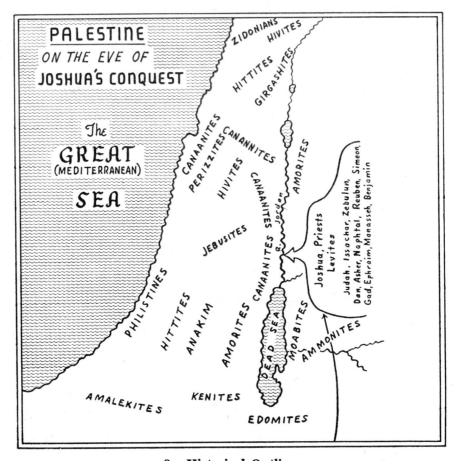

3. Historical Outline

I. **The Conquest of Canaan (Chapters 1-12)**

1. Joshua Ordered, Encouraged, and In Command (Chapter 1)
2. Spies Sent to Jericho (Chapter 2)
   (1) The help of Rahab
   (2) Return and report
3. Crossing of Jordan (3:1—5:1)
   (1) The order of the procession (3:1-17)
      1) Priests and ark "dipped in the brim"
      2) Priests and ark in the midst of Jordan
      3) People "clean" pass over

4) The priests called out
5) The waters roll down

   (2) The memorial stones (4:1-20)
      1) In Jordan
      2) At Gilgal
   (3) The time: 10th of first month (Nisan)
   (4) Effects:
      Upon future children
      Upon all people of the earth

4. Encampment at Gilgal (5:2-15)
   (1) Male children were circumcised
   (2) Passover was observed (14th of Nisan)

PALESTINE
AS ASSIGNED TO THE
TRIBES

The
GREAT
(MEDITERRANEAN)

SEA

ASHER
•Hazor
•Kedesh
NAPHTALI
Dan•

ZEBULON
ISSACHAR

MANASSEH
•Golan

MANASSEH
•Shechem
EPHRAIM
•Shiloh
•Timnath Serah
DAN
•Ai •Jericho
•Gibeon
•Ajalon
BENJAMIN

GAD
•Ramoth Gilead

R. Jordan

•Heshbon

SYRIAN

DESERT

JUDAH
•Gaza
■Hebron

REUBEN

DEAD SEA

■Bezer

SIMEON

Drawn by
Ralph N. Smith

(3) Manna displaced by corn and fruit

(4) Joshua's vision: captain of the LORD'S host

5. The Fall of Jericho (Chapter 6—7:1)

  (1) Instructions for the siege (6:1-5)

    1) Conditions and means (6:1-2)

    2) Order of march (6:3-16)

    3) Regarding the spoils (6:17-19)

    4) Regarding Rahab (6:17)

  (2) The outcome (6:20-25)

  (3) Curse upon a rebuilder (6:26; cf. I Kings 6:34)

(4) Secret: "The LORD was with Joshua" (6:27)

(5) Effect: "Fame" throughout the country (6:27)

(6) Israel's trespass causes God's anger (7:1)

6. The Taking of Ai (7:2—8:29)

  (1) Appraising the enemy (7:2-3)

  (2) Unexpected defeat (7:4-5)

  (3) Joshua seeks the reason (7:6-8)

  (4) The cause revealed (7:9-15)

  (5) Investigation reveals sin (7:16-23)

  (6) Punishment of the offender (7:24-26)

  (7) Ai successfully taken (8:1-29)

7. Worship and Instruction at Ebal (8:30-35)
  (1) An altar is erected at Ebal
  (2) Burnt and Peace offerings are made
  (3) Law of Moses is written and read
  (4) Ebal-Gerizim litany is used (see Deut. 27-28)
8. Southern Confederacy Is Formed (9:22)
  (1) Members: Hittites, Amorites, Canaanites, Perizzites, Hivites, Jebusites
9. Gibeonites make League with Israel (9:3-27)
  (1) The irrevocable commitment
  (2) The lot of the Gibeonites
  (3) Gibeonites remain Israel's confederates
10. The Battle against the Southern Kings (Chapter 10)
  (1) The attack of Gibeon by the Kings (10:1-5)
  (2) The appeal of Gibeon to Israel (10:6-7)
  (3) God mightily "fought for Israel"
    1) Stones fall from heaven
    2) The sun and moon stand still
  (4) Execution of the five kings (10:15-27)
  (5) Seven more kings taken (10:28-39)
  (6) Victory in south is complete (10:40-43)
11. The Conquest of the North (Chapter 11)
  (1) The northern league is formed (11:1-5)
    1) Numbers: "As the sands of the sea"
    2) Equipment: "Horses and chariots very many"
    3) Place: Near Lake Merom
  (2) God assures Joshua (11:6)
    1) "I will deliver them up . . . . tomorrow"
    2) "Thou shalt hough their horses and burn their chariots"
  (3) General victory in north is won (11:7-20)

12. The Anakims Destroyed (11:21-22)
II. **Division of the Land (Chapters 13-22)**
  1. The Inheritance of the Two and One-half Tribes (Chapter 13)
  2. Method of Division—By Lot (14:1-5)
  3. Hebron Given to Caleb (14:6-15)
  4. The Lot of Judah (Chapter 15)
  5. The Lots of Ephraim and Manasseh (Chapters 16-17)
  6. Tabernacle Is Set Up at Shiloh (18:1)
  7. Survey of Remaining Lands (18:2-9)
  8. The Lot of Benjamin (18:10-28)
  9. The Lot of Simeon (19:1-9)
  10. The Lot of Zebulun (19:10-16)
  11. The Lot of Issachar (19:17-31)
  12. The Lot of Naphtali (19:32-39)
  13. The Lot of Dan (19:40-48)
  14. Joshua's City (19:49-50)
  15. The Completion Affirmed (19:51)
  16. Cities of Refuge Designated (Chapter 20)
    (1) Kedesh
    (2) Shechem
    (3) Hebron
    (4) Bezer
    (5) Ramoth
    (6) Golan
  17. Forty-eight Cities for Levites Designated (21:1-42)
  18. Recognition of God's Fulfilled Promises (21:43-45)
  19. Two and One-half Tribes Return (Chapter 22)
    (1) Joshua's dismissal and blessing (22:1-7)
    (2) Sharing the spoils (22:8-9)
    (3) The altar of Ed incident (22:10-34)
III. **The Last Days of Joshua (Chapters 23-24)**
  1. Time: A Long Time after the Conquest (23:1)
  2. Assembly of Officers (23:2-16)
    (1) Exhortation to love and serve God (23:2-11)
    (2) Threats against failure (23:12-16)

3. Assembly of People (24:1-28)
  (1) Reminder of God's undeserved mercies (24:1-13)
  (2) The covenant reaffirmed and ratified (24:14-24)
  (3) The stone of witness set up (24:25-27)
4. The Death of Joshua (24:29-31)

  (1) His epitaph: "The servant of the LORD"
  (2) His age: 110 years
  (3) His burial place: Mount Ephraim
  (4) His influence upon Israel (verse 31)
5. Burial of Joseph's Bones (24:32)
6. Death and Burial of Eleazar (24:33)

4.   Qualifications of Joshua

Joshua was assigned to a point of responsibility soon after the Israelites left Egypt. It was he who in the power of Jehovah so valiantly led Israel to victory against the Amalekites at Rephidim (Exod. 18). He and Caleb were the two spies who returned a good report of the Land of Promise, giving evidence of a faith in the power of Jehovah which the ten spies did not possess. For their courage on this occasion they were promised the privilege of entering the Promised Land while all others over twenty years of age at that time were to be denied the privilege. It is remarkable that the very people who in unbelief complained that they had been unjustly brought into the wilderness to die, did die in the wilderness, while Joshua and Caleb whose faithfulness imperiled their very lives before the complaining mob, lived through the wilderness wanderings and a good while in the Land of Promise. How fitting that this nation of young men should have this courageous associate of Moses to lead them to victory over the Canaanites, of whose land he had, nearly forty years before, said, "Let us go up at once and possess it, for we are well able to overcome it." (Numbers 13:30). And who, better than he, could organize and establish the institutions of the nation according to the pattern shown to Moses? Who like God can prepare the leaders of his people according to the needs of each age?

5.   The Task Before the New Nation

Two main objectives were before the Israelites. First, they must subdue the Canaanites. These pagan people were given to the most repulsive forms of idolatrous worship and it was now God's purpose to visit them with judgment. It is marvelous to see how God dovetails developments. Simultaneous to the moral decay of these nations God had been stiffening the fibre and shaping the character of the new people who were to possess the land of the Canaanitish idolaters. The second phase of the new task was for the Israelites to establish themselves in the land according to the institutions given them of God. They were then to become not merely another nation but **the** nation by whom God had promised to bless the whole race.

6.   The LORD a "Man of War"

There is an erroneous idea regarding God which must be corrected if some readers are ever to have a real appreciation for the book of Joshua. It is that the attribute of justice is something less worthy in our concept of deity than the attribute of mercy. The Christian ethic precludes all war, it is maintained. If this view is true then the LORD is a very changeable person, for in the song of Moses, taught Israel after the judgment of Pharaoh at the Red Sea, the LORD is clearly stated to be a "man of war" (Exod. 15:3).

The fact is that the LORD is the only person competent to declare war. "Vengeance is mine saith the Lord, I will repay" (Rom. 12:9). Both Moses and Joshua had to learn this fact. Impetuously, Moses had presumed to kill an Egyptian, but it was forty years earlier than God's command for the judgment of Egypt. When at last God's hour struck, he from a burning bush declared his purpose to vindicate suffering Israel, to break the shackles of Egypt, and to wield the sickle of judgment against the ripened iniquity of the Canaanitish nations. To accomplish this he gave Moses a definite commission of leadership (Exod. 3:1-10).

Likewise with Joshua. Before the battle at Jericho, God appeared to Joshua as a man with a drawn sword and declared himself as the "captain of the LORD'S host." Before Joshua began his mission of war in Palestine he had first to bow in perfect submission to this captain of the LORD (Joshua 5:13-15).

The Conquest of Canaan must, therefore not be taken as a pretext for all or any of the wars of history. It is a precedent for war only when God has clearly commanded such action. While the New Testament does not set aside the functions of human government, it is clear that the Church has a commission from Christ involving a greater victory among the nations than the victory of physical combat. Jesus did not declare that the iniquity of the nations was full and that therefore his followers were to go forth and behead their opposers with the sword. The mistake of the Jesuits and of the Moslems has been that they have regarded as their precedent the historic conquests of Canaan rather than the particular commission of Christ for this age.

The point which we make here, however, is that faithful service of the people to God in Joshua's time required war, and that it therefore did not represent a lower ethic than obedience to Christ on a mission of mercy represents in the present age.

The LORD is "still a man of war." Once again judgments will break and the Son of God will come forth to execute fiery wrath upon those who obey not the gospel (See II Thess. 1).

7.   Miracles in the Conquest

Men do not ordinarily stop the Jordan to cross it. They do not ordinarily march around a city and then shout to get the walls to fall down. They do not ordinarily command the sun to stand still that they may continue a successful battle to its conclusion. Therefore, say agnostic critics of Joshua, these things did not take place in the history of Israel. On this assumption some men who are reputed as scholars have forsaken the laws of literary criticism in an attempt to read these miracles out of the records. To attempt to interpret these records by marking out the miraculous makes nonsense of the records, and leaves a greater literary problem than ever.

But why should a literary critic delete the miraculous elements from Israel's history? What reasonable grounds are there for such measures? Is it not to adjust the records to a theory of atheism? If God is a reality, then miracles are neither impossible nor improbable. If God is a reality then we should expect him to be cleansing this land of wickedness. We should expect him to have a purpose and a plan of making himself known to the world and of extending redemption through his chosen channel to all peoples. That is what we see him doing in the records, and it should please every reader to know that God has been and still is thus at work in the world.

8.   The Sparing of Rahab—Mercy in Judgment

The Bible clearly reveals that God has no delight in the judgment of the wicked, that he wants them to repent, to believe, and to return and live. The sparing of Rahab is a case in point, show-

ing that God does revoke the order of judgment when the conditions
of bestowing mercy are evident. "By faith the harlot Rahab perished
not with them that believed not (were disobedient, A. R. V.)," says
the writer of the Hebrew letter. Later the Ninevites were spared
the pronounced judgment upon them on the same grounds. So also,
in our times, says John, "He that believeth is not condemned (judged,
A. R. V.), but he that believeth not is condemned already, because
he hath not believed in the name of the only begotten Son of God"
(John 3:18).

9. The Accomplishments of Joshua—What Remained To Be Done

When the conquest was completed, the record states, "Joshua
took the whole land, according to all that the LORD said unto Moses,
and Joshua gave it for an inheritance unto Israel according to their
divisions by their tribes. And the land rested from war" (11:23;
21:43-45). This statement refers to the military victory which gave
to Israel a right to possess and occupy the land. It did not mean
that there was no further need for initiative upon Israel's part. It is
one thing to inherit a farm but another thing to farm the farm, to
produce crops and to keep the weeds down.

In the account of the division of the land to the tribes by lot
there is notice given of remaining Canaanitish peoples in the land
and the fact is given that down to the day of the editing of the
record they had not been removed (see 13:13; 15:63; 16:10).

Joshua observed the dilatory tendency of the people regarding
this condition and when the people ratified the covenant he challenged their sincerity (34:14-27). It remains for the book of Judges
to reveal the degeneracy which their complacency toward idols and
idol worshipers entailed.

10. Discussion and Review

1. Discuss the relation of Joshua to Deuteronomy.
2. What facts qualified Joshua as Moses' successor?
3. Define the task facing the new nation.
4. How do you justify the ethics of the book of Joshua in
which the Lord is represented as a "man of war"?
5. Compare the work of the spies at this time with that of
those who went into the land thirty-nine years before.
6. What lesson is taught by the sparing of Rahab?

7. Why did God lead the people over Jordan by a miracle (4:24)?

8. Do you suppose that he had the same purpose for the miracles which followed?

9. Tell of four important incidents which took place at Gilgal.

10. What was the effect of the fall of Jericho upon the Canaanites (6:27)? What was the flaw connected with their victory so far as Israel was concerned?

11. Why, in a time of war, did the Israelites have to take time out for such a matter as a single man's sin (7:2—8:9), and for worship (8:30-35)?

12. State the grounds of reasoning followed in the sparing of the Gibeonites (9:3-27). How do they compare with Rahab?

13. Show that the formation of a confederacy on the part of the southern nations simplified Israel's victory (9:22; chapter 10). Observe that the whole universe was engaged in God's judgment of the kings arraigned before him.

14. Compare the course of victory in the northern part of the land (chapter 11) with the southern victory.

15. Where had the Anakims been encountered before, and why are they mentioned separately now (11:21-22)?

16. Describe the method pursued in dividing up the land (chapters 13-22).

17. Appraise the state of the nation as Joshua left it, militarily and spiritually (Joshua 23-24).

18. What epitaph distinguishes Joshua?

11. Character Review

Identify:

Joshua	Achan	Perizzites
Rahab	Gibeonites	Hivites
Captain of the	Hittites	Jebusites
Lord's Host	Amorites	
Caleb	Canaanites	

12. Select Memory Passages

Joshua 1:9, 21:43-45

13. Bibliography

Albright, Wm. F. "The Israelite Conquest of Canaan in the Light of Archaeology," *Bulletin of the American Schools of Oriental Research.* Nu. 74. 1939, pp. 11-23.

Garstang, John. *The Foundations of Bible History: Joshua, Judges.* London, 1931.

Kuyper, Abraham. *Women of the Old Testament.* Grand Rapids: Zondervan. "Rahab," pp. 67-71.

Marston, Sir Charles. *The Bible Comes Alive.* Chapter IV, "Joshua, Captain of the Lord." New York: Fleming H. Revell Co., Sixth Edition Revised.

Meyer, F. B. *Joshua, and the Land of Promise.* New York: Fleming H. Revell.

Morgan, G. Campbell. *Living Messages of the Books of the Bible,* Vol. I. "The Message of Joshua." New York: Fleming H. Revell Co. Pp. 99-116.

Sangster, Margaret E. *The Women of the Bible.* Chapt. IX, "Rahab and the Scarlet Cord." New York: The Christian Herald.

Chapter 12

THE DARK AGES OF ISRAEL

(1426-1095 B. C.)

1. Reading Assignment: Book of Judges

2. Collateral: Book of Ruth

(Read the Bible first)

3. Introduction

The Judges of Israel

The name of the book of Judges comes from the fact that the rulers of the period were judges (shophetim). This title does not refer to ordinary judges such as those appointed in Exodus 18. These were deliverers or saviors at the beginning of their respective reigns. They were, generally, ordinary tribesmen upon whom God bestowed the gift of leadership to deliver Israel on occasions of trouble, foreign oppressions being the usual trouble. They demonstrated their leadership at such times so as to win the recognition of the nation or a part of the nation, and were then conceded judicial functions for an indefinite time.

The Literature of the Period

Three books give us our knowledge of this period, each making a distinctive contribution. The book of Judges covers the major

129

part of the period. It gives the account of seven oppressions and corresponding deliverers or judges (shophetim). Its last five chapters give special incidents which took place, evidently sometime during the period of the Judges, and are to be considered insets in relation to the history of the preceding chapters. The book of Ruth likewise belongs somewhere in this period and stands as a refreshing oasis of moral beauty in contrast to the general degeneracy of the times. The first ten chapters of I Samuel record the last two judgeships, those of Eli and Samuel. Since the books of Samuel are properly regarded as books of the kings, these last two judgeships may best be considered in the kingdom period.

4. Historical Outline

I. **Degeneracy after the Days of Joshua (Judges 1-2)**

  1. Failures (Chapter 1)

  2. Compromise; Departure; God's Anger (Chapter 2)

  3. Heathen Scourges (3:1-4)

II. **Oppressions and Deliverers (3:5—16:31)**

  1. Oppression by the Mesopotamians (3:5-11)
    Deliverer: Othniel

  2. Oppression by the Moabites (3:12-30)
    Deliverer: Ehud

  3. Oppression by the Philistines (3:31)
    Deliverer: Shamgar

  4. Oppression by the Canaanites (Judges 4 and 5)
    Deliverers: Deborah and Barak

  5. Oppression by the Midianites (Judges 6-10)
    Deliverers: Gideon, Abimelech, Tola, Jair

  6. Oppression by the Ammonites (Judges 11-12)
    Deliverers: Jephthah, Ibzan, Elon, Abdon

  7. Oppression by the Philistines (Judges 13-16)
    Deliverer: Samson

III. **Insets—Incidents of the Judges Period (Judges 17-21)**

  1. The State of Religion Depicted

    (1) Religion of Micah (chapter 17)

    (2) Religion of the Danites (chapter 18)

  2. The State of Social Life Depicted

    (1) The outrage of Gibeah (chapter 19)

    (2) Civil war (chapter 20)

    (3) The plight of Benjamin (chapter 21)

  3. Jewels of Character amidst Moral Chaos (Ruth)

    (1) Famine: Emmigration of Elimelech's family (1:1-2)

    (2) Naomi's bereavement (1:3-5)

    (3) Filial love tested (1:6-22)

    (4) Two saints brought together (chapters 2-4)

      1) A virtuous man discovers virtue (chapter 2)

      2) Kinsman claims investigated (3:1—4:8)

      3) Kinsman estate bought (4:9-10)

      4) Blessings and best wishes (4:11-12)

      5) Marriage (4:13-17)

(5) The genealogy of David (4:18-22)

Judah (See Genesis 38)	Nahshon
Pharez (of Tamar)	Salmon (of Rahab)
Hezron	Boaz
Ram	Obed (of Ruth)
Amminadab	Jesse
	David

5. Law Displaced by Individualism

The book of Judges describes a time when "every man did that which was right in his own eyes" (17:6). Obviously this was not the kind of economy intended by the instruction of the book of Deuteronomy. It was the farthest degree removed from that. God's law was ignored and to a great extent forgotten. This left no standards as a common basis of social life. The tribes were only very loosely held together and the distinctive institutions of the nation disintegrated sadly. The Canaanites still remained in the land and were a blight to Israel politically, religiously, and morally. Pagan nations harassed Israel enviously on every side, jealous of her lands and disrespectful of her God. With all of these troubles, the most hopeless fact was that no agency seemed anywhere at hand to break the trend of drift, and of further disintegration. But God's hand was not removed, and even in such times we are able to follow the course of his unfailing mercy.

6. The Pattern of History in This Period

The fact that history repeats itself is nowhere more fully demonstrated than in the Judges period of Israel's history. Joshua gave the nation rest (Joshua 21:43-45; 24:31). But after his generation passed, the weeds of compromise sprang up on every hand. Israel fell into a state of sin. God then withdrew his shielding hand, leaving her to experience the scourging of her illicit associates (2:1—3:7). The consequence was bondage to a foreign yoke (3:8). In her oppressed condition "Israel cried unto the LORD" (3:9). At this point God raised up a deliverer (3:9-10). The land again had rest (3:11). After eight years Israel was in sin again, and the cycle was repeated. This repetition took place not less than seven distinct times during the Judges period.

7. Degeneration Through Continued Idolatry

This pattern brings certain facts to relief. It demonstrates the overall disciplinary procedure of God, not against, but in behalf of

Cycles of the Judges Period

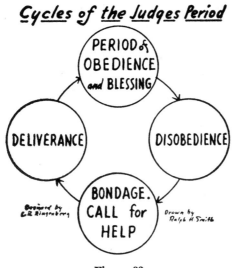

Figure 22

Israel. He endowed them with mercies to begin with. When they forsook him for idols and idol worshiping associates he lengthened the limits of their freedom until they learned the cruel end of their choice. Then he went the "second mile" to restore them and make them happy.

The pattern demonstrates, on the human side, how shortsighted men are in securing their own good. They will forfeit all for a mess of pottage. The Israelites demonstrated a strong tendency to revert to idolatry, in spite of the abundant proofs in their national experience of the supremacy of the LORD. With idolatry, of course, was associated fleshly gratification, and the absence of moral restraint. Moreover, idolatry was popular among the heathen, and it is not human to choose to be unpopular. Sex attraction on the part of the heathen was a common snare as was seen in the case of the Moabites and the Midianites (Numbers 26, 31). The primary peril in the days after Joshua was not military, but moral. Intermarriage with the Canaanites became common. But marriage is a matter of mutual love. Accordingly, it was a very natural step from intermarriage to idolatrous worship (Judges 3:5-7). In such compromise the worship which followed in the home was the lower and not the higher. A person who disobeys God to marry a godless person is not apt to influence his mate to obey God.

The consequence of continuance in idolatry is deeper degeneration. When one chooses a lower object of worship to accommodate wrong desires, he assimilates the characteristics of his god. When he makes another god it will represent his lowered standards. Thus, idolatry renders its devotees less glorious in each succeeding generation.

8. Sin's Darkest Hour—God's Silence

These repeated cycles resulted in a climax of evil that eventually shocked the whole nation. This is seen in the criminal outrage at Gibeah, in consequence of which the tribe of Benjamin was nearly exterminated (chapters 19-21). Thus, the age in which every man did "what was right in his own eyes" ended in moral chaos too intolerable to be endured. All Israel arose to vindicate the innocent against criminals who stalked abroad in the land. A war such as this reminds us of the American Civil war in which the evil of slavery had to be paid for by the sacrifice of many sons in both north and south.

What made this climax of moral chaos in Israel still more unbearable was the fact that spiritual darkness had fallen upon the nation. Personal standards had displaced God's law. But that was not all. God ceased to speak to the nation. The "word of the LORD was precious in those days; there was no open vision" (I Sam. 3:1). Had God withdrawn himself finally? If he had, then Israel would certainly have gone right on her downward course and found her level with the common idolatry of the surrounding peoples of the time. But God did not give her up. Even in this dark and silent hour, God by his gracious providence was working in the hearts of two humble, pious souls whose offspring would be the direct ancestor of David, yea of the Son of David. His promised dominion will bring final righteousness and rest to the whole world. Thus God is seen accomplishing redemptive ends in times when sin had brought on a harvest of chaos.

9. Discussion and Review

1. What is the Biblical literature covering this period?
2. Indicate the loss to Israel when Joshua died.
3. Characterize the individualism of the period.
4. Describe the pattern of cycles in Israel's history during this period.

5. Name the seven major oppressions and relate the experience of deliverance in each case.

6. Show the degenerating effect of continued idolatry.

7. Account for the darkness which prevailed in the latter part of this period.

8. What does the religion of the Danites indicate as to the apostasy of the times?

9. Show that religious apostasy takes its toll in crime (Judges 19-21).

10. In what respects is the book of Ruth the account of an "oasis in a spiritual desert." Trace God's providence during this dark period.

10. Select Memory Passages

Judges 2:11, 14, 16, 19; 17:6

11. Character Review

Identify:

Othniel	Abimelech	Abdon
Caleb	Tola	Samson
Ehud	Jair	Micah
Shamgar	Jephthah	Elimelech
Deborah	Ibzan	Naomi
Barak	Elon	Ruth
Gideon	Boaz	Obed

12. Bibliography

Blaikie, Wm. G. *A Manual of Bible History.* Chapter VIII, Section I, "The Six Great Invasions." New York: Thomas Nelson and Sons.
Kuyper, Abraham. *Women of the Old Testament.* Grand Rapids: Zondervan.
  1. "Deborah," pp. 71-75.
  2. "Jael," pp. 75-78.
  3. "Jephthah's Daughter," pp. 78-81.
  4. "Manoah's Wife," pp. 82-85.
  5. "Delilah," pp. 85-88.
  6. "Naomi," pp. 89-92.
  7. "Orpah," pp. 92-95.
  8. "Ruth," pp. 95-98.
Morgan, G. Campbell. *Living Messages of the Bible,* Vol. I. "The Book of Judges," Pp. 117-132. "The Book of Ruth," Pp. 133-146. New York: Fleming H. Revell Co.
Ockenga, Harold John. *Have You Met These Women?* Grand Rapids: Zondervan. Chapter I—"The Woman Who Ruined a Holy Man." Chapter III—

"The Woman Who Won a Husband."

Sangster, Margaret E. *The Women of the Bible.* Chapt. X, "Deborah, the Prophetess." New York: The Christian Herald.

Sangster, Margaret E. *The Women of the Bible. Chapt.* XI, "Jephthah's daughter." New York: The Christian Herald.

Sangster, Margaret E. *The Women of the Bible.* Chapt. XII, "Delilah, the Betrayer." New York: The Christian Herald.

Sangster, Margaret E. *The Women of the Bible.* Chapt. XIII, "The Story of Ruth and Naomi." New York: The Christian Herald.

PART FIVE

THE UNITED KINGDOM OF ISRAEL
(1095-975 B. C.)

Chapter 13

THE UNITED KINGDOM OF ISRAEL

—The Founding of the Kingdom
(1095-1055 B. C.)

1. **Reading Assignment:**   I Samuel; I Chronicles 10.

(Read the Bible first)

2.   Introduction

A Woman's Desire and a Nation's Need

Hannah belongs to the class of Mary, Sarah, Rachel, and Elizabeth, each of whom consecrated her powers of motherhood to God and gave to him and to the world a miracle son.   Little did Hannah know that her pleas for a son corresponded with God's need for a man.   God needed, not just any kind of a man, but one who would be consecrated to him even before conception.   Hannah vowed that her son would be so consecrated.   She kept her vow.   Doubtless from the first dawn of intelligence Samuel was told that he belonged to God.   A son who grows up with such a consciousness will come to have an open ear to hear God and a mental eye to see him.   Thus, Samuel was born and trained to be a prophet.   One wonders to what degree   Hannah, during her lifetime, came to know how well her labor of love became a part of the building of a kingdom.

139

The Last Days of the Judges

The Philistines were playing havoc at Israel's borders with impunity. Eli was old and his sons were unprincipled, wicked, and weak men. Individualism had left Israel without a law and the wickedness of the priests left her without God. The pathetic fact was that in her desperate need for help there was no "open vision." The word of God was "precious in those days."

Instead of seeking divine help from God, Israel superstitiously attempted to win by taking the ark into battle. As a result the ark was lost to the enemy. Eventually, Eli's sons were slain in battle, at the report of which Eli himself was overcome and fell over dead. Under these desperate circumstances it is said, "Israel lamented after the LORD" (7:2). At this point the prophet of God appeared and gave the instructions that brought victory (I Sam. 7). The instructions were simple. There was no new doctrine and no new law. Israel had but to "return to God" sincerely and God would deliver.

Samuel's formula worked. As he cried to God for the people and offered a consecration offering, God began to thunder and the Philistines were discomfited, smitten, and driven out.

Samuel the Prophet

If any man can be said to have been the man of the hour in this darkest period of Israel's history it is Samuel. Doubtless he was the peer of leaders from Moses and Joshua on to his day. He was God's man, supernaturally born, specially consecrated, trained, and unmistakably timed for an epoch-making work in Israel. The age was one of soft morals, selfish individualism, and weak government. It was a generation which was socially sick, yet which was disinclined to the discipline of law. To deliver such a generation a man would have to speak with the authority of God and with utter fearlessness of men. Such an age would of course need to have a leader who himself had been disciplined, who had a sensitive ear to God's voice and who made obedience his fixed purpose and rule of life.

Samuel stands out in a class with Moses and Joshua. He could not be moved from the law of God. He moved the people instead of letting them move him.

The age must have had a great immoral drag upon the average man. Even Samuel's sons, whom we may suppose were trained in the law, yielded to the easy policy of selling justice for lucre.

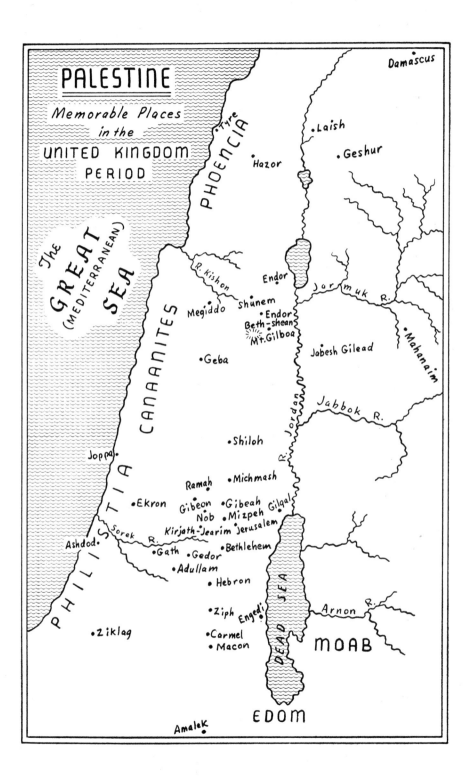

It appears that there was a stigma cast upon Samuel's character in the minds of many people because of the deeds of his sons. In this matter Samuel proved his moral courage by gathering the assembly and challenging anyone to produce any proof of wrong dealing on his part (I Sam. 12). Silence on the part of all vindicated Samuel.

The Prophetic Office

With Samuel, the prophetic office became a distinct part of the national life of Israel. Two reasons for this are evident. First, the priesthood had become formal and corrupted. It was a fixed order, and yet was not amenable to discipline. It came to be too un-wieldly as a means of powerfully communicating God's will to the people. In the second place, the institution of the kingly office needed the safeguard of the prophetic office. Kings, and the princes born to them, might or might not be men of God. Thus, in the prophetic office God continued to keep a way open by which to communicate truth and righteousness to the nation.

The Kingdom of Israel

The term "kingdom of Israel" must be defined. Under Saul, David, and Solomon there was the united kingdom of Israel. Then the kingdom was divided, the northern division comprised of ten tribes being designated as the kingdom of Israel, and the southern division comprised of the tribes of Judah and Benjamin being desig-nated as the kingdom of Judah. The northern kingdom, Israel, con-tinued for a period of 153 years and the southern kingdom, Judah, continued for a period of 389 years.

3. Historical Outline

I. **Years of Transition (I Samuel 1-10)**

1. The Judgeship of Eli (I Sam. 1—7:2)
   (1) Samuel prayed for, promised, born, presented (chapter 1)
   (2) Samuel instructed by Eli (2:11—3:18)
   (3) Samuel called of God (3:1-18)
   (4) Samuel recognized as a proph-et (3:19-20)
   (5) The end of Eli's house (4:1—7:2)
      1) Encounter with the Philis-tines
      2) Loss of the Ark and defeat
      3) Death of Eli
2. The Judgeship of Samuel (7:3—10ff)
   (1) The Philistines subdued (chap-ter 7)
      1) Israel's lamentation (7:2)
      2) Samuel declared terms of God's favor (7:3)
      3) Israel returns to God (7:4)

4) Israel gathered at Mizpeh (7:5-7)

5) Israel's fear and cry for help (7:8)

6) Samuel's burnt offering and God's thunder — Ebenezer (7:9-12)

7) Israel has rest (7:13-14)

8) Samuel's tenure as judge: life (7:15)

9) His circuit: Bethel, Gilgal, Mizpeh (7:16)

10) His permanent bench: Ramah (7:17)

(2) Samuel installs Israel's first king (8-10)

1) The unsatisfactory rule of Samuel's sons (8:1-4)

2) Request of the people for a king (8:5)

3) The request unfavorably appraised but granted (8:6-22)

4) Saul and Samuel meet by God's direction (chapter 9)

5) Saul anointed, prepared, and presented to the assembly (chapter 10)

II. **The Reign of Saul (I Sam. 11-31)**

1. Before His Rejection (Chapters 11-15)

(1) Saul establishes confidence by victory at Jabesh-Gilead (chapter 11)

(2) Samuel's address: acquittal by the LORD (chapter 12)

(3) Saul's first disobedience; rejection (chapter 13)

(4) Saul's hasty adjuration (chapter 14)

(5) Saul's second disobedience; rejection (chapter 15)

2. After His Rejection (Chapters 16-31)

(1) Samuel Anoints David (16:1-13)

(2) David at court as musician and armour-bearer (16:14-23)

(3) David delivers Israel from Goliath (chapter 17)

(4) Saul fears David; becomes his "enemy continually" (chapter 18)

(5) David's success, Saul's envy; David's flight (chapter 19)

(6) David's covenant with Jonathan (chapter 20)

(7) David's refugee experiences (21—28:2; 29, 30)

1) At Nob
2) At Gath
3) At the cave of Adullam
4) At Mizpeh
5) In the wilderness of Ziph
6) In the wilderness of Maon
7) In the stronghold of Engedi
8) In the wilderness of Paran
9) At the hill of Hachilah
10) At Gath
11) At Ziklag

(8) Saul's extremity; counsels Witch of Endor (chapter 28)

(9) Saul's defeat and death (chapter 29)

4. Israel's Desire and God's Sovereign Plan

"He (God) gave them their request; but sent leanness into their soul" (Psalms 106:15).

G. Campbell Morgan has described the act of establishing a king in the book of I Samuel as revealing two elements. First "its supreme revelation is that of Jehovah reigning by adaptation, in order to advance." Secondly, "it reveals the fact that under this government of God, men cooperate with him towards the final issues, either by failure or by loyalty." Dr. Morgan says further,

"It is one thing (for man) to reject Jehovah, but it is quite another to dethrone Him."

In keeping with these principles we may clearly observe two stories in this book of I Samuel. There is the history of human choice and resulting failure and concurrently there is the history of God's reigning by adaptation to accomplish an advancing purpose. In the importunate desire and vow of Hannah and God's gift of a son we see providence at work to prepare the man of God who would hold the nation to a true course even though at the people's choice an unprincipled and rebellious king sat upon the throne. Likewise, as Saul by defection plunged the nation into distress, God was preparing a shepherd boy to occupy the throne.

Viewing matters from a much longer range of viewpoint, God made the throne of David the symbol of the greater throne of the Son of David. Thus, while many people were making their choices, some worthy and some not, God was working to the scale of a greater purpose. Some persons glorified God in this on-going purpose by faith and obedience, others did so by disobedience and the demonstration of the folly of their rebellion. We may be sure that God is ever ruling from his throne and that his purposes will not fail. We had better not be too complacent, however, about the place we as individuals are filling. If we rebel against God, if we persist in our own ends, God may grant us what we require and it will be to our eternal loss. If we, on the other hand, give prompt and full adherence to his voice we shall receive a crown of righteousness in the eternal kingdom.

5. Saul's Good Beginning

At the time of Saul's anointing he had a high score of possibilities. In the first place, his rule was wanted; the people had asked for a king. Also, God chose him and prepared the way for his kingship. God's Spirit was upon him and "gave him another heart." His call from the quest of his stray asses was a miracle of God's arrangement, in which Saul must have been impressed with the hand of God. Three special signs were given to further convince him that his anointing had been the real appointment of God (I Sam. 10:1-13). In his initial encounter with Israel's enemy at Jabesh-Gilead he was enabled to so triumph that the people with one accord acknowledged him as their king. They celebrated with offerings and "rejoiced greatly" (chapt. 11).

6. Saul Under Test

What a man is by natural and spiritual endowment is one thing. What he is by personal choice when he faces issues is another thing. There is one thing that God could not supply in preparing Saul for successful leadership of Israel. That thing was a fixed purpose to obey God. It is easy to have a purpose before entering upon the scene of test, but it is constancy under test that determines one's course.

Excepting the victory over the Ammonites at Jabesh-Gilead, which was prior to the time that all Israel made Saul king (chapter 11), Saul's decisions were consistently wrong. His first encounter with the Philistines was a rash teaser which served only to infuriate the enemy and to terrify defenseless Israel (13:1-7). Saul disobediently and foolishly presumed to offer burnt offerings, contrary to the command of God (13:8-14). He spared king Agag of the Amalekites whom he had been commanded to destroy, and reserved spoils which he had been commanded to destroy (chapter 15). His conduct on this occasion was named by Samuel as rebellion and stubbornness. It provoked from God a final word of rejection of his kingship.

Saul's reaction to this final rejection was a pathetic but futile attempt to be restored to favor (15:24-35). His reaction had, apparently, some marks of genuineness. He confessed his sin. He asked for pardon. He asked for Samuel to be with him. He expressed the desire to worship God. Yet, if we examine these appeals more closely, we will have to say that they bore the marks of insincerity. While Saul admitted disobedience he nevertheless blamed the people and made them responsible for fear on his part (15:24).

While he said with his lips, "I have sinned," he followed in the same sentence with the request, ". . . . yet honour me now, I pray thee, before the elders of my people, and before Israel . . . . turn again with me that I may worship the LORD thy God" (15:30). Saul's primary concern was to save his face. He confessed sin, yet wanted honor; he wanted God's prophet to be with **him**, and wanted to be **classed** as a worshipper of God. Thus, at the penitent form, so to speak, Saul demonstrated essential selfishness and utter disregard for the sovereign claims of God.

Saul was not forced to leave the throne immediately, but rather he was left to occupy it alone, without God's favor, without the companionship of Samuel, without God's Spirit with him and with the affliction of an evil spirit instead.

From Saul we learn that no degree of initial grace can take the place of our yielding to the moral claims of God upon us. Grace does not abound as an individual goes on practicing rebellion and disobedience to God.

Saul's life from the time of God's rejection of him displays the sad alternative which one faces when he rejects the rule of God's Spirit. Saul became the prey of an evil spirit. While not all who resist God's sovereignty are immediately subjected to demon-possession, it is well to realize that persistent rejection of God may lead to God's rejection of us, and that beyond that point we face the enemy of our souls without help.

Saul appears to have contracted a split personality. At one time he expressed his sin and bestowed admiration upon David, and at another time murderously sent a javelin toward David's head. In the main, however, he was dominated by envy and murder. He sought help from Samuel, from David, and from his own family, all to the end that he might not have to lose the honor of position. He finally sought a witch, but under her auspices received no consolation. The height of tragedy was reached in his life, when eventually his vain life purpose of self-sovereignty ended in self-destruction.

7. God Uses a Rebellious King to Prepare a Good One

It is God's method, very commonly, to forge the character of his people in the fires of persecution at the hands of their enemies. David, though anointed by Samuel was driven from Saul's court and obliged to live the life of an outlaw refugee. God could have taken Saul's life and immediately put David upon the throne. David had many opportunities of killing Saul, but always refrained, because he regarded him as God's anointed. God's purpose in letting Saul live on is partly evident, at least. In the first place, Saul needed to live on to experience the consequences of his course of rebellion. Secondly, Saul had followers who also needed to see that Saul's dynasty was forsaken of God, as a condition to recognizing a new dynasty. Perhaps most important of all, was the preparation which this period afforded for David the anointed successor of Saul.

We have seen in Saul the consequence of exalting an unchastened novice to the high position of a kingly throne. David might also have been a failure, even though as a shepherd lad he was a "man after God's own heart," had he not been disciplined by a preparatory process. He learned from Saul's example, the folly of self-will and unadvised action. He learned to restrain his impulses, to refrain from rushing ahead of God's time and from taking matters belonging to God into his own hands. David learned to trust God in extremities, and to maintain courage in adversity. He learned how to work with men and to lead them. Most important of all, David learned to know God and to be led by him.

As David fled from Saul we are impressed with the undignified lengths to which he resorted at Nob and at Gath. Following him to the cave of Adullam, however, we see him become adjusted and established in a settled position of defense.

The cave of Adullam, according to commonly accepted opinion, is that located about six miles southeast of Bethlehem, in the site of the wild gorge el-Kureitun. It is an immense natural cavern in the side of a cliff, so difficult of access that once in it a few men might guard its entrance against the assault of an army. David as a shepherd boy had doubtless explored this cave and was familiar enough with it to convert it into a stronghold.

With such a stronghold David became the leader of the growing number of Saul's subjects who found Saul's rule too distasteful and too oppressive to be tolerable. This band was doubtless the nucleus of the army which later rallied to David's support. Psalms 34 and 62 should be read with this stronghold in mind. The Adullam fortress doubtless was the occasion for the analogy of God as a rock, and as a refuge, and as a secure hiding place, so common in the Psalms. When one finds a place of security, others who have experienced the insecurity of the world will rally to him. David, the rejected king during those days, affords an obvious type of Christ in this time of his general rejection by the world. His pilgrim followers, as David's band, will be identified with him in his Messianic kingdom. Those who suffer, we are told, shall also reign with him.

8. Discussion and Review

1. Show how a woman's desire, a nation's need, and the divine purpose centered in Samuel's birth.

2. Relate the circumstances which opened the way for Samuel's **leadership in Israel.**

3. How do you account for the wickedness of Eli's sons?

4. Relate the procedure of Samuel in subduing the Philistines (chapter 7).

5. How do you account for the wickedness of Samuel's sons?

6. Appraise Israel's request for a king. How do you harmonize the granting of it with God's sovereignty?

7. Relate the steps by which Saul was brought to the throne.

8. Did Samuel clear his character before the people (chapter 12)?

9. Trace the actions of Saul which led to his rejection (chapters 11-15). Note especially the fact of his good beginning, then of the situations under which he failed.

10. Trace the developments which led to an impasse between Saul and David (chapters 16-20).

11. Relate David's refugee experiences from Nob to Ziklag chapters 21-30).

12. Characterize the dual nature of Saul's personality as it may be seen after his rejection by God.

13. Why did God not dethrone Saul at the time David was first chosen?

14. Can you show in First Samuel the operation of a higher sovereignty which overrules human choices? Cite instances. Toward what higher end does this higher sovereignty work?

9. Select Memory Passages

I Samuel 15:22, 23; 16:7b

10. Character Review

Identify:

Eli	Achish	Abishai
Samuel	Hophni	Witch of Endor
Hannah	Phinehas	Baalim
Elkanah	Ichabod	Ashtaroth
Belial	Dagon	Saul
Nahash	Men of Bethshemesh	Kish
Kenites	Jonathan	Agag
Eliab	David	Jesse
Goliath	Abinadab	Shammah
Nabal	Michal	Ahimelech
Abigail	Abiathar	Doeg

11. Bibliography

Allis, O. T. "The Punishment of the Men of Bethshemosh," *The Evangelical Quarterly.* Vol. 15. 1943, pp. 298-307.

Kuyper, Abraham. *Women of the Old Testament.* Grand Rapids: Zondervan.
1. "Hannah," pp. 98-102.
2. "Ichabod's Mother," pp. 102-105.
3. "Rizpah," pp. 129-133.

Morgan, G. Campbell. *Living Messages of the Books of the Bible,* Vol. I. "The Message of I Samuel." New York: Fleming H. Revell Co. Pp. 147-160.

Olson, Bessie G. *Samuel a Man of Consecration,* in Bible Character Series. Des Moines: Boone Pub. Co., 1948.

Sangster, Margaret E. *The Women of the Bible.* "Hannah, the Woman Who Prevailed in Prayer." New York: The Christian Herald.

Sangster, Margaret E. *The Women of the Bible.* Chapt. XV, "Michal, Saul's Daughter." New York: The Christian Herald.

Sangster, Margaret E. *The Women of the Bible.* Chapt. XVI, "Abigail, The Wife of a Churl." New York: The Christian Herald.

Sangster, Margaret E. *The Women of the Bible.* Chapt. XVII, "The Witch of Endor." New York: The Christian Herald.

Sangster, Margaret E. *The Women of the Bible.* Chapt. XVIII, "Rizpah, the Desolate." New York: The Christian Herald.

Wilson, R. Dick. "The Books of Samuel," *The International Standard Bible Encyclopedia.* Vol. IV. Pages 2678-2681.

Chapter 14

THE UNITED KINGDOM OF ISRAEL

—The Times of David
(1055-1015 B. C.)

1. Reading Assignment: II Samuel; II Kings 1-2:11

2. Collateral: I Chronicles 11-29; Psalms of David
(Read the Bible first)

3. Introduction—David's Rise to Public Favor

Our study of the reign of Saul has already involved notice of the important preparatory period of David's reign. The anointing of David (I Sam. 16) was probably not a matter of general knowledge in Israel, though it certainly was clearly understood by Samuel and David as meaning that David should succeed Saul upon the throne. David, however, probably did not know that God had rejected Saul and he seemed to have no other thought in mind than that for the present Saul was to be regarded as the "anointed" king.

David, much like Joseph, made capital of adversity. Though the object of Saul's envy, he so conducted himself as to have Saul's approbation in his saner hours. He was loved in Saul's household, marrying Saul's daughter Michal, and being knit in love with Jonathan with a love that was tender and strong to the end. His successful combat with Goliath was a favorable score for him, in the minds of all Israel, which was never forgotten. While a fugitive from Saul's court David advanced in a twofold manner. He gathered

150

about him a band of leaders which became the nucleus of his army. On the other hand, he developed in the grace of self-control; he never lifted a hand against Saul and his household. Twice he could have killed Saul but spared him. David literally heaped fiery coals of grace upon the head of Saul.

At the report of the death of Saul and Jonathan, the messenger who brought the news claimed credit for Saul's death, hoping of course that David would reward him for the deed. To his great consternation, David ordered him killed. Instead of celebrating the event as a victory, he genuinely mourned. At this time he wrote his beautiful song in tribute to Saul and Jonathan (II Samuel 1:19-27).

Against the strong resentment of Joab the captain of David's host, David pursued a consistent policy of kindness to the remnant of Saul's house. It was by a rift in that house, between Ishbosheth the king and Abner his captain that the tribes were turned to favor David's rule. Assassins in his own house, not from David, finally brought the life of Ishbosheth to its end. When only Mephibosheth, Jonathan's lame son, remained of Saul's house, David, desiring to show a kindness to Jonathan, gave him a permanent home in the court at Jerusalem.

David, thus won both his friends and his enemies in the nation. When through the course of events no successor to Saul remained, the hearts of the people were already prepared to own David as their king.

David's attitude in all of this was in contrast to the attitude of Saul. Saul was wilful and jealous. He clung to power as though it was his right. He made his own decisions until he came to insurmountable odds and impossible extremities. David never manifested a covetous spirit in relation to the kingly office. Even after Saul had been slain, when on the basis of God's anointing he might have assumed that he should go ahead, he remained at Ziklag, and, the text says significantly, "David inquired of the LORD, saying, Shall I go up into any of the cities of Judah?" The expression, "David inquired of the LORD" is found repeatedly in the account of David's life (I Sam. 23:2, 4; 30:8; II Sam. 2:1; 5:19, 23; 21:1; I Chron. 14:10, 14). Because David fully regarded the sovereignty of God, God was able to make him the greatest king of Israel's history.

4. Historical Outline

I. **David King Over Judah (II Samuel 1-4)**

1. The Slayer of Saul Executed (1:1-16)

2. David Grieved for Saul and Jonathan (1:17-27)

3. David Made King of Judah (2:1-4)
   (1) Procedure: "David enquired of the LORD"
   (2) God ordered advance to Hebron
   (3) David anointed by men of Judah

4. David Commended Jabesh-Gilead (2:5-7)

5. Ishbosheth Made King over Israel (2:11)
   (1) Crowned by Abner, captain of Saul's host
   (2) Ishbosheth reigned 2 years at Mahanaim

6. Captains of Israel and Judah in Conflict (2:12-32)
   (1) Abner slew Joab's brother Asahel
   (2) Abner beaten
      1) Israel's loss, 360 men
      2) Judah's loss, 20 men

7. Rift between Ishbosheth and Abner (3:6-11)

8. League between Abner and David (3:12-39)
   (1) Israel inclined to David by Abner (3:12-21)
   (2) Abner treacherously slain by Joab (3:22-30)
   (3) David lamenting, disclaimed responsibility (3:31-39)

9. End of Saul's Dynasty (Chapter 4)
   (1) Ishbosheth assassinated by captains Baanah and Rechab (4:1-8)
   (2) Assassins are rewarded by David (4:9-12)

II. **David King over All Israel (II Sam. 5:24)**

1. The Nation Unified (5:1-5)

2. Jerusalem Made the Capital (5:6-16; note I Chron. 12:23-40)

3. Philistines and Others Subdued (5:17-25; 8:1-14; 10:1-19)

4. The Ark Returned (Chapter 6; Note I Chron. 16)

5. A New Temple Considered (Chapter 7; Note I Chron. 22; 28:11-21; Chapter 29)

6. Mephibosheth Remembered (4:4; Chapter 9)

7. David's Sin; Nathan's Probe (Chapter 11)

8. Family Troubles (Chapter 13)
   (1) The Amnon-Tamar incident (13:1-18)
   (2) Tamar in Absalom's house (13:19-22)
   (3) Amnon slain by Absalom (13:23-36)
   (4) Absalom's abode at Geshur (13:37-39)

9. David in Exile—Absalom's Supremacy (Chapters 14-18)
   (1) Joab's cunning intercession (chapter 14)
   (2) Absalom's conspiracy; David's flight (chapter 15)
   (3) Ziba's gifts; Shimei's curses; Ahithophel's counsel (chapter 16)
   (4) Hushai vs. Ahithophel; Amasa vs. Joab (chapter 17)
   (5) David's forces vs. Absalom's (chapter 18)
      1) Three leaders: Joab, Abishai, Ittai (18:1-2)
      2) David in the rear (18:3-4)
      3) David's charge regarding Absalom (18:5)
      4) Israel beaten; Absalom slain (18:6-18)
      5) Ahimaaz and Cushai report to David (18:19-32)
      6) David overwhelmed with grief (18:33)

10. David Restored to His Throne (Chapters 19-20)
    (1) Poise regained; escort home; pardons and rewards (chapter 19)
    (2) The revolt of Sheba (19:41—20:22)
    (3) Personal notices: concubines (20:3)
    (4) Famine and requital of the Gibeonites (21:1-14)

(5) David's mighty men (20:23-36; 21:15-22; 23:8-39)

(6) A Psalm of David (chapter 22)

(7) Numbering the people (24:1-18)

(8) Araunah's threshing floor (24:19-25)

(9) David's last days (I Kings 1—2:11; note I Chron. 29:10-19)

5.   The Founding of Jerusalem

The question of choosing a permanent site for a capital city arose, and the ancient citadel of Jebus was decided upon. The situation was unique, easily protected from within but difficult for attack from without. It consisted of four mounts in something of a horseshoe shape, with a valley between and valleys on each side, and with an opening to the south. This site then was surrounded by other hills.

David's admiration for this site is thus expressed in a psalm: "Beautiful for situation, the joy of the whole earth, is Mount Zion, on the sides of the north, the city of the great King" (Psa. 48:2).

The city has been called Zion, the city of David, and most commonly, Jerusalem. It became not only the capital but the center of the nation's worship. The Levites were dismissed from their tabernacle transportation duties in view of the permanent placing of the tabernacle and in view of the new temple to be built.

The taking of this city was David's problem, for it was still in the hands of the Jebusites. These people were so sure that they could not be taken that they ridiculed the forces of David. David made a challenge to his men, promising as a reward to the man who would take the stronghold, the position of captain of his host. It was Joab who successfully met the challenge, and began his important role as the military leader of Israel. He held his position until David's death.

6.   David's Military Conquests

David promptly subdued his enemies. Those named in the account of Samuel were Philistia, Moab, Hadarezer of Zobah, Edom, Ammon, and Syria. By these conquests the territorial boundaries of Israel were extended to the greatest area of all history.

Having subdued his enemies, David set up garrisons and placed over them the most capable leaders. The strength of David's kingdom was due in no small degree to David's descretion in choosing and committing authority to men. In all of this his dependence upon God was the secret of his leadership. Saul had failed because he

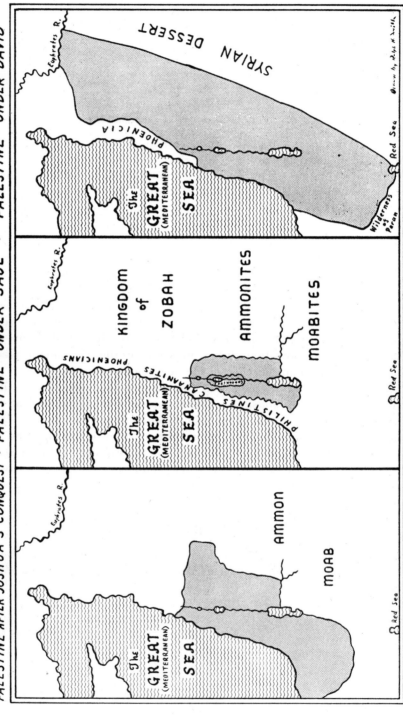

TERRITORIAL DEVELOPMENTS of PALESTINE

PALESTINE AFTER JOSHUA'S CONQUEST · PALESTINE UNDER SAUL · PALESTINE UNDER DAVID

The GREAT (MEDITERRANEAN) SEA

Euphrates R.

AMMON

MOAB

Red Sea

KINGDOM of ZOBAH

PHOENICIANS

CANANITES

PHILISTINES

AMMONITES

MOABITES

Euphrates R.

Red Sea

SYRIAN DESSERT

PHOENICIA

Euphrates R.

Wilderness of Paran

Red Sea

Drawn by Ralph M. Smith

rashly proceeded upon his own impulses. David proceeded by inquiring of God for wisdom and direction.

7. The Awful Sin of a Great Saint

The eleventh chapter of II Samuel records an ugly blot upon
the otherwise admirable David. The Bible is marked by its honesty.
Such men as David are not spared from exposure when their example runs amiss. After all, the Bible has only one hero—God.
Men are dependent upon his grace to keep them from falling into
sin and to save them from sin's consequence of destruction. How
David slipped from his high eminence into almost irretrievable
baseness is told us fully. Doubtless the Spirit of God intended this
adverse example to be an exhibition of the way sin may arise in the
life of any saint.

The sin started with two facts of the natural order. The first
was the human sexual propensity of David. The second was the
beauty of a woman. Both of these facts are a part of the normal
make-up of human beings. But both must be under the control of
the moral law of God. David had reached a place of ease in his life.
More than one man has done well until prosperity has made him
drunken with self satisfaction. Under God's blessing man tends to
forget that there is a line between what he may have and may not
have. Men of means sometimes drift into the assumption that they
may have whatever they can have. But once the moral law is ignored in any degree, an initial sin leads to a covering sin, and the
policy eventually leads to a degree of sin never contemplated in
the beginning. David stayed at home when he should have been
with the army. Whose responsibility it was that his eyes met the
scene which they beheld we do not know, probably both his and
Bathsheba's. But in short order the temptation developed into
collusion. The act of adultery was committed. The act resulted in
illegitimate pregnancy. Trouble was then inevitable and sins of
covering followed until the equivalent of murder had been
committed. The scheme worked. Uriah, Bathsheba's husband, was in the regular list of casualties of battle, apparently. David legally married Bathsheba, apparently. No one
knew the true story, David thought. If Joab who perpetrated the
death of Uriah knew the facts, he probably regarded it expedient
to hush them up. Also, considering David's authority, no one would

have cared to risk interference in such a matter on the ground of suspicion. Uriah, himself, was probably only a Hittite mercenary soldier and no one cared too much about him. "But the thing that David had done displeased the LORD" (11:27b).

It is almost inconceivable that one of David's spiritual stature would be the perpetrator of such scheming. Yet no one knows the degree of crime to which sin, once yielded to, will lead. One had better do as Joseph did in the face of a similar temptation—run from the spot. He who trusts himself to linger in the presence of forbidden fruit plays a dangerous game.

If the record had stopped with the eleventh chapter and this dark secret of David's life had never been brought to light, such a stigma would have remained upon David as to blemish his life forever. Such a sin unrepented of and unforgiven would have made him a misfit among the saints. Doubtless as the months wore on and as the crimes committed passed the likelihood of being brought to light by men, David's spirit must have felt an awful, woeful weight. To keep such sins covered would have had either of two results eventually. They would have brought a climax of irrepressible conviction to David's heart or they would have hardened his heart, making a beast of him. Fortunately for him, God strove with him and brought him to conviction. The parable with which Nathan, the prophet of God faced the king was too obvious in its application to be missed. Convicted, David uncovered and confessed his sin. Psalms 51 and 32 (studied in this order) are the expressions of the spiritual struggle by which David came to be restored from his sin.

8. Reaping Wild Oats

David learned the blessedness of God's forgiveness, as is readily seen in the 32nd Psalm. But David's seed-sowing of sin nevertheless came to a harvest of evil in his own family as the prophet Nathan said it would (I Sam. 12:10-12). Also, his sin had given occasion for blasphemy to the enemies of the LORD (I Sam. 12:14).

The account of David's sin in II Sam. 11-12 is followed by the record of similar sins in David's family. Amnon committed incest with his sister Tamar, and cruelly turned her away to bear her shame. Absalom killed Amnon in vengeance. Later Absalom nearly stole the throne from his father, but was defeated and lost his life at the hands of Joab. Absalom committed adultery with David's concubines in the sight of all Israel. One of Absalom's men committed the same sin with Abigail, David's wife.

In all of this we see David, previously so invincible in battle, as defenseless as a child. Why? Because he knew, as others did not perhaps, that these things were traceable to his seed-sowing of sin. There was a sense of justice, more than of mercy perhaps, in David's wish that he might have died in Absalom's stead (II Sam. 18:33). Also, it was doubtless a sense of his own responsibility in this schism which caused David to withhold punishment from such as Ziba and Shimei who had been implicated in Absalom's rebellion.

9. David's Problem Captain

Of the many personalities who surrounded David, one stands out in importance through his long reign, namely Joab the son of Zeruiah. Joab was the captain of David's host. With him were associated his two brothers, Abishai and Asahel.

Joab was both a boon and a problem to David. When David needed a strong man Joab filled the occasion with utmost efficiency. It was Joab who took the difficult citadel of Jebus for use as David's capital. Yet Joab continually overstepped his authority. He was too "quick on the trigger." He slew Abner, Amasa, and Absalom without authority from David. Upon the occasion of Joab's murder of Abner, David lamentingly complained to his servants, "Know ye not that there is a prince and a good man fallen this day in Israel? And I am this day weak, though anointed king; and these men be too hard for me: the LORD shall reward the doer of evil for his wickedness" (II Sam. 3:38, 39).

Joab's hard hand is seen in the slaying of Absalom, contrary to the bidding of David. Also when David mourned for Absalom, Joab reproved him. It seemed to Joab that David was more concerned about his son's life than about the lives of the people of the nation. Undoubtedly, Joab had a point, yet it is evident that he lacked the moral discernment to appreciate David's sense of personal responsibility for the evil ways of his son. He could not see why David should want to die for his son.

The issue between David and Joab came to full relief as David lay upon his death bed and as the question of a successor arose. Joab took undue initiative in promoting Adonijah for the position. Such an act led David to bring his whole career into review. In view of Joab's unauthorized shedding of blood Solomon was charged to see that he should not die a natural death. Realizing his plight, Joab took refuge by clinging to the horns of the altar. Solomon required that Benaiah, his newly appointed captain of the host, should carry out the execution order.

Joab was typical of the militarist who lacks the motive of right principle. He was a man of force and action, valuable in his place, but inclined to ignore the higher sovereignty which is the source of all authority. In this respect he shared the fault of Saul. Not even the horns of the altar to which he fled (I Kings 2:30) were of avail to appease the hand of judgment upon him.

10. The Writings of David

Seventy-three chapters of the book of Psalms are, by the psalm-titles, ascribed to David. There are fifty-three unidentified psalms of which quite probably many belong to David as author. David, who was renowned in his youth as a harpist, is also known as the "sweet psalmist" of Israel (II Sam. 23:1).

Some of the psalms clearly fit into recorded experiences of David (Psalms 3, 7, 11, 18, 24, 34, 55, 60, 72).

The value of the Psalms is threefold. They represent the spiritual experience of the writer and in this are inspiring by way of example. Secondly, they are valuable because they embody principles of spirituality applicable to all worshipers of God. Thirdly they are of distinctive value in their portrayal of the Messiah. Some Psalms in which the Messianic reference is prominent are the following:

Psalm 2 (See Acts 13:33; Heb. 1:5; 5:5)
Psalm 16 (See Acts 2:25-28; 13:35)
Psalm 22 (See Matt. 27:46; 27:35; Heb. 2:12)
Psalm 40 (See Heb. 10:5-10)
Psalm 41 (See John 13:18)
Psalm 45 (See Heb. 1:8-9)
Psalm 68 (See Eph. 4:8)
Psalm 69 (See John 2:17; Rom. 15:3; 11:9, 10; Acts 1:20)
Psalm 72 (Matt. 22:44; Mark 12:36; Acts 2:34, 35; I Cor. 15:25;
          Heb. 1:13; 10:12-13; 5:6)
Psalm 118 (Matt. 21:42; Acts 4:11; I Pet. 2:4-10)

Some of the Psalms have both historical and Messianic reference. Psalm 72, for example, is written in view of Solomon's succession to the throne, yet the glories of the reign described are universal in scope and perpetual as to time, and hence must refer to the goal of all prophecy—the kingdom of God.

11. The Family of David

Wives (II Sam. 3:2-5)	Sons
Ahinoam (Jezreelitess)	Amnon
Abigail (Widow of Nabal, the Carmelite)	Chileab
Maachah (Daughter of Talmai, King of Geshur)	Absalom
Haggith	Adonijah
Abital	Shephatiah
Eglah (David's wife)	Ithream

More wives and concubines at Jerusalem (II Sam. 5:13-16) including Bathsheba (II Sam. 12; I Kings 1). From these the following sons were born:

Shamuah	Ibhar	Elishama
Shobab	Elishua	Eliada
Nathan	Nepheg	Eliphalet
Solomon	Japhia	

Figure 23

12. Discussion and Review

1. Evaluate the gifts and the experiences which qualified David as he came to power.

2. How had David advanced during the period of Saul's adversity against him?

3. Show that David's attitude toward the house of Saul was both spiritually and politically correct.

4. Describe the founding of David's capital. Of what permanence is Jerusalem in the plan of God?

5. Summarize David's military achievements.

6. Show from David's life that a saint, though he be a king, cannot get away with sin.

7. Show the importance of the prophetic office in relation to the throne of the nation. Which was the higher office?

8. What would the result have been for David if he had succeeded in hiding his sin permanently?

9. Show the harvest of wild oats which David reaped following his sin with Bathsheba.

10. Why was David so defenseless against his son's sins?

11. Estimate the character of Joab.

12. What is the threefold value of the Psalms?

13. Select Memory Passages

Psalms 1; 8; 23; 24:1; 25:9; 32:1-2, 8, 9; 34:18; 85:10; 89:3, 4; Psalm 103.

14. Character Review

Identify:

David	Baanah	Amnon	Ahithophel	Ahimaaz
Isbosheth	Rechab	Tamar	Hushai	Cushai
Abner	Bathsheba	Absalom	Amasa	Sheba
Asahel	Mephibosheth	Ziba	Abishai	Araunah
Joab	Nathan	Shimei	Ittai	Uriah

15. Bibliography

Kuyper, Abraham. *Women of the Old Testament.* Grand Rapids: Zondervan.
  1. "Abigail," pp. 106-109.
  2. "Michal," pp. 109-112.
  3. "Bathsheba," pp. 112-115.
  4. "The Women of Tekoah," pp. 115-118.
MacCartney, Clarence E. *Trials of Great Men.* Chapter VI, "The Trial of David." Nashville: Abingdon-Cokesbury Press.
Meyer, F. B. *David, Shepherd, Psalmist, King.* London: Morgan and Scott.
Morgan, G. Campbell. *Living Messages of the Books of the Bible.* "The Message of II Samuel," Pp. 161-176. "The Message of the Psalter," Pp. 27-39. New York: Fleming H. Revell Co.
Robinson, George L. "David," *The International Standard Bible Encyclopedia.* Vol. II. pp. 790-797B.

Chapter 15

THE UNITED KINGDOM OF ISRAEL

—The Times of Solomon
(1015-975 B. C.)

1. Reading Assignment: I Kings 1-11; II Chronicles 1-9

2. Collateral: Song of Solomon, Proverbs, Ecclesiastes
(Read the Bible first)

3. Introduction—Solomon's Debt to David

The favorable conditions under which Solomon began his reign must be credited in no small measure to David. Wars of conquest were over; enemy military power had been broken. The peoples of adjoining kingdoms enjoyed prosperity under Israel's supremacy, and under such conditions were not resentful of the tribute required.

Solomon has been called, with propriety, a builder. Yet, if this is true, David must be recognized as the architect, and as the trainer of the builder. From the book of Chronicles it is evident that David devoted much of his time to plans and preparation of materials for the Temple. Solomon has been credited also as the organizer of a great state. Yet, it was David who had broken down resistance to Israel and had made her the number one power of Western Asia. David's "mighty men" (II Sam. 20:23-26; 21:15-22; 23:8-39) held the power of the nation intact in the days when David could no longer go into battle. The inauguration of Solomon (I Kings 1:32-

161

40) indicates impressively that Solomon's reign was to be a perpetuation of that of David. His men, exclusive of certain discordant persons such as Joab and Abiathar, continued in the state over which Solomon ruled. The kingdom which David turned over to Solomon extended from the Euphrates river in Mesopotamia to Egypt and included approximately fifty thousand square miles, the largest area in Israel's history.

4. Historical Outline

I. **Solomon's Appointment and Anointing (I Kings 1—2:11; Cf. I Chron. 22:9-10; 28:5-7)**

1. David's Infirmity (1:1-4)
2. Adonijah's Attempt to Take the Throne (1:5-10)
    (1) His pretext, bearing, and age rank (1:5-6)
    (2) His counsellors (1:7): Joab, captain of the host; Abiathar, the priest; his brethren; the King's servants (1:9)
    (3) Persons conspicuously excluded (1:8): Zadok, the priest; Benaiah, the son of Jehoiada; Nathan, the prophet; Shimei; Rei; David's mighty men; Solomon (1:10)
    (4) The feast (1:9-10; 41-49)
3. Solomon Made King (1:11-53; 2:1-11)
    (1) Appeal to David
    (2) David's oath
    (3) Instructions for anointing
    (4) Solomon's anointing
    (5) Adonijah's plea for mercy
    (6) Charges (I Kings 2:1-11)

II. **Solomon's Reign before the Building of the Temple (2:13—4)**

1. Judgments Administered (2:13-46)
    (1) Adonijah heard, executed (2:13-25)
    (2) Abiathar exiled to Anathoth (2:26-27)
    (3) Joab executed (2:28-34)
    (4) Shimei executed (2:36-46)
    (5) Appointments:
        Captain—Benaiah
        Priest—Zadok
2. Solomon's First Foreign Ally (3:1)
    (1) Affinity with Egypt
    (2) Pharaoh's daughter taken
3. Solomon's Worship (3:2-4)
    (1) He loved the LORD
    (2) He walked in David's statutes
    (3) Exception: offerings in high places
4. God's Gift of Wisdom (3:5-15)
5. Solomon's Wisdom Exhibited (3:16-28)
6. Solomon's Officers (4:1-19)
7. Statistics (4:20-21)
    Population—as the sand of the seashore
    State of the nation—eating, drinking, making merry
    Area—River Euphrates to River of Egypt
    Foreign relations—reigned over all kingdoms
    Provisions—for table and stable
    Home ownership—vine and fig tree for each
    Horses—40,000; horsemen—12,000
    Wisdom—Solomon excelled all men
    Proverbs—3000
    Songs—1005

III. **Solomon's Building Program (I Kings 5-9)**

1. The Cooperation of Hiram (5:1-12)
    (1) Hiram's identity:
        1) King of Tyre
        2) Lover of David
        3) Son of a man of Tyre and of a widow of Naphtali (7:14)
    (2) Request for cedar and fir
    (3) Hiram's gracious response
    (4) Solomon's annual payments: 20,000 measures of wheat; 20 measures of pure oil

(5) League of Hiram and Solomon

2. Solomon's Employees (5:13-18)
   (1) 30,000 men for Lebanon service
   (2) 70,000 burden bearers
   (3) 80,000 hewers in the mountains
   (4) 33,000 officers

3. Construction of the Temple (Chapter 6)
   (1) Time: Second month of 480th year after Exodus until eighth month of the 487th year
   (2) Dimensions:
       Length 60 cubits (90 feet)
       Height 20 cubits (30 feet)
       Breadth 30 cubits (45 feet)
       Porch: 20 times 30 cubits
   (3) Windows, chambers, walls, overlaying gold, carvings, doors
   (4) Materials:
       Main walls — stone "made ready"
       Inner walls—boards of cedar
       Floors and ceiling—cedar and fir
       (All interior was wood, no stone was seen)
       The Oracle (Holy of Holies) —interior completely overlaid with pure gold
       Altar of Incense—overlaid with pure gold

4. Other Buildings (7:1-12)
   (1) Solomon's house (7:1)
   (2) The house of Lebanon (7:2-8a)
   (3) The house for Pharaoh's daughter (8b)

5. Brass Work for the Temple (7:13-47)
   (1) Made by Hiram (7:13-14)
   (2) Two pillars for the porch: Jachin and Boaz
   (3) Chapiters
   (4) A molten sea
   (5) Bases
   (6) Lavers
   (7) Networks
   (8) Pots, shovels, and basons
   (9) Amount of brass, beyond calculation

6. Vessels and Instruments of Gold (7:48-51)
   (1) Altar of incense

(2) Table of shewbread
(3) The ten candlesticks (with flowers, lamp and tongs)
(4) The bowls, snuffers, basons, spoons, censers, hinges for two doors

7. The Feast of Dedication (8:1-11)
   (1) The Ark of the covenant placed
   (2) Sacrifices offered before the ark
   (3) The glory of the LORD occupied the house
   (4) Solomon blessed the congregation (8:12-21)
   (5) Solomon's prayer (8:22-61)
       1) Tribute to God for covenant keeping (22-24)
       2) Regarding God's dwelling place (25-30)
       3) Regarding future trespasses (31-32)
       4) Regarding future defeat (33-34)
       5) Regarding drouth, famine, etc. (35-40)
       6) Regarding strangers (41-43)
       7) Regarding battle (44-45)
       8) Regarding sin—and captivity (46-54)
       9) Blessing upon Israel (55-59)
       10) High motive and challenge of the prayer (60-61)
   (6) Dedicatory peace offering: 22,-000 oxen, 120,000 sheep (62-64)
   (7) A fourteen day feast (65-66)
       1) Attendance nationwide
       2) Thankfulness of the people for their felicity

8. God's Covenant with Solomon (9:1-9)

III. Solomon's Felicity in Wisdom and Wealth (9:10—10:29)

1. The Mutual Gifts of Solomon and Hiram (9:10-14)
   (1) Time: after 20 years

2. Solomon's Levies (9:15-23)
   (1) Projects requiring services and money (15-19)
   (2) Sources of income (20-23)

3. Pharaoh's Daughter's Abode (9:24; Cf. 3:1; 7:8)

4. Three Annual Sacrifices of Solomon (9:25)
5. Solomon's Navy (9:26-28)
   (1) Port at Ezion-geber
   (2) Hiram provides sailors
   (3) Imports from Ophir: gold, almug trees, and precious stones (note 9:11)
6. Visit of the Queen of Sheba (10:1-13)
7. Solomon's Gold (10:14-25)
   (1) By annual tribute, 666 talents (approximately 20 billion dollars)
   (2) Income by commerce and under-rulers
   (3) His golden targets
   (4) His golden shields
   (5) His throne of ivory and gold
   (6) His drinking vessels of pure gold
   (7) Summary of abundance: ". . . . it was not accounted of in the days of Solomon" (10:21) "And all the earth . . . . brought every man his present . . . ." (10:24-25) "And the king made silver to be in Jerusalem as stones, and cedars . . . . sycamore trees . . . ." (10:27)
8. Solomon's Horses (10:26-29; Note Deut. 17:16)
   1400 chariots
   12,000 horsemen
   Brought from Egypt in "droves"

IV. **Solomon's Apostasy (Chapter 11)**
1. Cause: Many Strange Wives
   (1) Of Egypt, Moab, Ammon, Edom, of Sidon, and of the Hittites
   (2) Number:
        700 wives
        300 concubines

2. Time of Solomon's Apostasy
   (1) "When Solomon was old" (vs. 4)
3. Nature of Solomon's Apostasy
   (1) "His wives turned away his heart unto other gods"
   (2) "Solomon went after" Ashtoreth and Milcom" (vs. 5)
   (3) "Solomon did evil . . . . went not fully after the LORD" (vs. 6)
   (4) Solomon built "an high place for Chemosh . . . . Molech . . . . and for all his strange wives" (vss. 7-8)
4. God's Judgment upon Solomon (11:9-40)
   (1) God's anger (11:9)
   (2) God's charge: covenant breaking (11:10, 11)
   (3) The penalty: kingdom to be rent
   (4) Considerations for David's sake:
        1) The rent will not be in his day
        2) Not all will be rent
   (5) Adversaries (11:14-40)
        1) Hadad (14-22)
        2) Rezon (23-25)
        3) Jeroboam (26-40)
5. Other Historical Sources (11:41; II Chron. 9:29)
   (1) The Acts of Solomon (11:41)
   (2) Book of Nathan the prophet
   (3) Prophecy of Ahijah the Shilonite
   (4) The visions of Iddo
6. Length of Reign—40 years (11:42)
7. Place of Burial—the City of David (11:43)

5. The Question of David's Successor

The appointment of Solomon as David's successor was made by God at the time that David had first asked for permission to build a house for God (II Samuel 7; I Chron. 22:9-10; 28:5-7). Thus, it is evident that the matter was clear in the minds of David, Bathsheba, Solomon, and Nathan, at least. It is possible that other members of David's family did not know that the matter had been definitely settled.

Adonijah had some grounds for attempting a claim, which, though not conclusive, constituted a pretext sufficiently strong to impress quite a following. He was possibly the oldest living son. He was a "goodly man." Furthermore, he had in earlier days playfully dramatized his anticipation of the time when he would be king, preparing horsemen and chariots and having fifty persons run before him, to which David, he said, had expressed no displeasure. His argument was that David must have intended that he should be the successor or he would have interfered.

Yet Adonijah's procedure in putting on his inaugural feast betrayed his scheming. He conspicuously excluded David, Bathsheba, Solomon, and Nathan from the feast. It appears that this feast was put on while David was in a coma and seemed unlikely to revive (I Kings 1:1-4). Providentially, he did revive and by his oath to Bathsheba and Nathan gave unquestionable positive instructions as to the succession. He set in motion active steps to crown Solomon king. The procedure completely unnerved the Adonijah party, and cleared the way for Solomon's reign, without rival.

Solomon's leniency with Adonijah in sparing his life was an act of graciousness marking the beginning of his reign. This act, of leniency, however, was necessarily conditional, and when Adonijah showed himself a continued aspirant to Solomon's heritage his life was taken.

6. Solomon's Commendable Beginning

To this great heritage Solomon added a wise choice at the beginning of his reign. This combined to make the outlook in his reign a happy one indeed. It seems that Solomon, after his copious sacrifices to the LORD (I Kings 3:4) became keenly conscious of his inadequacy for the great responsibility to which he had been appointed, and sought God for help. The dream followed, in which God's gift of wisdom was communicated to him.

Solomon's request, as set forth in the dream, pleased God. An "understanding heart," literally a "hearing heart," did not mean infinite wisdom. Rather, what Solomon requested was for the faculty to receive wisdom from the God of infinite wisdom. He was not asking for an endowment that would make him self-sufficient. Says

Stanley: "He showed his wisdom by asking for wisdom. He became wise because he had set his heart upon it. This was to him the special aspect through which the Divine Spirit was to be approached, and grasped, and made to bear on the wants of men."

Solomon's approach to his task is a worthy example to every one whose role in life involves leadership of others. To be a father, or a mother, to be a Sunday School teacher, or a pastor, or to be a civil ruler of township, state, or nation, is too big a job for anyone to undertake without seeking wisdom from God.

7. The Nature of Solomon's Wisdom

We have in the above paragraphs noted that Solomon's wisdom consisted primarily of an understanding heart. He appears to have had the gift of an intuition to discern and judge. This gift is exhibited in the manner in which he judged the two mothers (3:16-28). By this incident he gained the reputation in Israel for prudence in judgment (vs. 28). He was a keen psychologist. He understood the folly of pride and sin, and in contrast the wisdom of righteousness and virtue. His wisdom extended to the varied phases of human knowledge, and on all subjects he was a teacher. He was evidently an entertaining conversationalist, hearing and answering the questions brought from the wise and great of all nations, to the greatest satisfaction of all who came.

All of these achievements in wisdom stemmed from God's gift to Solomon of a wise and understanding **heart.** Since we have to face another side less favorable in Solomon's life, it may be well to call attention to the fact that when Solomon failed, it was because his **heart** was "turned away."

8. The Temple of Solomon

The temple was built, in general, upon the pattern of the tabernacle, except that the dimensions were doubled. It was built upon Mount Moriah, the spot which David had purchased from Araunah, and possibly also the location where Abraham offered Isaac. It is also of note that Jesus was crucified on the northern part of this mount.

The temple of Solomon was the feature of the greatest glory in Jerusalem for more than 400 years. It was a major factor in securing national centralization, although it was the seat of worship for the whole nation for only about thirty years.

The temple building task took seven years, even after much preliminary work had been done by David. People from remote parts of the world contributed to its structure as is seen by naval developments. The Holy of Holies, a room 30 x 30 feet, was completely inlaid with gold; walls, ceiling, and floors alike were covered with pure gold. The total cost of the structure has been estimated at $600,000,000.

9.   Solomon's Conception of God

The prayer offered by Solomon at the dedication of the Temple is remarkable for its comprehension of the twofold fact of God's infinitude on the one hand, and of his condescension to commune with people on the other hand. Now that the temple to the LORD was built, Solomon appears to be guarding against the dwarfing effect that such a center of worship might have (note I Kings 8:27). The temple must not be allowed to imply that God is finite.

This expression on Solomon's part is perfect and complete refutation of those modern critics who say that the Israelites had no conception of God as a supreme being until the eighth century, or later, before Christ. Jehovah was not, as these critics say, a tribal god. He is clearly conceived to be the God of the universe, yet in no wise to be contained in it.

Solomon's prayer (I Kings 8:27) suggests the vastness of the universe, leaving room for all that has since been brought to view by modern telescopes. On the expression, "heaven and heaven of heavens," Adam Clarke, who for our purpose is sufficiently up to date, comments:

"There are systems, and systems of systems, each possessing its sun, its primary and secondary planets, all extending beyond each other in unlimited space, in the same regular and graduated order which we find to prevail in what we call our solar system; which probably, in its thousands of millions of miles in diameter, is to some others, no more than the area of the lunar orbit to that of Georgium Sidus . . . Had God created a system like ours in every six days since the foundation of the world, and kept every seventh as a Sabbath . . . they would occupy but a speck in the inconceivable immensity of space. Reader, all this and millions more is demonstrably possible; and if so, what must God be . . . . who inhabiteth eternity?"

The word "yet" with which Solomon follows his reference to the greatness of the universe in this verse is significant. How can there be, it must be asked, the possibility of this word "yet" if God is infinitely beyond us? It is simply because there is something which means more to God than immensity. God is not only every where. He is everywhere in particular. As for particular places, he has special "respect" for some and relatively less for others. He delights to dwell in the midst of his people. Eden, the Tabernacle, the Church, and the New Jerusalem—these are his cherished dwelling places. The temple which Solomon had built would be his center of habitation because he could thus dwell at the heart of Israel's population.

Note the prominence of the word prayer or its equivalent in verses 28, 29, and 30. God's house is to be known as a house of prayer. Prayer is communion. God hears and speaks. God shows forth his power, his glory, his instruction. Man is thus enlightened, pardoned, sanctified, and vivified as he worships in God's presence.

10. Transition From Nomadic to Commercial Life

David had been a shepherd. His departure from that life is something of a symbol of what was about to take place in the nation. In Solomon's day the nation entered upon new and extensive foreign relations and commercial enterprises. In addition to the former commerce by caravans there was added a sizeable navy which sent ships to distant points in the Mediterranean sea and through the Red Sea to the Indian Ocean. The three year voyages of Solomon's ships indicate that great distances must have been traveled. Imports named in connection with these voyages included gold, silver, lumber, precious stones, ivory, apes, and peacocks. One shipload, it has been estimated, carried gold valued at $12,000,000.

Such a transition was bound to raise many new problems. The life of luxury occasioned by multiplied wealth was doubtless the first problem. The book of Proverbs is an attempt to raise up moral standards against the multiplied moral evils that attended this period of transition.

11. Solomon's Apostasy

One of the main problems regarding this great king is the tragic

course of sin in his own life. It appears that the deeds which led to
this sin came in the very beginning of his reign. The occasion for
his apostasy was integrally related to the development of his re-
nown.

There is room for question marks to be raised regarding his
first actions—the taking of Pharaoh's daughter and an affinity with
Egypt, and then the repetition of this policy with hundreds of foreign kings. How could Solomon enter into these relations?

Barring the moral issue, Solomon's alliance with Egypt on the
southwest was a masterstroke of diplomacy both politically and
commercially. This alliance immediately stepped up Solomon's
fame and comparative status among the nations. It also added to
his dominion (9:16).

A partial justification of Solomon's alliances and affinities is
pointed out in a paragraph by Whedon, who says:

"According to the letter of the law only marriage with the
Canaanitish tribes was forbidden (Exod. 34:16), and intermarriage with
nations outside of Canaan was not only not prohibited but tolerated
in the examples, never rebuked, of Joseph's marriage with the
daughter of an Egyptian priest (Gen. 41:45), of Moses' marriage
with a daughter of Midian (Exod. 2:21), and that of Boaz with
Ruth. But though the law did not forbid these marriages, they were
not in harmony with its spirit; and it was by foreign marriages that
Solomon's heart was seduced from the worship of Jehovah."

Had Solomon taken but one wife, and had she been like Ruth,
or had he possessed the self-control of Joseph, he might be justified by the consideration raised by Whedon. But the writer of I
Kings accompanies the record with no justification, by which we
may assume that there probably was none.

Such inconsistency seems nearly unbelievable in the life of a
wise man. Yet, we need only to realize the subtlety of temptation,
the susceptibility to vanity in human nature, and the perilous in-
volvements of compromise, to understand how naturally Solomon
was misled. It appears that an ambitious foreign policy, a toler-
ance of pagan religion, and an amorous nature were his undoing. It
is evident that Solomon's heart was right at first, else it could not
be said that his "wives turned away his heart."

While the Kings and Chronicles accounts say very little about
Solomon's last days, we may judge, perhaps, from the book of Ecclesiastes, that at the last, Solomon brought his whole life under

review and renounced his vain pursuits. In the closing part of that book, Solomon acknowledges that life is lived to the best end when it is under control of God's law. "Under the sun" is too limited a viewpoint. Man's life, he tells us, should take into account the judgment and the order of things beyond. Remembering the Creator in one's youth, he says, is the best assurance of a happy outlook in old age.

12.   The Writings of Solomon

Three books of the Bible are to be credited to the authorship of Solomon, namely, the Song of Solomon, Proverbs, and Ecclesiastes. These books, considered in the order stated, serve to represent three periods in Solomon's life. The first probably belongs to his early life and is expressive of his romantic nature. The second, with its moral instruction, belongs to the mature years of the king and is the expression of his wisdom in government. Ecclesiastes, according to the opinion of Jewish authorities, belongs to the latter years of Solomon, after he had repented and turned from the idolatry into which his heathen wives had led him.

13.   Discussion and Review

1.   Relate the controversy regarding David's successor.

2.   Show the fact of Solomon's great indebtedness to David for the glory of his kingdom.

3.   Show that Solomon had a good beginning.

4.   Discuss the nature of Solomon's wisdom.

5.   Describe Solomon's temple in relation to the tabernacle, as to its site, as to its duration of existence, as to its builders, and as to its costliness.

6.   Discuss Solomon's conception of God.

7.   What transition in the life of the people of Israel took place in this age?

8.   Discuss the moral and spiritual history of Solomon's life.

9.   What three literary works correspond to periods of Solomon's life?   Discuss.

14.   Select Memory Passages

Proverbs 3:1-2, 5; 4:7, 18, 23; 6:6; 8:13; 9:10; 28:2, 9; 29:1, 2; 31:4, 5, 10; Ecclesiastes 12:1, 13-14.

15. Character Review

Identify:

David	Nathan	Hiram	Molech
Solomon	Shimei	Ashtoreth	Hadad
Adonijah	Abiathar	Milcom	Rezon
Benaiah	Zadok	Chemosh	Jeroboam

16. Bibliography

Albright, Wm. F. *The Archaeology of Palestine and the Bible.* pp. 45-47.

Kuyper, Abraham. *Women of the Old Testament.* Grand Rapids: Zondervan.
1. "The Witch of Endor," pp. 119-122.
2. "The Real Mother of the Illegitimate Child," pp. 126-129.
3. "The Queen of Sheba," pp. 137-140.

Morgan, G. Campbell. *Living Messages of the Books of the Bible.* Proverbs, pp. 41-56. Ecclesiastes, pp. 57-72. Song of Songs, pp. 73-88. New York: Fleming H. Revell Co.

Robinson, George L. "Solomon," *The International Standard Bible Encyclopedia.* Vol. V. pp. 2822-2825B.

Sangster, Margaret E. *The Women of the Bible.* Chapt. XIX, "The Queen of Sheba." New York: The Christian Herald.

PART SIX

THE DIVIDED KINGDOM
ISRAEL AND JUDAH

Chapter 16

SECESSION: THE KINGDOM
OF THE TEN TRIBES

—From Jeroboam to Hoshea
(975-722 B. C.)

1. Reading Assignment: I Kings 12—II Kings 17

2. Collateral Reading: Jonah, Amos, Hosea
(Read the Bible first)

3. Historical Outline

See the Harmony of the Kings of Judah and Israel, pages 187-197

4. Secession of the Northern Tribes—Causes

God had told Solomon that because of his sins his kingdom should be rent. This was to take place in the time of his son Rehoboam. What took place in the revolt of Jeroboam, however, may be seen to have human historic causes which, under God, brought about the divine judgment.

Remote Causes. Tendency to division may be observed at points earlier in Israel's history than the reign of Rehoboam. Judah enjoyed a favored position by a destiny beyond human manoeuvring. Her tribe was at the head of the tribes in the camp of Israel in the days of Moses. Her location in Palestine was a matter of "the

175

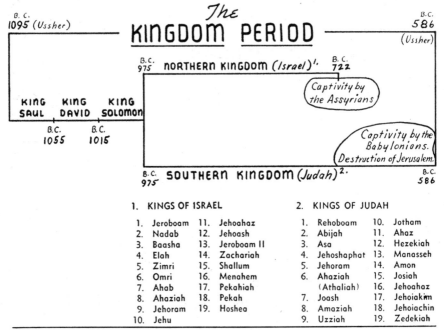

Figure 25

lot." After the death of Joshua God appointed Judah to take leadership against the Canaanites (Judges 1:1-8). The choice of David of Judah to displace Saul of Benjamin was altogether God's. Upon the death of Saul the people of Judah took prompt initiative in making David king, while the northern tribes followed the leadership of Ishbosheth, the son of Saul. In the latter part of David's reign Sheba was able to find a discordant element in the northern tribes to launch a rebellion which appears to have succeeded temporarily. The great developments of the nation under David and Solomon naturally brought a disproportionate wealth into the tribe of Judah. Those in more remote areas from the capital resented having to pay taxes to build up another tribe; especially was this true as they came to lose their fervor for the LORD and for the temple at Jerusalem.

Direct Cause. The immediate cause of the cessation was Rehoboam's rash treatment of those who appealed for tax adjustment. In reply to a suit representing the tribes brought by Jeroboam, a three day period for consideration was set. During this time, counsel was sought from two sources.   By the older men, Rehoboam was advised to lower the taxes.   By the young men, he was urged to rebuke the complainers and promise them only a heavier tax load. Presumably, the young men were ambitious friends of the court. Had the decision been made sincerely there might have been a different reaction, but Rehoboam's threat to chastise the people with scorpions clearly proved his despotism, and nothing could have been surer than revolt.

The sovereign hand of God is seen again, in this event, accomplishing a worthy purpose from the unworthy decision of man.   The prophet Ahijah had called and anointed Jeroboam, and God would have blessed his kingdom had he met the conditions.   Rehoboam reacted to the revolt with arms, but God intervened and gave him to understand that a higher power than that of Jeroboam had rent the kingdom, and that he did this as a measure of judgment.

5. The Kingdom of Israel

The Term.   The kingdom of the northern tribes came to be known as the kingdom of Israel.   It is necessary to understand in reading the Scriptures whether a given usage of the term refers to the limited usage or whether all of the tribes of Jacob are meant. The kingdom of Israel, in its more limited meaning, existed during a period of 253 years (Ussher).

Periods.   The history of Israel (the northern kingdom) falls into four rather distinct periods.   The first, covering about fifty years is the record of the policy of **idolatry taking root** in the nation.   It includes the reigns of Jeroboam I, Baasha, and Zimri.   The second, covering about the same length of time is the record of a nation under the **dominance of idolatry.**   It includes the reigns of Omri, Ahab, Ahaziah, and Jehoram.   The prophets Elijah and Elisha are the distinguished voices for God in this lawless period.   The third period, lasting about a hundred years, is distinguished by **God's hand of restraint** upon Israel's profligacy.   Jehu, Jehoahaz, Joash, Jeroboam II, and Zachariah were the rulers.   The prophets Jonah, Hosea, and Amos were the great prophets of the third period.   The fourth period, lasting about 50 years, is distinguished by the incoming of the Assyrians and the **final uprooting** of the kingdom of Israel. The kings were Shallum, Menahem, Pekahiah, Pekah, and Hoshea.

As an aid to memory the periods may be characterized as follows: idolatry rooting, reigning, receding, ruining.   In each of these

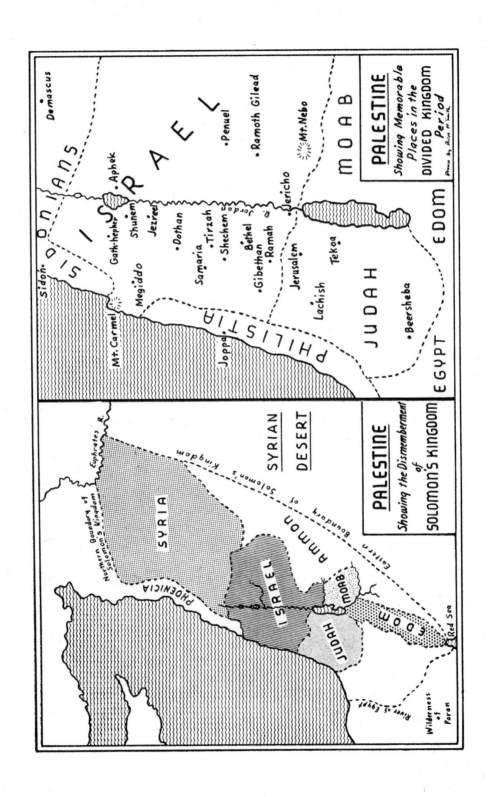

PALESTINE
Showing Memorable
Places in the
DIVIDED KINGDOM
Period

Drawn by Peter M. Smith

Damascus

SIDONIANS

I S R A E L

MOAB

Aphek

Gath-hepher

Shunem

Jezreel

Penuel

Ramoth Gilead

Mt. Nebo

Jordan R.

Dothan

Samaria

Tirzah

Shechem

Bethel

Gibethon

Ramah

Jericho

Jerusalem

Tekoa

Megiddo

Mt. Carmel

Joppa

Lachish

JUDAH

Beersheba

EDOM

P H I L I S T I A

EGYPT

PALESTINE
Showing the Dismemberment
of
SOLOMON'S KINGDOM

SYRIAN
DESERT

Euphrates R.

Northern Boundary of
Solomon's Kingdom

Eastern Boundary of Solomon's Kingdom

SYRIA

PHOENICIA

AMMON

ISRAEL

MOAB

JUDAH

EDOM

Red Sea

River of Egypt

Wilderness
of
Paran

periods, also, there was an outstanding typical man. In the first it was Jeroboam, in the second Ahab, in the third Jehu, and in the last it was Pekah.

6. Jeroboam the Standard-Setter of an Age

So far as we know him, Jeroboam had no unfavorable traits of character before he became king. On the contrary, he appears to have been a man of worthy character. His ability may be judged from the fact that Solomon had made him a collector of revenue in Ephraim, his native tribe. After Ahijah anointed him, and possibly with something of a premonition of what was ahead for his kingdom, Solomon sought to kill Jeroboam. To escape, Jeroboam sought and found refuge in the friendship of Shishak (Sheshonk), the pharaoh of Egypt. Shishak opened an attack on Jerusalem and looted the temple and the king's house while Rehoboam was waging war on Jeroboam.

Only very special grace would have kept Jeroboam faithful to worship at Jerusalem, considering the constant warfare between himself and Rehoboam. It was something of a diplomatic measure that a different worship was set up at Bethel and Dan. Enmity with Judah very easily resolved itself into antagonism in religion. It was moreover a popular stroke to legalize and establish idolatry considering the fact that it was Israel's perpetual tendency to revert to idols.

Under Jeroboam, idolatry became the fixed policy of the northern kingdom. Jeroboam's name became the symbol of evil in the land. The record describes his successors as evil "like Jeroboam." Jeroboam is an example of what happens to character where policies are not formed out of principle, and Israel affords the example of what happens to a people when they follow such leadership.

7.   The Capitals of Israel

The northern kingdom had three different capitals. Jeroboam first ruled at Shechem, but moved to the city of Tirzah, a few miles farther to the north. In the reign of Omri, Samaria was selected and built up as the capital.

Samaria, like Jerusalem, was built upon a unique hill. The city was built on the flattened top of the hill of Shemer, which occasioned Isaiah's reference to it as the "crown of pride," a city renowned for its combined beauty and vanity (Isaiah 28:1-6).

The building of Samaria was nearly identical with the establishment of Baal worship in Israel, for Omri's son, Ahab, while helping his father build the new capital, was also courting Jezebel, the daughter of the king of Zidon. When he ascended the throne of his father, the power behind his throne was the woman whom he married, and in the heart of this woman was enthroned the very spirit of heathendom. Samaria became the symbol of Baalism during the reign of Ahab. In it is seen the full harvest of the policy of Jeroboam, who sinned and made Israel to sin.

8. Baal Worship

Baal was the supreme male divinity of the Phoenician and Canaanitish nations. The worship of Baal was practiced by the Moabites and Midianites in the time of Moses, and from them spread to the Israelites (Num. 25:3-18; Deut. 4:3). During the reign of the kings it became the religion of the court and people of the ten tribes (I Kings 16:31-33), and never was permanently abolished. Temples to Baal were erected in Samaria (I Kings 16:32), and also later in Judah. According to Jeremiah (11:13) altars on which incense was burned to Baal were set up in all the streets of Jerusalem. In the reign of Ahab, Baal was served by 450 priests as well as by prophets. At times the priests danced around the altar, slashing themselves with knives (I Kings 18:26, 28).

The International Standard Bible Encyclopedia describes Baal worship as follows: "As the Sun-god, Baal was worshipped under two aspects, beneficent and destructive. On the one hand he gave light and warmth to his worshippers; on the other hand the fierce heat of summer destroyed the vegetation he had himself brought into being. Hence human victims were sacrificed to him in order to appease his anger in time of plague or other trouble, the victim being usually the first-born of the sacrificer and being burnt alive. In the O. T. this is euphemistically termed 'passing' the victim 'through the fire' (II Kings 16:3; 21:6)."

Baal worship included licentious rites (Num. 25) and should have been abhored by God's chosen people.

There seems to have been many Baals of different places, worshipped under different compounds, such as Baal-berith, Baal-zebub, and Baal-peor.

9. The Prophets of Israel

Though Israel's leaders marked out a trail of great wickedness, God at no time relinquished supreme control of Israel. His prophets had the final word, and in the eyes of the people God was glorified in the deeds of the most wicked kings. God, not primarily Jeroboam, ordered the schism in the nation. This is seen in the initiative taken by the prophet Ahijah. While Samaria was being built as the citadel of Baal worship, God was preparing the most colorful and powerful of the prophets, Elijah the Tishbite, to be the champion of the LORD against the prophets of Baal. Elijah not only struck a master blow at the priests of Baalism, but he anointed the terriffic soldier Jehu to completely exterminate the family of rulers which came from the union of Ahab and Jezebel, including Ahaziah, king of Judah who had married Athaliah, Ahab's daughter. Thus at the word of Elijah, Baalism was cut as a cancer from the breast of the two kingdoms. While Elijah wrote no book, his deeds stand as the great testimony of all times to the supremacy of the LORD over the powers of evil. His supernatural disappearance, as seen by Elisha, is testimony also of the reality of the eternal order. His appearance on the mount of Christ's transfiguration indicates something of his rank among those who surround the heavenly throne.

Elisha continued the ministry of Elijah. A list of the miracles of Elisha shows a power which approaches the mighty deeds later done by Christ himself. His power was a source of sure help. A grief stricken widow, a leper, a nation harrassed by the Syrians, all alike found in his power the deliverance they needed.

Jonah appears in the reign of Jeroboam II as the first among the writing prophets. The book of Jonah is a masterpiece in exhibiting the judgment and mercy of God in their operations. While the experience of Jonah relates to Nineveh, he was primarily a prophet to Israel. From the lesson of God's dealings with Nineveh there ought to have been a deep impression made upon Israel of the mercies of God which may be realized by penitent sinners.

The prophet Amos skillfully enumerated the sins of Israel's neighbors, of Philistia, Tyre, Edom, Ammon, Moab, and of Judah, soundly condemned them, and then turned his greatest fire upon Israel. For greed, dishonesty, adultery, and fornication, and for the pride and the selfishness of her nobles, the land would fall to the Assyrians, said Amos. Amos was not a professional prophet and pleaded no credentials. He was but a herdsman and a dresser of sycamore trees, upon whom the burden of the nation's sins called forth the voice of judgment. Though a prophet of rebuke and judgment, Amos also held out hope for a faithful remnant and the promise of a latter day restoration of Israel to her land.

The voice of the prophet Hosea was heard over a period of possibly sixty years, embracing the closing period of Israel's national existence. Hosea uttered and reiterated the message of judgment ahead. He spoke in metaphorical language based upon his own unhappy home life. Like his profligate wife, Israel had played the whore with God's enemies. Hosea waits and longs for his wife to tire of her lovers. He earnestly entreats her to return. So God even under impending judgment, pled for Israel to acknowledge her fallen condition and to return from her backsliding.

10. Israel's Foreign Relations

With Egypt. At the outset Jeroboam was in alliance with Shishak, king of Egypt. Shishak protected Jeroboam when Solomon in anger drove him into exile. When Rehoboam went against Jeroboam in war Shishak came up from the south and looted the temple and the king's house, thus enriching himself and weakening Jeroboam's enemy.

With Judah and Syria. Jeroboam and Rehoboam continued at war against each other all their days (II Kings 12:29-31). This war continued until the days of Jehoshaphat of Judah, of whom it is said that he made peace with Israel. This peace included a policy of putting up a united front against Syria who had been breaking over the northern boundary lines.

Notwithstanding Ahab's unworthiness, God marvelously assisted him in battle with Benhadad of Syria. Because of his disobedience, however, Ahab was slain at the hands of the Syrians.

In the reign of Ahaziah, the son of Ahab, the Moabites arose in rebellion against Israel. War with Syria continued intermittantly with loss to Israel until the reign of Jehoash. On his death bed the prophet Elisha energetically jogged the spirits of Jehoash, after which he went out and recovered cities which had been held by Syria (II Kings 13:10-25). This continued under Jeroboam II who, in keeping with the word of Jonah the prophet, restored the northern coast of Israel from the entering of Hamath to the sea of the Plain (Mediterranean) (II Kings 14).

With Assyria. Following the relatively prosperous reign of Jeroboam II, affairs at home and abroad plunged Israel into new troubles. While the prophet Hosea called upon the nation to return to God, the foundation of national life began to break up. A series of assassinations took place at the capital and the ten year reign of Menahem left marks of terror upon the land. On the foreign horizon appeared a foe far more terrible than Syria had been. From the north the Assyrian armies marched, irresistably, under king Pul. Israel was placed under tribute. Later, in the reign of Pekah, Tiglath Pilesar of Assyria invaded the land again and carried away captives. Finally, in the reign of Hoshea, when Shalmaneser observed that Israel was seeking aid against him from King So of Egypt, he marched against Samaria. After a three year siege, he destroyed it and carried the inhabitants captive. Thus ended, forever, the kingdom founded by Jeroboam "who sinned and made Israel to sin."

11.   Where Are the Ten Tribes?

Northern Palestine was left with a small remnant of Israelites with whom were mingled a planting of foreigners. Over these were placed a non-Levitical priesthood. They used a Samaritan version of the Pentateuch as their Scriptures. Thus a kind of Israelitish economy was set up. It was not, however, such as Zerubbabel, Ezra, and Nehemiah, at a later time, were willing to recognize as belonging to the LORD.

The major part of the ten tribes were taken to the lands of Shalmanesar IV, mainly to Media, perhaps. Doubtless most of them settled there. Some may have migrated to India, Armenia, and other lands. Very few, if any, returned to Palestine. In later times the distinction between the two divisions had no real significance, for Judah as well as the other tribes became subject to Gentile sovereignty. The prophet Ezekiel, who prophesied after Judah had also been carried captive, gives us an object picture of sticks signifying a restoration in which there will no longer be two nations but one (Ezek. 37:15-19). In New Testament times the term Israel always refers to the whole nation, even though it is true that the remnant who returned to the land were mainly of the tribe of Judah (note James 1:1).

12. Discussion and Review

1. Discuss the causes of the secession of the northern tribes.
2. What is meant by the "kingdom of Israel"?
3. Discuss the policies of Jeroboam.
4. Speak concerning Israel's (the northern kingdom) capitols.
5. Show the role of the prophets in Israel's history.
6. Name her prophets and briefly characterize the message of each.
7. Trace the course of Israel's foreign relations.
8. What happened to the ten tribes?

13. Select Memory Passages
Amos 5:21-24; 8:11; 9:9; I Kings 17:14

14. Character Review

Identify:

Jeroboam	Elah	Pekah	Benhadad
Baal	Zimri	Hazael	Athaliah
Ahijah	Zachariah	Elisha	Jehoahaz
Shemaiah	Rekahiah	Naboth	Jehoash
Abijah	Omri	Ahaziah	(Joash)
Jonah	Ahab	Jehoram	Jeroboam II
Menahem	Elijah	(Joram)	Shallum
Nadab	Jezabel	Naaman	Shalmaneser
Baasha	Micaiah	Hosea	
Jehu	Amos	Hoshea	

15. Bibliography

Free, Joseph P. *Archaeology and Bible History.* "Jeroboam's Calf Worship; Liberal View; Light from Archaeology," pp. 180, 181. "Archaeological Light on Baal Worship in the Northern Kingdom," pp. 182, 183. "Archaeological Light on Ahab's Ivory House," p. 193. Wheaton, Ill.: Van Kampen Press.
Kuyper, Abraham. *Women of the Old Testament.* Grand Rapids: Zondervan.
  1. "Jeroboam's Wife," pp. 141-144.
  2. "The Widow of Zarephath," pp. 144-147.
  3. "Jezebel," pp. 147-150.
  4. "The Shunammite," pp. 150-153.
  5. "Naaman's Wife's Little Jewish Maid," pp. 153-157.
MacCartney, Clarence E. *Trials of Great Men of the Bible.* Chapter VII, "The Trial of Elijah." Nashville: Abingdon-Cokesbury Press.
Meyer, F. B. *Elijah, the Secret of His Power.* New York: Fleming H. Revell.
Mosiman, S. K. "Jeroboam," *The International Standard Bible Encyclopedia.* Vol. III. pp. 1593-1594.

Olson, Bessie G. *Elijah a Man of Miracles,* in Bible Character Series. Des Moines: Boone Pub. Co., 1948.

Rawlingson, George. *The Kings of Judah and Israel.* New York: Fleming H. Revell.

Sangster, Margaret E. *The Women of the Bible.* Chapt. XX, "The Widow of Zarephath." New York: The Christian Herald.

Sangster, Margaret E. *The Women of the Bible.* Chapt. XXI, "Jezebel and Athaliah." New York: The Christian Herald.

Sangster, Margaret E. *The Women of the Bible.* Chapt. XXII, "The Shunammite, A Great Lady." New York: The Christian Herald.

Sangster, Margaret E. *The Women of the Bible,* Chapt. XXIII, "The Little Captive Maid." New York: The Christian Herald.

Sayce, A. H. "Baal," *The International Standard Bible Encyclopedia.* Vol. I. pp. 343-346.

HARMONY OF THE KINGS

HISTORY OF JUDAH

(Harmonized with the History of Israel)

REIGN	OUTLINE

1
REHOBOAM
Time: 17 years
Sources:
  I Kings 12; 14:21-31;
  II Chron. 10-12
Prophet:
  Shemaiah
	1. **A Bad Beginning.** All Israel assembled to crown Rehoboam. Jeroboam led in a suit for lower taxes. Rehoboam adjourned the counsel for three days (12:1-5). He counseled the old men, then the young men, and returned a rough answer to the assembly (I Kings 12:6-15). Ten tribes revolted and crowned Jeroboam king (12:16-20). Shemaiah intercepted Rehoboam's plan for war with Israel (12:21-24).
	    Jeroboam cut off traffic of worshippers to Jerusalem; he erected calves at Bethel and Dan, made high places, ordained priests of non-Levites, and scheduled feasts simultaneous with those at Jerusalem (I Kings 12:25-35).
	2. **Chronology.** Rehoboam began reigning at the age of 41 years and reigned 17 years (I Kings 12:21).
	3. **Family.** His mother was Naamah, an Ammonitess; he had 18 wives, 60 concubines, 28 sons, and 60 daughters (Chronicles).
	4. **Character.** "Judah did evil in the sight of the LORD"; they built many high places; they tolerated sodomy and all Canaanitish vices (I Kings 12:22-24).
	5. **Plunder of the Temple.** Shishak, king of Egypt, looted the temple and the King's house. Golden shields were replaced with brass shields (I Kings 14:25-28).
	6. **War.** Rehoboam and Jeroboam were at war all their days (I Kings 14:29-31).

3
ABIJAM
Time: 3 years
Sources:
  I Kings 15:1-8
  II Chron. 13
	1. **Chronology.** He began to reign in the 18th year of Jeroboam.
	2. **Character.** He "walked in all the sins of his father."
	3. **Wars.** There was war with Jeroboam all his life.

4
ASA
Time: 41 years
Sources:
  I Kings 15:9-24
  II Chron. 14-16
Prophets:
  Azariah
  Hanani
	1. **Chronology.** He began to reign in the 20th year of Jeroboam.
	2. **Character.** He "did that which was right in the sight of the LORD as David his father."
	3. **Reforms.** He took away sodomites; he removed idolatrous Maachah from being queen. High places were not removed.
	4. **Foreign Relations.**
	    (1) Zerah, an Ethiopian menaced Judah with 1,000,-000 men. Asa called upon God; marvelous de-

186

OF JUDAH AND ISRAEL

HISTORY OF ISRAEL

(Harmonized with the History of Judah)

REIGN	OUTLINE
2 **JEROBOAM** (First Dynasty) **Time:** 22 years **Sources:** I Kings 12:12—14:20 **Prophets:** Ahijah "A man of God" from Judah An "old prophet" from Bethel	1. **Identity.** Jeroboam, an able soldier under Solomon, had in Solomon's day been appointed by the prophet Ahijah as ruler of ten tribes (I Kings 11:26-40). Jeroboam led Israel in a suit against the new king, Rehoboam (12:12-20), and brought about the existence of the Kingdom of Israel under his reign. 2. **Character.** Jeroboam made idolatry a matter of policy in Israel, establishing calf worship at Bethel and Dan. His name became the symbol and perpetual example of evil in Israel. 3. **Presumption.** Jeroboam acting as a priest at Bethel was rebuked by a "man of God" from Judah. Attempting to seize the man of God, Jeroboam's hand instantly withered, but was restored in mercy. In this incident a prophecy was made of Josiah's reign (see II Kings 23:15-16). "The man of God from Judah" refused to eat with Jeroboam, but yielded to eat with the "old Prophet" of Bethel. For disobedience to God he was slain by a lion (13:1-32). 4. **Heavy Tidings.** Jeroboam stealthily sought help for his sick son Abijah from the prophet Ahijah. The prophet delivered "heavy tidings": The child will die and because of Jeroboam's sins Israel will be uprooted from the land (14:1-8).
5 **NADAB** (First Dynasty) **Time:** 2 years **Sources:** I Kings 15:25-28	1. **Chronology.** He began in the 2nd year of **Asa of** Judah. 2. **Character.** "Evil . . . . walked in the way of his father and in his sin wherewith he made Israel to sin." 3. **Death.** He was assassinated by Baasha, who succeeded him. This ended Jeroboam's house.

REIGN	OUTLINE
	liverance came (Chronicles). Azariah the prophet called the nation from apostasy. Great revival followed, with participation by many of the tribes of Israel. There was peace until Asa's 35th year.
	(2) War with Baasha of Israel was resumed. Baasha built Ramah to prevent traffic to Judah. Asa made a gift to Benhadad, king of Syria, and invited him to a league against Baasha. Baasha quit building Ramah. Asa razed it and built Geba in Benjamin. Hanani, the prophet, reproved Asa for his league against Baasha. Asa was smitten in his feet, but sought physicians instead of God (Kings and Chronicles).

11
JEHOSHAPHAT
Time: 25 years
Sources:
  I Kings 22:1-50
  II Chron. 17-20
	1. **Chronology.** Began in the 4th year of Ahab of Israel, at the age of 35.
	2. **Character.** "Walked in the ways of Asa his father; he turned not aside from it, doing that which was right in the sight of the LORD."
	He destroyed remaining sodomites.
	Exception: High places were not destroyed.
	3. **Foreign Relations.**
	  (1) He made peace with Israel and assisted Ahab against Syria.
	  (2) He failed in naval undertakings.
	  (3) Chronicles supplement to the Kings account.

188

REIGN	OUTLINE
6 **BAASHA** (Second Dynasty) **Time:** 24 years **Source:** I Kings 15:27—16:7 **Prophet:** Jehu	1. **Chronology.** He began in the 3rd year of Asa of Judah. 2. **Character.** "Evil . . . . walked in the way of his father and in his sin wherewith he made Israel to sin." He came to power by assassination and usurpation, yet as an agent of God to punish the house of Jeroboam. Jehu the prophet pronounced the end of his house because he sinned like Jeroboam.
7 **ELAH** (Second Dynasty) **Time:** 2 years **Source:** I Kings 16:8-14	1. **Chronology.** He began in the 26th year of Asa's reign. 2. **Character.** He was a drunkard. 3. **Death.** While drunk, he was slain by Zimri, his servant, who then usurped the throne.
8 **ZIMRI** (Third Dynasty) **Time:** 7 days **Source:** I Kings 16:15-20	1. **A Rejected Usurper.** He came to the throne by assassination and usurpation, but was rejected by the people, who made Omri, captain of the host, king. 2. **Death.** He set fire to the king's house and burned within it.
9 **OMRI** (Fourth Dynasty) **Time:** 12 years **Source** I Kings 16:21-28	1. **The People's Man.** He came to the throne by the choice of the people. A party also supported Tibni, but Tibni was defeated (slain). 2. **Chronology.** He began to reign in the 31st year of Asa of Judah. 3. **New Capital.** He removed his capital from Tirzah to Samaria. 4. **Character.** He "did worse than all before him . . . . provoked the LORD."
10 **AHAB** (Fourth Dynasty) **Time:** 22 years **Source:** I Kings 16:29 to 22:40 **Prophets:** Elijah Micaiah	1. **Chronology.** Began to reign in the 38th year of Asa of Judah. 2. **Character.** He "did evil in the sight of the LORD above all that were before him." He married Jezebel, daughter of the king of Zidon, worshipped Baal, and set up Baal worship at Samaria. Jericho was rebuilt in his day contrary to the command of God (See Joshua 6:20). 3. **Elijah the Prophet.** The bright star shining in this darkest of reigns was Elijah the Tishbite prophet. Like a signal, he appeared to announce to Ahab a three year drought; and then disappeared. During this time Elijah is seen at the brook Cherith, fed by ravens, and at the house of the widow at Zarephath in Zidon, who fed him and whose son he healed. At the close of the period he appeared to Ahab, exchanged rebukes with him, and then staged a meeting of the people at Mount Carmel to prove whether Baal or the LORD is God. Baal was put to shame and at Elijah's command his prophets were slain. Then at Elijah's word came

189

REIGN	OUTLINE
	1) Jehu, the son of Hanani the prophet, reproved Jehoshaphat for helping and loving them that hate the LORD, but commended him for his reforms (II Chron. 19:1-4).
	2) Judges and teachers were stationed in cities of Judah (II Chron. 19:5-11).
	3) Foreign foes (Moab, Amon, and others) occasioned fear, prayer, and fasting, and led to a great spiritual revival in Judah. Victory followed.
	4) Jehoshaphat formed a league with wicked Ahaziah of Israel, contemplating a naval project. Because of God's displeasure his ships were destroyed at Ezion-geber (II Chron. 20:35-37).
14 **JEHORAM** (JORAM) (Son of Jehoshaphat) **Time:** 8 years	1. **Chronology.** Began in the 5th year of Jehoram (Joram) of Israel. 2. **Character.** "Walked in the ways of the kings of Israel." He married Athaliah, daughter of Ahab and Jezebel, and killed his six brothers.

190

REIGN	OUTLINE
	a great rain, breaking the famine. Elisha retired to Beersheba, out of reach of angry Jezebel, where angels fed him, and where a still small voice spoke to him. Three significant anointings close his work, of Hazael, of Syria, of Jehu of Israel, and of Elisha his successor. Elijah's departure to heaven without death classifies him with Enoch whom God took to heaven without death.
	4. **The Naboth Incident.** The taking of Naboth's vineyard demonstrated the peevishness and the moral weakness of Ahab, and it demonstrated the utterly monstrous spirit and influence of Jezebel (Note 21:25).
	5. **War With Syria.** Notwithstanding Ahab's unworthiness, God marvelously assisted him in triumph over Benhaded who taunted Israel. Yet, before the battle was finished Ahab had disobeyed God's express command and incurred judgment (I Kings 21).
	6. **Ahab's Penitence.** Ahab humbling himself, was granted a deferrment of judgment.
	7. **Death.** At the hands of the Syrians, against the word of the lying prophets, and according to the word of Micaiah, Ahab was slain.
12 **AHAZIAH** (Fourth Dynasty) (Son of Ahab) **Time:** 2 years **Source:** I Kings 22:51-53 II Kings 1:1-18 **Prophet:** Elijah	1. **Chronology.** He began in the 17th year of Jehoshaphat of Judah. 2. "He did evil in the sight of the LORD and walked in the way of his father and . . . . mother . . . . and of Jeroboam . . . . served Baal and worshiped him." 3. **Foreign Relations.** Moab arose in rebellion in this reign. 4. **Death.** Ahaziah fatally injured, sent fifty men to Elijah for help. These being consumed he sent fifty more. These being consumed he sent fifty more. Elijah, at God's word came. After reproving Ahaziah for worship of Baalzebub, he affirmed that he must die.
13 **JEHORAM** (JORAM) (Son of Ahab) (Fourth Dynasty) **Time:** 12 years **Source:** II Kings 1:17—9:26 **Prophet:** Elisha	1. **Chronology.** He began to reign in Jehoshaphat's 18th year. 2. **Character.** He "wrought evil" but not as his parents. He put away their image of Baal. 3. **Elisha.** When Elijah was taken to heaven his mantle fell upon Elisha. Elisha, by miracles, brought victory over Moab (II Kings 3) and over the Syrians (II Kings 6:8—8:15). Notable miracles of the period by Elisha were the healing of defiled water (II Kings 2:19-22), the cursing of mocking children (II Kings 2:23-25), replenishing the widow's oil (II Kings 4:1-7), the healing of the widow's son (II Kings 4:8-37), the purifying of the deadly pottage (II Kings 4:38-41), feeding of 100 men (II Kings 4:42-44), the healing of Naaman the leper (II Kings 5), causing the axe to float (II Kings 6:1-

191

REIGN	OUTLINE
Sources II. Kings 8:16-24 II Chron. 21	3. **Foreign Relations.** Revolt of Edom became a permanent condition. Philistines and others also revolted.
15 **AHAZIAH** (Son of Jehoram of Judah) **Time:** 1 year **Sources:** II Kings 8:25—9:29 II Chron. 22:1-9	1. **Chronology.** Began in the 11th year of Jehoram of Israel, at the age of 22 years. 2. **Character.** "He walked in the ways of the house of Ahab, and did evil in the sight of the LORD, as did the house of Ahab." 3. **Foreign Relations.** He allied himself with Jehoram (Joram) the son of Ahab against Syria. 4. **Death.** While visiting with Jehoram who had been wounded in battle, the two were overtaken by Jehu and slain.
(ATHALIAH) (Daughter of Ahab) (Widow of Jehoram) (Mother of Ahaziah) (Usurper) **Time:** 6 years **Sources:** II Kings 11:1-21 II Chron. 22:10—23:21	1. **Chronology.** When Ahaziah, her son, died, Athaliah attempted to destroy all the royal seed in order to inherit the throne. She reigned for six years. 2. **The Child Joash.** Jehosheba, sister of the late king Ahaziah, hid one son Joash and his nurse. 3. Jehoiada the priest anointed and installed Joash as king. The people rejoiced, but Athaliah cried, "Treason." Athaliah was executed with one of David's swords. 4. **Reform.** Worship of the LORD was restored.
17 **JEHOASH** (JOASH) (Grandson of Athaliah and son of Ahaziah) **Time:** 40 years **Sources:** II Kings 12:1-21 II Chron. 24 **Prophet:** Hazael	1. **Chronology.** Began to reign six years after the death of his father Ahaziah. 2. **Character.** He "did that which was right in the sight of the LORD all his days wherein Jehoiada the priest instructed him." Exception: High places were not removed. 3. **Temple Repair.** He carried on, on a voluntary basis, extensive temple repairs. 4. **Temple Impoverished.** Jehoash stripped the temple of valuable hallowed things to make an appeasement offer to Hazael of Syria. 5. **Death.** He was slain by his servants.
20 **AMAZIAH** **Time:** 29 years **Sources:** II Kings 14:1-20 II Chron. 25	1. **Chronology.** Began in the second year of Jehoash of Israel at the age of 25 years. 2. **Character.** He "did that which was right in the sight of the LORD, yet not like David his father; he did according to all things as Jehoash his father did." The high places were not destroyed. 3. **Relations.** He slew the assassins of his father but not the children, in keeping with Deut. 24:16. He won a major war with Edom, completely subduing it. Feeling his power, he challenged Jehoash of Israel to war, but was severely beaten. 400 feet of wall about Jerusalem was destroyed and the temple was looted. 4. **Death.** Conspirators at Jerusalem assassinated him.

REIGN	OUTLINE
	7), smiting of the Syrians with blindness (II Kings 6:8-23), the terrifying noise causing the Syrians to flee Samaria (II Kings 7:1-20). Elisha was counselled by Benhadad, king of Syria. He foretold his death and reaffirmed his anointing of Hazael as his successor (II Kings 8:7-15). 4. **Death.** He was slain by Jehu (9:24-26).
16 **JEHU** (Fifth Dynasty) Time: 28 years Source: II Kings 9:30—10:36	1. **God's Agent of Judgment.** Jehu was anointed by Elisha and commissioned to completely destroy the house of Ahab, including King Joram of Israel (II Kings 9:1-29). This he dramatically accomplished. First he slew Joram, then Jezebel, then seventy sons of Ahab, then 42 of the brethren of Ahaziah (son of Ahab), and finally the remnant of Baal's prophets with their worshippers. He also slew Ahaziah, king of Judah, who had been in league wih Jehoram of Israel and had married Athaliah, Ahab's daughter. Thus, thoroughly did Jehu wield the sword of judgment to purge both Israel and Judah. 2. **Character.** Though fierce in his eradication of the system of Baal, he had no regard for God's law, but followed in the sins of Jeroboam. 3. **Chronology.** He reigned 28 years. Note: Notice of cutting off of Israel is given in connection with Jehu's life (II Kings 10:31).
18 **JEHOAHAZ** (Fifth Dynasty) Time: 17 years Source II Kings 13:1-9	1. **Chronology.** He began to reign in the 23rd year of Joash of Judah. 2. **Character.** He did evil . . . . as Jeroboam, incurring for Israel God's anger. 3. **Foreign Relations.** God sent the king of Syria to afflict Israel. By seeking God she was saved. Yet she continued to sin.
19 **JEHOASH** (JOASH) (Fifth Dynasty) Time: 16 years Source: II Kings 13:10—14:16	1. He began to reign in the 39th year of Joash of Judah. 2. **Character.** He did evil . . . . as Jeroboam. 3. **Foreign Relations.** (1) Elisha upon his deathbed, inspired Joash to energetic battle with Syria. (2) Joash retrieved cities of Israel held by Syria. (3) Wars with Judah (Amaziah) continued (II Kings 14:8-16).
21 **JEROBOAM II** (Fifth Dynasty) Time: 41 years Source: II Kings 14:23-29 Prophets:	1. **Chronology.** He began to reign in the 15th year of the reign of Amaziah of Judah. 2. **Character.** He did evil, "departed not from the sins of Jeroboam." 3. **Foreign Relations.** He restored the northern coast of Israel from the entering of Hamath to the sea of the Plain (Mediterranean).

193

REIGN	OUTLINE
22 **UZZIAH** (AZARIAH) **Time:** 52 years **Sources:** II Kings 14:21, 22 II Kings 15:1-7 II Chron. 26 **Prophets:** Joel Hosea Isaiah	1. **Chronology.** He began in the 27th year of Jeroboam II, at the age of 16 years. 2. **Character.** He "did that which was right," except that high places were not removed. He reigned prosperously in the earlier part of his reign. "His name spread far abroad; for he was marvelously helped, till he was strong." Then he presumed, in his pride, to usurp the functions of a priest. When dissuaded by the priests he became angry. God smote him with leprosy, which he had until the day of his death. He was obliged to remain in isolation while his son Jotham reigned. 3. **Death.** Leprosy was, presumably, the cause of his death. 4. Isaiah the prophet was called in the year of Uzziah's death (Isa. 6:1).
28 **JOTHAM** **Time:** 16 years **Sources:** II Kings 15:32-38 II Chron. 27 **Prophets:** Micah Isaiah Hosea	1. **Chronology.** Began in the 2nd year of Pekah of Israel, at the age of 25 years. 2. **Character.** He "did . . . . right in the sight of the LORD . . . . like his father Uzziah had done." Exception: High places were not removed. 3. **Work.** He built the high gate of the house of God. 4. **Foreign Relations.** In those days the LORD began to send against Judah Rezin, king of Syria and Pekah, king of Israel.

REIGN	OUTLINE
Jonah Amos Hosea	4. Israel had sore oppressions but was delivered. Note: Jonah, the first of the prophetic writers, appears.
23 **ZACHARIAH** (Fifth Dynasty) Time: ½ year Source: II Kings 15:8-12 Prophet: Hosea	1. **Chronology.** Began in the 38th year of Azariah of Judah. 2. **Character.** Did evil, "as fathers . . . . departed not from the sins of Jeroboam." 3. **Death.** Shallum assassinated him publicly and succeeded him to the throne. This terminated the reign of the house of Jehu, according to God's word (II Kings 10:30).
24 **SHALLUM** (Sixth Dynasty) Time: 1 month Source: II Kings 15:13-15 Prophet: Hosea	1. **Chronology.** He began to reign in the 39th year of Uzziah of Judah. 2. **Character.** He gained power by assassination. 3. **Death.** Menahem assassinated him.
25 **MENAHEM** (Seventh Dynasty) Time: 10 years Source: II Kings 15:16-20 Prophet: Hosea	1. **Chronology.** He began to reign in the 39th year of the reign of Uzziah of Judah. 2. **Character.** He "did evil . . . . departed not from the sins of Jeroboam . . . . made Israel sin." He smote resisting cities and ripped up their women with child. 3. **Foreign Relations.** Assyrian conquest of Israel began. Tribute of 50 shekels per man was exacted by king Pul.
26 **PEKAHIAH** (Seventh Dynasty) Time: 24 years Source: II Kings 15:23-26 Prophet: Hosea	1. **Chronology.** He began to reign in the 50th year of Uzziah of Judah. 2. **Character.** He "did evil . . . . departed not from the sins of Jereboam . . . . made Israel to sin." 3. **Death.** Pekah assassinated him.
27 **PEKAH** (Eighth Dynasty) Time: 20 years Source: II Kings 15:27-31 Prophet: Hosea	1. **Chronology.** He began to reign in the 52nd year of Uzziah. 2. **Character.** He "did evil . . . . departed not from the sins of Jeroboam . . . . made Israel to sin." 3. **Foreign Relations.** Assyrian conquest of Israel continued. Tiglath-pileser carried away captives. 4. **Death.** Hoshea conspired against, assassinated, and succeeded him to power.

195

REGN	OUTLINE
29 **AHAZ** **Time:** 16 years **Sources:** II Kings 16 II Chron. 28 **Prophets:** Micah Isaiah Hosea	1. **Chronology.** Began in the 17th year of Pekah of Israel at the age of 20 years. 2. **Character.** Did not right "like David," but walked in the "way of the kings of Israel." He made his sons pass through fire and burnt incense in high places. 3. **Foreign Relations.** Rezin of Syria and Pekah of Israel waged war against Ahaz. Syria recovered Elath from the Jews. (The first use of this term for Israel is observed here.) Ahaz sent temple money as a gift to the Assyrian Tiglath-pileser requesting his assistance against Rezin and Pekah. Damascus was taken and Rezin was slain. 4. **Temple Alterations.** Seeing an altar at Damascus that struck his fancy, Ahaz had Urijah, the priest at Jerusalem, build one like it to be used in the temple. He took other great liberties in altering the temple equipment.
31 **HEZEKIAH** **Time:** 29 years **Sources:** II Kings 18:1—20:21 **Prophets:** Micah Isaiah Hosea	1. **Chronology.** Began in the 3rd year of Hoshea of Israel, at the age of 25 years. 2. **Character.** He did right as David. Removed the high places, cut down the groves, broke to pieces the brazen serpent that Moses made and which Israel now worshipped, he "trusted in the LORD God" as no other king, he "clave to the LORD" . . . . "kept his commandments." "The LORD was with him." 3. **Foreign Relations.** (1) He broke off relations with Assyria. (2) He drove the Philistines to their borders. (3) Shalmaneser, king of Assyria, captured Samaria in the fifth year of Hezekiah of Judah. (4) Sennacherib, Shalmaneser's successor, was given appeasement money from the Temple treasury. Unsatisfied, he sent a host against Jerusalem. Hezekiah apologized and offered to pay greater tribute. To make good, Hezekiah stripped not only the Temple treasury but the golden hinges off the Temple doors and the golden overlay of the woodwork. (5) Hezekiah became ill but by God's mercy was given a fifteen year extension of life. (6) Envoys from Babylon visited Jerusalem and were shown the treasures of the Temple, in connection with which, Isaiah foretold the future destruction of Jerusalem by the Babylonians. 4. **The Chronicles Viewpoint.** Chronicles gives fuller light on Hezekiah's reforms. He opened the doors of the house of God and repaired them. He called together the priests and Levites and prepared them for a national revival. God's house was cleansed. He assembled the people for the Passover observance. The depth and sincerity of this revival was unprecedented.

REIGN	OUTLINE
30 **HOSHEA** (Ninth Dynasty) **Time: 9 years** **Source:** II Kings 17:1-41 **Prophet:** Hosea	1. **Chronology.** He began to reign in the 12th year of Ahaz of Judah. 2. **Character.** Did "evil . . . . but not as the kings of Israel that were before him." 3. **Foreign Relations.** Assyrian conquest became final. Shalmaneser made Hoshea his servant. Hoshea gave him a yearly present. Hoshea bid for favor from So of Egypt and discontinued his gift to Shalmaneser. Detecting conspiracy, Shalmaneser shut him up and besieged the city three years. In the ninth year of Hoshea, Samaria was taken, and the people were scattered into Assyrian countries. In II Kings 17:6-23 God's case against Israel is given. Shalmaneser repopulated Israel with foreigners, but because of their wickedness, God permitted lions to terrify them. To overcome this a Jewish priest was installed at Bethel to teach the people. Thus a very mixed race, culture, and religion came to make up Samaria. They are aptly characterized by I Kings 17:33: "They feared the LORD and served their own gods."

CAPTIVITY, 722 B.C.

REIGN	OUTLINE
32 **MANASSEH** **Time:** 55 years **Sources:** II Kings 21:1-18	1. **Chronology.** He was 12 years old when he began to reign. He reigned 55 years. 2. **Character.** He did "evil . . . . after the abominations of the heathen, whom the LORD cast out before the children of Israel." He built up the high places and the altars of Baal, made altars to the "host of heaven" in the house of God, made his sons pass through fire, used enchantments, and shed innocent blood. 3. **Judgment.** For these evils God pronounced judgment. He would wipe the nation inside and out as a dish. The captivity was specifically foretold. 4. **Repentance.** II Chronicles 33:1-18 tells of the repentance of Manasseh in his latter years and of the reforms which he promoted.

33
AMON
Time: 2 years
Sources:
  II Kings 21:19-26
  II Chron. 33:21-35
	1. **Chronology.** Began to reign at the age of 22 years.
	2. **Character.** He "did evil in the sight of the LORD, as his father Manasseh did (before his repentance)." He "forsook the LORD God of his fathers."
	3. **Death.** He was assassinated by his servants. The people slew the servants, and made his son Josiah king.

34
JOSIAH
Time: 31 years
  (B. C. 639-608)
Sources:
  II Kings 22—23:30
  II Chron. 34-35
Prophets:
  Huldah
  Jeremiah
  Zephaniah
	1. **Chronology.** Began to reign at the age of 8 years.
	2. **Character.** He "did right . . . . as David."
	3. **Reforms.**
	  (1) He repaired the Temple (18th year).
	  (2) The Book of the Law was found in the house of the LORD, which when read to Josiah greatly moved him because of the departure of the nation from the law of God. He inquired of the LORD by the prophet Huldah, who promised that the judgment of God would not fail in his time.
	  (3) The Law was read, the passover kept, and the covenant renewed.
	  (4) The land was cleansed of idolatrous priests, groves, sodomites, horses and chariots of the sun, pagan altars, and other idolatrous equipment.
	  He cleansed Bethel, slaying the idolatrous priests and burning their bones on their altar (Note I Kings 13:2).
	  He destroyed spirit-mediums according to the Law.
	4. **Death.** He was slain in battle against Pharaoh-necho at Megiddo.

35
JEHOAHAZ
  (Son of Josiah)
Time: 3 months
Sources:
  II Kings 23:31-34
  II Chron. 36:1-5
Prophet:
	1. **Chronology.** Began to reign at the age of 23 years.
	2. **Character.** He did evil according to all that his fathers had done.
	3. **Foreign Relations.** He was crowned by the people of Jerusalem but was promptly subdued and imprisoned, and then carried into Egypt by Pharaoh-necho. The land was placed under tribute. Eliakim, another son of Josiah, was made king

REIGN	OUTLINE
Jeremiah	under Pharaoh-necho. He was renamed Jehoia-kim. 4. **Death.** He died in Egypt.
36 **JEHOIAKIM** (ELIAKIM) (Son of Josiah) **Time:** 11 years 608-597 B. C. **Sources:** II Kings 23:34—24:6 II Chron. 36:5-8 **Prophets:** Jeremiah Habakkuk	1. **Chronology.** Began to reign at the age of 25 years. 2. **Character.** He did "that which was evil" in the sight of the LORD, according to all that his fathers had done." 3. **Foreign Relations.** (1) He was enthroned by Pharaoh-necho, and became his tax collector. (2) After three years he became servant of Nebuchadnezzar, king of Babylon (II Chron. 36:6; Jeremiah 25:1, 9; Dan. 1:1). He rebelled against Nebuchadnezzar in the 7th year of his reign. (3) Bands of Chaldees, Syrians, Moabites, and Ammonites plundered Judah (II Kings 24:2). (Note: The invasion of Nebuchadnezzar in the 4th year of Jehoiakim marks the beginning of the 70 year captivity. Daniel and his companions, and others were carried to Babylon at that time (Dan. 1:1).
37 **JEHOIACHIN** (Son of Jehoiakim) **Time:** 3 months **Sources** II Kings 24:8-16 II Chron. 36:9-10 **Prophets:** Ezekiel Jeremiah	1. **Chronology.** Began to reign at the age of 18 years. 2. **Character.** He "did that which was evil in the sight of the LORD, according to all that his fathers had done." 3. **Captivity.** After 3 months (Nebuchadnezzar's 8th year), Nebuchadnezzar made his return and besieged Jerusalem. He carried captive Jehoiachin, his mother, his servants, princes, and officers; persons of skill and power were removed. Only the poor remained. The prophet Ezekiel was included. (Note: Ezek. 1:1-3). The Temple was looted in fulfillment of Isaiah's prophecy to Hezekiah (II Kings 20:12, 13). Jehoiachin faired well in Chaldea (II Kings 25:27-30).
38 **ZEDEKIAH** (MATTANIAH) (Son of Josiah) **Time:** 11 years 597-586 B. C. **Sources:** II Kings 24:17—25:30 II Chron. 36:11-14 **Prophets:** Nahum Jeremiah	1. **Chronology.** Began to reign at the age of 21 years. 2. **Character.** He "did evil in the sight of the LORD according to all that Jehoiakim had done." 3. **Relations with Babylon.** (1) He rebelled against Nebuchadnezzar all his reign. (2) Jerusalem was besieged for a year and a half, from the 9th to the 11th years of Zedekiah. (3) Zedekiah was taken and his eyes put out. (4) Nebuzaradan, the Babylonian captain, burned the Temple, broke down the walls, and carried away all but the poor who were left as vine-dressers. The nobles were destroyed. Gedaliah was made ruler of the remnant.

CAPTIVITY, 586 B.C.

Chapter 17

THE KINGDOM OF JUDAH
First Cycle—Decline and Revival

(Rehoboam to Jehoshaphat)
(975-ca. 889 B. C.)

1. Reading Assignment
2. Historical Outline: See pages (..)
3. Introduction—
   (1) The Kings of Judah
   (2) Cycles of Decline and Revival
4. Foreign Relations—With Egypt, Israel, Syria, Ethiopia, Amon, Moab, Edom

5. Elements of Judah's Religious Revivals
6. Failures of Good Kings
7. Discussion and Review
8. Select Memory Passages
9. Character Review
10. Bibliography

---

1. **Reading Assignment:** I Kings 12—22; II Chronicles 10—20
   (Read the Bible first)

---

2. Historical Outline

See the harmony of the histories of Judah and Israel, pages 186-190

3. Introduction

The Kings of Judah

The kingdom of Judah existed over a period of about 389 years (975-586 B. C.), about 136 years longer than that of the ten tribes. Like the northern kingdom it had 19 kings. It will be observed that the average length of reign was much longer than it was in Israel. This represents the greater stability of Judah. There was a continuous dynasty in Judah instead of nine dynasties as in Israel. There were seven assassinations and one suicide among the kings of Israel. Whereas in Israel every king is recorded as evil, there were a number of very godly kings in Judah. Israel had no revival in the sense of a return to the worship of God, while Judah had notable periodic revivals.

200

Cycles of Decline and Revival

The four centuries of Judah's national life were characterized by periodic cycles of religious declension and spiritual revival. In all, there were three and one-half such cycles, three full cycles of decline and revival and a final period of decline culminating in the Babylonian captivity. The first cycle (approximately 975-889 B. C.) includes the reigns of Rehoboam, Abijam, Asa, and Jehoshaphat. The second (about 207 years) includes the reigns of Jehoram, Ahaziah, (Athaliah), Joash, Amaziah, Uzziah (Azariah), Jotham, Ahaz, and Hezekiah. The third (about 88 years) includes the reigns of Manasseh, Amon, and Josiah. The final half cycle (about 23 years) includes the reigns of Jehoahaz, Jehoiakim (Eliakim), Jehoiachin, and Zedekiah.

For the completion of the fourth half-cycle we must await the study of the partial restoration at the close of the seventy year Babylonian captivity.

It is appropriate that we should devote more time to the history of Judah than to the history of Israel. The period is longer. The Spirit of inspiration has given us a much fuller history of Judah. The books of Chronicles are little concerned with Israel's kings but they add considerably to First and Second Kings in regard to Judah's history. Also the writings of the major prophets Isaiah, Ezekiel, and Jeremiah afford important historical literature for our use in understanding and interpreting Judah's history.

The student will be well rewarded for his pains in thoroughly studying these cycles. In this history we see the externalities of religion degenerate to the point of God's rejection of them; but we have in the word of the prophets an increased emphasis upon the spiritual, the personal, and the unchanging elements of true religion.

4. Foreign Relations

With Egypt

Solomon began his reign by entering into an affinity with Egypt. Rehoboam's reign was marked by the menacing enmity of Egypt. The invasion of Shishak may have been induced by Jeroboam. While Solomon lived, no one ventured to dismantle Jerusalem's costly buildings, but now that Egypt found herself the friend of the enemy of Rehoboam there was a temptation to yield to the spirit of covetousness.

Perhaps nothing could have depicted more clearly the passing of the earthly glory of Solomon's golden age than the replacing of the golden shields of the king's house with shields of brass. And nothing could have depicted better her loss of spiritual power than the necessity of appeasing the king of Egypt with the consecrated money of the LORD's treasury.

Shishak, (Sheshonk), according to late discoveries, headed a new Egyptian dynasty which gives an additional explanation for the changed relations between Judah and Egypt after Solomon's day. An Egyptian inscription recently discovered shows Shishak holding several captive Jews by the hair and dealing heavy blows upon them with a club. The inscription indicates that other towns of Judah than Jerusalem were plundered.

The Chronicles account (II Chron. 12) indicates that the invasion of Shishak was a direct judgment against Rehoboam for forsaking the law of the LORD. The prophet Shemaiah faced Rehoboam and his princes with their responsibility in the matter, whereupon they humbled themselves and acknowledged the righteousness of the LORD. God stayed the hand of Shishak from the degree of destruction which he planned. The inscriptions correspond to the Chronicles account in indicating that Shishak intended to completely subjugate the kingdom of Solomon.

With Israel and Syria

War with Israel continued through the reigns of Abijam (3 years) and Asa (41 years). Abijam succeeded in a signal victory on one occasion and won back certain cities of the northern kingdom to Judah.

Asa also gained some ground religiously against the northern kingdom in attracting large numbers of people from the tribes of Simeon, Ephraim, and Manasseh to the worship at Jerusalem, and in securing from them a pledge—"They entered into a covenant to seek the LORD God of their fathers with all their heart and with all their soul."

Asa's later tactics against Israel, in which he hired Benhadad, king of Syria, to attack Israel's northern frontier were reproved by the prophet Hanani. Asa's otherwise worthy reign is marred by his failure to receive this reproof, and by his imprisonment of the prophet of God.

Jehoshaphat reversed the discredited policy of Asa but adopted another lamentable policy. He formed an alliance with King Ahab of Israel against Syria, thus "helping and loving them that hate the LORD" as the prophet Jehu charged. At this very time, it appears that the prophet Elijah was a refugee from Ahab's fury. In the united effort against Syria, Ahab was slain, and Jehoshaphat very nearly lost his life.

With Ethiopia

An almost incredibly huge army of a million men under one Zerah approached Judah in the days of Asa. This was clearly a chastisement of God intended to awaken the people to their need of God. After Asa cried to God, God smote the attacking army and Israel drove them away. The prophet Oded made of the occasion a basis of appeal to Asa for thorough-going reform in the land.

With Amon, Moab, and Edom

During the reign of Jehoshaphat, combined forces of these old-time enemies of Israel set themselves against Jehoshaphat. Victory for Judah was again scored on a high level. Judah's troops advanced, singing Psalms. The enemy began quarreling amongst themselves, and were defeated without battle on Judah's part.

5. Elements of Judah's Religious Revivals

Certain factors contributing to religious revival in Judah are noteworthy. While in the reign of Rehoboam there was no great revival, we do observe that the invasion of Shishak was the means of getting Rehoboam and his princes to acknowledge the LORD and that their humbled attitude led God to turn military disaster from swallowing up the land. The ministry of the prophet Shemaiah in this experience is important. In this incident three factors may be seen. There was a critical need for help, there was a prophetic voice, and there was a responsive leadership.

A similar pattern may be observed in the time of Asa. The invasion of Ethiopian hordes brought a major national crisis. There was a responsive king who cried unto God, and there was a fervent prophet of God (Oded) who made of the crisis an occasion to turn the whole nation back to God. (Note the account of Chronicles).

In the reign of Jehoshaphat the pattern occurs again (I Chron.

20). The league of Moab-Ammon-Edom constituted a menace that brought Judah to the point of crisis. King Jehoshaphat was afraid. He sought the LORD and assembled the people to do so. He led them in an appealing prayer to God. ". . . . all Judah stood before the LORD, with their little ones, their wives, and their children." A special prophetic gift came upon Jahaziel and he gave God's word of assurance to the waiting assembly. The procedure in this crisis was uniquely spiritual. The joy of the LORD was indeed the strength of his people. As the people of Jehoshaphat went out singing, the gathered armies destroyed themselves. The effect of this revival was salutary and extensive. ". . . . the fear of God was on all the kingdoms of those countries when they had heard that the LORD fought against the enemies of Israel."

Jehoshaphat affords the example of a ruler who vigorously promoted religious instruction in the land. In Asa's reign there had been an impressive movement of the people to Jerusalem where a solemn covenant was made with God. Under Jehoshaphat, religious instruction was carried to the people. The princes cooperated with the Levites in putting on regional schools of instruction. Jehoshaphat himself, apparently, participated in a kind of itinerant teaching movement.

The pattern of revival appropriate to any nation professing trust in God would seem to be evident. Face the facts and recognize the need for God, let God's ministers faithfully declare and teach God's word, and let governmental leaders order their policies accordingly. This procedure will bring new life wherever it is followed.

6. Failures of Good Kings

Of Rehoboam and Abijam the text tells us that they did evil. Of Asa and Jehoshaphat it says that they did right. These judgments describe what these men were "in the sight of the LORD." They are general statements. On the whole, Rehoboam was an evil ruler, even though when the Ethiopians threatened to destroy the land, he acknowledged God's righteousness and found a degree of mercy. On the other hand, Asa and Jehoshaphat were in general good rulers, even though in certain respects they failed.

Asa's alliance with Syria deserved reproof because by it he sought a pagan ruler's help against his sister nation **instead** of relying upon the LORD. Likewise when his feet were diseased, he sought physicians **instead** of the LORD. We are bound to fail whenever our reliance is upon any person or thing **instead** of the LORD.

Hanani's words to Asa lifted up the positive standard for a fully victorious faith and deserve to be made a memory passage of this lesson. They are: "For the eyes of the LORD run to and fro throughout the whole earth, to shew himself strong in the behalf of them whose heart is perfect toward him" (II Chron. 16:9).

Asa's failure was magnified because he took a wrong attitude toward it. His imprisonment of Hanani and his oppression of some of the people express an unworthy resentment against the truth. Asa's last days ended in war for the nation and in disease for himself.

Jehoshaphat's failure was that he was too willing to be agreeable with a man who was unworthy of his companionship. We have already observed this wrong relationship. We shall have occasion to look back upon it with an increased realization of the great evil which it entailed, as we study the lives of Jehoshaphat's son and grandson and the dark era which resulted from their rulership. While it is true that fathers are not to be made wholly responsible for the moral outcome of their children, we can readily see that Jehoshaphat's alliance with Ahab established a trend which turned radically to the left after he died.

7. Discussion and Review

1. Characterize the kings of Judah as compared with the kings of Israel (in general).

2. List the kings of Judah according to the cycles of her history.

3. Indicate Judah's relations with Egypt, Israel, Syria, Ethiopia, Amon, Moab, and Edom during the first cycle.

4. Characterize Judah's religious revivals during the first cycle.

5. Who are designated the good kings of this cycle? What were some of their failures?

8. Select Memory Passages

II Chronicles 15:2b; 16:9; 20:20b

9. Character Review

Identify:

Rehoboam   Azariah   Maachah
Shemaiah   Oded   Zerah
Shishak   Hanani   Jehoshaphat
Abijam   Jehu
Asa   (Judah)

10. Bibliography

Davies, W. W. "Asa," *The International Standard Bible Encyclopedia.* Vol. I.
    pp. 261-262.
Free, Joseph P. *Archaeology and Bible* History. "Archaeological Confirmation
    of Shishak's Invasion," pp. 181. Wheaton: Van Kampen Press.
Guthrie, Thomas. *Studies of Character.* "Rehoboam the Foolish Man." New
    York: E. B. Treat and Co. Pp. 399-417.
Mosiman, S. K. "Jehoshaphat," *The International Standard Bible Encyclopedia.*
    Vol. III. pp. 1582-1583.
Mosiman, S. K. "Rehoboam," *The International Standard Bible Encyclopedia.*
    Vol. IV. pp. 2551-2552.

Chapter 18

THE KINGDOM OF JUDAH
Second Cycle—Decline and Revival

(Jehoram to Hezekiah)
(889-696 B. C.)

1. **Reading Assignment:** II Kings 8:1-20; II Chronicles 21:32

---

2. Collateral Reading: Micah and Isaiah

(Read the Bible first)

3. Historical Outline

See the harmony of the histories of Judah and Israel, pages 190-196

4. The High Cost of a Wrong Alliance

The tolerant relation of Judah with Israel became, in the life of Jehoshaphat's son, Jehoram, a far more serious matter than mere military alliance. Jehoram's marriage with Athaliah, the daughter of Ahab, brought to Jerusalem the dark prospect of complete apostasy. Vicious policies, intended to secure himself, were taken by the evil king. The slaying of his six brothers was doubtless to get rid of their protests, and to remove the prospect of a revival. Jehoram openly practiced idolatry, and under the influence of Athaliah, "walked in the ways of the kings of Israel."

In judgment, God permitted foreign scourges to invade Jehoram's realm, and other ills plagued him until he died. When he died the disdain in which he was held was so great that he was not permitted burial in the tombs of the kings.

When Jehoram died the throne was left to Ahaziah, his youngest and only remaining son. Under the influence of his mother, Athaliah, it was only natural that Jehoram's policies were continued. It was natural, also, that Ahaziah allied himself with his uncle Jehoram of Israel (Athaliah's brother), and that together they carried on war with the Syrians. God's hour of judgment struck at one time for both kings, as Jehu, the divinely ordained agent of execution, met them on their return from battle and slew them at Jezreel.

Athaliah's action, upon the death of her son, King Ahaziah, shows the fiendish tenacity of an evil personality once it is in power. Her way of holding power was to kill all other eligible persons. In this way she retained the throne for herself for six years. But God completed his purging process and Athaliah the usurper was displaced by Joash whom she had supposedly slain. Thus came to an end, approximately fifteen years of idolatry-dominated rule in Judah. How costly to Judah's well-being and honor was the despotism of evil which a wrong relationship had admitted to the nation!

5.   A Good Person Behind the Throne

Just as Athaliah had been the power on the throne during the reigns of Jehoram and Ahaziah, so, after her death the real power upon the throne was that of an aged priest Jehoiada and his wife Jehoseba. While Athaliah sat upon the throne this godly couple were nursing and teaching the lad Joash in preparation for his reign. It was Jehoiada's initiative and influence that dethroned Athaliah and enthroned Joash. While Jehoiada lived, we are told, Joash did right "wherein the priest instructed him." The implication of this characterization is that when Jehoiada's influence for good was gone, defection set in. This is borne out by the record. Whereas in the earlier part of his reign Joash carried on reforms, in the latter part he succumbed to evil influences and was preyed upon by both foreign and internal foes. When reproved by Zechariah the son of Jehoiada, he retorted with death for the reprover. Attacks by Hazael of Syria and from the Philistines, and finally, assassination by his own servants were the unhappy end of the man who had never learned to stand upon his own feet for the right.

6. Pale Copies of David's Righteousness

It is noteworthy that the reigns of the three kings following were characterized by similar instability. While all three are credited as doing right, yet there was discoloration in their records. Amaziah did right, yet "not like David," but "like Joash his father." Uzziah also did well until he prospered. Then in his pride he presumed to be a priest and was smitten with leprosy. Jotham who succeeded him as a pale character who did right, but only "as Uzziah his father." He did very little to raise the nation's life above its previous low religious level.

7. A New Low Under Ahaz

While Jotham was a pale personality, Ahaz his son was not. He was a resourceful young fellow. However, his originality was always positively to the left. Not satisfied with the altar in the temple, nor with borrowing from Baal temples, he had a new altar made for the Jerusalem temple on the pattern of one which he observed in Damascus. While Pekah resorted to an alliance with Syria against him, he did not hesitate to urge the Assyrians to assist him against Pekah. In this he doubtless hastened the capitulation of the northern kingdom. It would seem that if there had been any new evil to be imported into Judah, Ahaz would have introduced it. Fortunately for Judah he died at the early age of 36 and gave place to a good king who in God's providence guided the nation through the critical days of the Assyrian menace.

8. Salvation Through Revival

Hezekiah began to reign in Judah six years before the final overthrow of the northern kingdom. From all natural considerations Judah would have gone into captivity to Assyria just as Israel did. Certainly, so far as the administration of Ahaz was concerned, it was ripe for judgment.

But something had been going on in Judea within the hearts of many people. Isaiah the prophet had been calling the people to repentance ever since the death of Uzziah. The nation was ripe for revival, only awaiting a king who would give leadership to the necessary reforms, in order to make it a general fact. King Hezekiah matched the fervor of Isaiah and made thorough-going religious reform the primary policy of his administration. He washed Jerusalem of its idolatry, repaired the temple, and reinstated the institutions of Moses. Hezekiah performed a master stroke in inviting all Israel to the Passover observance. Posts were sent to the remotest borders sounding forth a call for all sincere souls to pull away from Israel's idolatry and to meet at God's appointed place for the Passover. Thus, revival became a means of grace to the faithful of all Israel, preparing them for the crisis through which they would soon pass. One wonders whether many of these faithful of Israel did not move permanently to Judah and thus escape the judgment of the Assyrian captivity under Shalmaneser. This much is evident, Hezekiah had learned the source of supernatural help, and Judah was spared because of it.

9.   The Prophets and Their Messages

The prophets Micah and Isaiah specify that they uttered their prophecies during the reigns of Jotham, Ahaz, and Hezekiah. Isaiah's call came in the "year that king Uzziah died." Joel probably appeared early in this period.

Micah

Micah's prophecy was addressed to both Samaria and Jerusalem. He laid bare the social evils of the times, championing the cause of the common people against their corrupt leaders. Micah had not merely a message of social reform, however. Though the existing order might not be reformed, nevertheless he set forth to the faithful a hope. This hope did not center in Samaria, nor in historic Jerusalem, but in unpretentious Bethlehem, of Judah, out of whom should come the Messiah.

Isaiah

Isaiah is undoubtedly the most significant figure in this second cycle of Judah's history. His prophecy from the beginning lays the nation low because of her sins. He repudiates her hypocritical worship, and calls for sincere cleansing from sin. He promises God's sure mercy. Pleadingly he cries, "Come now, and let us reason together, saith the LORD: though your sins be as scarlet, they shall be as white as snow, though they be red like crimson, they shall be as wool. If ye be willing and obedient ye shall eat the good of the land: but if ye refuse and rebel, ye shall be devoured with the sword: for the mouth of the LORD hath spoken it" (Isa. 1).

Isaiah's prophecies concerning Judah, Israel, and foreign nations are very explicit. Syria and Israel will be taken by Assyria (Isa. 7-8), but Assyria will herself fall because of her pride, and will not succeed in conquering Zion (Isa. 10). The destinies of Babylon, Philistia, Moab, Damascus, Ethiopia, Egypt, Arabia, Tyre, and, summarily, of the whole earth are brought into view (Isa. 13-24). The mountain of Zion is seen, ultimately, to be the seat of the LORD'S dominion over all the earth (Isa. 25-27).

While Isaiah prophecied specifically that Assyria would not take Zion, his prophecy rose to a far higher height of triumph, and it is to this that he hopefully directs the eyes of that distracted age. "Come my people," he cried, "enter thou into thy chambers, and shut thy doors about thee, hide thyself as it were for a little moment, until the indignation be overpast. For behold the LORD cometh out of his place to punish the inhabitants of the earth for their iniquity: the earth also shall disclose her blood, and shall no more cover her slain" (Isa. 26:20-21).

Isaiah denounced the policy of resorting to Egypt for aid (Isa. 28-35).

Chapters 36-39 give Isaiah's account of Judah's encounter with the Assyrian Sennacherib and of the marvelous divine intervention in behalf of Judah.

Chapters 40-48 center in the Babylonian period, which Isaiah had foretold in connection with the visit of the Babylonian envoys in the temple (II Kings 20:12-19). He foretold the restoration of Judah under the Persians, naming Cyrus as the LORD'S servant by whom this would be accomplished (44:28; 45:1-4).

Israel's final deliverance will not come from the LORD'S servant Cyrus, however, but from the seed of Israel as is set forth by the Servant of the LORD pictured in chapters 49-59. The glory of the Messianic kingdom protrudes throughout the book (chapters 2, 7, 9, 11), and becomes resplendent in the final part (chapters 60-66).

10. Assyrian Kings of the Period

Tiglath Pileser III (Pul)[1]—746-728 B. C.

After 750 B. C. Assyrian approaches began to fill the foreign

---

[1] I Chronicles 5:26 together with archaeological findings have established with fair certainty that Pul and Tiglath Pileser III are identical persons. For a fuller study see Joseph P. Free, *Archaeology and Bible History*, Van Kampen, 1950, chapters 17 and 18.

horizon of Israel and Judah. The first of these was under Pul, King of Assyria (II Kings 15:19, 20) in the reigns of Menahem of Israel and Uzziah (Azariah) of Judah. He placed Israel under tribute of 50 shekels per man. Later in the reign of Pekah of Israel this same king invaded Israel and carried away captives (II Kings 15:29).

Because Rezin of Syria and Pekah of Israel joined together against Judah in the reigns of Jotham and Ahaz, Ahaz sought an alliance with Tiglath Pileser III, paying money from the temple treasury to enhance his appeal. The Assyrian King responded with aid (II Kings 16:5-9).

Shalmaneser V—728-722 B. C.

He is the king usually credited with laying siege to and destroying the city of Samaria in 722 B. C.

Sargon III—722-705 B. C.

This king made an invasion into southwestern Palestine (Isa. 20:1). Some think he, rather than Shalmaneser, took the city of Samaria as related in II Kings 17:6.[1]

Sennacherib—705-681 B. C.

This is the king who invaded Judah in 701 B. C. taking northern cities and threatening to take Jerusalem likewise. Hezekiah paid tribute to him, hoping to stave off invasion. But appeasement did not satisfy Sennacherib, who sent a blasphemous, threatening letter and three envoys to taunt Hezekiah into surrender of his sovereignty. God's word came through the prophet Isaiah to the godly Hezekiah assuring Judah of safety from Sennacherib. The special divine intervention by which the angel of the Lord smote 185,000 soldiers (II Kings 19:35; Isa. 37:36) is uniquely consistent with the findings of archaeology. The inscriptions indicate that while Sennacherib took other Palestinian cities there is a strange exception made in the case of Jerusalem. Speaking in the inscription, Sennacherib says, "As for myself, like a bird in a cage in his royal city Jerusalem, I shut (him) up."[2]

---

[1] Ibid, pp. 199-200.

[2] Ibid, pp. 209.

The death of Sennacherib at the hands of his sons is substantiated by the subscription which says, "In the month Nisan, on a favorable day, complying with their exalted command, I made my joyful entrance into the royal palace, the awesome place, wherein abides the fate of the kings. A firm determination fell on my brothers. They forsook the gods and turned to their deeds of violence, plotting evil. . . . To gain the kingship they slew Sennacherib, my father."[1]

Esar-haddon—681-668 B. C.

It was Esar-haddon who returned to Palestine, subdued Manasseh, carried him to Babylon a prisoner, and then brought him back to Jerusalem a converted man (II Chronicles 33:11).

Ashurbanipal—668-626 B. C.

Ashurbanipal is known as a scholar-king, and is the last great ruler of Assyria. He is noted for the library of tablets and documents which he collected at Nineveh, and thereby for his service in transmitting learning, ancient already in his day, down to later times. After his death Assyria declined rapidly, culminating in the fall of Nineveh in 612 B. C. to a coalition force of Babylonians, Medes, and Scythians.

11. Discussion and Review

1. Show the price Judah had to pay for Jehoshaphat's intimacy with Ahab and Ahaziah of Israel. Note the results in the times of his son (Jehoram) and his grandson (Ahaziah).

2. What good work did the priest Jehoida do for Judah? What happened when his influence was gone? Evaluate the character of Joash (Jehoash).

3. Characterize the three kings who followed Joash.

4. What were some of the novel ideas of Ahaz? What happened to Judah's moral score under his reign?

5. Relate how salvation from the Assyrian menace came to Judah through spiritual revival.

6. State briefly the messages of Micah, Isaiah and Hosea for their times. Are their messages confined to their times? Discuss.

7. Name the successive Assyrian kings of this period with a note as to the points at which they touch Judah's history.

---

[1] Luckenbill, D. D. *Ancient Records of Assyria and Babylonia*, U. of Chicago Press, 1924, chapter II, pp. 200, 201.

12. Select Memory Passages

Joel 2:12-14; Micah 6:6-8; Hosea 3:4-5; Isaiah 1:18-20; 7:14-16; 9:6-7; 43:2; 52:7; chapter 53; 54:5; 55:3, 6-7; 59:1-2, 20; 61:1-3.

13. Character Review

Identify:

Jehoram	(Joash)	Hosea	Rezin
(Joram)	Hazael	Isaiah	Tiglath Pileser
Ahaziah	Amaziah	Jotham	Urijah
Athaliah	Uzziah	Ahaz	Shalmaneser
Jehosheba	(Azariah)	Hezekiah	Rabshakeh
Jehoash	Joel	Micah	Sennacherib

14. Bibliography

Cheyne, T. K. *Introduction to the Book of Isaiah.* 1895.

Cheyne, T. K. *Micah with Notes and Introduction.* 1882.

Free, Joseph P. *Archaeology and Bible History.* Chapter XVIII, Topics: "Isaiah and Hezekiah," p. 203; "Archaeological Light on Isaiah's Words to the Vain Women of His Time," pp. 203, 204; "Discovery of an Ancient Isaiah Manuscript," pp. 205-207; "Sennacherib's Invasion of Judah; Archaeological Confirmation of Hezekiah's Payment of Tribute," p. 208; "Hezekiah's Conduit; Archaeological Light from the Siloam Inscription," pp. 211-212. Wheaton: Van Kampen Press.

Kuyper, Abraham. *Women of the Old Testament.* Grand Rapids: Zondervan.
  1. "Athaliah," pp. 157-160.
  2. "Jehosheba," pp. 160-163.

Miller, Dorothy Ruth. *A Handbook of Ancient History in Bible Light.* Chapter XII, "The Assyrian Empire." New York: Fleming H. Revell Co.

Orelli, C. von. "Micah," *The International Standard Bible Encyclopedia.* Vol. III. pp. 2046-2047.

Robinson, George L. "Isaiah," *The International Standard Bible Encyclopedia.* Vol. III. pp. 1495-1508.

Chapter 19

THE KINGDOM OF JUDAH
Third Cycle and Final Declension

(Manasseh to Zedekiah)
(696-586 B. C.)

---

1. Reading Assignment: II Kings 21-25; II Chronicles 33-36

---

2. Collateral Readings: Nahum, Zephaniah, Habakkuk,

Jeremiah, Obadiah, Ezekiel

(Read the Bible first)

3. Historical Outline

See the harmonized histories of Judah and Israel, pages 198-199

4. Introduction

This period of nearly a century has the distinct marks of Judah's national nightfall. The marks of sin were made deep and permanent during Manasseh's fifty-five year reign. While there was in the period a gracious eighteen year revival under Josiah the results were not effective in changing the general downgrade of morality. Sin had produced weakness, and the Chaldean hordes which threatened the west would eventually find Judah an easy prey.

After the death of Josiah there was little real strength of leadership left. Judah was left in the hands of boys, with neither principles, judgment, nor policies. The hereditary weakness of the rulers was evident. Josiah was born when his father was only a boy of sixteen. Jehoahaz was born when his father was sixteen. Jehoiakim was born when his father was eighteen. Jehoiachin was born when his father was eighteen. Zedekiah was twenty-one when he became king, but was less than a man in character. His vacillation between the false patriotism of his nobles and the godly counsel of Jeremiah is conspicuous. Had he listened to Jeremiah, destruction and waste, and the dispersion of the people might have been much less severe. But judgment and wise policy were no longer a possibility in a land so perforated with sin. Godly people, as Jeremiah, knew that the political system of Judah must drop as a plum over-ripe for judgment.

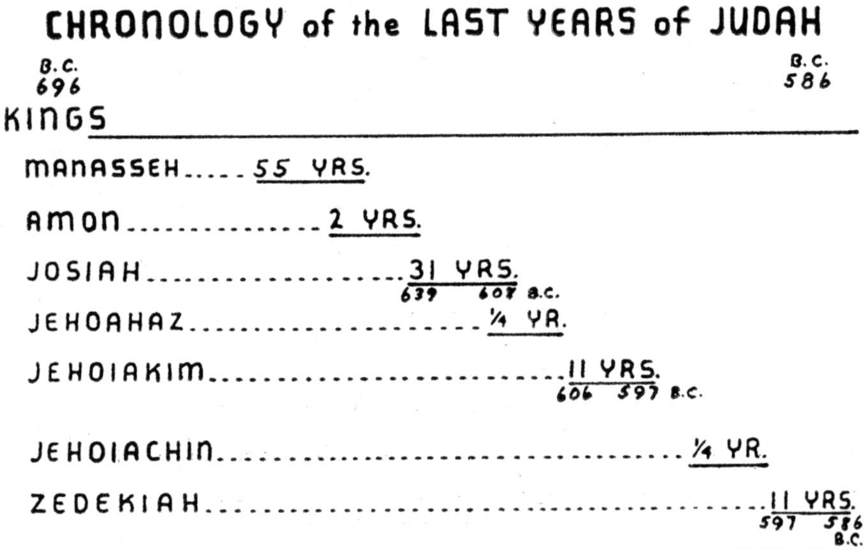

CHRONOLOGY of the LAST YEARS of JUDAH

B.C.
696

B.C.
586

KINGS

MANASSEH......55 YRS.

AMON..............2 YRS.

JOSIAH..................31 YRS.
639   607 B.C.

JEHOAHAZ......................¼ YR.

JEHOIAKIM................................11 YRS.
606   597 B.C.

JEHOIACHIN...¼ YR.

ZEDEKIAH..11 YRS.
597   586
B.C.

Figure 25a

5. The Moral Ledger of Manasseh

The Bible record sets to Manasseh's account one of the completest lists of sins engaged in by any king. It is difficult to explain such a turn from the godly ways of his father Hezekiah. Perhaps there is some explanation in the fact that Manasseh was born late in the life of his father. Being only twelve years old at his father's death, he had only second hand information of the reforms which had been carried out. Also, it is sometimes the case that children of public servants must be reared by others, and thus it is possible that in preoccupation Hezekiah may have missed an important opportunity in the life of his son. Twelve years is a very early age for a son to become a king, and it is entirely possible that influence arose which begat prodigality in his youthful spirit. The fact that Manasseh repented under chastisement may imply that he returned to the instruction of his youth.

Manasseh's example teaches that while one may be forgiven for a course of sin, it is impossible to undo the public damages. Though he tried with all sincerity and energy, he was unable to turn the national current from the evil which his long reign had fostered. His son Amon followed, not the reformed Manasseh, but the profligate one. Evil came to such a harvest under Amon that his servants slew him.

6. The Last Revival in Judah's National History

Josiah appears as a star of brief hope upon the national horizon in the last days of Manasseh. If Manasseh's last year aspirations for the kingdom had a dismal shadow cast upon them by the fact that the evilly-inclined Amon was to succeed him, there may also have appeared for his encouragement the prospect for better things from the wise heart of his six year old grandson. Undoubtedly, the example of reformed Manasseh, the only Manasseh Josiah knew, made its mark in the little lad.

Since Josiah began to reign at the age of eight, it may be assumed that other officers carried for a time the responsibility of major decisions, which meant that conditions in the nation were permitted to continue in their degenerate course. At the age of 16, Josiah "began to seek the LORD." Four years later in his 12th year, at the age of 20, his ideals and policies began to be manifest. He initiated a program of purging which swept before it all forms of idolatry. He went up into the territory of Ephraim, Manasseh, Simeon, and Naphtali and vigorously demolished idol worship. It is to be noted that he engaged in the cleansing of the land for six years before he undertook the repair of the house of the Lord, indicating that moral and spiritual reform was given precedence over ceremonials. The house of God was not neglected, however, and in due time, in his 18th year, at the age of 26, repairs began.

The reforms of Josiah up to this time appear to have been the result of his seeking the LORD, and they were largely iconoclastic.

Thorough-going reform began when the book of the Law was found in connection with the repair of the temple. Finding and reading it, Josiah was greatly astonished to learn of the extent of ignorance and neglect into which the nation had drifted. He became alarmed, for he realized that according to God's law the nation was doomed for judgment.

One of the requirements of the Law to which Josiah gave himself was the observance of the annual Passover Feast. This involved the convening of the people from all parts of the kingdom at Jerusalem. At this assembly Josiah caused the book of the Law of the LORD to be read and received a covenant renewal pledge from all the people. The zeal of his leadership is seen in the indignation with which he publicly evicted the paraphernalia of Baal worship from the temple, burned it, and stamped it into small powder. The altar at Bethel he broke down, and stamped to powder. He burned the bones of the idolatrous priests with their altar as predicted by the man of God in the days of Jeroboam.[1]

The book of Chronicles says that the reforms of Josiah were unprecedented in their thoroughness. "And like unto him was there no king before him, that turned to the LORD with all his heart, and with all his soul, and with all his might, according to all the law of Moses." The Passover observance is said to have been the greatest celebration since the days of Joshua.

It was made clear to Josiah both from the book of the Law and by direct word from God that the time of Judah's judgment was at hand. Because of his devotion, Josiah was promised that it should not occur in his day, but not even such a revival as had been experienced could longer prevent God's purpose to bring about the end of the kingdom. Thus, it is evident that there may be a revival of the faithful even while a nation passes into judgment.

7. Foreign Relations

With Assyria

It has been made evident by Assyrian inscriptions that Hezekiah did not cease paying tribute to Assyria but that this continued into the times of Manasseh. Esar-haddon, the successor of Sennacherib speaks of his dominion over realms extending from Syria to Egypt,

---
[1] I Kings 12:28-33; 13:1-2.

including Manasseh, in particular, as his subject. This is in full accord with the record of II Chronicles 18:11-13 which speaks of the time Manasseh was obliged to serve in Babylon, Babylon being at that time a part of the Assyrian realm.

Beginning about 626 B. C., the hordes of Scythia, who were allied to the Babylonians, overran Assyria, preparing the way for the final downfall of Nineveh (612-606 B. C.). The date 626 B. C. seems significantly crucial in that it was the date of the death of Assurbanipal, the last main stay of Assyrian power, and the date of Jeremiah's call as a prophet (Jer. 1).

With Egypt

The weakened condition of Assyria in her latter years left her dependencies the easy prey to conquest. Babylon had not yet begun her conquest of the east, and the moment appeared opportune for Egypt to assert her imperialistic instinct. In 608 B. C. Necho II of the twenty-sixth Egyptian dynasty made his way to the northeast with the hope of getting at least a share of the Assyrian dependencies. On his way he was resisted at Megiddo by King Josiah of Judah. Josiah was slain. His son Jehoahaz succeeded him but in three months was taken captive into Egypt where he died. Judah was placed under tribute to Egypt. Jehoiakim (Eliakim), another son of Josiah, received the favor of Egypt and was placed upon the throne of Judah on the condition that he should collect tribute for Egypt faithfully.

The armies of Necho proceeded from Megiddo to their anticipated prey in the north, but they were destined to reverses. Nabopolasser, king of Babylon, was soon on the grounds and met the forces of Necho in battle at Carchemish on the Euphrates (606 B. C.). The Egyptians were entirely routed, and the pursuing army followed them, bringing under the control of Babylon all lands which had been gained by Pharaoh Necho II from the river of Egypt to the river Euphrates. (II Kings 24:7).

With Babylon

In the third year of Jehoiakim (ca. 606 B. C.) the first Babylonian invasion of Judah was made, at which time Daniel and other of the nobility were carried away captive (Dan. 1:1-2; II Kings 24:1; II Chron. 35:5-8). Jehoiakim was threatened with deportation, but evidently was spared on the condition of paying tribute to Babylon. At the end of three years Jehoiakim rebelled against Babylon with the result that bands of Chaldeans and pro-Chaldeans visited Judah with grievous plunder (II Kings 24:2).

In 597 B. C. Jehoiakim was succeeded by his son Jehoiachin, who reigned only three months until Nebuchadnezzar laid siege to Jerusalem. The king, his mother, his servants, his princes, his officers, his wives, his best men for industry, battle, and government— all these to the number of ten thousand were deported. Ezekiel the prophet was among these captives (Ezekiel 1:1-3; II Kings 24:12-15).

Nebuchadnezzar placed Zedekiah (Mattaniah), another son of Josiah upon the inglorious throne of Judah. In the eleven years of this vacillating king the hold of the Babylonians continually strengthened. It was Zedekiah's policy to resist. This resistance was based upon a twofold misapprehension, first, of the tremendous military strength of Babylon, and secondly, of the fact that captivity as the judgment of God had become Judah's inevitable lot. Sentiment and vain patriotism determined the fatal policies by which the administration of Zedekiah led the nation to its worst.

After a year and six months of siege the city of Jerusalem fell (586 B. C.). Zedekiah's sons were slain before him, his eyes were put out, and he was bound and taken to Babylon. The chief religious and political heads were slain. The army was scattered, and the city walls were demolished. The poorer people and such as were known to be submissive to the invasion, were left in the land. Among these were Gedaliah whom Nebuchadnezzar appointed ruler of the remnant, and Jeremiah the prophet, whose counsels had been observed with favor by the Babylonians. Gedaliah was assassinated by a band under the leadership of one Ishmael, a relative of Zedekiah. Jeremiah was coerced to go with some of the remnant down into Egypt and nothing more is heard of him. During the fifty years following, the land lay desolate, with little taking place of historic interest. The historians of Scripture, however, take us with them to scenes in Babylon where the people of the covenant continued to make history.

8. Prophets of Judah's Last Years

Nahum

Nahum the Elkoshite (of Galilee), writing probably some time during the reign of Manasseh, prophesied against Assyria. It is ex-

pressive of the LORD'S goodness that, after he had allowed Assyria to judge Israel, he should turn about and through the prophet
Nahum, vindicate God's people against the Assyrians. The name
Nahum means "consolation and vengeance" and denotes the twofold message of his prophecy.

Zephaniah

Zephaniah, a relative of King Josiah, prophesied probably in the
early part of Josiah's reign, sometime before the revival and reformation which began in Josiah's 12th year. We may think of him as associated with, and possibly a strong promoter of the reforms of
Josiah's time. He must accordingly, have been associated with
Jeremiah. Considering the fact that he wrote of evil in the land
as though it were still unrepented of, it has commonly been supposed
that this ministry may have been confined to the early part of
Josiah's reign. His message centered in a single theme, namely,
the judgment of the "day of the LORD." Nevertheless, he gave his
message a silver lining as is seen in his projection of the Messiah's
kingdom in the last chapter of his prophecy.

Habakkuk

Habakkuk prophesied probably sometime between the destruction of Nineveh (612 B. C.) and Nebuchadnezzar's first invasion of
Judah (606 B. C.), probably during the reigns of Jehoahaz and
Jehoiakim. He is fitly regarded as the philosopher-prophet. Habakkuk raised two questions which he put to the LORD. First, he
asked why God allowed evil to dominate his land. When God answered his question by saying that the Chaldeans would soon put
an end to that domination, he raised the second question, which was,
"Why should God's people be judged by Chaldea who is less righteous?" To this, God, acknowledging the pride and unworthiness of
Chaldea, proclaimed the divine principle which has ever been the
consolation of God's true people, "The just shall live by faith." It is
of interest to note that Jeremiah was concerned with the very same
problem (chapter 12).

Jeremiah

Undoubtedly, Jeremiah is the greatest figure of this period. He
was a descendant of the priests of Anathoth, a village about three

miles north of Jerusalem. He was called to prophesy when but a child and began in the 13th year of Josiah's reign (Jeremiah 1). This was a year after Josiah had begun to purge the land, and it was five years before the law of the LORD was found in the temple. He was commanded not to marry. The whole assumption of his life and message was that the existing order of things in Judah was about to be dissolved. Accordingly, his counsel to the people was that they should bare their necks to accept the God-appointed Chaldean yoke. So long as Josiah lived Jeremiah had the support of the throne for his work. After Josiah's death, the times changed and Jeremiah was no longer countenanced. Forbidden to appear publicly, he wrote his messages and had them delivered by Baruch. Sometimes in stocks, in prison, and in the court of the guard, and sometimes summoned by the troubled kings for much needed counsel, Jeremiah ministered to the nation until the conquering Chaldeans had done their final work of destruction.

After the destruction of Jerusalem, Jeremiah opposed a movement on the part of the remnant to go down into Egypt, but was forced to go with them. So far as we know this is where he spent his last days. The book of Jeremiah, contrary to the attitude of some people, is one of the most interesting books of the Bible. Jeremiah was no mere weak complaining prophet. He stood in one of the toughest spots of history and his personality was a moral rock of Gibralter while all around, men of expediency without principle succumbed to their vanity.

Obadiah

Nothing is known about Obadiah except what is made evident from his short prophetic book. He prophesied against Edom for taking advantage of the fleeing captives when Jerusalem was being destroyed. Since Nebuchadnezzar's conquest proceeded from the destruction of Jerusalem (586 B. C.) to the destruction of Edom (581 B. C.) it is evident that Obadiah belongs between these dates, for he writes of the doom of Edom for having done violence against his brother in the day of his calamity.

Ezekiel

Ezekiel, of priestly descent, was one of the captives who were carried away with King Jehoiachin (II Kings 24:8-16; Ezekiel 1:1-3) in 597 B. C. His detachment of captives were settled on the river Chebar, probably a branch of the Euphrates. Here his home became a center of consolation and spiritual counsel to his fellow captives (Ezek. 1:1-3; 3:15; 8:1; 24:15-18; 33:30-32). Ezekiel continued to prophesy on into the period of captivity, his last dated prophecy being the 27th year of Jehoiachin's captivity, in 570 B. C., sixteen years after the destruction of Jerusalem.

Shut from the means of instruction afforded by the temple, Ezekiel taught by means of a multitude of symbols suitable to the exile's mind. His pen pictures made vivid the link of hope between Israel's captivity and the promised restoration. In no book is there a more graphic portrayal of God's purpose to bless all nations through the chosen race.

9. Discussion and Review

1. Appraise the effect of Manasseh's reign upon the destiny of Judah.

2. Tell the account of the last spiritual revival in Judah's national history.

3. What was the nature of Judah's relation with Assyria after the times of Sennacherib?

4. How did Egypt react to the diminishing supremacy of Assyria in world affairs and how did this affect Judah?

5. Relate the account of the three major invasions of the Babylonians, including the final siege and destruction of Jerusalem.

6. Name the six prophets of this period stating briefly the main features of the message of each.

10. Select Memory Passages

Jeremiah 1:13; 3:13; 4:4; 9:25; 31:33, 34

11. Character Review

Identify:

Manasseh	Nebuchadnezzar	Pharaoh-necho	Zedekiah
Amon	Jehoiachin	Jehoahaz	(Mattaniah)
Josiah	(Jeconiah)	Jehoiakim	Nahum
Huldah	Ezekiel	(Eliakim)	Gedaliah
Jeremiah	Esarhaddon	Habakkuk	Daniel

12. Bibliography

Allis, Oswald T. "A Modernistic View of Jeremiah," *The Princeton Theological Review*. Vol. 23. 1925, pp. 82–132.

Free, Joseph P. *Archaeology and the Bible*. Chapter 19, dealing with various archaeological confirmations of Biblical history. Wheaton: Van Kampen Press.

Gordon, T. Crouther. *The Rebel Prophet. Studies in the Personality of Jeremiah*. London, 1931.

Miller, Dorothy Ruth. *A Handbook of Ancient History in Bible Light*. Chapter XIII, "The Second Babylonian Empire." New York: Fleming H. Revell Co.

Miller, Dorothy Ruth. *A Handbook of Ancient History in Bible Light*. Chapter XIV, "Babylon a Type." New York: Fleming H. Revell Co.

Morgan, G. Campbell. *The Prophecy of Jeremiah*. New York: Fleming H. Revell Co.

Morgan, G. Campbell. *Living Messages of the Books of the Bible*, Vol. I. "The Message of Jeremiah," pp. 109–124. New York: Fleming H. Revell Co.

Morgan, G. Campbell. *The Prophecy of Jeremiah*. New York: Fleming H. Revell and Co.

Sangster, Margaret E. *The Women of the Bible*. Chapt. XXIV, "Huldah, the Discreet Counsellor." New York: The Christian Herald.

Welch, Adam C. *Jeremiah: His Time and His Work*. Oxford, 1928.

PART SEVEN

GENTILE SUPREMACY

Chapter 20

THE BABYLONIAN CAPTIVITY

(606-536 B. C.)

1. **Reading Assignment:** II Kings 23:36—25:30; II Chronicles 36:5-23; Jeremiah 28, 29; Ezekiel 1-48; Daniel 1-12

(Read the Bible first)

2. From Babylon to Babylon

The life of the Abrahamic nation had moved in an inglorious cycle. Abraham had been called out of Ur of Chaldea (Babylonia). Now, after a millennium and a half, his descendants were back in Babylon. Abraham had left Babylon in faith and obedience to God. His descendants now returned to Babylon because of unbelief and disobedience to God.

God had been faithful to Abraham. His descendants had grown to be a great nation, they had been given a good land, and God's glory had been manifested to this nation and in this land in a manner without parallel in history. Israel, on the other hand, had never ceased to backslide. In connection with this perpetual backsliding, the captivity had been repeatedly foretold (Deut. 29-30; II Kings 8:46-53; 20:17; 21:10-15; 22:14-17; Jeremiah 25:9-11; 34:2, 3; Micah 3:8-12).

227

536 B.C.

--BABYLON--------- PERSIA -------------------

333 B.C.

B.C. 586

B.C. 482

B.C. 458

B.C. 445

B.C. 432

B.C. 400

B.C. 323

Destruction of Jerusalem by Nebuchadnezzar's army, according to Jeremiah's prophecy (Jer. 25). II Kings 25, II Chron. 36.

Return of Ezra and a second caravan to Jerusalem.

Return of Nehemiah to build Jerusalem.

Old Testament canon completed.

Second visit of Nehemiah to Jerusalem.

Persian dominion succumbs. Alexander the great conquers the world, spreading Greek culture everywhere. His attitude toward the Jews was favorable but short. Upon his early death his empire fell to his four generals.

Return of the first caravan of Babylonian captives to Jerusalem, under Zerubbabel and Jeshua. Temple foundation laid; Temple completed 20 years later. II Chron. 36; Ezra 1.

Esther and Mordecai save the Jewish people from Haman's plot for their extermination

For a century and a half two of the surviving four divisions mad Judea the arena for their rivalry. The Seleucidaes were from Syria the north and the Ptolemies from Egypt in the south. Under the Ptol maic supremacy (208-165 B. C.) Palestine and Coele-Syria were sep arated into the five divisions known in New Testament times, namel Judea, Samaria, Galilee, Trachonitus, and Perea. The Greek transla tion of the O. T (LXX, Septuagint) was written 288 B. C.

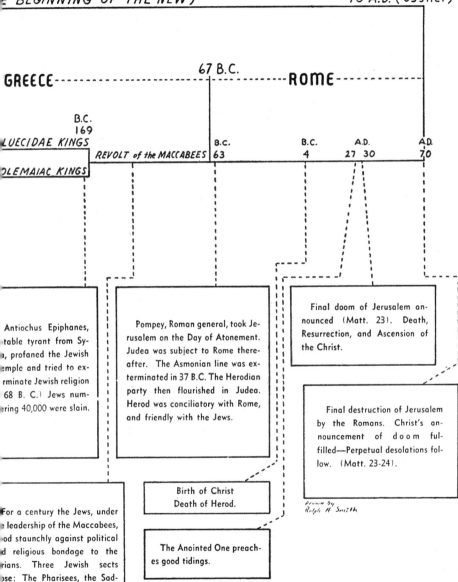

OVERTHROW

70 A.D. (Ussher)

67 B.C.

GREECE - - - - - - - - - - - - - - - - ROME - - - - - - - - - - -

B.C.
169

LUECIDAE KINGS

REVOLT of the MACCABEES

| B.C. | | B.C. | A.D. | | A.D. |
| 63 | | 4 | 27 30 | | 70 |

PLEMAIAC KINGS

Antiochus Epiphanes, table tyrant from Syria, profaned the Jewish temple and tried to exterminate Jewish religion 68 B. C.) Jews numbering 40,000 were slain.

Pompey, Roman general, took Jerusalem on the Day of Atonement. Judea was subject to Rome thereafter. The Asmonian line was exterminated in 37 B.C. The Herodian party then flourished in Judea. Herod was conciliatory with Rome, and friendly with the Jews.

Final doom of Jerusalem announced (Matt. 23). Death, Resurrection, and Ascension of the Christ.

Final destruction of Jerusalem by the Romans. Christ's announcement of doom fulfilled—Perpetual desolations follow. (Matt. 23-24).

Birth of Christ
Death of Herod.

Drawn by
Ralph H. Smith

For a century the Jews, under the leadership of the Maccabees, stood staunchly against political and religious bondage to the Syrians. Three Jewish sects arose: The Pharisees, the Sadducees, and the Essenes. Division destined the noble aim of achieving Jewish freedom to failure.

The Anointed One preaches good tidings.

3. God's Unchanging Sovereignty

It should be observed that God's purpose, as expressed in Genesis 12:1-3, is not fully contained within the destiny of Israel's national existence. God has ever thought and planned in terms of humanity. Abraham's seed was chosen as the instrument by which God purposed to bring blessing to "all families of the earth." That successive reigns of earthly kings had produced a zig-zag line of national history, ending in the loss of earthly sovereignty, did not frustrate the redemptive purpose of God in the world. Israel's kings had made a bad record in history, but God's sovereignty never ceased to be supreme. Israel's inglorious disestablishment was in itself a vindication of God's throne. It had been shown that not even God's chosen people could rebel against him and escape judgment. When eventually Israel gave the world the Messiah, it was not at the high point of her greatest national strength but at its lowest ebb, and only by faith in God's invisible throne could one interpret the result as hopeful for either Israel or the world.

Our study of Israel from Zedekiah's time on is always in relation to two outside sovereignties. There is the earthly sovereignty of Babylon, and the higher and supreme sovereignty of their God. Babylon in the scriptures includes not only the government which existed at the time of the Babylonian captivity, but the sequence of governments beginning with that of Nebuchadnezzar under whom Israel was to exist as a subject people until the eternal kingdom of the promised Messiah should be established on earth. This view of things is clearly set forth by the prophetic image of Daniel's dream (Dan. 2). Babylon, considered in this sense, will in a future day be up for judgment and for the termination of her sovereignty. Then Israel's Messiah will reign upon the earth in righteousness and peace. If the passing of sinful Judah as a nation served to direct God's people to this greater kingdom, it was indeed a capital gain.

4. Captivity Chronology

Jeremiah prophesied that the captivity should last three score and ten years. This seventy year period can be accounted for by recognizing transitional periods of twenty years at the beginning and at the end. At the beginning there were three major deportations of captives (B. C. 606, 597, and 586). At the close there was the date of Cyrus' decree for the return of the captives (536 B. C.), and the date of the completion of the rebuilding of the temple (516 B. C.). These dates may readily be remembered as forming an oblique parallelogram.

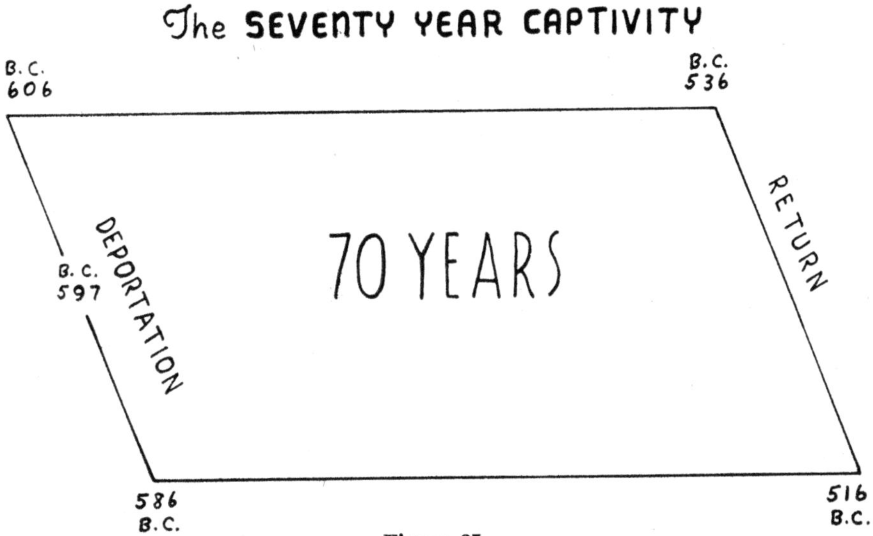

The SEVENTY YEAR CAPTIVITY

Figure 27

5. Kings of the Neo-Babylonian Empire

Nebuchadnezzar—604-561 B. C.

Nebuchadnezzar is first seen as the general of his father Nabopolassar, king of Babylon (609-604 B. C.). As such he carried out his first conquests of the west, driving the Egyptians from Carchemish, and then extending his dominion over Syria and Palestine (605 B. C.) He may be regarded as the builder of the new Babylonian Empire, which included the complete subjugation of Palestine and the removal of its people to Babylon. He marks the beginning of a succession of world powers to which the Israelites were destined to be subject in centuries to come. His reign lasted forty-three years.

Evil-Merodach—561-559 B. C.

He was the son of Nebuchadnezzar, and reigned for two years. In kindness he raised up Jehoiachin, and bestowed care and honor upon him (II Kings 25:27-30). He was assassinated and succeeded by his assassin.

Neriglissar—559-555 B. C.

Neriglissar (Nergal-sharezer) is first observed as a general under Nebuchadnezzar, who at Nebuchadnezzar's command, released Jeremiah from prison (Jer. 39:3). Profane history assigns considerable importance to him, recording the fact of his usurpation of the throne.

Labashi-Marduk—555 B. C.

He was but an infant and was deposed by the priestly party after nine months.

Nabonidus—555-538 B. C.

He was a Babylonian of the priestly party, and a leader, in previous times, of the Babylonian army. History records him as the last king of the new Babylonian Empire. It is evident from Daniel 5 and late archaeological findings that Belshazzar, Nabonidus' son, was actually co-ruler with his father, reigning up to the capture of Babylon by the Medes and the Persians in 538 B. C.

6.   Jeremiah's Prophecy of a Seventy-Year Captivity

Jeremiah explains why the time of the captivity was seventy years. It was that the land might enjoy the sabbatic years which she had been denied in the course of the nation's history. From the beginning of the monarchy (B. C. 1095) until the beginning of the captivity (B. C. 606) there should have been 70 sabbatic years, none of which had been observed (Lev. 25:4; 26:33; II Kings 25:21).

7.   Jeremiah's Letter to the Captives of Babylon

Two things are very important contributing factors to the complex commonly called "the jitters," namely, a frustrated sense of time and of place. Jeremiah was the stabalizer of the captives in both respects. He had foretold and prepared the minds of the people for their displacement to Babylon. He also told them how long they would have to stay away from their homeland.

Within the land, during the reign of Jehoiakim, a false prophet, Hananiah, had falsely consoled the people that within two years Nebuchadnezzar's yoke would be broken. In that instance, Jeremiah was vindicated at the expense of death to the false prophet (Jeremiah 28).

Similarly, in Babylon, false prophets in the name of the LORD fostered and spread abroad the idea of a very short captivity (Jeremiah 29). It appears that the prophets named were not only self-appointed, but their doctrine was accompanied by immoral living and immoral influence. In a letter Jeremiah denounced them and counselled the people to settle down, and to adjust themselves in keeping with a seventy-year captivity. He encouraged them to raise families, to build homes, and thus to develop national strength. Thus, Jeremiah taught the Jews the attitude which in subsequent centuries they have never failed to manifest, which is that of making the best of their circumstances.

8.　Ezekiel's Ministry to the Captives

It is necessary to ponder the lot of the captives in order to fully appreciate the nature of Ezekiel's ministry to them. Away from the temple, out of their promised land, and in a relation of slavery to a pagan people, there was every opportunity for doubt and futility to sieze their minds. No associations in their lives seemed to point them to God. This is the temptation of every believer when he must be separated from home, from the church of his youth, and must go forth into a strange environment. His sense of God's presence and power, in fact of God's reality, are apt to suffer.

Under such circumstances Ezekiel was led to employ teaching strategy remarkably suited to the occasion. His prophecy begins with a new and revitalized picture of God's sovereignty; there is a transcendently high and glorious throne, and from the throne there is a voice, the voice of God; and to the prophet there is a commission to prophesy (chapters 1-3). Thus, the basic facts of religion were established: God's existence, his supreme sovereignty, his revelation, and his appointment of a prophet.

There follows in chapters 4-24 a series of object lessons conveying for the most part rudimentary instruction, direct guidance, and vivid disclosures signifying the meaning of the times.

In chapters 25-32 and 35 there are pictured the destinies of Israel's former national neighbors, a realistic recital of the roll of Sheol.

In chapters 33-34 God is contrasted with Israel's past unfaithful shepherds.

Chapters 36 and 37 are chapters portraying Israel's restoration.

Chapters 38 and 39 picture the judgment of God upon godless hordes gathered against God's restored people.

The final chapters of the prophecy (40-48) picture restored Israel as the source of glory and grace to the whole world.

Thus, Ezekiel was God's teacher, sent to minister grace to a people who were under severe divine chastisement, to teach people who had forsaken God for things, but who now, having nothing left, needed to know the source of all things.

9.   Daniel the Prophet of the Times of the Gentiles

Daniel's life spanned the full length of the captivity, extending from 606 B. C. and continuing into the times of the Medo-Persian supremacy. It may have seemed, as Daniel left Jerusalem among the first captives, and as he risked the king's wrath for refusing his meats, that it was indeed a very venturesome thing to "dare to be a Daniel." Yet, after Nebuchadnezzar and all of his successors were dead, Daniel was much alive.

Daniel lived in an altitude that transcended human sovereignties. At this height God gave him a perspective that affords the key of all later history. Across the bleak landscape of subsequent times he saw the successive imperialists under whom the saints of God would be subjects, and at the end of this succession he saw, unmistakably, though mysteriously, the establishment of God's eternal kingdom upon earth.

The book of Daniel is the primer of prophecy. The first lesson of this primer is chapter two. The lesson is set forth in terms of an image seen by King Nebuchadnezzar in a dream. The interpretation of the dream is fully given. All that remains for the reader is to compare the dream and its interpretation with the facts of history. As a result he will discover the times in which we are now living, and he will be made aware of the great crisis which still awaits the world.

Some significant observations and considerations may be made of the facts of the accompanying diagram. First, the course of human history is set forth as a succession of governments of declining glory, from gold to clay. In the times of the feet the divided condition and the vulnerability of government are the noteworthy characteristics. There is no natural unifying element.

Secondly, it is to be observed that this image is to be regarded

Daniel's Prophetic Image

THE DREAM (Daniel 2:31-35)   THE INTERPRETATION (2:36-45)

Parts	Interpretation	Suggested Fulfillment
Head of gold	Nebuchadnezzar's kingdom Babylon	The Neo-Babylonian Empire (606-538 B. C.)
Breast and arms of silver	An inferior kingdom	The Medo-Persian Empire (538-333 B. C.)
Belly and thigh of brass	A world kingdom	The Grecian Empire (333-63 B. C.)
Legs of iron	A kingdom strong as iron. It breaks into pieces and subdues.	The Roman Empire (63 B. C.-476 A. D.)
Feet of iron and clay	Division of the iron kingdom and mingling with other nations. Parts fall apart.	Romance, Germanic, and other nations (476 A. D. to ....)
Destroying stone: Great mountain	God will set up a kingdom. It will not be destroyed. It will not pass on its sovereignty. It will break up and consume all other kingdoms. It will stand forever.	God's kingdom is now being preached to all nations and entered into by repentance and faith. The stone has not yet been cast. Christians are to pray for the coming of God's kingdom.

Figure 28

as in existence until the whole is destroyed. The picture given us is that of human imperialism, particularly the imperialism which dominates Israel and the Church. The whole image might be named, after its head, Babylon. Thus, we have the explanation for the fact that in the Apocalypse, Babylon appears for judgment (Rev. 17-18)—Babylon, not in the head stage, but in the toe stage.

Thirdly, the declension of human governments and the destruction of the toe kingdoms, casts out as erroneous, any view which rests our faith and hope in the achievement, through social evolution, of an ideal world order.

Fourthly, it is significant to consider the preparatory phase of God's kingdom. The stone of destruction is fashioned without hand. This brief word reminds us of Isaiah's prophecy of the child which would be born, upon whose shoulder authority would rest, and whose sovereignty was to increase without end upon the throne of David (Isa. 9:6-7). That stone has already been manifest to the world. Some have fallen upon it in repentance and faith.

Upon others, impenitent and rebellious, the stone will be cast and it will grind them to powder (note Psalms 118:22; Matt. 21:42-44). Those who spurn the blood of the Lamb (John 1:29) will finally encounter the wrath of the Lamb (Rev. 6:16).

Simultaneous with this passing of successive human governments, Daniel was told, God would be accomplishing a personal redemptive work. "Many shall be purified, and made white, and tried; but the wicked shall do wickedly: and none of the wicked shall understand; but the wise shall understand." These, with Daniel, will first rest, then be resurrected, and then be permitted to stand in their lot "at the end of the days" (Daniel 12).

The pattern of prophecy thus set forth in the second chapter of Daniel is further supplemented by other chapters in the book of Daniel. Chapter seven presents the same succession of governments under different symbols, and with significant details not given in the more general pattern of chapter two. Chapter eight it is commonly believed, gives symbols corresponding to the second and third divisions of the image of chapter two. Chapter nine, under a calendar of seventy weeks ("times" of unspecified length), sets forth what was to be accomplished between the time of the restoration proclamation of Cyrus and the times of the Messiah. Daniel's prophecy closes with a picture of military conquests in the Persian, Grecian, and later periods, and with a picture, not clearly understood by Daniel himself, of intensified tribulation for God's people. Wickedness would increase, but at the same time many of God's people would be purified, made white, and tried. At the end of it all, Daniel clearly saw the deliverance of God's people, the resurrection, and the new order established by the "God of Heaven."

10. Discussion and Review

1. Since it was God who led Abraham out of Babylonia, why did he now condemn Abraham's nation to be delivered to Babylon?

2. Distinguish between the sovereignty of Israel as a nation and God's sovereignty. How was God's sovereignty related to the sovereignty of Babylon? What comfort is there for God's people in God's sovereignty?

3. Draw from memory the parallelogram of captivity dates.

4. Name the six Babylonian rulers of this period in their proper sequence and relate identifying features of each.

5. Why was the captivity seventy years in length?

6. What issue did Jeremiah clarify in his letter to the captives?

7. Characterize Ezekiel's ministry as to time, place, manner of prophesying, and his message.

8. Depict the main features of Daniel's view of the future. Was it hopeful? Explain.

11. Character Review

Identify:

Jeremiah	Nebuchadnezzar	Nabonidus
Ezekiel	Evil-Merodach	Belshazzar
Daniel	Neriglissar	Hananiah

12. Select Memory Passages

Ezekiel 3:17; 18:20; 31-32; 22:30; 33:11, 31; 34:34; 36:25-27; 39:7; Daniel 2:44; 12:13.

13. Bibliography

Moller, Wilhelm. "The Book of Ezekiel," *The International Standard Bible Encyclopedia*. Vol. II. 1071-1081.

Morgan, G. Campbell. *Living Messages of the Books of the Bible*, Vol. I. "The Messages of Ezekiel," pp. 127-144. "The Message of Daniel," pp. 145-164. New York: Fleming H. Revell Co.

Nichols, T. "The Captivity," *The International Standard Bible Encyclopedia*. Vol. I. pp. 569-576.

Torrey, Charles Cutler. *Pseudo-Ezekiel and the Original Prophecy*. New Haven: 1930.

Young, Edward J. *The Prophecy of Daniel*. Grand Rapids: Eerdmans. 1951. This is a new commentary on Daniel which brings to the student a wealth of assistance in arriving at the true meaning of the book. Though scholarly, it can be used successfully by students on all levels.

Wilson, R. Dick. "The Book of Daniel," *The International Standard Bible Encyclopedia*. Vol. II. pp. 783-787.

Chapter 21

THE JEWS UNDER PERSIAN SUPREMACY

—Restoration under the Decrees of Cyrus and Darius
(536-485 B. C.)

1. Reading Assignment: I Kings 25; II Chronicles 36;

Ezra 1-6; Haggai; Zechariah

(Read the Bible first)

2. Introduction

Limits of the Restoration

In speaking of the Restoration period, we must not suppose that anything like a full national restoration took place. Only a handful, relatively, of about 50,000 persons returned to Jerusalem under Zerubbabel in 536 B. C. There was no restoration to political independence. Spiritual restoration was, with a few exceptions, spasmodic and very feeble. Furthermore, beyond the quite favorable Persian rule lay times in which the yoke of tyranny would severely remind the Jews that they had not yet realized a restoration to former blessings.

The Continuing Divine Purpose

The Restoration period continued to be proving ground for Israel. Many made nothing of the opportunity to return and reestablish worship to their God in the land promised to Abraham. Those who returned exhibited a chronic tendency to become discouraged, to set aside God's law, and to permit evils of one kind or another to arise. God continued, however, to keep his spiritual leaders among them during these days. As Daniel had prophesied, many would be purified, and made white, and tried.

RESTORATION CHRONOLOGY

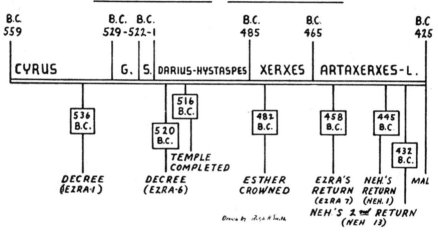

Figure 29

3. Historical Outline

I. **Return of Jews under Zerubbabel (Ezra 1-2)**

1. The Decree of Cyrus (1:1-4; II Chron. 36:22-23)
   (1) Isaiah's prophecy was fulfilled (Isa. 44:28; 45:1-4)
   (2) Jeremiah's prophecy was fulfilled (Jer. 25:12)
   (3) Date: First year of Cyrus (536 B. C.)
   (4) The prime mover: "the LORD"
   (5) Provisions: The decree included an order to build the house of God by a policy of free participation of Jews, and voluntary free gifts of materials and help

2. Personnel of the Returning Company (1:5—2:67)

   (1) Tribes: Judah, Benjamin, and others
   (2) Census: 42,360 people; 7337 servants; 200 singers; 736 horses; 245 mules; 435 camels; 6720 asses

3. Arrival and Settlement (2:68-70)
   (1) Contributions for the house of God (2:68-69)
   (2) They all dwelt "in their cities" (2:70)

II. **Reestablishment of Worship (Ezra 3-4)**

1. Worship and Work (Chapter 3)
   (1) The altar of burnt offerings was observed (3:4-6)
   (2) Time: seventh month of 536 B. C.

(3) Morning and evening offerings were made

(4) The Feast of the seventh month was observed

(5) Appropriations were made for temple rebuilding (3:7)

(6) Leadership and labor pool for the task was provided (3:8)

(7) Procedure by work and praise (3:9-11)
Workmen at the task
Priests with trumpets
Sons of Asaph with cymbals
The people with the shout of their voices

(8) Mingled lamentation and joy upon the completion of the temple foundation (3:12-13)

2. Adversaries — Rebuilding Halted (Chapter 4)[1]

(1) Early opposition (4:1-5, 24)

(2) Later opposition (4:6-23)

3. Temple Rebuilding Resumed and Finished (Ezra 5-6)

(1) Haggai and Zechariah prophesy (Ezra 5:1; see their messages)

(2) Zerubbabel and Jeshua "rose up" and "began to build" (5:2)

(3) Governor Tatnai questions leaders (5:3-5)

(4) Tatnai writes to Darius (5:6-17)

(5) Decree of Cyrus is recovered (6:1-5)

(6) Darius issues a vigorous decree (6:6-12)

(7) The decrees are executed (6:13-14)

(8) The building completed (6:15)

(9) The rebuilt house dedicated (6:16-22)
1) It was done with joy
2) The tribes offered sacrifices
3) The priests were assigned to service
4) The Passover was kept
5) The people separated from the filthiness of the heathen
6) The feast of unleavened bread was kept

---

[1]Chapter four deals with the subject of opposition in a general way. Various attempts have been made to explain the order of the Persian Kings in whose reigns the persecutions of this chapter occurred. The student should fix clearly in mind the order of the Persian kings as presented in the Introduction. The kings referred to are Darius (vs. 5), Ahasuerus (vs. 6), Artaxerxes (vss. 7-23), Darius (vs. 24). Some historians have felt that an intelligible interpretation of the chapter makes it necessary to assume that Ahasuerus refers to Gambyses and that Artaxerxes refers to Pseudo-Smerdis, and that the chapter therefore describes opposition through these two reigns up to the time of Darius' decree of chapter six. The trouble with this view is that it has no historical support, since these two kings are nowhere given these names. Rather, it would seem that the author, in treating the general subject of opposition, projects the reader ahead of the immediate oppositon, giving the course of opposition under the whole history of the Restoration. The following simple formula sets forth this parenthetical projection: vss. 1-5 (6-23) 24.

Coming to chapter five, the "Then" with which it begins refers back to the "Then" which introduces verses four and five of chapter four. The prophets Haggai and Malachi encouraged the drooping spirits of the builders and kept them at the job until the decree of Darius in his second year put down the opposition.

4. Leadership Personnel in the Restoration

Foremost in the restoration leadership personnel was God himself. He planned for the restoration long before the Israelites were carried captive and made known the time and the means for its accomplishment to the prophets Isaiah and Jeremiah.

Next in order is Cyrus. The "Lord stirred up the spirit of Cyrus," and ordered him to rebuild the house of the God of heaven in Jerusalem. The decree issued by Cyrus was the basis for a favorable attitude in the Persian Court toward the Jews during the whole two hundred year period of Persian supremacy.

Zerubbabel (Sheshbazzar), a Judahite of royal blood, was the general leader of the returning captives in 536 B. C.

Jeshua, a representative of the priests, was Zerubbabel's right hand associate.

Under these men were the priests, the Levites, the singers, the porters, and the Nethinims (non-Levitical servants of the priests).

The prophets Haggai and Zechariah deserve a much larger place in the Restoration history than they are accorded in the book of Ezra. (Ezra 5:1). Referring to the books of these prophets we observe that it was they who stirred the people to action under the leadership of Zerubbabel.

5. The Prophecies of Haggai and Zechariah

Of these two men, Ewald suggests that Haggai was the senior prophet. This may be implied from the fact that his time appears first (Ezra 5:1; 6:14), and from the speech of Haggai in Haggai 2:3. An ancient tradition says that he was born in Jerusalem, carried into captivity by Nebuchadnezzar, and commissioned by Cyrus to return with Zerubbabel. Tradition also accords these prophets places in the Great Synagogue established in Ezra's time.

Ezra 6:1 indicates, simply, that these two prophets prophesied, when through adversity the rebuilding of the temple was halted. The context indicates that when they had prophesied, Zerubbabel and Jeshua led the people in resuming the work. It is only by referring to the two books of these prophets that we learn what it was in their prophecies that inspired the people.

Haggai's prophecy is made up of four short discourses. In the first (Haggai 1), he probed the excuses of the people who were saying that it was not an opportune time to build. Haggai pointed out to them that they did not reason in this way when it came to building their own "cieled houses." In the second discourse (2:1-9) Haggai encouraged the people by assuring them that the latter glory of this temple would be greater than that of the first (2:9 A. R. V.). In the third discourse (2:10-19) the prophet taught the principle that God takes special interest in the prosperity of those who put his interests first. In his closing discourse (2:20-23) the prophet pictured the Messiah's acquittal of his people, and their larger final restoration.

The prophecy of Zechariah begins with a simple thesis: Your fathers displeased God and went into captivity—see that you profit by their mistake (1:1-6).

Eight night visions were seen by the prophet:

1. The vision of the horsemen who declare God's jealousy for Jerusalem (1:7-17).

2. The vision of the four horns and the four carpenters, signifying God's judgment in the captivity in relation to his mercies in restoration (1:18-21).

3. The vision of the measuring line, indicating that Jerusalem is to be rebuilt and that the LORD will be in her midst (chapter 2).

4. The vision of mitred Joshua and the Branch, signifying the blessed existence of God's people in a future day (chapter 3; also 6:9-14).

5. The vision of the golden candlestick signifying the finished glory and future power associated with the house, the foundation of which is being laid (chapter 4).

6. The vision of the flying roll, signifying the curse of evil to be visited upon the houses of evil-doers (5:1-14).

7. The vision of the ephah and the woman, signifying how evil had been contained and carried into Shinar (Babylon) through the captivity (5:5-11).

8. The vision of four chariots signifying God's messengers into all parts of the earth, their present mission being to still the spirit of vengeance from the north (6:1-8). (Assyria, Babylon, and Persia make their way into Palestine from the north.)

An interesting inquiry from the people of Bethel is considered in chapters seven and eight. During the captivity four fasts had been ordained commemorating four events respectively:

1. The capture of Jerusalem by Nebuchadnezzar
2. The burning of the temple
3. The murder of Gedaliah
4. The siege of Jerusalem

The question was this: Shall these fasts continue to be observed? Zechariah's answer, though given somewhat indirectly, was that

God's greatest concern is not that his people fast but that they heed his word. Had that been done, there would have been no occasion for these fasts. Beyond this, Zechariah pointed the inquiries, in chapter eight, to the time when, through God's mercies, fasting would give way to the joyful feasts of the LORD.

In chapters 12-14 Zechariah turns the eyes of the restored captives from their past unfaithful shepherds to the shepherd-care of their God. The section is rich in its portrayal of the mercies and the blessings of the future Messiah.

6. The Adversaries

Who were the "adversaries" who wanted to build with Zerubbabel, and why were they rejected? Reference to our past studies contains the answer.

Samaria had been desolated by Shalmaneser, king of Assyria. He carried the Israelites into captivity. Then Esar-haddon colonized Samaria with people from Babylon and other foreign provinces who brought with them their idols. Upon this planting of idolatry Esar-haddon provided the teaching work of a Levitical priest. Samaria, accordingly, became a mixed race with a mixed religion. These facts make obvious the wisdom of rejecting these too-willing helpers.

7. The Temple of Zerubbabel

The Restoration, in its primary significance, centered in the temple of the LORD. God's command to Cyrus specified this. Not the walls, the streets, nor the dwellings, but this house was to be built; all other construction would of course follow. A temple might have been built in Babylon, but that could have none of the associations of God's covenant with Israel. That covenant had to do with the promised land.

Zerubbabel's temple may have been built upon the foundation of Solomon's. We do not know how much of the old structure could be reconditioned. It was obvious to the older men who had been carried captive that the finished structure would not compare with the Solomonic temple. This they lamented (Ezra 3:10-13). Haggai's second discourse assures them, however, that the true glory of the latter house will be even greater than that of the former (2:1-9). Why? Because it would be associated with fuller manifestations of

the times of the Messiah. There was less gold but there would be
greater glory.

8. Kings of the Persian Period

Cyrus the Great (549-529 B. C.)

Cyrus the Great, the founder of the Persian Empire was a remarkable character. He brought Persia from the status of a group
of disorganized provinces to a well organized state. He loosed it from
the political dominion of Media and then induced the Medes to throw off
allegiance to their king Astyages and to annex their domains with
Persia thus forming the Medo-Persian empire. Cyrus was a statesman by nature. His policy differed from that of the Babylonians
regarding subject peoples. While Babylon ruthlessly over-rode the
customs and religious beliefs of her peoples, Cyrus, being a poly-
theist was disposed to show honor to the gods of the various con-
quered peoples over whom he ruled. This fact was of great significance so far as the Jews were concerned. No one but God could
have set the time for the rise of Cyrus, and he did it with remarkable
precision long in advance of the time of need (Isa. 44:28—45:4).

Gambyses (529-521 B. C.)

Cyrus, before his death, appointed his eldest son Gambyses as
his successor. To a younger son Bardes or Smerdis he left several
provinces. Shortly after Gambyses began to reign he ordered Smerdis
to be secretly killed. While Gambyses was suppressing an uprising in
Egypt a psuedo-Smerdis arose and usurped the emperial title. Some
question remained in Gambyses' mind as to whether his servants
whom he had commanded to secretly slay Smerdis had betrayed
him or whether the usurper was a stranger. The opinion appears to
have prevailed that the usurper was Gomates whom Gambyses had
left in charge of the court. Under these circumstances Gambyses
took his own life.

Pseudo-Smerdis (521 B. C.)

Pseudo-Smerdis was never substantially seated in power. Upon
his death in battle, Darius Hystaspes, of royal succession was prepared to take the emperial title.

Darius I (Hystaspes) (521-485 B. C.)

When Darius Hystaspes came to power he faced revolts in the provinces on every hand. In putting down these revolts Darius distinguished himself as an organizer. He relaxed the terrorism of Gambyses and gave fuller recognition to the Privy Council of each state. Over these he appointed satraps; not less than twenty such satrapies were formed.

Darius showed great kindness to Israel as is shown in Ezra 5-6, practically underwriting the temple rebuilding project, which was completed in 516 B. C.

The latter part of his reign was taken up with war against the Greeks, in which is seen the beginning of the transition from the second to the third division of sovereignty prophetically set forth in the dream-image of Daniel 2.

Ahasuerus (Xerxes I, 485-465 B. C.)

Xerxes the father of Artaxerxes I has been described as "handsome in person and kingly in bearing; but weak, vain, fickle, and despotic." Early in his reign he successfully subdued discordant elements in Egypt. He is characterized as the fourth king of Persia in the prophecy of Daniel (11:2; 10:1). It was said concerning him: He "shall be far richer than they all: and by his strength and through his riches he shall stir up all against the realm of Grecia." In history he is famous for his wars with Greece, although the Greeks finally poured disastrous defeat upon his armies and cut short his power in the west.

Our historical knowledge of Ahasuerus in relation to God's people Israel is confined to Ezra 4:6 and the book of Esther. It is evident that the rebuilding of the walls of Jerusalem suffered stoppage during his reign.

Artaxerxes I (Longimanus, 465-425 B. C.)

Artaxerxes (the long handed), the son of Ahasuerus, early in his reign exhibited an approachable spirit, which turned out to great advantage for the Jews. It is very possible that Esther's influence is reflected in this attitude. Artaxerxes' acquaintance with Jerusalem was progressive. His attention was first called to it by Rehum his chancellor who impressed him with the idea that it was a dangerous city and that its rebuilding must stop. He accordingly ordered a temporary stoppage of work in Jerusalem (Ezra 4:7-22). Evidently, Artaxerxes informed himself regarding the decrees of Cyrus and Darius, for in the seventh year of his reign he fully supported Ezra's return to Jerusalem, and in his twentieth year he sponsored the return of Nehemiah to promote the reconstruction of the Jerusalem walls.

Other Persian Kings

Later Persian kings, not referred to in Scriptures, were: Xerxes II who reigned two months, Sogdianus who reigned seven months, Darius II (Nothus, 423-405 B. C.), Artaxerxes II (Mnemmon 405-358 B. C.), Artaxerxes III (Ochus, 358-337 B. C.), Arses (337-335 B. C.), and Darius III (Codomanus, 335-331 B. C.).

9. Favorable Conditions of Persian Rule

The two hundred years of Persian rule were, in general, favorable to the Jews. The Persian kings were not the absolute monarchs which the Babylonians had been. Most of them were Zoroastrians and adhered to or were favorable to monotheism. They adhered to a policy of permitting each province to have its own religion. Through these two centuries the Jews, therefore, were perfectly free to worship God. In fact, other peoples were required to permit them to do so, which meant that they were actually protected in carrying on their worship.

10. Discussion and Review

1. Show from Isaiah, Ezra, and II Chronicles the fact of God's early planning for the restoration of the captives.

2. Show that the decree of Cyrus was the fulfillment of Jeremiah's prophecy.

3. What were the provisions of Cyrus' decree?

4. Indicate the extent by numbers and tribes of the return under Zerubbabel. In what other respects was the restoration limited?

5. What continuing divine purpose may be observed in the restoration?

6. Who were the important leaders in the restoration?

7. What part did the prophets Haggai and Zechariah play?

8. What were the leading ideas of Haggai's prophecy?

9. What was the thesis of Zechariah?

10. Enumerate Zechariah's eight night visions.

11. What counsel did Zechariah give regarding fasts?

12. What was the relevancy of the last three chapters of Zechariah's prophecy to the need of those times?

13. Who were the adversaries and why was their help refused?

14. Appraise the architectural importance of the rebuilt temple. Appraise its importance otherwise. Explain.

15. Enumerate the principal Persian rulers of this period identifying them in relation to the captives.

16. State briefly the actual state of well-being enjoyed by the Jews under Persian rule.

11. Character Review

Identify:

Zerubbabel	Haggai	Darius-Hystaspes
Cyrus	Zechariah	
Jeshua	Tatnai	

12. Select Memory Passages

Zechariah 1:14b-15; 2:10-12; 4:6b; 8:22-23; 9:9; 12:10; 13:1, 8-9; 14:9

13. Bibliography

Fairweather, William. *From the Exile to the Advent.* Book II, Chapt. I, "The Jews under Cyrus and His Successors." Chapt. II, "The Jews under Darius." Edinburgh: T. & T. Clark.

Mears, John W. *From Exile to Overthrow.* Chapt. VI, "The Return from the Exile." Chapt. VII, "The Second Temple." Philadelphia: Presbyterian Board of Publication.

Miller, Dorothy Ruth. *A Handbook of Ancient History in Bible Light.* Chapter XVII, "The Persian Empire." New York: Fleming H. Revell Co.

Robinson, George L. "Haggai," *The International Standard Bible Encyclopedia.* Vol. II. pp. 1317-1319.

Robinson, George L. "The Book of Malachi," *The International Standard Bible Encyclopedia.* Vol. III. pp. 1969-1970.

Robinson, George L. "Zechariah," *The International Standard Bible Encyclopedia.* Vol. V. pp. 3136-3140.

Chapter 22

THE JEWS UNDER PERSIAN SUPREMACY

—The Times of Esther
(483-479 .... B. C.)

1. **Reading Assignment:** Book of Esther

(Read the Bible first)

2. Introduction—Time Setting of the Book of Esther

The book of Esther, although classed by the Jews with the Writings, is of great historical value. It is important for the picture which it affords of the state of the great majority of Jews still scattered through the Persian Empire.

Between the sixth and seventh chapters of Ezra there is a sixty year period of silence, except for the brief notice of Ezra 6:4 and the account of the book of Esther. The book of Esther opens in the third year of Ahasuerus (483 B. C.), thirty-three years after the rebuilt temple was dedicated at Jerusalem and twenty-five years before the return of the second company of captives to Jerusalem under Ezra in 458 B. C.

The book begins with tremendous but vain display of the "riches of his (Ahasuerus') glorious kingdom and the honour of his excellent majesty" for a period of 144 days. All of his princes and servants attended. It climaxed with a seven day feast for all the people present in the palace. Queen Vashti made a feast for the women of the court. Wine was set forth in abundance in costly vessels of gold. This scene of vanity closed unhappily as Vashti declined the king's request that she openly display her beauty. Such refusal, the king and

248

and his counsellors agreed, would have to be punished. Vashti accordingly was deposed from her throne.

It is of interest that this protracted show just preceded and was perhaps designed to foster morale for what was intended to be an overwhelming military invasion of Greece (Note Daniel 11:2).

During the three or four years following the deposing of Vashti (482-479 B. C.) Ahasuerus assembled the forces of his realm in his historic abortive attempt to conquer Greece. In 481 B. C. he invaded Greece, but was stopped at Thermopylae by a small but gallant band of Spartans. In the following year at the naval battle of Salamis he witnessed with his own eyes the annihilation of a large part of his fleet. He returned to his palace at Shushan. The remaining part of the book of Esther (chapters 2-10) obviously belongs to the times following 479 B. C.

3. Historical Outline

I. **The Show of King Ahasuerus (Chapter 1)**

1. Extent of His Kingdom: 127 Provinces Reaching from India to Ethiopia (1:1)
2. Place of His Palace: Shushan (Susa) (1:2)
3. Time: Third Year of His Reign (482 B. C.) (1:3)
4. Guests: His Princes and Servants, the Nobles and Princes of the Provinces (1:3) Also Many People (1:5)
5. What He Shows: ". . . . the riches of his glorious kingdom and the honour of his excellent majesty . . . ." (1:4)
6. Duration of the Show: 151 Days
7. Special Feasts:
   (1) For the people (1:5-8)
   (2) Vashti's feast for the court women (1:9)
8. Intoxication: All who care to drink are given freely of the king's wine
9. The Intoxicated King's Request: That His Queen Vashti Appear before the King to Show the People and the Princes Her Beauty (1:10-11)
10. Vashti's Response: Refusal (1:12)
11. Ahasuerus' Reaction: Anger (1:12)
12. The Reasoning of the King's Counsellors: That in Order to Maintain the Authority of Husbands over Their Wives, Vashti's Disobedience Must Be Punished (1:13-20)
13. The King's Decree: That Vashti Come No More before the King, and That Her Royal Estate Be Given to Another That Is Better Than She (1:21-22)

II. **Esther Succeeds Vashti (Chapter 2)**
1. Search for a Successor Extends to All Kingdoms
2. Esther as a Prospect (2:5-20)
   (1) Her identity: a foster daughter of Mordecai, her cousin, whose parents had been among the Benjamites in the captivity of Jehoiachin's time
   (2) Her beauty: She easily becomes a contestant, and wins the king's favor, and the favor of all.
   (3) Her concealed identity (2:10)
3. Mordecai in the Background (2:5-23)
   (1) His position: He sits in the king's gate
   (2) His counsel: He advises Esther secretly
   (3) His vital service: He has spared the king's life

4. Time of Esther's Succession: Seventh Month of the Seventh Year of Ahasuerus (478 B. C.)

III. Haman's Plot against the Jews (Chapter 3)

1. Haman's Identity: an Agagite Official

2. His Promotion: above All the Princes
   Homage to him is commanded

3. His Problem: Mordecai will not do obeisance to him.

4. His Appeal to a Weak King: There is a people scattered in the realm who should be destroyed because (1) they have different laws, and (2) they do not keep the king's laws. By way of further appeal, Haman makes it clear that if they are destroyed, the spoils for the king's treasury will be 10,000 talents ($10,000,000)

5. The King's Decree: ". . . . to destroy, to kill, and to cause to put to death all Jews, both young and old, little children and women in one day . . . . and to take the spoil of them for a prey"

6. Time of Haman's Appeal: 12th Year (472 B. C.), 1st Month (3:7)

7. Time of the Scheduled Execution: 12th Year, 12th Month, 13th Day (3:13)

IV. Esther Responds to Challenge (Chapter 4)

1. The Appeal: Mordecai and the Jews in all the realm being in a state of mourning, Hatach informs Esther and conveys an appeal from Mordecai to make supplication to the king (4:1-9)

2. Esther States the Risk: No one may come into the king's presence uncalled for, unless the king holds out his sceptre. To appeal to the king might involve death

3. Mordecai Interprets the Occasion (4:13-14)
   (1) The Jews are doomed, Esther included
   (2) Providence has placed Esther in the place of opportunity in the crisis
   (3) God may raise up help elsewhere

4. Esther Takes Up the Challenge (4:15-17)
   (1) All Jews are to fast for three days
   (2) Esther's Memorable Decision: "I go in unto the king, which is not according to the law: and if I perish, I perish"

V. Esther's Banquets (Chapters 5-7)

(Accepted by the King, Esther invites the king and Haman to a banquet (5:1-5).)

1. The First Banquet (5:6-8)
   Esther, given the opportunity of a request, asks that there be another banquet on the following day at which she will disclose her request

2. An Eventful Night between Banquets (5:9—6:14)
   (1) Haman, elated, reports his advancements to his family, but also, with resentment tells of Mordecai's unbending will (5:9-13). Gallows are built for Mordecai (5:14)
   (2) The King, unable to sleep, has the court records read. He discovers that no reward has been given to Mordecai for having saved his life (2:21-23). Haman, happening in to request permission to hang Mordecai, is consulted as to a suitable way of honoring a very worthy person. Thinking that no person other than himself (Haman) can be in the king's mind, he advises that royal garments be given him and that he be led through the streets seated upon a horse led by the king's most noble prince
   (3) Haman, the most noble prince, is assigned the task of thus honoring Mordecai
   (4) Haman and his house discuss the forebodings of doom (6:12-13)
   (5) It being banquet time, Haman is hurried off by the king's chamberlains (6:14)

3. The Second Banquet (Chapter 7)
   (1) Esther pleads for her life and the life of her people against a plotting foe, Haman being unmasked as the foe

(2) The king in wrath goes aside; Haman throws himself upon the mercy of Esther, only intensifying the king's anger

(3) Learning of the gallows which Haman has built, the king o r d e r s Haman's execution thereon

(4) Haman's position is given to Mordecai (8:1-3)

VI. **The New Decree (8:3—10)**
  1. Esther's Appeal for a Reverse order (8:3-6)
  2. The Appeal Granted (8:7-10)
    Note: While the first decree can not, by Persian jurisprudence, be revoked, yet Mordecai is permitted to give a decree which may have an equivalent value.
  3. Mordecai's Letter (8:11-14)
    Note: It gives to all Jews the right to exercise vengeance upon their enemies on the day which has been set for their execution.
  4. The Favorable Position of the Jews (8:15-17)
    Note: Considering that Mordecai, the highest officer of the realm is a Jew, the power of the empire is actually back of the second decree. The situation actually makes it desirable to become a Jew in order to be safe.
  5. The Day of Execution (13th of Adar) (9:1-11)
    (1) All people fear the Jews
    (2) Provincial rulers, lieutenants, deputies, and officers of the king help the Jews, in fear of Mordecai
    (3) Extent of enemy victims: 500 men in the palace are slain

10 sons of Haman are included (No spoil is taken)

(4) Esther requests a second day extension of Mordecai's decree and the hanging of Haman's sons upon the gallows

6. The Second Day of Execution (14th of Adar)
  (1) Extent of victims:
    10 sons of Haman are hanged
    300 men of Shushan are slain
    (No spoil is taken)
    75,000 in provinces are slain
    (No spoil is taken)
  (2) Rest, feasting and gladness follow

7. The Third Day (15th of Adar)
  (1) Rest, feasting, and gladness continue

8. The Days of Purim Officially Set Apart (9:20-32)
  (1) Features of the days:
    Rest
    Feasting and joy
    Sending portions to one another
    Giving gifts to the poor

VII. **Mordecai's Greatness (Chapter 10)**
  1. The Wealth Which He Commands (10:1)
  2. The Record of His Deeds—in the Chronicles of Media and Persia (10:2)
  3. His Position and Influence (10:3)
    (1) Next to Ahasuerus
    (2) Great among the Jews
    (3) Accepted of the multitude of his brethren
    (4) Known for his beneficence
    (5) Speaks "peace to all his seed"

4.   The Identity of Mordecai

He was a Jewish inhabitant of Shushan whose great grandfather, Kish, a Benjamite, had been carried captive to Babylon with King Jeconiah (Jehoiachin) of Judah in 597 B. C. He was the cousin, and became the foster-father of Esther. The fact that he was stationed at the king's gate probably indicates that he had a task there, perhaps that of watchman. His discovery of a plot against the king's life would have been in keeping with such responsibility (2:21-24). The position to which he rose made of him an important figure in Jewish history, and the Jews to this day hold him in very high regard.

5. The Identity of Haman

He is introduced in Esther 3:1 as the son of Hamadetha the Agagite. The Targum and Josephus fancifully construe the term Agagite as referring to the Amalekite king of I Samuel 15:33, but this is groundless. Agag is known from an inscription of Sargon to be a province of Medo-Persia. He was elevated to the place of highest authority under the king sometime after the crowning of Esther.

6. The Feast of Purim

The deliverance of the Jews from Haman has been celebrated from the 12th year of Ahasuerus to this very day. The word "Purim" comes from "pur" meaning lots in reference to Haman's casting of lots for a date upon which to destroy the Jews (3:7). As is indicated in chapter nine, the feast lasted two days, the 14th and 15th of the twelfth month (Adar).

In modern times celebration begins on the evening before the 14th when the stars begin to shine. Candles are lighted as a sign of rejoicing. The people assemble in the synagogue for a service. After a prayer of thanksgiving, the book of Esther is read. When the reader comes to the word Haman, the congregation cries out, "May his name be blotted out." After the whole book has been read the congregation exclaims in concert, "Cursed be Haman; blessed be Mordecai; cursed be Zoresh (the wife of Haman); blessed be Esther; cursed be all idolaters; blessed be all Israelites, and blessed be Harbonak who hanged Haman."

The whole book is reread in the manner described above. Then, when all is over, all the congregation give themselves to merriment.

7. God in the Book of Esther

Some have questioned the canonicity of this book because in it there is no mention of the name of God. Such an objection has little weight as an argument against the fact, which, in the words of Urquart, is that "in the Jewish Canon Esther had not only a recognized, but also a distinguished place."[1] Maimonides, affirms that the book

---

[1] I. S. B. E., *The Book of Esther*, Vol. II, p. 1006.

was dictated by the Holy Spirit, and adds: "All the books of the Prophets, and all the Hagiographa shall cease in the days of the Messiah, except the volume of Esther; and too, that shall be as stable as the Pentateuch, and as the constitutions of the oral law which shall never cease."[1]

---

[1] Ibid.

The absence of the name of God certainly does not lessen its importance as religious literature. God is implicit in the book. Even though the atuhor does not specifically attribute Israel's deliverance to God he gives all of the facts which embody God's providence. The book simply tells the story without interpreting it.

The value of the book of Esther does not depend upon the spiritual level of the Jews of the dispersion anymore than the deliverance of the children of Israel from Egyptian bondage depended upon the spiritual state of the captives in Egypt. The important thing in both cases was that the people cried unto God. The three day fast after which Esther made her successful appearance before Ahasuerus clearly implied faith in God. Mordecai recognized the fact of a higher providence in Esther's coming to the kingdom to meet the crisis of the Jewish people.

The book of Esther stands as an assurance of God's continued providence in behalf of the Jews, not merely those who returned to Palestine after the Babylonian captivity, but of "all Israel." The Hamans of history have been numerous, but there has never failed to be a virile Jewish remnant. While the spiritual state of that remnant may be low, yet God's purging fires continue, as Daniel (chapter 12) said would be the case, and God will eventually "reverse" their oppression, reestablishing their sovereignty under the Messiah and purging the world of all their enemies.

Just as, under the decree of Mordecai, many Gentiles became Jews (8:17), so under the Messiah many Gentiles are, through faith, being grafted into the vine of the purged seed of Abraham (Romans 9).

8. Discussion and Review

1. Discuss the time setting of the Book of Esther.
2. Identify Mordecai.
3. Identify Haman.

4. Identify Xerxes (see Chapter XX).

5. Discuss the extent of Jewish influence in the Persian court after the rise of Mordecai. How does it compare with the influence of Joseph in Egypt?

6. Describe the modern observance of the Feast of Purim.

7. Answer the criticism that there is no mention of God in the book of Esther. Show that God is in the book.

9. Character Review

Identify:

Esther	Haman	Vashti
Mordecai	Ahasuerus	

10. Select Memory Passages

Esther 4:13-14, 16; 8:17b

11. Bibliography

Kuyper, Abraham. *Women of the Old Testament.* Grand Rapids: Zondervan.
   1. "Vashti," pp. 170-173.
   2. "Esther," pp. 173-176.
McGee, J. Vernon. *Exposition of the Book of Esther.* Wheaton: Van Kampen, 1951.
Morgan, G. Campbell. *Living Messages of the Books of the Bible.* "The Message of Esther." New York: Fleming Revell Pub. Co. Pp. 267-282.
Sangster, Margaret E. *The Women of the Bible.* Chapt. XXV, "Vashti, the Deposed." New York: The Christian Herald.
Sangster, Margaret E. *The Women of the Bible.* Chapt. XXVI, "Esther, the Savior of Her People." New York: The Christian Herald.
Urquart, John. "The Book of Esther," *The International Standard Bible Encyclopedia.* Vol. II. pp. 1005-1009.

Chapter 23

THE JEWS UNDER PERSIAN SUPREMACY

—The Leadership of Ezra, Nehemiah, and Malachi
(458-425 B. C.)

---

1. Reading Assignment
2. Introduction
3. Historical Outline
4. Ezra, the Vital Reformer
5. Nehemiah, A Statesman of Stature

6. Malachi, the Herald of a New Day
7. Character Review
8. Discussion and Review
9. Select Memory Passages
10. Bibliography

---

1. **Reading Assignment:** Ezra 7-10; Nehemiah; Malachi

(Read the Bible first)

---

2. Introduction

Seventy-eight years had passed since Zerubbabel had led the first band of captives in their return to Jerusalem. For fifty-eight years the Temple had been rebuilt. Haggai and Zechariah, whose inspiration had stirred the people from indifference when they ceased building, were now gone. One wonders why no mention is made of Jerusalem in the book of Esther. Had it ceased to be a matter of thought and concern? Had the Jews in Jerusalem stopped making history of sufficient importance to be noted? Was the cause of restoration at a stalemate?

The books of Ezra and Nehemiah tell all too plainly that the cause of God at Jerusalem needed to be championed by leaders who were men of God—men who loved his law, who regarded his honor, who would raise a banner for his cause. Such men were Ezra, Nehemiah, and Malachi.

3. Historical Outline

I. **The Return and Labors of Ezra (Ezra 7-10)**

1. Ezra's Lineage and Profession (7:1-6)

   (1) Of Hilkiah and Aaron

(2) A ready scribe in the law of Moses

2. Time: They journeyed from the first day of the first month until the first day of the fifth month of

255

the 7th year of Artaxerxes I (458 B. C.)

3. Personnel (1:7; 8:1-23): 1754 Males Or Approximately 7000 Persons
   (1) People
   (2) Priests
   (3) Levites
   (4) Singers
   (5) Porters
   (6) Nethinims

4. Ezra's Preparation (7:10)
   (1) He prepares his heart
   (2) He seeks God's law
   (3) He purposes to do God's law
   (4) He purposes to teach:
       1) Statutes
       2) Judgments

5. Artaxerxes' Decree (7:11-26)
   (1) Salutation (vss. 11-12)
   (2) Silver and gold shall be supplied
       1) To purchase animals for offerings
       2) For any other purposes
   (3) Vessels for the house of God to be provided
   (4) Order to treasurers beyond the river to give Ezra all needed assistance up to:
       1) 100 talents of silver
       2) 100 measures of wheat
       3) 100 baths of wine
       4) 100 baths of oil
       5) Salt (unlimited amount)
       6) "Whatsoever is commanded by the God of heaven"
   (5) Full tax exemption to be accorded to:
       1) Levites
       2) Singers
       3) Porters
       4) Nethinims
       5) Ministers of God's house
   (6) Judges and teachers are to be assigned
   (7) Full power of execution is given Ezra
   (8) Ezra's grateful response (7:27-28)

6. A Test of Faith—Need for a Military Escort (8:21-23)
   (1) Fast and humiliation
   (2) God's assurance of protection

7. Keepers of Treasures Appointed (8:24-30)
   (1) The treasures weighed
   (2) Delivery to be made at the temple chambers in Jerusalem
   (3) The keepers consecrated

8. Arrival at Jerusalem (8:31-36)
   (1) God's assurance made good (vs. 31)
   (2) Three days (of rest) (vs. 32)
   (3) Checking in of the treasures (vss. 33-34)
   (4) Burnt offerings sacrificed (vs. 35)
   (5) The king's commissions delivered to the satraps and governors, who respond with help (vs. 36)

9. Reforms of Ezra (Ezra 9-19)
   (1) The princes inform Ezra of mixed marriages (9:1-2)
   (2) Ezra mourns, confesses, and places the nation upon God's mercies (9:3-15)
   (3) Shechaniah points to the way of hope (10:1-4)
       1) By putting away all strange wives and children born to them (10:1-3)
       2) By assuring Ezra of backing (10:4)
   (4) Ezra assumes authority (10:5-44)
       1) A pledge of reform is required of priests, Levites, and people (10:5)
       2) An assembly of all Israel is required (10:6-8)
       3) The people assemble, trembling (10:8-14)
          a. Because of their sin
          b. Because of "great rain"
       4) Authority to make adjustments delegated to Jonathan and Jahaziah (10:15)
       5) Time of the reforming court session: From the first day of the tenth month to the first day of the first month —3 months (10:16-17)
       6) The roster of the offenders (10:18-44)

II. **The Return and Labors of Nehemiah (Neh. 1-12)**

1. Nehemiah in Persia (Chapters 1—2:8)
    (1) His position: Artaxerxes' cup-bearer
    (2) Hanani's report of Jerusalem saddens Nehemiah
    (3) Nehemiah accorded a leave of absence
    (4) Artaxerxes' commission
        1) Nehemiah made governor of Jerusalem
        2) Given an escort, letters, and access to supplies
2. Nehemiah's Governorship of Jerusalem (Neh. 2:9—12)
    (1) He surveys the dilapidated conditions (2:9-20)
    (2) The people are inspired to "rise up and build" with Nehemiah (2:18)
    (3) Nehemiah organizes the people to rebuild the walls (chapters 3-4)
        1) Each laborer and his helpers work a section
        2) Watchmen are placed
        3) The workmen are armed
        4) A signal system is effected
        5) They lodge within the walls in their work clothes
    (4) External opposition to the work (2:10, 19; chapters 4, 6)
        1) Successive forms of enemy reaction:
            a. Grief (2:10)
            b. Laughter and scorn (2:19)
            c. Anger (4:1)
            d. Ridicule (4:2-3)
            e. Greater anger (4:7)
            f. Conspiracy to fight (4:8)
        2) Israel's defense:
            a. Prayer and work (4:4-6)
            b. Prayer, guards, trumpets, work (4:9-23)
    (5) Internal Opposition (chapter 5)
        1) The people are oppressed by the usury of brethren (1-5)
        2) Nehemiah rebukes the nobles and rulers (6-10)
        3) Usury relinquished and property restored (11-13)
        4) Nehemiah's example: He serves without salary (14-19)

    (6) External opposition continued (chapter 6)
        1) By craft—three proposals:
            a. Four repeated appeals for a conference on the plains of Ono (vss. 1-4)
            b. False letter (verses 5-9)
            c. Appeal for a meeting in the house of God (verses 10-14)
        2) By envy—shame and defeat (vs. 16)
        3) By relationship complications (vss. 17-19)
    (7) Completion of the walls (6:1, 15)
    (8) Appointments (7:1-4)
        1) Rulers: Hanani and Hananiah
        2) Guards by watches
    (9) The lack of people in Jerusalem noted (7:4)
    (10) The register of Zerubbabel's company discovered (8:1-69)
    (11) Contributions of various groups (8:70-73)
    (12) Instruction in the Law (chapters 8-10)
        1) Reading by Ezra (8:1-8)
        2) Response: sorrow and joy (8:9-12)
        3) The Feast of Tabernacles kept (8:13-18)
        4) Continuation of the assembly with fasting, confession, reading, separation, worship, and with a covenant (chapter 9)
        5) The signers of the covenant (10:1-27)
        6) The points of the covenant:
            a. The people will not intermarry with other people (10:30)
            b. They will keep God's sabbaths (10:31)
            c. They assess themselves for the temple needs (10:32-33)
            d. They provide for the wood offering (10:34)
            e. They pledge the first fruits (10:35-37)
            f. They promise to give their tithes (10:38-39)

g. Volunteers offer to live in Jerusalem (11:1-2)

(13) Settlements and appointments (11:3 to 12:47)

  1) The names of Jerusalem dwellers (11:3-20)

  2) The names of outsiders (11:21-36)

  3) Register of priests and Levites and their succession (12:1-26; 44-47)

(14) Dedication of the walls with great rejoicing (12:27-43)

III. **Nehemiah's Second Labors in Jerusalem (Chapter 13)**

1. Time (432 B. C.)
(Nehemiah had first come to Jerusalem in 445 B. C. After 12 years he returned (13:6), which would have been in 433 B. C. Then after some months, perhaps in response to reports of new sins at Jerusalem, he returned to rectify matters.)

2. Conviction is wrought by reading the law (13:1-3)

3. Forbidden Relationships (13:4-9; 23-31)

  (1) Tobiah the Ammonite given temple quarters

  (2) Jews have married foreign wives

  (3) Nehemiah throws out Tobiah's things, and cleanses the people of mixed marriages

4. Temple Support Withheld (13:10-14)

5. The Sabbath Commercialized (13:15-22)

IV. **The Close of the Period of Old Testament Prophecy (Malachi)**

1. The LORD Affirms His Love for Israel (1:1-5)
Proof: In the favor shown her in comparison with his dealings with Esau

2. Malachi Denounces the Sins of the Priesthood (1:6—2:9)

  (1) They despise God's name (1:6-14)

    1) By offering polluted bread
    2) By saying that the table of the LORD is contemptible
    3) By offering crippled animals

    4) By regarding sacrifice as "a weariness"

  (2) A curse is pronounced upon the priests (2:1-9)

    1) God will curse the blessings of those who will not glorify his name
    2) The covenant requires such a curse
    3) The priest has ceased his function when the law of God no longer proceeds from his lips, therefore God will remove the honor of the priests

3. Malachi Denounces the Sins of the People (2:10-17; 3:7-15)

  (1) Treachery is committed among brethren (2:10-16)
Note: While a highly sentimental worship was displayed, the people (men) were guilty of leaving their wives for younger pagan women.

  (2) God's indignant ultimatum (2:16):
"I hate putting away"

  (3) The people have wearied God (2:17)

    1) By misrepresenting God's attitude toward evil doers
    2) By regarding the God of judgment as absent

  (4) The people have robbed God (3:7-12)
Note: By not paying tithes and offerings they have robbed both God and themselves.
They have also robbed themselves of showers of blessing. Their land has been "cursed" and not a "delightsome land," hence, the challenge to return (vs. 7).

4. The Day of the Lord (3:1-6; 4:1-6)

  (1) Two coming messengers:

    1) The preparatory messenger
    2) The messenger of the covenant—the Lord

  (2) The nature of the day of the Lord's coming

    1) It is greatly desirable: "ye seek," "ye delight in" (3:1)
    2) But it will be a day of testing (3:2-6)

      a. Like a refiner's fire

b. Like fuller's soap

c. The offerings will be made pleasant again

d. Sorcerers, adulterers, false swearers, oppressors of labor, of widows, of orphans, and of strangers, and all who do not fear God will be purged from the land by the Lord's swift witness

e. Like an oven against the proud (stubble) (4:1)

3) It will be a new day for those who fear God's name (4:2-3)

   a. The Lord will heal them

   b. They will help God judge the wicked

(3) Preparations in view of the day of the Lord (4:4-6)

1) Moses' law is to be regarded

2) Elijah is to come first

   a. To restore the hearts of children and parents

   b. Thereby, to prevent a curse upon the earth

4. Ezra the Vital Reformer

Reformation, to be thoroughgoing, must be motivated by more than police action. It has its source in a teaching ministry. This we are led to conclude from the ministry of Ezra.

It appears that after the passing of Zerubbabel, Jeshua, Haggai, and Zechariah, the early leaders of the restoration, Israel's spiritual condition bogged down to a lamentable state. Not only had the people stopped observing God's law, but many of them it appears were ignorant of it.

Under such circumstances, Ezra, touched by God's spirit, made preparations to meet Israel's need. His example is noteworthy for all spiritual leaders. He first prepared his own heart. This is the only kind of heart in which the truth can bear the fruits of righteousness. He sought to understand the law, not merely to be a teacher, but to do it. Beyond this, then, he prepared to teach statutes and judgments, which meant the application of the law of God to the new order in Jerusalem.

Ezra's chagrin, upon returning to Jerusalem, almost turned him to hopelessness, for he saw how extensively the life of the people had departed from the word of God. Intermarriage had literally reduced them to a condition of estrangement from the God of Israel. But Shechaniah and others, and finally all the people determined that there should be a reformation "according to the law." Drastic as the steps to be taken were, it was better to break up the mixed marriages than for the remnant to drift further and hopelessly from God's covenant.

The picture of the procedure is salutary. Ezra's hand was firm. An assembly of all Israel was ordered, anyone failing to respond being subject to expulsion from the congregation and the forfeiture of his property. The response was touching. Trembling with fear, and because of the great rain, the whole assembly heard Ezra's indictment of the offenders. In succeeding days all involved were summoned to appear before an appointed court for the correction of their social relations. Priests and common people alike were checked, and the register of bona fide Israelites was cleansed.

The spiritual growth of the remnant is seen in the fact that after the walls had been rebuilt the people of their own accord appealed to Ezra to read the law of God to them, and "gathered themselves together as one man" to hear him (Nehemiah 8). They stood before him from morning until noon. "So they (Nehemiah and Ezra) read in the book of the law of God distinctly, and gave the sense, and caused them to understand the reading." The people wept when they heard and understood. Their weeping was restrained and they were encouraged to rejoice. During a large part of this seventh month, it appears, the people tarried at Jerusalem, offering sacrifices and hearing the law. The covenant with which this season was climaxed indicates that the reform of Ezra had touched the people deeply and that they really purposed to yield their lives to God.

It is evident that copies of the law were very few at that time. Also, it appears that when Ezra "gave the sense" he had to reckon with a linguistic change that had taken place since the days of Moses. Thus, it is shown that when the word of God really gains entrance into the understanding it has vital spiritual power. It changes the thinking and the sentiments of people, and provides a source of motivation which changes life. It does this because it brings the mind of man under the influence of God.

5.   Nehemiah A Statesman of Stature

Nehemiah, as the cupbearer of Artaxerxes was a man of dignity and influence. Doubtless he enjoyed a good salary in the position which he held. But Nehemiah was a son of Abraham first, and an associate of the Persian king secondly. His heart was in Jerusalem and his primary concern was to see the restoration of his people to covenant relations with their God. It was this deep devotion within him, more than the backing of the king, that made him such an effective governor of Jerusalem.

Nehemiah gave authority to the teaching ministry of Ezra while Ezra gave spiritual foundation to the building projects which

Nehemiah managed. There was teamwork between the teaching and governing phases of the restoration movement.

Nehemiah trusted God, as is seen in the great place given to prayer in connection with his going to Jerusalem and in connection with the building operations. Yet, Nehemiah did not hesitate to use force when there was resistence to government. When Eliashib permitted Tobiah, a foreign ally, to set up quarters in the sacred chambers of the temple, he threw out his "stuff" and restored the appropriate furniture. It took courage also to force those who had married illicitly to separate from their foreign wives and children, especially considering that persons of high rank were involved. When he saw foreigners lined up at the city wall to lure Jews into Sabbath trading he warned them to get out and that if they returned he would "lay hands on" them. Nehemiah knew that the future realization of the covenant interests of the remnant depended upon discipline in this restoration period. To prevent racial, spiritual, and moral degeneracy and disintegration meant that it was necessary to effectively break up these early alliances and intermarriages and the irregularities into which the people so easily drifted.   In Nehemiah we see a government motivated by high and worthy purposes. The remnant, so graciously restored to the status forfeited by their fathers, must not again sacrifice the blessings of their covenant for a mess of pottage.

Nehemiah backed up his disciplines with an exemplary spirit. He could order the usurers to restore the property which they had extorted from unfortunate debtors, because he himself was not a profiteer. By receiving no salary for his services he had proved this beyond question to his fellow Jews and was successful in averting internal dissension which might have wrecked the restored economy before the rebuilt walls had been dedicated.

On the occasion of Nehemiah's last visit to Jerusalem, when he met the spectacle of reversion of leaders and people into sickening sins, this noble patriot's heart appears to have been literally wrung with chagrin. After twelve years the remnant seemed still to have no spiritual legs. In his disheartenment he prayed, "Remember me, O my God, concerning this, and wipe not out my good deeds that I have done for the house of my God, and for the offices thereof" (13:14). After chasing a pesky pagan son-in-law of Sanballat from his premises, he turned again to God, beseeching, "Remember them,

O my God, because they have defiled the priesthood, and the covenant of the priesthood, and of the Levites" (13:29).

6. Malachi the Herald of a New Day

While the book of Malachi is silent as to date, the unanimous opinion is that it belongs to the period of Ezra and Nehemiah (458-425 B. C.), and that Malachi was the last of the Old Testament prophets whose writings were recorded in the sacred canon.

As Nehemiah is last of the historical books so Malachi closes the prophetical section. Judging from the subject-matter of Malachi it could easily belong to the times of the reforms of Ezra and Nehemiah. Since no mention is made of him in their connection it is probable that Malachi dealt with a condition that arose after Nehemiah's last reforms in 432 B. C. There was no reason to expect, from Israel's past record that after Nehemiah's governorship ended, Israel would not again soon need the purging ministry of a reformer. In keeping with Israel's long history of moral failure, it was necessary for the last prophet to chide with her about the most elementary principles of righteousness, such as hypocritical worship, mixed marriage, and oppression of the unfortunate of society.

This last voice portrayed the cherished hope of a coming deliverer, indeed, but it frankly probed the complacency of some who professed a "delight" in that day. There would have to be preparations for that day, Malachi insisted, for when it came it would purge the land of wickedness. That day would bring, not the abrogation of moral law, but its true fulfillment. There would be a powerful prophet coming in the spirit and power of Elijah who would probe beneath ritual and restore the hearts of the people.

While the Old Testament era closes with a picture of Israel's failure, it by no means allows us to assume that God had finished with his own people, and that he had no further plans. Rather, as the shadows of Israel's desolation deepened, the converging and cumulative rays of Messianic hope from the prophets brightened. During the four centuries following, such expressions as "the coming of the Lord," "the coming of the Messenger of the Covenant to the temple," and the "rising of the Sun of Righteousness" kept before Israel a high destiny against the background of gloom and hopelessness which literally filled the world.

7. Character Review

Identify:

Ezra	Jahaziah	Sanballat
Artaxerxes I	Nehemiah	Geshem
Nethinims	Hanani	Malachi
Shechaniah	Hananiah	
Jonathan	Tobiah	

8. Discussion and Review

1. What is the source of thoroughgoing reformation?

2. What spiritual developments followed the early labors of Zerubbabel, Haggai and Zechariah?

3. Who was Ezra? Where did his work of reform begin?

4. Describe the conditions which Ezra found upon returning to Jerusalem.

5. Picture Ezra's salutary procedure in dealing with the situation.

6. Who was Nehemiah? Why did he return to Jerusalem?

7. What work did Nehemiah accomplish and how was it related to Ezra's work?

8. Characterize Nehemiah as a builder, as a governor, and as a reformer.

9. Against what sins did Malachi address himself? What hopes did he raise? How did he relate these two features?

10. Show how the book of Malachi is related to the Gospels.

9. Select Memory Passages

Ezra 7:10; Malachi 3:1-3; 4:2, 5-6

10. Bibliography

Dods Marcus. *Post-exilian Prophets: Haggai, Zephariah, and Malachi.* (Handbook for Bible Classes), J. M. P. Smith, ICC, 1912.

Fairweather, Wm. *From the Exile to the Advent.* Book II, Chapt. III, "The Jews under Xerxes and Artaxerxes." Chapt. IV, "Inner Life of Israel During the Persian Period." Edinburgh: T. & T. Clark.

Mears, John W. *From Exile to Overthrow.* Chapt. VIII, "Ezra and Nehemiah." Philadelphia: Presbyterian Board of Publications.

Rawlinson, George. *Ezra and Nehemiah and Their Lives and Times.* New York: Fleming H. Revell.

Robinson, George L. "The Book of Malachi," "*The International Standard Bible Encyclopedia.* Vol. III. pp. 1969-1970.

Chapter 24

THE INTER-TESTAMENTAL PERIOD

—Malachi to Christ
(425-4 B. C.)

1.   Introduction

For this study our historical materials must be drawn from Greek, Roman, and Jewish historians and from the Apocryphal books. We shall endeavor to sketch an outline of Jewish history in the light of these sources, sparing the student from the time-consuming and arduous task of gathering the facts, and yet, at the same time providing him with the important connections between Old and New Testament times.   If the student desires to read further he is referred to the Bibliography at the close of the chapter.

2.   The Persian Supremacy (536 B. C.-335 B. C.)

The 200 year Persian supremacy began approximately one hundred years before Malachi's time and extended approximately one hundred years beyond it.   It will be recalled that the Persian kings extended every favor possible, short of complete governmental autonomy, to the Jews.   After the defeat of Ahasuerus (Xerxes, 483 B. C.) by the Greeks, the Persian sun began to pale.   Palestine, as a part of the satrapy of Syria was, under these conditions, left to exercise a still greater degree of self-government.   The Jewish high

RULERS of the JEWS DURING the INTER-TESTAMENTAL PERIOD

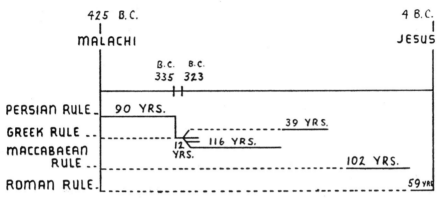

Figure 30

priests, acting under the Syrian satraps, virtually ruled. The office of high priest became an object of political ambition. Apart from this observation it may be said that during the times of the later Persian kings life in Palestine was not especially eventful.

3. The Supremacy of Alexander the Great (335-323 B. C.)

No historical personage is more clearly marked out in prophecy than Alexander of Macedon. The kingdom which Alexander founded was the third great division of the prophetic image of Nebuchadnezzar's dream (Daniel 2). He is the leopard with four heads who succeeds the slow moving but powerful Medo-Persian bear (Daniel 7). He is the great horn between the eyes of the rough he-goat which mightily subdued the Persian two-horned ram, but which was, after a short time, destroyed and replaced by four subordinate horns (Daniel 8).

The rise and the conquests of Alexander are notable. His sudden rise to power was occasioned by the assassination of his father, Philip of Macedon. His leopard-like nature went into operation at once. Rebellious elements in Macedonia were silenced. Entering Greece, he scored several decisive victories over Theban resistance. Thence he flew against the Persian bear, encountering and defeating Darius III in the memorable battles of Granicus in Mysia and Issus in Cilicia. After several months he subdued Tyre, the main stronghold of Syria.

Alexander's southward movement involved Jerusalem (333 B. C.) where, according to tradition, a procession of robed priests so influenced him as to lead him to spare the city and grant favour to the Jews. In all probability he was shown the prophecies of Daniel, which so clearly marked out his career, and which doubtless pleased him.

From Jerusalem he moved southward into Egypt where he founded the city of Alexandria, which still bears his name, and which became notable as a center of Graeco-Jewish learning. He then returned to Asia where at Arbela on the plains of Assyria he dealt the finishing blow to the Persian Empire.

Still not satisfied, he laid plans for conquests further east. In the midst of these plans he took down with a fever, brought on by too much drinking at a banquet, and died. Thus at the early age of thirty-two years (323 B. C.), his sun which had seemed to have such unlimited prospects, had its untimely setting.

The twelve years of Alexander's reign were most favorable to the Jews. While Alexander's ambition was to stamp upon the world the impress of Greek culture, he saw in the intelligence, thriftiness, and industriousness of the Jews an element which he prized. He, therefore, encouraged them to settle in the chief cities of his empire. In Alexandria, particularly, he encouraged the Jews to settle, giving them the status of first class citizenship. The Jews, which in the times of Mordecai and Esther attained to a place of high standing in all the one hundred twenty-seven provinces of the Persian empire, thus continued to hold a place of great influence in the Grecian empire.

Separated from the temple at Jerusalem, the ritual element of Jewish worship diminished. Greater attention came to be given to the Law, the Prophets, and the Writings, and to the hope of their promised Messiah. Unconsciously, the Jews constituted a missionary influence among the nations. Thus, their loss of national autonomy and of normal temple privileges, accomplished, in God's providence, the high purpose of conditioning the heathen for the coming of the incarnate Son of God.

4. The Jews Under the Ptolemies (320-204 B. C.)

Upon the death of Alexander, his kingdom fell, not to a son, but to his four generals, Ptolemy, Lysimachus, Cassander, and Seleucus. Of these, two developed into political figures of importance, Ptolemy as the ruler of Egypt, and Seleucus as the ruler of Syria. After ten years of conflict these two divisions became independent kingdoms. Between them lay Palestine which at first came under Ptolemaic rule (320-204 B. C.), and then under the rule of the Seleucidae of Syria (204-165 B. C.). All of this is in amazing fulfillment of Daniel's prophecy (Daniel 8, 11).

There were three notable Ptolemies, Ptolemy Soter, Ptolemy Philadelphus, and Ptolemy Philopator.

Ptolemy Soter, who had been Alexander's general, at first dealt severely with the Jews, but soon learned the greater wisdom of his father's attitude. Observing their strength of character he sent thirty thousand of them to various parts of his realm, some of whom the historians of this period mention with high honor.

Ptolemy Philadelphus who succeeded Soter is unquestionably the most significant ruler of this period. He erected one of the seven wonders of the world—the lighthouse of Pharos. He founded the great library of Alexandria by collecting the works of authors from all nations. Most noteworthy is the patronage which he gave to the work of translating the Hebrew Scriptures into the Greek language (285 B. C.), giving to the world what is known as the Septuagint (LXX). This was nothing less than the gift of God's providence to bring to the world, through the widely diffused Greek tongue, the Word of God. Thus, in a measure, which many do not realize, the world was being prepared for the coming of its Redeemer.

Ptolemy Philopater lacked the appreciation of his predecessors for the Jews. Visiting Jerusalem after a victorious battle in Syria, he approached the temple to desecrate it. He was strenuously opposed by the Jews but would not be dissuaded, until, as he neared the holy of holies he was stricken with terror and fled. Upon returning to Alexandria, the resistance which the Jews had manifested so stirred his anger that he plotted their wholesale destruction. He gathered large numbers into the hippodrome, and turned loose upon them elephants which had been made wild with intoxicants. Contrary to plans, the elephants centered their attack upon the great crowd of spectators rather than upon the Jews. So manifest was God's favor upon the Jews that the king reversed his policy of persecution.

Several Jewish personalities attained eminence during this period. **Simon** the just, is characterized in the apocraphal book of Ecclesiasticus as a man of wisdom, integrity, and of piety. **Antigonus** of

Socho was a president of the Sanhedrin who is reported to have taught that God should not be served for reward but out of love and appreciation. **Sadoc,** who is thought to have furnished the ideas for the sect of the Sadducees, drew out the teachings of Antigonus to imply that there are to be no rewards at all after this life, not even a resurrection, nor any future felicity in heaven or anywhere else.

5. The Jews Under the Seleucidae (204-165 B. C.)

While the Ptolemies reigned in Egypt, Palestine, and Coele-Syria, Seleucus and his successors were attaining recognition as ranking monarchs in Syria. From Antioch as capital, the Seleucidae extended their dominion to include all Asia. Seleucus, as the Ptolemies, recognized the wisdom of favoring the Jews. War between the Seleucidae of Syria and the Ptolemies of Egypt was constant, and Palestine was their favorite bone of contention.

Upon the death of Ptolemy Philopator, the five year old Ptolemy Epiphanes was left ruler of Egypt. Antiochus III, (the Great) of Syria saw his opportunity and seized it. Palestine and Coele-Syria were his easy prey and they were made a part of the Syrian empire.

The Syrian supremacy lasted thirty-nine years and was a time of almost continuous persecution for the Jews. The outstanding figure of the period was Antiochus IV (Epiphanes). When he became king the high priesthood was in the worthy charge of Onias. It was the purpose of Antiochus to displace the Hebrew spirit of Jerusalem with a Greek spirit. Onias was displaced by his brother Jason who was Greek in spirit. Jason is said to have paid Antiochus 360 talents for the office. This marked the emergence of a Greek party in Palestine in opposition to the orthodox party. Jason in his zeal for Greek culture, sent an embassy to Tyre to take part in Greek games and to sacrifice to Hercules. Notwithstanding the subserviance of Jason to Antiochus, another brother who was still more of a liberal than Jason, was permitted to displace Jason in the office of high priest.

The occasion for open persecution against the true Jews of Palestine came when Antiochus, who was in war against Egypt, was falsely reported to be dead. The Jews showed such joy upon hearing this report that Antiochus rose up against them with vengeful reprisal. He slew 40,000 Jews and profaned the Temple by offering a sow upon the altar and sprinkling the broth from the flesh all through the Temple interior. An altar was erected to Jupiter. At a later time Antiochus sent his general, Apollonius on a mission of terror against Jerusalem. When the people were in their synagogues the general struck. The men were slain and women and children were carried captive. The city and its walls were torn down and the fortress of Acra built with the materials. Such Jews as escaped capture fled, leaving the city depopulated. The only reason that the temple was spared was that it had been turned into a pagan institution.

The peril of the Jews under Antiochus Epiphanes may be judged from Antiochus' edict and from the measures by which he enforced it. All people under his dominion were to worship the same gods. In Samaria the decree was accepted. Mount Gerizim was consecrated to the Grecian Jove by consent of the Samaritans. The Temple at Jerusalem was so consecrated by force. A statue to Jupiter Olympus was erected upon the altar of burnt sacrifice. Circumcision was prohibited. By way of enforcement of this prohibition, two women, charged with circumcising their children, were hurled with their children clinging to their necks from the steepest part of the city wall. The clear purpose of Antiochus was to completely terminate all faithful Jews. This condition lasted for three and one-half years at which time the Jewish patriot, Judas Maccabaeus, retrieved the Temple and removed its pollution (165 B. C.).

6.   The Rule of the Maccabees (165-63 B. C.)

The Maccabees (Asmoneans) were a body of Jewish patriots who rallied to the leadership of Mattathias, a devout priest, and his five sons. Much like David in exile from Saul, this band of Maccabees developed a powerful defense, operating from the caves and hilly fortresses of Judea. When Mattathias died, his son Judas was recognized as the new leader.

Antiochus had failed in three attempts to crush the Maccabees when his efforts were cut short because of a loathesome disease from which he died.

At the time that Antiochus the Great (not Epiphanes) seized supremacy of Palestine from the Ptolemies, the latter made a bid for Roman aid. From that time Rome's hand began to be felt in the East, and rested with no little weight upon Antiochus Epiphanes during his last cruel undertakings in Palestine. This situation so neutralized the Syrian supremacy that upon the death of Antiochus Epiphanes, Judas Maccabees' leadership in Palestine was left undisputed.

Judas took steps to restore the religious life of the people. The temple was cleansed and rededicated. Syrian hostility in time revived, however, and Judas was slain in battle.

Leadership then fell to Judas' brother Jonathan. He also was killed, by murder.

Simon, another brother, assumed leadership. He appealed to the Romans for support and found them waiting. He became Rome's appointee, which, strictly speaking, marks the beginning of the supremacy of the Roman state in Palestine. It was the beginning of the Hasmonean line of priest rulers in Judea.

Simon was succeeded by his son, John Hyrcanus. It was at this time that the two-party system of Pharisees and Sadducees had its rise in Jewish history. The party system had very little freedom within which to operate, however. When the two grandsons of John Hyrcanus, Aristobulus and Hyrcanus, disputed for the ruling position, the dispute had to be submitted to Pompey for settlement. His appointment of Hyrcanus was resisted by the disappointed Aristobulus party, and Pompey promptly took the city of Jerusalem. This event marks the passing of the Jews under the supremacy of the fourth world power prophetically marked out by Nebuchadnezzar's dream image (Daniel 2).

7. The Jews Under the Roman Supremacy (63-4 B. C.)

It was at the time of the First Roman Triumvirate composed of Julius Caesar, Pompey, and Crassus, that Palestine came under the dominion of Rome. This triumvirate had established the rule of Palestine under Hyrcanus the Asmonean Jew. Such an arrangement seemed to be very satisfactory to the Jews.

The fortunes of Roman politics were, however, very uncertain grounds for confidence. With the death of Julius Caesar and of Pompey, Antony was left in charge of Syria and the East, which included Palestine. It was this Antony who had so shamefully fouled history by his illicit relations with Cleopatra, queen of Egypt. He further fouled Jewish history by appointing Herod king of Judea. Antony, always ambitious for himself, yielded readily to bestow patronage upon Herod for the sake of the career which he sought to carve for himself.

Herod was, by blood, not a Jew, but an Idumaean (Edomite). His father, Antipater, had been appointed by Julius Caesar to serve as the procurator of Judea under the Asmonean Hyrcanus, king of Jerusalem. It was the intention of Caesar that the kingship of Jerusalem should continue under the family of Hyrcanus. A combination of factors, however, led to the elevation of Herod's procuratorship to the status of kingship. First, Antigonus, a son of Aristobulus, who coveted the office of priest-ruler at Jerusalem, had managed to have Hyrcanus' ears cut off. With such a defection Hyrcanus was disqualified for the priesthood according to the law of Moses. At this time Herod added Miriamne, a granddaughter of Hyrcanus, to his many wives, in this way gaining increased favor with the Jews. Proceeding further, he then made a report of the pathetic state of affairs to Antony and convinced him that if he were made king the condition in Judea would be corrected.

Herod was made king of Judea (37 B. C.). The Jews never approved domination by an Idumaean, except for the Herodian party which arose to promote Herod's ends. Herod must have sensed this for he constantly exhibited fear that some member of the Asmonean party would displace him. Upon being made king, he promptly executed Antigonus. After some time he began to eye with jealousy the favor enjoyed by Aristobulus, his wife's brother, who was high priest. At a bathing pond, under the pretense of sport, he had Aristobulus held under so that he drowned. Hyrcanus, though grown old, without ears, and an exile in Parthia, also came under Herod's suspicion. He was brought to Jerusalem, falsely charged, and executed. Miriamne naturally became disaffected from Herod by such atrocities against her kin; her changed countenance brought her under suspicion, and although Herod had greatly delighted in her, she was executed. When he realized what he had done he was nearly beside himself with remorse. Yet, his suspicious heart did not repent, but grew more cruel. Greater bloodshed followed. His two sons were among those who fell victims of his murderous jealousy. A large number of Pharisees were slain on one occasion. Finally, in the days of the infancy of Jesus, jealousy led him to shed the blood of all new born boys in the land (4 B. C.).

Herod followed the psychological pattern common to politicians of his kind. To offset his crimes, he went great lengths to please the Jews. He could not afford to risk a complaint from them to

Rome. For the amusement of the worldly minded liberal Jews, of whom there were many, he erected a large amphitheatre at Jerusalem. He built Caesarea to give Palestine a much needed first class seaport. His chief benefit, and that which was calculated to please the more devout element of the Jews, was the rebuilding of the temple at Jerusalem. Zerubbabel's Temple was now five hundred years old and doubtless was obsolete and worn.

The Temple rebuilding project was a very absorbing interest. A thousand priests with skill in architecture superintended the work. Ten thousand workmen were employed. A thousand wagons were engaged in conveying materials to the Temple site. Because the Jews were not willing to risk a miscarriage of the project, they insisted that materials for construction be assembled and prepared before the old structure was discommoded for use. Once the rebuilding began, nearly ten years were required to prepare the temple for dedication and use. After this there remained much more to be done on the exterior. Forty-six years, the Jews remarked to Jesus (John 2:20), was the total time during which the building project continued. It is evident that the completed structure was looked upon with a great deal of pride by the Jews (Matt. 24:1).

8. Palestine Boundary Lines under the Herods

The kingdom over which Herod the Great ruled included all of Palestine. At his death in 4 B. C. Judea and Samaria were made a Roman province and assigned to Herod's son Archelaus; Galilee and Perea were assigned to a second son, Herod Antipas; the northwest territory was assigned to a third son, Philip; a small portion to the north of Herod's dominion made up the fourth part of the Tetrarchy (government by four). This Tetrarchy was the political set-up in Palestine during the main part of Christ's lifetime.

In 41 A. D. Emperor Caligula bestowed the title of king upon Herod Agrippa, the grandson of Herod the Great, and gave him dominion over all the dominions of Herod the Great plus Abilene. Herod did not wear this honor well, however. After having slain James the apostle, he imprisoned Peter. He illicited worship from the Caesareans for which God smote him with judgment so that he died (44 A. D.).

Herod's son, Agrippa II, inherited only the northeast territory and the district of Abilene; this dominion he held until 70 A. D. It was Herod Agrippa II who heard Paul at Caesarea and was almost persuaded to become a Christian (Acts 25, 26). After 44 A. D. the province of Judea was made up of Idumea, Judea, Samaria, Galilee, and Perea, and was ruled by procurators who resided at Caesarea. Felix and Festus were the notable rulers at the time of Paul's arrest. Palestine continued with these two provinces until the destruction of Jerusalem in 70 A. D., at which time Judaea became a part of the province of Syria.

9. Religion in Judea at the Time of Christ

The Rabbinical System

The system of religion in Judea when Jesus was born had its root developments back in the periods of inter-testamentary history which we have surveyed. Extra-biblical sources report that Ezra, the scribe, associated with himself more than a hundred scholars who constituted a Great Synagogue and gave rise to the formation of the Jewish supreme court known as the Sanhedrin. This court reflected the religious scholarship of Judea at the close of the inter-testamental period. Surrounding and constituting the court were expert scribes and doctors of the Law. These were the rabbis or teachers of the nation who zealously and with great authority dictated the standards of religious faith and life in the temple to which Jesus came. It was these leaders whom Jesus, at the age of twelve, instructed concerning his Father. It was the Sanhedrin which tried and condemned Jesus to death.

Schools of Interpretation

Two men, Hillel and Shammai, represent two important lines of teaching common in the last century of the inter-testamental period. Hillel, a Babylonian Jew, a man of recognized learning, who came to Palestine about 112 B. C., advocated greater freedom for the individual conscience in the interpretations and application of the Law. Shammai, also a rabbi of reputation, contended for rigid adherence to traditions, pressing the letter of the Law in some matters to a point of self-contradiction. Both were diligent students of the Law. Gamaliel, the teacher of Saul of Tarsus and president of the Sanhedrin at the time of the apostles, was a grandson of Hillel.

Jewish Parties

There were four prominent parties in the Jewish life of the

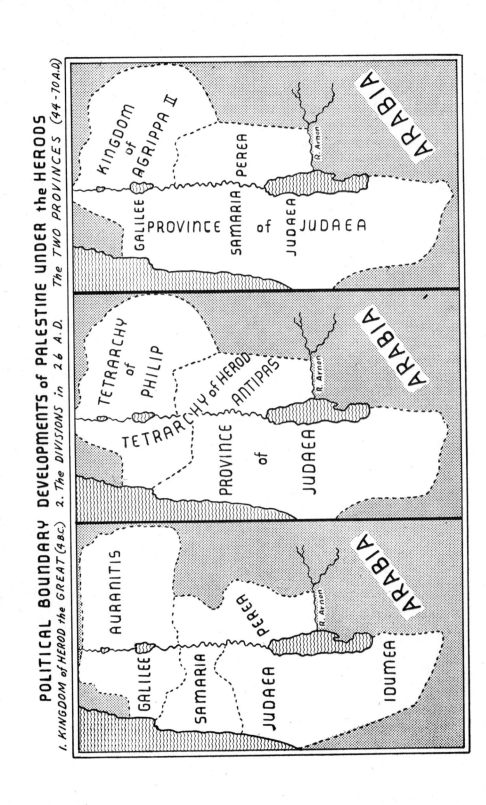

POLITICAL BOUNDARY DEVELOPMENTS of PALESTINE UNDER the HERODS

1. KINGDOM of HEROD the GREAT (4 B.C.)   2. The DIVISIONS in 26 A.D.   The TWO PROVINCES (44-70 A.D.)

Panel 1:
GALILEE
AURANITIS
SAMARIA
JUDAEA
PEREA
IDUMEA
R. Arnon
ARABIA

Panel 2:
TETRARCHY of PHILIP
TETRARCHY of HEROD ANTIPAS
PROVINCE of JUDAEA
R. Arnon
ARABIA

Panel 3:
KINGDOM of AGRIPPA II
GALILEE
PROVINCE of JUDAEA
SAMARIA
PEREA
JUDAEA
R. Arnon
ARABIA

Herodian period, the Pharisees, the Sadducees, the Essenes, and the Herodians.

The **Pharisees** had their rise in the Grecian period. They distinguished themselves by supporting the Maccabees, although they later, in the time of John Hyrcanus, disassociated themselves from them. At first known as Assidaeans (Holy Ones), they came to be known as Pharisees (Separatists), due especially to their stand against Hyrcanus and the Roman government which supported him.

Against the liberalism of the times, the Pharisee believed in a personal God whose will was providence, and in a future life with rewards and punishments. To the Law they added many traditions. They interpreted the Law with regard to external conduct in the most minute fashion, but they failed to sense the spirit of the Law. They held a definite Messianic doctrine, though here also they thought more of a displacement of the Roman yoke than of moral and spiritual allignment with God. They stressed almsgiving in a way which contrasted with the common neglect of the poor by the Greeks and Romans, yet this virtue too often deteriorated into self-righteousness. They had a very high regard for formal learning, but their learning came to lack the common sense requirements of life.

Paradoxically, their regard for learning and strict conduct, begat in the Pharisees an overbearing arrogance, trite scrupulosity, and a spirit of hypocrisy. The Talmud describes seven varieties of latter day Pharisees: (1) the "shoulder" Pharisee who wears his good deeds on his shoulders; (2) the "wait a little" Pharisee, who always begs for time to do a deed of merit; (3) the "bleeding" Pharisee, who in his eagerness to avoid looking on a woman shuts his eyes and so bruises himself to bleeding by stumbling against a wall; (4) the "painted" Pharisee who advertises his holiness so that none will touch and thus defile him; (5) the "reckoning" Pharisee, who is always saying, "What duty must I do to balance any unpalatable duty which I have not done?"; (6) the "fearing" Pharisee, whose relation to God is that of trembling awe; (7) the Pharisee from "love." It is evident that in all of these varieties except the last, there is a dominant element of hypocrisy.

The **Sadducees**, though less numerous than their opponents, the Pharisees, were not less significant in influence. Their wealth, political prestige, and their worldliness were the points in which they scored. Most scholars trace the name Sadducee from Zadok, the high priest of David's time. If this is tenable, it must not be assumed that the Sadducees as a party originated so far back. The party appears to have arisen, rather, from the fact that after the restoration of the Jews under Cyrus, the high priest came to be the Jewish figure with whom the Roman emperors dealt. The position accorded the high priests and the corresponding numerous civil duties which they came to perform tended to secularize their viewpoint. Under Greek superiors they yielded to the leavening influence of Greek culture and became promoters in what was known as the Hellenizing movement. They were only negatively religious. Disbelief in the spiritual world, in the resurrection, and in the future life were their conspicuous tenets. They stressed ceremonial exactness. They had a very low regard for any other Scriptures than the Pentateuch. The moral law, the prophets, and the Messianic hope were practically despised. While there was no real connection, the Sadducees bear resemblance to the Greek Epicureans. Josephus describes their religion as "within the limits of sensation." He also describes them as "very boorish," which can be born out by observations of them in the New Testament.

A Talmudic account says of them, "They are high priests and their sons are treasurers of the temple, and their sons-in-law assistant treasurers; and their servants beat the people with sticks."[1]

Edersheim speaks of the booths of Annas and his sons in the courts of the temple, for the sale of temple necessities, and for changing monies of the worshippers into the shekels of the sanctuary, from which profiteering became a notorious practice.[2]

In relation to Jesus the Sadducees were at times pleased as Jesus upbraided the Pharisees. In later times, however, when the resurrection of Christ became the issue, their antagonism against the church grew fanatical.

The Essenes (pious) were the ascetics of Judea. They were characterized by strong aspirations for perfection. To this end they bound themselves to strict rules. They lived a communistic life, having all property held in a common store. They practiced self-denial and temperance. They were thrifty, usually following an agricultural life. They repudiated war, slavery, and commerce. Their

---

[1] Pesalim 57a.
[2] Edersheim, *Life and Times of Jesus*, I, 371 ff.

peculiar beliefs almost of necessity bound them to a life of retirement from society.

The Herodians, as we might suppose from the name, were the supporters of the rule of the Herodian family in Judea. These supporters usually were Jews who had some personal benefit from supporting the Herodian arm of the Roman government, or they were persons who reasoned that the Herodian rule was a good compromise between complete foreign tyranny and freedom. Better go along, these Jews reasoned, with a quasi-Jewish Herod who can bargain with Rome than to run the risk of a break for freedom.

10. The Religious Meeting Places of the Jews

The rise of the synagogue as an institution was an important phase of the providence of God by which the world through the dispersion of the Jews came to be lighted up with the knowledge of God; this was the case, particularly, with the prospect of the coming Messiah. In the Herodian period there was scarcely a town in the areas of the dispersion which did not have one or more synagogue. Where there were smaller groups of Jews insufficient to afford a building there was the **proseucha** or place of prayer, sometimes in the open air at a water's edge or in a shaded spot. Such a meeting apparently is pictured at Philippi (Acts 16:13). There was reading, prayer, and possibly a discourse, depending upon the persons present and the circumstances. There was an absence of ritual and little occasion for ostentation. The truth and the spirit were the important elements in such meetings.

In the synagogue the tendency to fixed forms naturally was stronger than in the **proseucha.** Forms of prayer were taught as is seen in Luke 11:1. Special portions of Moses were read on stated occasions (Acts 15:21). A calendar of synagogue events was naturally adopted. While the synagogue could not hope to reproduce the whole religious order of the Temple, it did have its ablutions, its set postures for worship, its rituals and responses, and its benedictions by the elders.

The functions of the synagogue were very practical. It constituted a school where children received the rudiments of learning, particularly a knowledge of the Scriptures. It had certain judicial functions varying more or less with the need and the degree of liberty under which a community lived.

In the itineraries of Jesus and the missionary journeys of Paul we observe something of the naturalness with which the Gospel fitted itself into the synagogue situation. The common procedure (in early gospel preaching) was to show that Jesus was the fulfillment of the Law and the Prophets. Ordinarily there was a great degree of latitude given, for such as could read and teach, to stand up and do so. The synagogues, each with its almost complete autonomy, made it possible for the Jews of a given community to hear, consider, and receive or reject the Gospel.

11. The Failure of Israel's Teachers at the Time of the Messiah's Coming

It is obvious that the coming of the Messiah was not timed to occur at the high point of spirituality in the history of Jewish leaders. Despite their zeal, Israel's very teachers of God's law were due to be set aside as useless in furthering the Messiah's mission. Though literally drunk with a sense of their authority as teachers of the people, they were both blind to the knowledge of God and fundamentally deficient with regard to the spirit of righteousness in God's holy Law. Their arrogance demonstrated that they had completely lost the spirit of the Abrahamic covenant which had as its end the bestowal of blessings upon all nations.

Israel's failure, however, does not mean God's failure. Like Joseph's brethren, whose evil lives God overruled and even used for good, so national Israel, though perpetually evil, was nevertheless God's instrument. The dispersion carried the knowledge of the true God to the many parts of the ancient world. Their captivity bore witness of the holiness of God, though it was by default on their part. Their longings implied a hope and bore testimony of a God who does not forsake his people, who is merciful, and whose plan includes redemption. Their hope for a coming Messiah, though set forth in the Old Testament scriptures from Genesis to Malachi, came to shine with a fuller light against the dismal background of the times. Thus it was that godly people such as Simeon waited devoutly for "the consolation of Israel."

Jerusalem had failed, but God could bring the victor for his kingdom out of little Bethlehem, and so he did. In it a child was born, and a son given, upon whose shoulder authority rested to establish the kingdom of God among men (Micah 5:2; Isa. 7:14-16; 9:6-7;

Luke 1:31-33). He was the promised seed of the woman, come to crush the head of the Serpent (Gen. 3:15). He fulfilled the blessing of the Lord God upon Shem (Gen. 9:26). He was the son of Abraham through whom the covenant of the fathers was to be realized (Gen. 12:1-3). He was the predicted Shiloh assigned to assume the sceptre of Judah (Gen. 49;10). He was the star whom Balaam knew would arise out of Jacob (Numbers 24:17-19).

Judaism as an institution had grown old. It was now to be put aside. This, however, was only to the end that the Messiah whom it had brought forth should be free to establish the universal kingdom embracing those from all nations who through faith are privileged to be the children of God. Christ's sanctuary henceforth would be in heaven—and in the midst of all true believers. He himself has provided a sacrifice which procures a timeless atonement. He is the great high priest heard by all who come through the sacrifice which he has made. He fulfills the law through the manifestation and giving of grace and truth. Through this ministry of the Messiah redemption is being extended to all nations. He who lives in our century sees the extension of this gospel of the Messiah's kingdom with facilities and speed unknown to ages past. Many devout Bible scholars believe that the preparatory stages of the Messiah's kingdom near completion, and that the day of universal blessing is at hand. Yet, although we, as Daniel (Dan. 12:13), are bidden to go the way of the saints of history and rest, we know that we shall stand in our lot with the Savior whom we have served "at the end of the days."

12. Discussion and Review

1. Characterize Jewish life under Persian supremacy during the century following Malachi.

2. State from memory the four successive political rulers of the Jews in the inter-testamentary period, with approximate dates of their supremacy.

3. What facts predisposed Alexander to favor the Jews? What was the unconscious accomplishment of the Jews in relation to Alexander's empire?

4. What happened to Alexander's empire?

5. Give a brief account of the three notable Ptolemies.

6. Who were Simon, Antigonus, and Sadoc of the Ptolemaic period?

7. What was the purpose of Antiochus Epiphanes regarding the Jews? Relate the account of his procedures in gaining his purpose. Can you find the picture of this man in Daniel's prophecy?

8. Relate a brief account of the rule of the Maccabees.

9. What circumstances led to the rise of Roman supremacy over the Jews? Was this supremacy an apparently good thing for the Jews? Explain.

10. Show by what fortunes the Jews were brought under the Herodian rule.

11. Write a biographical sketch of Herod the Great.

12. Evaluate Herod's statesmanship.

13. Trace the rise of the Rabbinical system.

14. Characterize the Hillel and Shammai schools of interpretation.

15. Trace the rise of the Pharisees. How did the element of hypocrisy become so strong in this party?

16. Trace the rise of the Sadducees. What were the distinctive traits of this party?

17. Characterize the Essenes. The Herodians. Describe the religious meeting places of the Jews of the dispersion.

18. In what sense was the Jewish religion of this period a preparation for the Messiah? In what sense was it useless to the Messiah's purpose? State the abiding element of Judaism.

13. Character Review

Identify:

Alexander the Great	Simon the Just	Herod the Great
Ptolemy (Soter)	Antigonus	Hillel
Seleucus	Antiochus Epiphanes	Shammai
Lysimachus	Maccabees	Pharisees
Cassander	John Hyrcanus	Sadducees
Ptolemy	Aristobulus	Essenes
Philadelphus	Pompey	Herodians
Ptolemy Philopator	Antony	

14. Bibliography

Blaikie, Wm. G. *Bible History*. *Chapter* XIV, "Interval between the Old and New Testaments." New York: Thomas Nelson and Sons.
Davis, Thomas Witton. "The Apocrypha," "*The International Standard Bible Encyclopedia*. Vol. I. pp. 178-183.

Fairweather, Wm. *From the Exile to the Advent.* Books III, VI. Edinburgh: T. & T. Clark.

Grant, C. M. *Between the Testaments.* New York: Fleming H. Revell Co.

Gregg, David. *Between the Testaments.* New York: Funk and Wagnals.

Latimer, Elizabeth Wormerly. *Judea, from Cyprus to Titus.* 525 to A. D. 70. Chicago, 1889, pp. 382.

Mears, John W. *From Exile to Overthrow.* Chapters IX—XX. Philadelphia: Presbyterian Board of Publications.

Miller, Dorothy Ruth. *A Handbook of Ancient History in Bible Light.* Chapter XXIV, "Alexander the Great and His Empire." Chapter XXV, "The Divisions of Alexander's Empire, and the Kingdom of the Seleucidae." Chapter XXVI, "The Early Ptolemies." New York: Fleming H. Revell Co.

Moss, R. Waddy, *From Malachi to Matthew.* London, 1893, pp. XIV, 256.

Robertson, A. T. *The Pharisees and Jesus.* New York: Charles Scribners.

Thackeray, H. St. J. "The Septuagint," *The International Standard Bible Encyclopedia.* Vol. IV. pp. 2722-2732.

Willet, Wm. M. *Life and Times of Herod the Great.* Philadelphia.

PART EIGHT

LIFE AND TIMES OF CHRIST

Chapter 25

THE SON OF GOD BECOMES MAN

1. Introduction

The lines of Old Testament emphasis converge in a babe at Bethlehem. The children of God of the passing generations had awaited the high moment of history when the promised seed of the woman should rise to triumph over the serpent and its seed.

The time span of this lesson stretches all the way from eternity past to the thirty year period of Christ's birth and growth into manhood. The prologue of John and the genealogies of Matthew and Luke presuppose that we know the Old Testament Scriptures. The New Testament does not give us a new set of truths. Rather, it places the cap sheaf on all previous revelations of God. It is the climactic disclosure of the Son of God to the world of men.

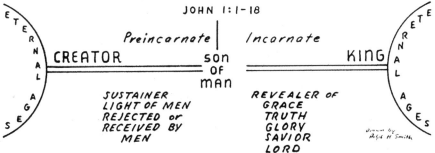

Figure 31

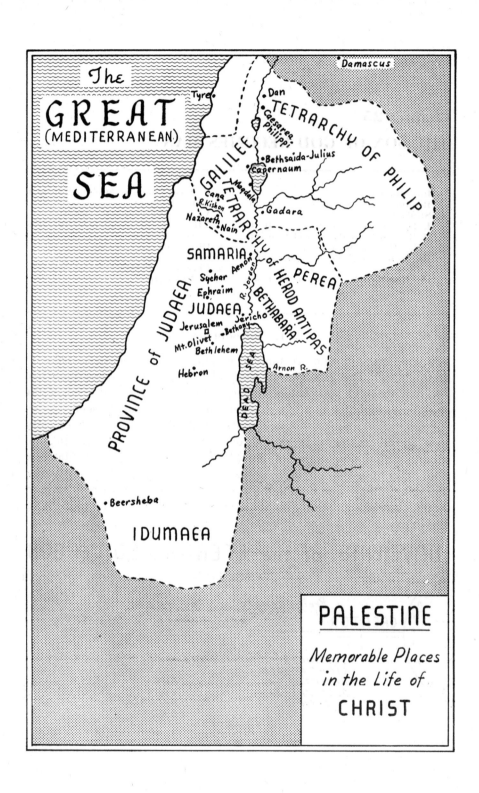

The GREAT (MEDITERRANEAN) SEA

Damascus

Tyre

Dan

Caesarea Philippi

TETRARCHY OF PHILIP

Bethsaida-Julius
Capernaum

GALILEE

Cana
R. Kishon
Magdala
TETRARCHY of HEROD ANTIPAS

Nazareth
Nain

Gadara

SAMARIA

PEREA

Sychar
Ephraim

Aenon
R. Jordan

JUDAEA

BETHABARA

Jerusalem
Mt. Olivet
Bethany
Bethlehem

Jericho

PROVINCE of JUDAEA

DEAD SEA

Arnon R.

Hebron

Beersheba

IDUMAEA

PALESTINE

Memorable Places in the Life of CHRIST

Our study of the earthly life of Christ will be made from the harmonized accounts of the four Gospel writers. The harmony below conforms to the standard works in this field, with special acknowledgements to **A Harmony of the Gospels for Historical Study** by Stevens and Burton, Scribners, N. Y.

A Harmony of the Gospels

PREPARATION			
Matthew 1:4—4:11	**Mark** 1:1-13	**Luke** 1:1—4:13	**John** 1:1-18

MINISTRY (January 27 A. D. to April 30 A. D.)				
Place	**Matthew**	**Mark**	**Luke**	**John**
Perea (1 mo.) Galilee (3 mo.) Judea (8 mo.) Samaria (visit)				1:19-42 1:42—2:12 2:13—3:36 4:1-42
Galilee (22 mo.)	4:12—18:35	1:14—9:50	4:14—9:50	4:43—6:71
Samaria (visit)				5:1-47
Galilee to Jerusalem via Perea (6 mo.)	19-20	10	9:51—19:28	7:10—12:11
Jerusalem (Passion week)	21-27	11-15	19:29—23:56	12:12—19:42
Resurrection to Ascension (47 days)	Chap. 28	Chap. 16	Chap. 24	Chaps. 20, 21

Figure 32

2. **Reading Assignment:**   John 1:1-13; Matthew 1—4:11;

Mark 1:1-13; Luke 1—4:13

(Read the Bible first)

3. Study Outline

I. **The Son of God before 4 B. C.** (John 1:1-13)

The Greeks gave the world a term which, after some modification, the apostle John employed to designate the eternal Son of God in his manifestation of himself to the world. This term is the "Word" (Logos) of John 1:1-13, which to the Greek mind stood for the uncaused cause of things. The Word as used by John refers to a personal being, the creator of all things, and eternal. Life and light have had their source in him. He is the Light lighting every person born into the world. Not all, John says, had recognized him nor received Him, but some had. Those who "received him," "believed on his name," or were "born of him," were accorded the power (right) to become sons of God. Thus, we learn that from the dawn of creation the Son of God has been striving with the hearts of men to win them into the family of God.

II. **The Birth of the Son of God into the Human Race** (John 1:14; Matt. 1-2; Luke 1-2)

John brushes aside all details and states the essential fact that the Word (Logos) who had thus been at work, "became flesh" and "dwelt among" men (1:14). He then relates the testimony of six persons who beheld his glory and received of his fulness of grace and truth (1:15-51).

Matthew and Luke relate more fully how this marvelous event, heralded from of old (Gen. 3:15; Isa. 7:14-16; 9:6-7; Micah 5:2), came to pass. The accounts indicate the unique parentage of the child Jesus. Mary was his mother. The Holy Ghost was his Father. He was truly man. He was truly God. Yet he was not merely man and he was not only God. He was both God and man, the God-man. God the Creator thus became a member of the human race, that he might lead men into his eternal kingdom. Obviously, this redemptive undertaking involves mystery, yet not such mystery as to prevent reasonable faith.

III. **Jesus' Genealogical Qualifications as the Messiah** (Matt. 1:1-17; Luke 3:23b-38)

Tiresome as the reading of genealogies may ordinarily be, these tables are recorded with good reasons. Two important reasons may be stated. First, every Jew knew from the Old Testament Scriptures that the promise of a Messiah was to be expected within a special lineage—the seed of Abraham, the tribe of Judah, and the royal line of David were genealogical tests. Secondly, these tables show Jesus to be the promised seed of Eve (note Gen. 3:15 and Luke's genealogy) and as such they suggest that the whole race is entitled to be the benefits of the Messiah's coming.

There is no catering, in these genealogies, to Jewish pride of race.   While Matthew represents Jesus as the son of Abraham, of Judah, and of David, he also shows him to be the descendant of personages with the least to recommend them from the standpoint of nationality and pedigree. He introduces four women, each of whom was connected with something irregular.   **Tamar**, the daughter-in-law of Judah, by the signet and bracelet in her hand, bears witness to every proud Jew of the hypocrisy in the life of Israel's first tribal head.   **Rahab**, the Canaanitish harlot, is a case which should have testified to all generations that salvation is by faith and not by pedigree.   **Ruth**, the Moabitess, the great grandmother of David, attained a place in Israel's royal line by her sterling faithfulness and not by rank of race.   **Bathsheba**, the wife of Uriah the Hittite, became the wife of David in connection with a multiple crime on the part of the otherwise highly accredited David.

Thus these genealogies stand as a two-fold witness, proving, on the one hand, that Jesus is eligible by ancestry to the throne of David, and on the other hand, that this ancestry is in itself unworthy of Jesus.   How fitting that the angel should announce regarding the coming of Jesus that he should "save his people from their sins" (Matt. 1:21).

IV. Heaven's Introduction of God's Son to Men

God's plan to save his people by sending his Son in human form involved the necessity of such an introduction of him that all would know that he was the Son of God, and not merely a man. How this was accomplished may readily be seen from the accounts of the Gospel writers.

1. The birth of John the Baptist was announced to Zacharias by a special visit of the angel of the Lord. In keeping with what Malachi had foretold, Zacharias was now told that through his barren wife Elisabeth this messenger of preparation should be born, and that in the spirit and power of Elias he would prepare the people for the Lord's coming (Luke 1:5-20).

2. The angel of the Lord likewise appeared to the virgin Mary announcing that she should conceive by the Holy Ghost and bring forth the son whose rise and eternal dominion was foretold by Isaiah (Luke 1:26-38; cf. Isa. 7:14; Dan. 2:44).

3. At the meeting of Mary and Elisabeth the unborn babe of Elisabeth (John the Baptist) leaped in her womb for joy (Luke 1:39-45). After exchanging what they knew, these women clearly understood that through Mary's offspring the Messiah should be born. The **Magnificat** of Mary, which followed their meeting, indicates that this was the case.

4. After Joseph's espousal (approximating engagement) to Mary, and after Mary's conception by the Holy Ghost, the angel of the Lord appeared to Joseph in a dream explaining the fact of Mary's conception and announcing to him the birth of the Savior, who should be called JESUS (Matt. 1:18-25).

5. When Jesus had been born in the stable at Bethlehem, the angel of the Lord appeared to shepherds of Judea breaking to them the glad news of the Savior's birth and giving as a sign the fact that they would find the babe wrapped in swaddling clothes in a manger of Bethlehem. With this announcement there was heard a chorus of angels singing, "Glory to God in the highest, and on earth peace, and good will toward men."

Coming with haste to the appointed place they found the facts as announced. They made news of what they experienced and returned with satisfaction and great joy (Luke 2:8-20).

6. Wise Men from the east were guided to Jerusalem by a star, where, according to their understanding a child was born destined to be King of the Jews (Matt. 2:1-12).

7. When Christ was baptized, thirty years later, heaven opened, the Holy Ghost descended upon him as a dove, and a voice from heaven said, "Thou art my beloved Son; in thee I am well pleased" (Luke 3:21-23). Since baptism was a public ceremony it is probable that this voice was heard by a large number of people. This was something of a cap sheaf to all previous introductions and announcements, making known the heavenly source of the Person who was to minister among men.

V. Jesus Comes to Manhood through Development (Luke 2:21-52; 3:21-23a; Matt. 3:13-17; Mark 1:9-11)

Growth, training, and development were elements in the constituting of the Son of Man just as was true of any other boy born in Judea. At the age of eight days he was circumcised. Later, after Mary's purification, he was presented for consecration at the Temple. At Nazareth he "grew and waxed strong in spirit, filled with wisdom: and the grace of God was upon him," which implies not only physical development but personal, and not only personal but spiritual. At the age of twelve he is seen to be subject to his parents, and in the subsequent years, we are told, he continued to be subject to them. It is evident, however, that from this year, at the latest, he was conscious, to a certain degree, of his mission from his heavenly Father. When, eighteen years later, he had reached the age of full manhood, he still adhered to the policy of fulfilling the Judean pattern of righteousness, and insisted, against John the Baptist's objection, upon being baptized. Thus, when Jesus began his ministry, those who knew him were made conscious of his normal humanity. Yet at the same time, Mary, and others no doubt, weighed in their hearts the unmistakable evidences of his unique divine origin.

In full keeping with the Judean pattern of righteousness, also, Jesus entered upon his ministry at the recognized age of maturity, which was thirty years (Luke 3:23). David became king at Jerusalem at the age of thirty. Priests ordinarily entered their ministry at this age. It was the normal time for a man to enter upon his life work.

VI. The Forerunner's Ministry (Matt. 3:1-12; Mark 1:1-8; Luke 3:1-20)

The very life of John the Baptist pulsated with the single purpose of heralding the coming of the Messenger of the Lord. As an unborn infant John leaped for joy in the womb of his mother Elisabeth at the presence of the Lord's appointed mother. When finally, through his public ministry, he had introduced the Lord, he made it a policy to fade out of the scene, to "decrease" that Christ might "increase."

The preparatory ministry of John was simple. He was but a voice, and he had a very limited message. There was no ostentation, no fan fare. His clothing of camel skin and a leathern girdle and his food of locusts and wild honey fitly symbolized the ruggedness of the truth which he spoke. He did not, primarily, announce the Lord's coming. That had already become a general expectation. Rather, he took up the question put by Malachi, "But who may abide the day of his coming? and who shall stand when he appeareth?" (Mal. 3). Transposing the question to positive and imperative form, John preached in all Judea, "Repent ye: for the kingdom of heaven is at hand." Those who responded by confessing their sins were baptized as a mark of their confession.

While John's message was simple, it did not permit any superficiality. Confession of sin meant just that. When therefore the Pharisees and Sadducees confessed their sins from one side of the mouth and boasted, from the other side, of their pedigree, they were told in John's straightforward terms that they were the offspring of vipers. Their pride, John said, was not the fruitage of true repentance.

As John probed the hearts of the multitudes who followed him, one after another they came to him concerned about knowing the will of God for their lives. Instead of telling them to quit their occupations in view of the coming of Christ, he told them **how** to fill their occupations.

Many asked, "What then must we do?" John answered them, "He that hath two coats, let him impart to him that hath none; and he that hath food, let him do likewise."

Publicans, coming to him for baptism, asked, "Master, what must we do?" To them John replied, "Extort no more than that which is appointed you."

Soldiers came to him, asking, "What must we do?" To them John replied, "Do violence to no man, neither exact anything wrongfully; and be content with your wages."

John was diligent to create in his followers a sense of Christ's greatness and of the high character of the work which he would do. In answer to the question put to John as to whether he were the Christ, he emphatically replied, "I indeed baptize you with water; but there cometh he that is mightier than I, the latchet of whose shoes I am unworthy to unloose: he shall baptize you with the Holy Ghost and with fire, whose fan is in his hand, thoroughly to cleanse his threshing floor, and to gather the wheat into the garner; but the chaff he will burn up with unquenchable fire."

VII. **Jesus' Preparation for His Mission Is Proved** (Matt. 4:1-11; Mark 1:9-13; Lk. 4:1-13)

The Temptation of Jesus in the wilderness was an experience marked with design. Before entering upon a mission to reconcile rebellious men to their God, Jesus in this experience demonstrated his complete devotion to the Father's will against the most extreme allurements of the god of this world. In this, Jesus rose above the common level of men, who, from Adam to Herod, had proved willing to serve Satan for a price. In this Temptation experience Jesus repudiated the course of rebellion against God which is the moral condition of the race. Henceforth, he would preach and teach, with the purpose of leading men to repudiate their rebellion, and through God's offered mercy, to enter into a life of faith and obedience to God.

The issues drawn in the Temptation were consistently followed to the Cross, where Jesus demonstrated to the whole world and for all time that one man had broken with sin and its Satanic chain, and led the way for the liberation of a multitude of captives. By receiving this man's lordship, men would be led out of sin into glorious liberty, and hence into the blessed righteousness of the Father's kingdom.

4. Discussion and Review

1. What do we know about the preincarnate activities of the Son of God?

2. Relate the account of the fuller hope which developed from the germ-hope announced in Gen. 3:15.

3. What is meant by the God-man idea?

4. Show that Jesus qualified genealogically as the Messiah. Was the genealogy worthy of him? Discuss.

5. Indicate the seven occasions in which heaven introduced the Son of God to men.

6. Trace Jesus' development to manhood.

7. Give an account of the early ministry of Jesus' forerunner.

8. What was proved by Jesus' temptation in the wilderness? How is this related to Jesus' role as the captain of our salvation?

5. Select Memory Passages
John 1:1-14; Matt. 1:21b; Luke 1:31-33

6. Character Review

Identify:

The Word (Logos)	Zacharias	The Shepherds
John the Baptist	Elisabeth	The Wise Men
Jesus	Mary	

7. Bibliography

Athanasius. *The Incarnation of the Word of God* (Translation). New York: Macmillan Co., 1946.

Blaikie, Wm. G. *Bible History.* Chap. XV, "Birth and Childhood of Jesus," pp. 412-422. New York: Thomas Nelson Co.

Edersheim, Alfred. *The Life and Times of Jesus the Messiah,* (2 volumes). Longmans.

Free, Joseph P. *Archaeology and Bible History.* Chap. XXVI, "The Life and Ministry of Christ." Wheaton: Van Kampen Press. Special Topics:
1. Prophecies of Christ in the Old Testament, p. 283.
2. The Amazing Significance of the Three Hundred Thirty-two Prophecies Concerning Christ, pp. 283, 284.
3. The Birth of Christ at Bethlehem, p. 284.
4. The Date of the Birth of Christ, pp. 284-285.
5. Evidence outside of the Bible of the Existence of Jesus Christ, p. 287.
6. Christ's Birth at Bethlehem; the Manger; the Inn, pp. 287, 288.
7. The Years of Silence, p. 288.

Kuyper, Abraham. *Women of the New Testament.* Grand Rapids: Zondervan.
1. "Elisabeth," pp. 7-10.
2. "Mary," pp. 11-20.
3. "Anna," pp. 21-23.

Morgan, G. Campbell. *The Crises of Christ.* New York: Fleming H. Revell. In this volume Dr. Morgan gets to the heart of seven great aspects of the Lord's life, i. e., the Incarnation, the Baptism, the Temptation, the Transfiguration, the Crucifixion, the Resurrection, and the Ascension.

Ockenga, H. J. *Have You Met These Women?* Grand Rapids: Zondervan.
Chapter V—"The Woman Whose Son Was the Greatest of Men."
Chapter X—"The Noblest Woman of All."

Orr, James. *The Virgin Birth of Christ.* New York: Charles Scribners.

Reich, Max I. *The Messianic Hope of Israel.* Grand Rapids: Eerdmans Pub. Co., 1940.

Sangster, Margaret E. *The Women of the Bible.* Chapt. XXIX, "Mary, the Mother of Jesus." New York: The Christian Herald.

Sangster, Margaret E. *The Women of the Bible.* Chapt. XXX, "Elisabeth, the Wife of Zacharias." New York: The Christian Herald.

Stevins, William Arnold and Burton, Ernest DeWitt. *The Harmony of the Gospels for Historical Study.* New York, 1905.

Warfield, Benjamin B. *The Person and Work of Christ.* Philadelphia: Presbyterian and Reformed Pub. Co., 1950.

Zwemer, Samuel. *The Glory of the Manger.* New York: American Tract Society.

Chapter 26

EARLY MINISTRIES OF JESUS

(27 A. D.)

1. Introduction

At the age of twelve Jesus had said, "I must be about my Father's business." Yet he was obliged to return to Nazareth and be subject to his earthly parents, waiting, although in preparation, for his time of ministry.

The beginning of his ministry was accentuated, as we have seen, in a signal way, by his baptism, his anointing by the Holy Spirit, and by making proof, in the Temptation, of his purpose. Following these events he began to preach and to do signs, and to make disciples.

At Bethabara, John the Baptist introduced Jesus as the Lamb of God to those who were to be his first disciples. After three days, during which John (unnamed), Philip, Andrew, Peter, and Nathanael were enlisted, Jesus, with his disciples, ministered for brief periods in Galilee, Judea, and Samaria.

The duration of this period of early ministry is usually considered to be from January to December of 27 A. D., a period of about a year.

I. John the Baptist Testifies of Christ (John 1:19-51; 3:22-36)

The Scriptures blocked out for study in this lesson cover the time when Jesus and John were both preaching. Jesus was beginning and John was coming to the close of his public ministry. During this time John bore testimony to the presence of the Christ in their midst.

2. Reading Assignment

Matthew	Mark	Luke	John
			1:19—2:12
			2:13-22
			2:23—3:36
4:12	1:14		4:1-3
			4:4-42

(Read the Bible first)

3. Study Outline

In Bethabara. While John preached in Bethabara certain inquirers came from the Pharisees of Jerusalem to learn of his identity. They wished, particularly, to know whether he was the Christ. John, denying that he was, bore witness to the fact that the Messiah was another, who was already in their midst, though they knew him not (John 1:19-28).

The next day, as Jesus was seen coming, John bore witness to the presence of the pre-existent One of whom he had been speaking, saying, "Behold the Lamb of God which taketh away the sin of the world!" "This is he," said John, "of whom I said, after me cometh a man which is preferred before me: for he was before me" (John 1:29-34).

It appears evident from this passage that John did not know Jesus to be the one whose coming he had been announcing until at Jesus' baptism the voice from heaven pointed him out. Now, similarly, he was pointing out the very person whom he had announced. Perhaps the representatives of the Jerusalem Pharisees were present on this occasion.

The next day Jesus was pointed out with similar words, "Behold the Lamb of God." On this occasion two of Christ's first disciples were called, John (the son of Zebedee) and Andrew. Andrew thrilled to know Jesus, hastened to bring Simon Peter, his brother. He also became Jesus' follower, obtaining on this occasion from Jesus his new name, Cephas or Peter, meaning rock or stone (John 1:35-42).

On the third day, Jesus called Philip, who like Peter and Andrew, was from Bethsaida in Galilee. Philip in turn found Nathanael, against whose reluctant faith he declared that in Jesus of Nazareth they had found the Messiah. Nathanael, upon meeting Jesus, was soon convinced and became the fifth disciple (John 1:43-51).

At Aenon. After three days Jesus and his disciples (five) went into Galilee for a brief ministry and then Jesus continued to preach and baptize in Judea (John 2:1-2; 2:13—3:24). During this time John the Baptist continued to preach and baptize in Aenon. An interesting conversation between John and his disciples about purifying arose as it became known that many persons, possibly some whom the Jews held unclean, were being baptized by Jesus. John took the occasion, not only to justify, but to extol Jesus. Jesus was from the Father. He was to John as the bridegroom is to the friend of the bridegroom. He must increase, John must decrease. Bearing on the subject of purification, John declared that acceptance with God is not merely a matter of ceremonial cleansing, but of receiving the One whom the Father sent. "He that believeth on the Son," John said, "hath everlasting life: and he that believeth not (obeyeth not) the Son shall not see life; but the wrath of God abideth on him" (John 3:25-36).

II. Jesus' Early Ministry in Galilee (John 2:1-12)

After choosing five disciples Jesus took them with him and went into Galilee (John 1:43). At Cana, not far from Nazareth, Jesus performed the miracle of turning water into wine. This was the first of Jesus miracles by which he manifested his glory and led his disciples to believe (2:11). Of the purpose of these miracles (signs) John said, ". . . . these are written that ye might believe that Jesus is the Christ, the Son of God; and that believing ye might have life through his name" (John 20:21).

Leaving the vicinity of his native home, Jesus, accompanied by his mother, his brethren, and his disciples went to Capernaum which was near the home of Philip, Andrew, and Peter, and which became a kind of adopted home of our Lord. After a brief visit here Jesus made his way to Jerusalem where the feast of Passover was to be observed (John 2:12-13).

III. Jesus' Early Ministry in Judea (John 2:13—3:36)

1. The First Cleansing of the Temple (2:13-22)

Jesus made his first public appearance at Jerusalem on the occasion of the Passover. The only recorded instances of his presence in the Temple prior to this were at his consecration in infancy, and at the age of twelve when he came with his parents. It is very possible, however, that after the age of twelve he attended the annual Passover regularly.

This was his first attendance at the Passover following full preparation for his ministry. Accordingly, he entered the Temple now with an authority that was not in evidence before.

2. An Interview with Nicodemus (2:23—3:21)

We are told that at this Passover season Jesus did miracles (signs). No record is given of the particular miracles which he did in Judea at this early time, but it is simply stated that many believed on his name as a result of the miracles. This belief was shallow, and Jesus knew it. He did not yet trust himself to these people (2:23-25).

Nicodemus is perhaps typical of many of the believers who followed Jesus at this Passover season. He was a Pharisee, and a ruler and teacher of the Jews, yet he did not understand the experience of a new birth by the Spirit of God. The clear implication of Jesus' word to him is that he ought to have understood this subject. In dealing with Nicodemus, several distinct steps are seen in Jesus' procedure. First, Jesus stated positively the fact that a new birth by the Spirit is an essential entrance requirement of God's kingdom. Next, Jesus made it clear that it is neither necessary nor possible to understand the mystery of the new birth. Thirdly, he illustrated the manner of experiencing the new birth by the incident of the serpent in the wilderness; the Son of Man lifted up is the appointed way of salvation. Fourthly, eternal life, that is, the new birth, is realized by believing in the Son of Man. In final emphasis, Jesus told Nicodemus that the way of salvation is simply a matter of desiring and receiving the knowledge (light) which God has revealed. Condemnation (or judgment) rests upon all who love darkness rather than light (John 3:1-22).

It is of interest to observe that later when Jesus faced the cross, Nicodemus defended him against the Pharisees, which would support the supposition that he became a true believer after the interview of the third chapter of John (John 7:50; 19:39).

The imprisonment of John the Baptist by Herod the tetrarch of

Peraea (Matt. 4:12; Mark 1:14) became the signal for Jesus to leave this area. Naturally, such an action carried the implication of peril for Jesus. The particulars of John's clash with Herod are found in the following passages: Matt. 14:3-5; Mark 6:17-18; Lk. 3:19-20. The fact is, however, that it was now time in Christ's schedule of ministry to begin his larger labors in Galilee.

IV. Jesus' Early Ministry in Samaria (John 4:1-42)

In going from Judea to Galilee, John tells us, "he (Jesus) must needs go through Samaria" (4:4). While this probably refers to no more than geographical necessity, there proved to be an appointment of no small importance for Jesus in Samaria. Other Jews might by preference have gone the circuitous route east of the Jordan to reach Galilee. Jesus on purpose, we may be sure, went through it.

Two phases of significance to our present study may be noted in this incident. 1. It reveals the attitude and the method of Jesus toward an unpedigreed sinner. At Jerusalem Jesus had just revealed the way of life to Nicodemus, a man of note in Judea. Now, we see him revealing the well of life to one of a discredited race.

As in the interview with Nicodemus, here again Jesus orders each step of the interview according to his purpose of leading a soul to believe. He first of all put aside the racial barrier between himself and the woman. He then by analogy directed her mind to the eternal life which he desired to give. Having awakened a sense of desire, he put his finger upon the woman's sinful life. His offer of eternal life, together with his convicting searchlight upon her life, led her to recognize him as a prophet, and then as the Messiah.

2. This incident reveals the beginnings of a harvest in Samaria. The testimony of the Samaritan woman and the two day ministry of Jesus led many Samaritans to believe. Jesus referred to Samaria as a whitened harvest field. Doubtless the parable of the Good Samaritan, which Jesus spoke later, reflected something of the spiritual harvest of Samaria. Jesus made it clear that God was seeking people regardless of race or place and that the true worship of God was the result of such a meeting. There were later harvests in Samaria for which this early ministry of Jesus was doubtless an important preparation.

4. Discussion and Review

1. What was the relation of Jesus and John the Baptist during the period under study in this chapter?

2. Name the five men whom Jesus called to be his disciples in this Bethabara ministry.

3. What question arose at Aenon and how did John the Baptist deal with it?

4. Relate the account of Jesus' first miracle (sign) as to place, persons present, the occasion and need, and the divine purpose (compare John 20:30, 31 and 2:11).

5. What interests made it natural for Capernaum to become the adopted home of Jesus and his disciples?

6. Upon what occasion did Jesus return from Galilee to Jerusalem?

7. With what new authority did Jesus go to the temple at this time? How did he manifest it?

8. Evaluate the reality of the belief which many proposed at this time.

9. Identify and characterize the man who came to Jesus by night. What did Jesus teach him as to the way of salvation? What was the outcome of the interview?

10. What circumstance occasioned Jesus' departure from Judea at this time?

11. In going to Galilee, why did Jesus say he "must needs go through Samaria"? (John 4:4).

12. Indicate the twofold significance of the Lord's ministry in Samaria on this occasion.

5. Select Memory Passages
John 3:3-16, 18, 36

6. Character Review

Identify:

Andrew	Philip	Peter
John	Nathanael	Nicodemus

7. Bibliography

Free, Joseph P. *Archaeology and Bible History.* Chap. XXVI, "The Life and Ministry of Christ." Topic: The Baptism of Christ and the Early Judean Ministry. Wheaton: Van Kampen Press, 1950. Pp. 289-291.

Kuyper, Abraham. *Women of the New Testament*. Grand Rapids: Zondervan. "The Woman of Samaria," pp. 46-49.

Sangster, Margaret E. *The Women of the Bible*. Chapt. XXXI, "Salome, the Mother of James and John." New York: The Christian Herald.

Sangster, Margaret E. *The Women of the Bible*. Chapt. XXXII, "The Woman at the Well of Samaria." New York: The Christian Herald.

Sangster, Margaret E. *The Women of the Bible*. Chapt. XXXIII, "Mary of Magdala." New York: The Christian Herald.

Chapter 27

CHRIST'S GREATER GALILEAN MINISTRY

—Part One
(28 A. D.)

1. Introduction

More than half of Christ's forty-month ministry was spent in Galilee. In fact Galilee, rather than Jerusalem, was the home of our Lord. Though born in Judea he grew to manhood in Galilee. His ministries in Jerusalem were in the nature of visits. When finally he left Galilee and went toward Jerusalem it was with the consciousness that it would involve his death at the hands of Jerusalem leaders.

The Greater Galilean ministry falls rather naturally into three parts. The first begins at the close of Jesus' early Judean ministry and extends to the choosing of the twelve disciples. The second extends from the choosing of the twelve to Christ's withdrawal into northern Galilee. The third leads to Christ's final departure for Jerusalem. In our study we shall devote one chapter to Part I, two chapters to Part II, and one chapter to Part III.

2. Reading Assignment

Part I—From Jesus' Return to Galilee to the Choosing
of the Twelve

Matthew	Mark	Luke	John
4:12, 17-22	1:14—3:6	4:14—6:11	4:43—5
8:14-17			
8:2-4			
9:2-17			
12:1-14			

(Read the Bible first)

3. Study Outline

I. In the Vicinity of Nazareth

As we remember, Jesus' public ministry began in Cana of Galilee where he performed his first miracle (John 2). At Cana again,
he now performs his first recorded miracle of healing in this greater
Galilean ministry, the case being that of the son of a nobleman from
Capernaum (John 4:43-54). It is conspicuous that the only recorded
miracle in this part of Galilee was performed upon the faith of a
stranger to the country itself and in spite of the unbelief of Jesus'
countrymen.

At Nazareth Jesus came to an issue with the religious leaders of
the area when he read from the Scriptures and preached in their
synagogue. After reading from Isaiah 61, he forthrightly identified
himself with Isaiah's servant of the Lord. But Jesus read not only
from Isaiah; he also read and declared the unbelief which he saw in
the hearts of those present. This so angered them that they would
have destroyed him had he not slipped from their grasp (Luke 4:16-
30).

It should be observed that the message of Jesus in his early
ministry was identical with that of John the Baptist. The kingdom
was at hand, and in view of this, people were to repent for the remission of their sins. His native country folk made little response
to this spiritual appeal. Their unbelief rendered any real manifestation of his glory impossible.

II. From Nazareth to Capernaum (Luke 4:16-30)

Being rejected by his countrymen at Nazareth Jesus went to Capernaum, which, it appears, became his adopted home and the returning point of his journeys into Galilee. Jesus had now felt a major impact of rejection both at Jerusalem and at Nazareth. Consequently, as Isaiah had foretold, the "great light" of God was to shine upon "Galilee of the Gentiles," upon the people which sat in darkness" (Matt. 4:14-16). It should be noted that Bethsaida, which was the home of Philip, Simon Peter, and Andrew (John 1:44), was only about a mile from Capernaum. This was also the home vicinity of Zebedee and his sons.

III. The Call of Four Fishermen (Luke 5:1-11)

Not long after Jesus' arrival at Capernaum, he came to Peter, Andrew, James, and John as they washed their nets by the seashore of Lake Galilee. They had made no catch during the night before and were giving up. Jesus took a position in one of their boats and taught them. Then he gave orders to the fishermen by which they took in a miraculously large catch of fish. Jesus gave the whole incident a turn in keeping with his higher purpose. While the fishermen were marveling at the catch, Jesus drew another net. Upon Jesus' promise to henceforth make them fishers of men, "they left all and followed him." It will be remembered that three of these disciples had previously been called. This was now a call to specific preparation for service.

IV. A Typical Sabbath Day's Ministry at Capernaum (Mark 1:21-34. Also Matt. 8:14-17 and Luke 4:31-41)

Fulfilling Jewish custom, Jesus went to the synagogue on the sabbath day. He taught. But the teaching of that day was different from a regular synagogue service. The Son of God spoke, and whereas in other times the order of service was very regular, on this occasion lurking demons were probed from their restful abodes and responded to the authority of the speaker. There is little wonder that upon disbanding from service that morning news of the Christ speedily circulated into all Galilee.

Leaving the synagogue service Jesus went to the home of Simon Peter where his healing touch rebuked the fever of Peter's mother-in-law. Upon being healed, she in turn ministered to those present.

At evening, after the passing of the sabbath ban on travel, the people came in with their sick and demon possessed, and he healed "every one of them." It appears from the accounts that Capernaum must have had an unusually high health rating after that day. Matthew clearly states that these activities were the direct fulfillment of Isaiah's prophecy (Isa. 53), "Himself took our infirmities and bare our sicknesses."

V. A Tour into Galilee (Mark 1:35-45; Luke 4:42-44; 5:12-16)

In this block of Scripture we have a brief report of Jesus' first of three recorded tours through Galilee. We are not told where Jesus went except that it was "throughout all Galilee." The account leads us to assume that the typical sabbath day's ministry which we have observed, characterized the tour. It is important to observe the sense of mission expressed by Jesus in regard to this tour. Against the clamor of the people of Capernaum who followed him into the desert, he insisted that he must "go elsewhere into the next towns" to "preach there also." This, he said, was the purpose for which he had been sent. Only one among the many miracles which he did on this tour is recorded, which is the healing of a leper.

VI. Christ Teaches His Power to Forgive Sins (Matt. 9:2-8; Mark 2:1-12; Luke 5:17-26)

As soon as it was known in Capernaum that Jesus had returned, the crowds of needy people regathered. Among the many our attention is focused upon a certain paralytic, four of whose friends let him down through an opening in the roof of the crowded house where Jesus was ministering.

Keeping first things first, Jesus spoke the word of forgiveness to the paralytic, and then while all were in attention, awaiting the healing miracle he affirmed his authority to forgive sins. When Jesus healed the man it was to the end that those present might trust him for the forgiveness of their sins. The man, of course, had the advantage of the twofold benefit, and went away glorifying God.

VII. The Call of Matthew the Publican (Matt. 9:9-13; Mark 2:13-17; Luke 5:27-32)

The account of the call of six disciples up to this time has been observed. Levi or Matthew is the seventh. The call and the response are given in few words. Matthew's response was immediate and magnanimous. The incident involved Jesus in social intermingling with those regarded by the scribes and Pharisees as sinners. It must be borne in mind that the word sinner referred primarily to social outcasts. We are told nothing about the moral and spiritual status of Matthew, but Jesus must have seen in him the making of an apostle, one who would be able to reach others of his class. Matthew, in his list of the apostles, refers to himself, humbly, as Matthew the publican. He was manifestly, a man of deep spiritual insight as is seen from the aptness by which in his Gospel account he reproduces the teachings of Jesus.

VIII. The Underlying Principle of Fasting—Two Types of Followers (Matt. 9:14-17; Mark 2:18-22; Luke 5:33-39)

It appears that the disciples of John the Baptist were characterized by fasting. The Pharisees fasted regularly and methodically. Jesus' disciples seemed to be committed to no rigorous rules along this line. In fact, they did not fast at all, Mark says.

Why, Jesus was asked, is this so? Jesus' answer was given by three analogies, that of the bridegroom and the sons of the bridechamber, that of the patched garment, and that of the wine skins.

The principle enunciated set aside fasting as an end in itself. Fasting ought to be a sincere expression of sorrow, but where there is no occasion for sorrow, fasting has no real meaning. This cancelled out the legal and meritorious considerations with which fasting was then commonly practiced.

This incident should not be taken to indicate that Jesus did not fast, nor that spiritual people never will. It simply means that fasting should be genuine, sincere, and appropriate.

IX. Jesus Heals a Thirty-Eight Year Case—Receives a Twofold Charge of Criticism (John 5)

This incident took place at Jerusalem, where Jesus went to attend a Feast, probably the Feast of Tabernacles. There was there, among a multitude of sick, blind, halt and withered, a man more feeble than all the rest and perhaps the most hopeless of all. Jesus directed his attention upon this hardest case and healed him. He also gave him sober counsel against continuing to live a life of sin.

The characteristic objections of the Jewish leaders followed. First, he was reproved for doing the miracle on the sabbath. In answer to this charge Jesus laid the responsibility for the deed back upon the Father whose work he was doing. This served but to provoke hotter objection, for in claiming to be from God, he was regarded as a blasphemer.

In connection with this miracle Jesus discoursed very definitely concerning the future resurrection and the inevitable issues of judgment involved. The decisive issue for all men is their faith in Christ.

Jesus then set forth four sources of testimony upon which his claim rested, namely John the Baptist, the character of his works, the Father's direct utterance, and the Scriptures. On the basis of their Scriptures, particularly, Jesus charged the Pharisees with unbelief.

X. **The Principle of the Sabbath and a Test Case Regarding Corn Plucking** (Matt. 12:1-8; Mark 2:23-28; Luke 6:1-5)

On their way back to Capernaum, the disciples being hungry, plucked handfuls of grain from the wayside cornfield. This was not considered wrong according to the custom of Palestine. But it was done on the sabbath day and this was the point of objection by the Pharisees.

In reply Jesus cited as a parallel case the instance of David's use, in a time of need, of shewbread, which ordinarily was eaten only by the priests. He also cited the fact that the priests profane the sabbath and are considered guiltless, i. e., they do so because the conduct of worship itself requires it.

Two principles are expressed in Jesus' handling of this question. First, the sabbath was made **for** man, to serve his need and to do good to him. It is a merciful provision of God. It is not intended to prevent the satisfaction of his need. Secondly, the giver of the sabbath law is greater than the law itself. He is its lord. It is his right and his duty to allow such exceptions as are essential to the ends of the law itself.

XI. **The Principle of the Sabbath and the Healing of a Withered Hand** (Matt. 12:9-14; Mark 3:1-6; Luke 6:6-11)

Another case involving the principle of the sabbath arose as Jesus went into the synagogue. In the presence of a man with a withered hand were Jesus and the Pharisees. The Pharisees waited to see what Jesus would do that they might find an accusation to criticize him. Matthew says they asked Jesus whether it would be lawful to heal on the sabbath day. Mark and Luke indicate that they asked this question in their thoughts.

Jesus answered by putting other questions to them. If your sheep fell into a pit would you rescue it on the sabbath day? They did not answer. Is it lawful to do good or harm on the sabbath? Again they did not answer. Jesus looked upon them with anger because of the hardness of their hearts. Turning to the man with a withered hand he answered his own question by "doing good." The Pharisees were mad and conjured with the Herodians "how they might destroy him." Ordinarily, they were unfriendly with the Herodians.

XII. **The Wide-spread Popularity of Christ** (Matthew 4:23-25; 12:15-21; Mark 3:7-12; Luke 6:17-19)

The Pharisees' hardness of heart was more than matched by Jesus' popularity. There was enough discernment in the common man to recognize that Jesus, whoever he was and in spite of his clash with the Pharisees, was the person whom they needed.
Matthew describes his ministry at this time as follows:

1. It included all of Galilee.
2. The synagogues were the common meeting places.
3. It consisted of teaching, preaching, healing, and deliverance from demons.
4. The subject of his preaching was "the gospel of the kingdom."

From the various parts where he had ministered the people followed Jesus, attempting if possible to touch him that his healing power might be realized. From all parts of Galilee, from Decapolis, from Judea, from Perea, from Idumea, and from the coasts of Tyre and Sidon the people came.

The manifestation of demons was a constant phenomenon among these who came for help. The demons were subject to Christ. Wherever he went he proved that he had the power, foretold by God at the dawn of human history, to crush the serpent's head.

4. Discussion and Review

1. What proportion of Jesus' ministry was devoted to Galilee? How do you explain this?

2. Give the bounding events of the Greater Galilean ministry.

3. Relate the account of the first recorded miracle of healing in this Greater Galilean ministry. Who was healed?

4. Characterize the attitude of Jesus' countrymen toward Jesus' ministry. How do you explain it?

5. What made Capernaum rather than Cana or Nazareth the appropriate headquarters of Jesus' ministry?

6. Describe the call of the four fishermen.

7. Describe a typical Sabbath day's ministry of Jesus at Capernaum.

8. Depict Jesus' sense of mission as seen in his tours of Galilee.

9. Show how Jesus turned to spiritual account the healing of the paralytic let down through the roof.

10. Name and characterize the seventh man called to be a disciple of Jesus.

11. Characterize Jesus' disciples regarding the practice of fasting. How did Jesus explain the matter?

12. What objections were raised against Jesus in relation to his healing of the thirty-eight year invalid at the temple? Upon what four sources of testimony did Jesus rest his claims?

13. When the Pharisees complained to Jesus because the disciples plucked corn on the Sabbath, how did Jesus reply?

14. What principle of Sabbath observing did Jesus teach in relation to the healing of the man with a withered hand?

15. Give Matthew's description of Jesus' Ministry.

5. Select Memory Passages

Luke 4:18, 19; Matt. 4:19; Luke 5:31, 32

6. Character Review

Identify:

Jesus	Andrew	John
Peter	James	Matthew

7. Bibliography

Blaikie, Wm. G. *Bible History.* Chap. XV, Section II. New York:　Thomas Nelson Co.
Topics:
1. The Lake of Galilee: Accounts of Travelers, pp. 429, 430.
2. Plain of Gennesaret, p. 430.
3. Cities of Galilee, pp. 430, 431.
4. Fishing, pp. 431, 432.
Free, Joseph P. *Archaeology and Bible History.* Chap. XXVI. Wheaton: Van Kampen Press, 1950.
Topic: The Galilean Ministry, pp. 291, 292.
Kuyper, Abraham. *Women of the New Testament.* Grand Rapids: Zondervan. "Peter's Mother-in-Law," pp. 24-27.

Chapter 28

CHRIST'S GREATER GALILEAN MINISTRY

—Part Two
—From the Choosing of the Twelve to
the Withdrawal into Northern Galilee
(28-29 A. D.)

1. Introduction

In Jesus' ministry up to this point there had been a great response on the part of the masses. Many had sought Jesus for help. Many had believed. Among these we have observed six who were especially called to follow Jesus, namely Philip, Andrew, Peter, Nathanael, James, and John. They had chosen Jesus, but that was not all, Jesus had chosen them. Now Jesus is seen to concern himself further with this selective procedure. "He goeth up into a mountain," Mark says, "and calleth unto himself whom he himself would." After a whole night spent in prayer Jesus added to the seven already chosen five more men, and called them apostles (sent ones). While he himself continued to minister, he reckoned with the fact that if all people for whom the gospel was intended were to hear, he would have to **send** others who were prepared to preach it. The immediate purpose of this call to apostleship was that those selected "might be with him" (Mark 3:14) in view of the time when they they would be sent forth.

In keeping with the above purpose it is to be observed that in the part of the Galilean ministry which we are about to study occurred the great discourses on the kingdom, particularly the Sermon on the Mount and the parables of the Kingdom.

311

2. Lesson Assignment

Matthew	Mark	Luke	John
10:2-4	3:13-19a	6:12-19	
5, 6, 7		6:20-49	
8:5-13		7:1-10	
		7:11-17	
11:2-30		7:18-35	
		7:36-50	
		8:1-3	
12:22-45	3:19b-30		
12:46-50	3:31-35	8:19-21	

(Read the Bible first)

3. Study Outline

I. **The Choosing of the Twelve** (Matt. 10:2-4; Mark 3:13-19; Luke 6:12-19)

The complete list of the apostles includes the following names:

John	James the Son of Zebedee
Andrew	James the Son of Alphaeus
Simon Peter	Thomas
Philip	Simon the Canaanite
Bartholomew	Judas, the brother of James
or Nathanael	(Lebbeus, Thaddeus)
Matthew	Judas Iscariot

It is estimated that the full college of apostles was made up about a year and a half after Jesus began his public ministry. Doubtless, of course, these twelve had been among the many who followed Jesus and exhibited the qualities which led him to make them his choice for special training and for special service. It is evident, however, that these were not chosen because they were perfect, nor in all cases because of their special capacity for instruction. Peter was slow to learn and temperamental. Thomas was a chronic doubter. Judas Iscariot grew increasingly wicked in the course of the Lord's disciplines and ceased being an apostle altogether. It would appear that this group was not characterized by any special distinctions. They were rank and file people. They were not called to impress the world with their own personalities but to be effective witnesses of Christ. To this end their prime qualification was that they be just ordinary people, willing to learn and tell the truth. Why Jesus should have chosen one such as Judas we may not fully explain, except perhaps to say that he was not a thief at the time Jesus called him. It is evident that Judas' character deteriorated so that eventually he was not with Christ but against him. The Scriptures say that he fell. A high office does not mean immunity to evil.

II. **The Sermon on the Mount—Principles of the Kingdom** (Matt. 5, 6, 7, 8:1; Luke 6:20-49)

The exact mount which provided the meeting place for the Sermon on the Mount is not known. The rather late view of tradition points to Karn Hattin (Horns of Hattin). While this is uncertain, it was quite probably one of the mounts of the ranges which stretch north from Capernaum.

The discourse was doubtless delivered at one time, although Luke in his account connects different parts with various occasions. It is likely that the sermon may have embodied elements which were also given on other occasions. It is important to note that the Sermon on the Mount came not at the beginning of Jesus' ministry but late in the second year, after the inner circle of twelve disciples had been formed.

Principles of righteousness have to do with the heart—with the inner motives of life. Such principles rest not upon academic instruction, not upon the declaration of a law, but upon spiritual life and spiritual relationships. On this Edersheim writes with appropriate insight:

"Christ came to found a Kingdom, not a School; to institute a fellowship, not to propound a system. To the first disciples all doctrinal teachings sprang out of fellowship with Him. They saw Him, and therefore believed; they believed, and therefore learned the truths connected with Him, and springing out of Him. So to speak, the seed of truth which fell on their hearts was carried thither from the flower of His Person and Life."

Two characteristics of this sermon are significant. It is vitally related to the Old Testament law—its distinction being that of fulfillment. On the other hand it stands in contrast to the rabbinical teachings of contemporary Judaism. It is the out-flowering of God's earlier and progressively revealed law of life for his people.

The following diagram will afford a general analysis of the sermon and at the same time a comparison with the common elements of the earlier instruction of God.

The Pentateuch and the Sermon on the Mount

The Pentateuch	The Sermon on the Mount

Part I. Exod. 20, 21, 22, 23
  Prologue (20:1)
  The Ten Commandments
  47 laws against common sins
  The supremacy of love (Deut. 6)
	Part I. (Matt. 5)
	  The Beatitudes (vss. 1-12)
	  Epilogue (vss. 13-16)
	  Laws against prevailing unrighteousness (vss. 17-42)
	  The supremacy of love (vss. 43-48)

Part II. (Exod. 25-40; Leviticus)
  1. Tabernacle Worship:
    Offerings for equipment
    Priestly service
    Sacrifices
    Sacred seasons
  2. God to dwell in the midst of his people (Exod. 25:8)
	Part II. (Matt. 6)
	  1. Religious Exercises:
	    Alms
	    Prayer
	    Fasting
	
	  2. God and his kingdom to be first (6:33)

Part III. Numbers and Deuteronomy
  The Test of Life:
  The inclination to low levels of desire with chastenings
  God's providences spurned
  Resentment of authority
  Fumbling of opportunity
  The people were tested on the basis of faith and obedience. The promised land was for those who faithfully obeyed
	Part III. (Matt. 7)
	  The Test of Life:
	  Hypocrisy and false prophets
	  Effectual prayer
	  The golden rule
	  The strait gate and narrow way
	  Fruits of righteousness
	  Hearing and doing in relation to final reckoning with God

Figure 33

Both the Old Testament law and the New Testament law require faith and obedience for their fulfillment. Both rest back for spiritual power upon redeeming grace. Both were given after great manifestations of God's person, and both looked forward to a great inheritance. Both outlined the good, the perfect, and the acceptable will of God for redeemed people.

III. **The Amazing Faith of a Gentile—A Contrast** (Matt. 8:5-13; Luke 7:1-10)

The centurion of this occasion reminds us of the nobleman who came to Jesus at Cana near the beginning of Jesus' greater Galilean ministry (John 4:46-54). Both were from Capernaum. One came in behalf of a very sick son, the other in behalf of a palsied servant. The nobleman at first asked Jesus to come from Cana to Nazareth to perform the healing but upon Jesus' word he believed that the healing could be accomplished at a distance. The centurion, we suggest, doubtless knew of the nobleman's experience, hence his bold request that Jesus heal his servant without coming to his house.

The centurion drew a very significant analogy in his appeal to Jesus. He was an officer and understood proper regard for authority. Surely, his mind reasoned, the Son of God needs only to speak the word and all in his world should promptly respond to his will.

Jesus counted the centurion a prize among the multitudes. He was amazed that while some with so much knowledge were slow to believe, this man of the Gentiles accorded him full faith, fully recognizing both his sovereignty and his goodness.

A significant picture of the ultimate kingdom of God upon earth is simply depicted here. Abraham, Isaac, and Jacob, whom we are to regard as resurrected, will be there. Joining them are pictured this centurion and "many" other persons like him without religious or racial pedigree who came from all directions of the compass. Excluded from the kingdom, in contrast, Jesus said, will be the "sons of the kingdom," i. e., such as are only nominally sons, who have accorded Jesus no faith and have denied his authority.

IV. **Raising of the Nain Widow's Dead Son** (Luke 7:11-17)

Of the three recorded instances in which Jesus raised persons from the dead, two of the instances occur in this first third of the greater Galilean ministry. Nain was a village lying about five miles south of Nazareth along the Galilee-Samaria border.

The incident was dramatic. There are pictured a widow mother in a funeral procession following the bier of her only son whose body was being borne by the customary pallbearers. The woman wept. Jesus, in compassion said, "Weep not." He touched the bier. The procession stopped. Jesus addressing the dead, commanded, "Arise." The son arose and was restored to his mother.

The record includes the responses of the witnesses. They feared. They concluded that a great prophet had arisen. The report was circulated in the surrounding region. It is significant that history records no refutation of the genuineness of this act, nor even so much as an attempt at refutation. Had it been spurious, surely Jesus had plenty of enemies to take advantage of any misrepresentation.

V. John and Jesus Correspond—Jesus Upbraids and Comforts (Matt. 11:2-30; Luke 7:18-35)

This block of Scriptures centers in John the Baptist, who continued a prisoner of King Herod. John sent messengers to Jesus requesting a confirmation of Jesus' claim to be the Christ. This request was not, evidently, an indication of bad faith on John's part, for Jesus returns no rebuke.

Jesus' answer to John was not a simple positive affirmation. Affirmations are not proof. Rather Jesus returned a report of the works which were accompanying his mission. By these, such a student of the Old Testament as John could judge for himself. Jesus added, however, what was probably a needed word of encouragement, saying, "Blessed is he, whosoever shall find none occasion of stumbling in me."

From this conference with John's messengers, Jesus turned to the mutlitude of bystanders and to them spoke of John as a peer of greatness. Yet John's greatness was limited to the preparatory stage of the kingdom. Any position in the kingdom, Jesus said, is greater than the highest position in the preparatory stage. The spirit and power of Elijah were the marks of the preparatory messenger, but a far greater glory radiated from the presence of the messenger of the Covenant himself.

On the other hand, those who despised the kingdom brought from Jesus a solemn pronouncement of woe. Not less amazing than the marvelous works of Christ was the fact that in cities such as Chorazin, Bethsaida, and Capernaum, anyone could still remain cynically outside the kingdom. Such rejectors, Jesus said, would rank lower in the day of judgment than Sodom and Gomorrah.

The discourse closes with a prayer of gratitude to the Father and an invitation of welcome to all humble souls. Jesus offers a yoke—that is the occasion of offense to some, but it is the true answer to human need, and the fullest assurance of blessing is given to those who take it.

VI.   Jesus in the House of Simon the Pharisee (Luke 7:36-50)

Here is a somewhat typical situation. Simon the Pharisee and the woman who anointed Jesus are not otherwise known to us. Though not to be identified with Mary at Bethany (John 12) this woman reminds us of her. The willingness of the Pharisee to discredit Jesus because he took no account of the character of the woman is a trait which appeared many times in the Pharisees. The woman was a sinner in the sense that she was not a Jewess. We are not told what kind of life she lived. Jesus did not carry a set of balances to weigh her sins but judged her according to her heart. On this score, he proved to Simon, she ranked above him, and on this basis he freely forgave her sins.

VII.   Christ's Second Preaching Tour (Luke 8:1-3)

Again Jesus made a circuit through Galilee. We are not told where the tour led him. The party included the twelve, and certain women who ministered to Jesus and his disciples. It appears that these women represent the type of devotion which the "sinner" in Simon's house had shown. Much indeed had been done for them. It appears that persons freed from evil spirits were known for their personal attachment to their new master.

VIII.   Christ Warns the Scribes and Pharisees of Their Peril (Matt. 12:22-45; Mark 3:20-30)

Jesus had completely restored a man who had the multiple affliction of demon possession, blindness, and deafness, and the multitudes confessed that Jesus must be the son of David. On the contrary, certain Pharisees went to the greatest conceivable extreme to explain away this evidence of Christ's deity. They secretly charged that he was in collusion with Beelzebub, the prince of devils. Jesus read their minds and replied. First of all this would be impossible. Satan could have no purpose in casting himself out. The Lord's question, "By whom do your sons cast them out?" had the effect of playing up the impotence of the Pharisees to do anything about demons. Their sons were not casting them out. What was needed was something powerful enough to bind up the "strong man." Jesus had come to do that job. He had come to crush the head of the Serpent. The Pharisees by taking sides against Jesus thereby became the allies of the Serpent. Hence, Jesus called them a generation of vipers. Jesus declared that everyone classifies himself—one either gathers or scatters.

Christ warned of the peril into which the Pharisees were moving. It was not unforgivable that they should reject Christ. The Lord later prayed for the forgiveness of those who crucified him. The sin which could not be forgiven was blasphemy against the Holy Spirit who is the agent in the world accomplishing repentance and the spiritual new birth. To misrepresent his work by attributing it to Satan is to cut off the source of forgiveness. Such a reprobate attitude as calls evil good and good evil is not only wrong but it is wicked. There is no moral ground on which it can be forgiven. Some asked Jesus for a sign, as though the nature of his works, already observed, was not sufficient ground for faith. Jesus declared that such a request arose from an evil and adulterous condition. Men who are set upon selfish ends must have the last ounce of proof before they will accept a matter. When all proof is in, they will try to win their case by calling a thing what it is not. Jesus would allow them but one sign, the type of Jonah. If after his resurrection, they were in earnest about evidence, there should have been no further difficulty. But Jesus knew that many were too wicked to weigh evidence. For their obstinate unbelief, Jesus declared, the Ninevites and the queen of Egypt would pass judgment upon them.

IX. **Christ Speaks Concerning Relatives** (Matt. 12:46-50; Mark 3:31-35; Luke 8:19-21)

The question of family relationship was to Jesus a spiritual matter. Jesus did not neglect his blood relatives. This is proved by the concern which he had for the future of his mother as he provided for her from the cross. But had Mary sought to stand against the will of God, Jesus would promptly have disowned her claims.

The "fatherhood of God" is a misnomer when applied to men in general. Some men are of their father the devil, Jesus said. Others by faith and obedience are the children of God.

4. Discussion and Review

1. What were the underlying considerations in Jesus' choice of the Twelve?

2.   Name the twelve apostles.

3.   When was the full college of apostles made up?

4.   Would you say that Jesus chose extraordinary men?   Discuss.

5.   Discuss the Sermon on the Mount as to place and time, as to its relation to the Old Testament law, as to its requirement, as to the spiritual power which it presupposes and as to the present and future life which it anticipates.

6.   What would you say regarding the idea that the Sermon on the Mount is not applicable to this age?

7.   What insights and foresights regarding the kingdom of God are afforded in connection with the healing of the centurion's servant?

8.   Relate the first of the three recorded instances in which Jesus raised persons from the dead.   How is its genuineness attested?

9.   Relate the correspondence between Jesus and John the Baptist and the remarks to Jesus' bystanders which it occasioned.

10.   Relate the incident in the home of Simon the Pharisee and indicate its typical significance.

11.   What were some particular features of Christ's second preaching tour in Galilee?

12.   Discuss the peculiar peril concerning which Jesus warned the Scribes and Pharisees in relation to the healing of a man's multiple affliction.

13.   Give a true statement of Jesus' attitude toward his relatives.

5.   Select Memory Passages

Matthew 5-7, or special portions: 5:1-12; 13-16; 48; 6:9-13, 33; 7:21; 24-27.

6.   Character Review

Identify:

Andrew	James	Simon the Canaanite
John	(Son of Zebedee)	James
Simon Peter	Thomas	(Son of Alphaeus)
Philip	Judas	Judas Iscariot
Bartholomew	(Brother of James)	Herod Antipas
(Nathanael)	Lebbeus	Simon the Pharisee
Matthew	Thaddeus	Beelzebub

7. Bibliography

Blaikie, Wm. G. *Bible History.* Chap. XV, Section IV. New York: Thomas Nelson Co. Topic: Scenes of Christ's Ministry: The Sermon on the Mount, pp. 433, 434.

Jones, E. S. *The Christ of the Mount.*

Kuyper, Abraham. *Women of the New Testament.* Grand Rapids: Zondervan. "The Penitent Sinner," pp. 62-65.

Miller, Russell Benjamin. "The Sermon on the Mount," *The International Bible Encyclopedia.* Vol. IV. pp. 2732-2736.

Ringenberg, J. A. *Blessed Are Ye.* Fort Wayne: Bible Truth Publishers. 1949. (Ten expository chapters on the Beatitudes suitable for special study).

Chapter 29

CHRIST'S GREATER GALILEAN MINISTRY

—Part Two Continued

—From the Choosing of the Twelve to
the Withdrawal into Northern Galilee
(29 A. D.)

---

1. Introduction

In Jesus' recent warning to the Scribes and Pharisees we observed the peril toward which they were moving. They were becoming increasingly set in their opposition to Christ and in their
opposition to the truth. In the topic which follows, dealing with
the parables, we note the change in the teaching method which
Jesus employed with special reference to the closed minds of these
opponents. The parables were given to conceal instruction from unworthy hearers and at the same time to impart instruction to diligent
minds.

321

2. Reading Assignment

Matthew	Mark	Luke	John
13:1-53	4:1-34	8:4-18	
8:18, 23-27	4:35-41	8:22-25	
8:28-34	5:1-20	8:26-39	
9:1, 18-26	5:21-43	8:40-56	
9:27-34			
13:54-58	6:1-6a		
9:35	6:6b		
9:36—11:1	6:7-13	9:1-6	
14:1-12	6:14-29	9:7-9	
14:13-23	6:30-46	9:10-17	6:1-15
14:24-36	6:47-56		6:16-21
			6:22-71
15:1-20	7:1-23		

(Read the Bible first)

3. Study Outline

I. **Parables of the Kingdom** (Matt. 13:1-53; Mark 4:1-34; Luke 8:4-18)

The eight parables of this section are designed to set forth various features of the kingdom which Jesus had been announcing and into which he had been pointing the way. The parable teaches an unfamiliar truth by viewing it alongside a familiar one with which there is a basis of similarity. The first and second of these are explained by our Lord and the other five are left for us to interpret as we read.

Evidently Christ intended the meanings to be caught by the normal common sense type of mind desirous of knowing the truth. The parable of the sower and the soils shows six types of response to the word of the kingdom. The intention of the word is to gain a place in the understanding of the hearer and thus to bring forth an abundance of corresponding good works in life. Three hindrances to this result are pictured. First, in some cases Satan removes the truth from the mind before it gains a place in the understanding. Secondly, in some cases the word is received in a sentimental manner but with no depth of purpose. As a consequence such persons give way at the least opposition. Thirdly, in other cases persons are obsessed either with deceitful riches or with the cares of life so that they have not sufficient time to study the word. In positive cases, the word is understood, and bears varying degrees of fruitage in life, thirty-fold, sixty-fold, and a hundred-fold.

The parable of the tares is an extension of the parable of the sower, describing the presence of evil along with good in the present world. In this parable the seed is more than abstract truth. It is the person in which the truth has gained acceptance. Likewise the tares are the persons who have received the word (lies) of Satan. The disciples of the Son of Man are thus seen along with the disciples of Satan. The picture represents the spread of the gospel in the world, and in connection with this, the spread of error intended to simulate the gospel. This, however is more than a matter of wrong ideas; it is a matter of obedience to Christ as master in the one case and obedience to Satan as master in the other. This condition, Christ teaches, we must not attempt to correct. The two must develop during the present age, after which the Son of Man and the angels will garner in the precious seed (those who have received the word of Christ) but will bundle the tares (those who have received the lies of Satan) and burn them.

The parable of the blade and the ear again shows the growth of the word. It is to be a gradual growth, Jesus taught. After the sowing it rises and develops as a result of silent coordinating forces. The growth looks forward to full development when the principles of the kingdom find their expression in a world order of righteousness. This parable sees the present time of the worldwide dissemination of the gospel as an early stage of the kingdom for which we are taught to pray.

The parable of the mustard seed shows the small beginning and the proportionately great resulting development of the kingdom. Christendom began in lowly Bethlehem. Palestine was little more in size than a county of America. The apostles were men of no eminence and the world was against them. Yet today the Bible is the world's greatest seller and is read in more than a thousand languages. The greatness of the kingdom of course awaits the return of the king and the final establishment of his kingdom upon earth.

The parable of the leaven is usually understood to show the secret, penetrating power of the word as it comes into contact with people. It suggests the fact that God is preparing a people in whom his word has free operation. There is in this a principle of unity. The result is to be a loaf, suggestive of the church.

The parable of the hid treasure suggests the supreme value of the kingdom of heaven. In the sermon on the mount Jesus had urged that Christians should not regard earthly things as their heart's treasure. The kingdom of heaven is worthy of first place in one's life interests, even to the extent of selling all else.

The parable of the pearl of great price suggests the supreme beauty or charm of the kingdom. It is a thing to be admired beyond the power of money to measure.

The parable of the net reemphasizes the truth taught in the second parable. Both parables teach clearly that within Christendom are both genuine and false professors, but that the age is to end in judgment. The kingdom will be purged of all discordant members.

II. Christ Calms a Tempest (Matt. 8:18, 23-27; Mark 4:35-41; Luke 8:22-25)

This is one of two recorded cases in which Christ showed that he was master of the seas. In this case Jesus was himself in the boat with the disciples. He was asleep, however, even though the waves were enveloping the boat and it was filling with water. Naturally speaking, they would be lost. But in reality there was no peril at all, for the master of the seas and of death itself was in the boat. Under the strain of the storm, the disciples were provoked to accuse Jesus of not caring, to which he responded with rebuke to the storm and reproof of the disciples for unbelief. The question fostered in the minds of those who witnessed this miracle was, "Who can this man be that the winds and sea obey him?"

III. Christ Frees Gadarene Demoniacs (Matt. 8:28-34; Mark 5:1-20; Luke 8:26-39)

The miracle which Jesus performed on this occasion has not

only interesting but significant features. It is a complete miracle in the sense that it frees a man under the complete domination of Satan and makes of him a sane, normal, worshipper of God. That is the perfect miracle.

While Matthew speaks of two men possessed with devils, Mark and Luke speak of but one. This is of course not necessarily a contradiction. There may have been more than two for that matter, since not all of Jesus' miracles could be recorded.

The man described shows the lengths to which Satan's power in a man may go. In some cases demon possession appears as a dual or multiple personality. In this case the personality seems to have been totally possessed and the misuse of the man was terrific. It is indicated, in fact, that while one demon spoke, he spoke for a whole legion of others who inhabited the man.

It is of interest that these demons recognized and feared Jesus as the Son of the Most High God. It is of interest also that they had forebodings and fear of the abyss, and shrank from its torment. It is further of interest to note that demons crave embodiment and that human form is their choice. It is amazing that one man could be the abode of such demon power as drove a herd of swine to commit suicide in the ocean.

The feature of this miracle most difficult to understand is that when the Gadarenes saw the delivered man dressed, in his right mind, and worshipping Jesus, they requested Jesus to leave their country. Could it be that this request came from a hog growers' union which had come to dominate society in Gadara?

IV. The Raising of Jairus' Daughter (Matt. 9:1, 18-26; Mark 5:21-43; Luke 8:40-56)

Just as the widow of Nain had lost an only son, so in this case Jairus, a synagogue ruler, had lost an only daughter. As the girl lay dying, Jesus was sent for and made his way to her bedside. He was interrupted by a woman who pressed through the crowd, touched the hem of his garment and was healed.

The scene of mourning at Jairus' house told the story that the daughter had died. The scorn of those present when Jesus stated that she was but sleeping indicates that from the human viewpoint the girl was truly dead. Her restoration serves as a reminder of what will one day take place when the dead in Christ shall rise to die no more.

V. Jesus' Third Preaching Tour (Matt. 9:35; Mark 6:6b)

We have observed two previous statements of the fact that Jesus toured Galilee. This third reference leads to the Lord's expression of concern for the unreached multitudes and to his request that the disciples pray the Lord of harvest for more laborers (9:36-38).

VI. The Twelve Sent Forth (Matt. 9:36—11:1; Mark 6:7-13; Luke 9:1-6)

Jesus had toured Galilee repeatedly and the multitudes from all directions continually hung on his heels. Never do we read that he sent them away, although he did steal away for rest and communion with the Father. Jesus looked upon these as sheep without a shepherd waiting to be gathered into the fold, and as a ripened harvest ready to be reaped. The burden of this he laid upon his disciples for prayer. There must be more laborers.

Months before, as we have learned, Jesus had chosen twelve disciples with the declared purpose of sending them forth. The time had now come for the twelve to be sent. Certain particulars of this commission are noteworthy.

They were sent exclusively to the house of Israel, not to the Gentiles nor the Samaritans. Their message was simply that the kingdom of heaven was at hand. In relation with this they were to do what Jesus had been doing, heal, cleanse, cast out devils, and "freely give." The implication is evident that these acts were to serve as tokens of the coming of the kingdom of heaven. As a financial policy, they were to rely upon those to whom they were sent for their necessities. This relieved them of the necessity of cumbersome luggage, but also, it served the more important purpose of testing the response of those to whom the kingdom of heaven was preached. They were forewarned, but challenged, regarding the opposition which they would receive. Though they would meet wolves they were to be wise as serpents and harmless as doves. God would give them appropriate words to speak when they needed to stand before their accusers in court. They were faced with the fact that the gospel would bring schism to homes, that men would hate them. They were to be prepared to endure these things "to the end," that is to death, if need be, just as Jesus himself would eventually do. They were urged not to fear such a stand, but rather to fear him who is able to destroy both soul and body in hell. Along with this rugged challenge, Jesus assured them that they would never be outside the watchful eye of him who notes the sparrow's fall and who knows the number of hairs on one's head.

Confessing Christ was an issue which none could evade. Those who confessed him, Christ would confess before the Father. Those who shrank from confessing him would be denied before the Father. The issue at the judgment would be just that simple.

It appears that Jesus sent forth the twelve, and then followed them up (Matt. 10:23; 11:1).

VII. **The Death of John the Baptist** (Matt. 14:1-12; Mark 6:14-29; Luke 9:7-9)

The death of John the Baptist had taken place some time before this point in Jesus' ministry. The account is related here as an explanation of the fears of Herod the tetrarch, who having beheaded John, now surmised that the One whose marvelous works were being reported to him was actually John the Baptist risen from the dead.

VIII. **Feeding of the Five Thousand** (Matt. 14:13-23; Mark 6:30-46; Luke 9:10-17; John 6:1-15)

This is the one miracle of such significance that it is reported by all four gospel writers. The whole incident bears the design of revealing to the world the source of its life. The situation, briefly stated, was that a whole multitude were with Jesus in a desert place too far away from food to return without eating. Realizing the gravity of the situation, the disciples began to discuss it. Jesus, we are told, knew what he would do about it, but he waited to see what the disciples would suggest. There were three suggestions: 1. The first was that the people should be sent away, but this was not Jesus' way of doing. 2. The second suggestion was given by Philip who spoke of money, but realizing that they had enough money to buy only 200 pennyworth, repudiated his own suggestion. 3. Andrew mentioned the boy's lunch of five loaves and two fishes, only to set aside the idea as impossible. Then Jesus went into action. He did not send them away. He did not use money. He used the food on hand. What he did with it is an object lesson to humanity. He took it, blessed it, brake and distributed it, and after all had eaten, conserved what was left. In the whole procedure, there was a process of multiplication clearly indicative of God's creative power.

The multitudes readily recognized that they had witnessed an act of God and concluded that Jesus must be "that prophet that cometh into the world." Such an admission, however, was not necessarily a dependable mark of their acceptance of Christ's kingdom, and Jesus evaded their clamor to make him their king. He knew well enough that what many of them really wanted was a permanent free grocer, not a king to rule their lives.

IX. Walking on the Troubled Waters (Matt. 14:24-36; Mark 6:47-56; John 6:16-21)

The feeding of the five thousand occurred in a desert place located some distance across the sea from Bethsaida. After that incident Jesus withdrew into a mountain to pray, and the disciples went to their boat. Since Jesus did not come to them they started across the sea alone. Darkness came on and with it a storm. In the fourth watch (3 A. M.) Jesus came walking to them on the sea. A multiple miracle followed. Christ and Peter walked on the sea. The moment Jesus was admitted into the boat the wind ceased. The fears of the disciples were quelled. And they "straightway" arrived at their destination. It is little wonder that those in the boat worshipped Jesus and declared him to be "of a truth . . . . the Son of God." Nor is it strange that upon arrival, the people again crowded in upon him, with their needy ones, seeking, if they might, to touch but the hem of his garment.

X. Jesus' Discourse on the Bread of Life—Many Stop Following (John 6:22-71)

It is not difficult to see that in the feeding of the five thousand Jesus had laid the basis for a discourse on the Bread of Life. The miracle had attracted a widespread profession of discipleship. The discourse served as a sieve to eliminate many whose motives were spurious.

Confronted with the multitudes at Capernaum, Jesus charged them with too low a motive. They were laboring for temporary physical sustenance of life; Jesus wanted to give them the provision for eternal life. They did not understand and asked how they might labor to accomplish such a work of God. Jesus coming to the point, declared that the most important work a man can do is to believe on the one whom the Father had sent. To such the Father is pleased to give eternal life. All such the Son will raise up at the last day.

It was at this point of vital teaching that the destinies of the two types of followers was reached. When Jesus declared himself to be the source of eternal life he cast a sure stumbling block before many of his followers. They could not see in him more than the son of Joseph and Mary. They stumbled at his symbolic declaration, "I am the bread of life." Finally, Jesus led his impatient hearers from bread, and flesh and blood to that which is the source of these. "It is the spirit that quickeneth (makes alive)," Jesus said, "the flesh profiteth nothing." The flesh may be destroyed and even eaten, but not the spirit. Christ's blood would be shed but his life would not be lost. What men took from Jesus was flesh and blood. But they could not destroy the source of flesh and blood which is the spirit. Granting the mystery, the fact is that he who is the eternal Word, in his own way, made alive that body which men destroyed, and in this he stands as the guarantor of resurrection and eternal life for all who commit themselves to him in faith.

While many quit Jesus' school at this point, not all did. In spite of the mystery some believers went on to learn more. Peter expressed their confidence rightly in saying, "Thou hast the words of eternal life." Surely Jesus had given enough evidence of this to be the basis of continued faith, even in spite of mystery.

XI. Jesus' Discourse on Eating with Unwashed Hands (Matt. 15:1-20; Mark 7:1-23)

Against the weighty discourse which Jesus had just given, aimed at turning men to the source of eternal life, Jesus' critics now come up with an indictment against him for letting his disciples violate the tradition of the elders regarding ceremonial washings.

Jesus' reply included first of all a counter charge in which he pointed out the anti-moral tendency of Jewish traditions. In the instance cited, he showed that they were guilty of actually setting aside the fifth commandment through one of their traditions.

On the subject of purification, Jesus probed the shallow aversion to physical uncleanness so prominent in the traditions and pointed to the heart and the lips as the source of the sin which really defiles a person. Among the evils of a sinful heart Jesus named evil thoughts, murders, adulteries, fornications, thefts, false witness, and railings.

The Pharisees, Jesus said, were blind guides. Consider why. Was it not because they lacked the first principles? They proceeded to make declarations of righteousness without the necessary basic truths to guide them. They lacked love, justice, and mercy in their hearts; that is why they labored endlessly to define rectitude for the people, binding heavy duties upon them, yet never leading them into true righteousness.

4. Discussion and Review

1. What was the occasion for Christ's employment of parables in his teaching? (Matt. 13).

2. Name the parables of Matthew 13. Be able to relate each with its meaning.

3. Relate the first of the two recorded accounts in which Jesus stilled the sea.

4. Relate what may be learned concerning demons as seen in the Lord's freeing of the Gadarene demoniacs. Learn all you can about humans who cooperate with demons.

5. Relate the account of the second recorded miracle of raising a person from the dead.

6. Quote from memory our Lord's appeal to the disciples at the close of this third preaching tour in Galilee (Matt. 9:37, 38).

7. Summarize Jesus' instruction to the Twelve before sending them forth.

8. What fears regarding Jesus had developed in the mind of Herod Antipas?

9. Relate the account of the feeding of the five thousand, noting our Lord's procedure and the responses to the miracle.

10. In the account of the stilling of the sea (John 6) trace the indication of our Lord's care. What higher purpose did this experience serve?

11. What spiritual truth was drawn from the miracle of the loaves? Discuss the meaning of the designation "Bread of Life." Why did some quit following on this occasion?

12. What was Jesus' teaching on the subject of eating with unwashed hands?

5. Select Memory Passages

Matthew 9:37, 38; 13:44; 45-46

6. Character Review

Identify:

Gadarenes   Jairus   Widow of Nain

7. Bibliography

Bible Dictionary (Smith-Peloubet: Teacher's Edition). Chicago: John C. Winston
  Co.
  Articles:
  1. Demoniacs.
  2. Washing the Hands and the Feet.
Kuyper, Abraham. *Women of the New Testament.* Grand Rapids: Zondervan.
  1. "The Woman with an Issue of Blood," pp. 31-33.
  2. "Herodias," pp. 58-61.
McQuilken, Robert C. *Studying Our Lord's Parables.* 2 vol. Columbia Bible
  College, Columbia, S. C.
Sangster, Margaret E. *The Women of the Bible.* Chapt. XXXIV, "The Ruler's
  Little Daughter." New York: The Christian Herald.
Sangster, Margaret E. *The Women of the Bible.* Chapt. XXXVI, "The Daugh-
  ter of Herodias." New York: The Christian Herald.
Trench, R. C. *Notes on the Parables of Our Lord* (Popular Edition). Chapt. I,
  "On the Definitions of a Parable." Chapt. II, "On Teaching by Parables."
  Chapt. III, "On the Interpretation of Parables." Grand Rapids. Baker Book
  House.

Chapter 30

CHRIST'S GREATER GALILEAN MINISTRY

—Part Two Concluded

—From the Withdrawal into Northern
Galilee to the Departure from Galilee
(29 A. D.)

1. Introduction

The pressure of opposition which Jesus had felt when he left Judea for the Greater Galilean ministry had followed him up. Jesus did not go to the Passover which took place about the time of the feeding of the five thousand because of the opposition. Many of Jesus' disciples dropped off at this time (John 6:4, 66).

The issue at Capernaum about eating with unwashed hands, we observe, was created by Pharisees and Scribes who came up from Jerusalem. Jesus' answer nettled them.

Jesus appears to have avoided the development of the crisis of his death because his hour had not yet come. For this reason, partly, he went into northern Galilee to minister for a period of about six months. In addition, of course, there were Gentiles to be reached. Then also, Jesus had special instruction for his disciples which retirement to the north would make possible. On the one occasion that Jesus came south (to Dalmanutha or Magadan) the Scribes and Pharisees were at hand to entrap him.

2. Reading Assignment

Matthew	Mark	Luke	John
15:21-28	7:24-30		
15:29-38	7:31-37; 8:1-9		
15:39—16:12	8:10-21		
	8:22-26		
16:13-20	8:27-30	9:18-21	
17:1-13	9:2-13	9:28-36	
17:14-23	9:14-32	9:37-45	
17:24—18:35	9:33-50	9:46-50	
		~~████████████~~	7-8

(Read the Bible first)

3. Study Outline

I. Tour about Tyre and Sidon (Matt. 15:21-28; Mark 7:24-30)

The region of Tyre and Sidon lay just to the north of the area originally allotted by Joshua to the tribe of Asher. Since the days of David, trade relations existed between the Israelites and these coastal cities. It appears that Jesus made his way into this area several times, although he forbad the twelve from going outside the house of Israel. These Phoenicians had no reputation for piety, yet we have noted that Jesus predicted that it would be more tolerable for Tyre and Sidon in the day of judgment than for such cities as Chorazin and Bethsaida (Matt. 11:21; 15:21).

The healing of the Syrophoenician woman's daughter is the only recorded miracle of this tour. It is likely that, in general, Jesus directed his ministry to the Jews of the area. This, however, was certainly only a matter of procedural tactics, not because the gospel was not intended ultimately to be preached unto these people. When this Canaanitish woman presented her need, so humbly and with such great faith, Jesus put aside the present conventionality of ministry to the "Jew first" and responded to her faith with the full answer to her petition. This deed was a gracious token of the fact that God's provision of redemption is for all people. After Pentecost the apostles would be coming back to these parts with the gospel.

II. Three-day Ministry in the Decapolis Area (Matt. 15:29-38; Mark 7:31-37; 8:1-9)

Returning to the region of the sea of Galilee, Jesus seems to have avoided Capernaum and made his way to the region of Decapolis south of the sea. Here Jesus had left on a previous occasion at the request of the hog-raisers of Gadara. Upon returning a great multitude of needy human beings awaited him. He healed them and "they glorified the God of Israel."

Something of the public pressure upon Jesus on this occasion is seen from the fact that the multitudes had stayed with him for three continuous days. The sincerity of these people is proved by the fact that they had forgone food for their bodies in order to be with Jesus. Jesus was touched by this, and knowing that some would have a long way to travel in returning home, he performed a miracle similar to that which was performed some weeks before in the feeding of five thousand. On this occasion there were seven loaves and a few fishes, and after all were satisfied, there were seven baskets remaining.

III. At Magdala—Reproof to Sign-seekers and Warning to the Disciples (Matt. 15:39—16:12; Mark 8:10-21)

Entering a boat Jesus crossed the lower tip of the sea of Galilee and landed at Magdala. The chief incident of this stop was a conversation with the Pharisees and Sadducees. Jesus was asked to show a sign from heaven. Jesus upbraided his inquirers. It was not another sign that they needed, but discernment. They needed to have the same common sense in discerning the signs of the times as people generally have in forecasting the weather. Jesus left his critics the sign of the prophet Jonah, a sign which he appears to have pressed upon the consciousness of his hearers repeatedly.

Turning from his critics to his disciples, Jesus warned them against the leaven of the Pharisees and the Sadducees. As a matter of coincidence the disciples had forgotten to take bread with them and supposed that Jesus' remark had to do with this fact. Jesus made it clear that he referred to the subtle teaching of these religious leaders.

IV. At Bethsaida—A Unique Healing (Mark 8:22-26)

It is supposed that there were two cities called Bethsaida, the one located about a mile from Capernaum and the other on the northeast coast of the sea of Galilee. The latter was probably the city of this incident.

The healing of the blind man here is the only incident on record in which Jesus healed a person by degrees.

V. At Caesarea Philippi—A High Point of Confession and Revelation (Matthew 16:13-20; Mark 8:27-30; Luke 9:18-21)

All along, as Jesus performed his mighty deeds, there were spontaneous responses from those who witnessed as to who Jesus was. He was that prophet who should come into the world, he was the Son of David, he was the Christ, he was a great teacher, he was a teacher sent from God—these and various other designations described the person of Jesus. Certitude, however, was often lacking in these opinions. Speaking privately with the disciples, Jesus drew from them a clear cut confession which they expressed through the mouthpiece of Peter, who said, "Thou are the Christ, the Son of the living God." Upon this bedrock declaration of his identity, Jesus announced that he would build his church. The concept of the church, introduced here, marks out a body of believers whose faith rests in Jesus the Christ, the Son of God. This church is marked off from other people of the earth, the term **ekklesia** signifying called out ones. The basis of inclusion and exclusion, however, must not be drawn on any other principle than that set forth in this text. Such special theories as have been developed by the Roman hierarchy and by other eccentric sects have obscured the circle of faith and fellowship which ought to unify the church of Christ in the world.

From this high point of revelation and confession there followed, with what must have impressed the disciples as unreconcilable contrast, Christ's announcement of his death and resurrection. He was to build his church, yet, he was to die. Peter curtly and strongly resisted the idea. "This," Peter said, "shall not be."

Then he who received so high a point of credit for his true confession was given the lowest point of discredit for his failure to discern the mission of Christ. He was lending his influence to the use of Satan to deter Jesus from the work he had come to do, which was to die and then come forth in triumph over death.

Finally, Jesus carried the fact of his death and resurrection to its further point of providing a pattern for his disciples. The church would be built upon sacrifice, first by himself, and secondly, on the part of his consecrated followers. They, as he, must lay down their lives (psyche) that they may take them up again.

VI. Christ's Transfiguration—Two Historic Kingdom Characters Counsel with Jesus about His Death (Matt. 17:1-13; Mark 9:2-13; Luke 9:28-36)

Not far north of the area of Caesarea Philippi there rises to the highest point of all Palestine the lofty Mount Hermon. It is one of the chief sources of the Jordan and contrasts with the Dead Sea which is the lowest point and provides the mouth of the Jordan. It was probably this mount to which Jesus, after six days, took Peter, James, and John and permitted them to see transfigured before their eyes, the person of their Lord in counsel with Moses and Elijah, the great representatives of the Law and the prophets respectively. Luke tells us that the subject of conversation was Christ's coming death in Jerusalem.

In announcing this transfiguration Jesus had said that it would be a portrayal of the Son of Man in his coming kingdom. Here is an encouraging indication of the fact that in the final realization of the kingdom there will be a recognition of those who have died in the faith. The blessedness of this kingdom existence is also borne out from the expressed desire of the disciples. They were so pleased that they wanted to make permanent tabernacles and remain in the realm of this kingdom glory.

The most significant presence manifest upon the mount, however, was the Father himself who, a second time, bore verbal witness concerning Jesus, saying, "This is my beloved Son, in whom I am well pleased: hear ye him."

VII. Valley Experiences in Upper Galilee (Matt. 17:14-23; Mark 9:14-32; Luke 9:37-45)

A demoniac boy at the foot of the mount of transfiguration represented the great multitudes whose condition called for the return of the healer from the realm of kingdom glory. Not even the disciples had learned to minister in the absence of their Lord for they had tried and failed to heal the demoniac. Jesus, in considerable indignation, attributed the failure of the disciples to two things, namely, lack of faith and lack of prayer. It is indicated clearly that this was an exceptionally difficult case, yet only a mustard seed quantity of faith with true prayer would have accomplished deliverance.

Before returning southward Jesus restated the fact that death and resurrection on the third day were the experiences that lay before him. He also repeated the precaution that this should not be published until after his resurrection; evidently Jesus desired that no announcement should interfere with the free operation of the human agents involved in this crisis.

VIII. **A Passing Visit at Capernaum** (Matt. 17:24—18:35; Mark 9:33-50; Luke 9:46-50)

We have observed that Jesus spent very little time during Part III of his Greater Galilean ministry in his adopted home at Capernaum. It would actually appear that he avoided the town. He returns now, possibly only overnight, on his way to Jerusalem to attend the Feast of Tabernacles.

Upon coming to Capernaum Peter was reminded by the collectors of Temple revenues of the half-shekel assessment which Jews commonly paid for the support of the Temple. Whether there were funds to pay this bill we are not told. Anyway Jesus took the responsibility, even though from his relation to the kingdom of God he reasoned that there was ground for exemption. The miracle of taking a coin from a fish's mouth exactly sufficient to pay two tax bills, "for me and thee," must have been a personal favor to Peter that he did not soon forget.

Before going on to Jerusalem Jesus discoursed in a somewhat informal way to his disciples, probing to the depths of their hearts and planting the seed of vital kingdom principles within them.

In reply to their inquiry as to who is greatest in the kingdom, Jesus demonstrated his answer by placing a child before them and making its humility the standard of real greatness.

Little children, and big ones who are little children in humility, Jesus said, are the objects of his jealous care. To cause such to stumble will bring judgment upon the offender; to minister to such a little one is the equivalent of ministering to himself. The parable of the Lost Sheep was given to demonstrate the Father's outreach of love for one of his lost "little ones."

Jesus gave a very specific formula to the disciples for settling wrongs which arise in the church between brethren. First, he said, go to your brother personally and show him his fault. Secondly, if he will not listen, take one or two others with you and seek by their counsel to settle the matter. Thirdly, if the offender will not hear them the matter should be brought before the whole church. Fourthly, if he will not hear the church, he is to be regarded as a Gentile, or a publican. The purpose in this order of procedure is obviously to win the man to the fellowship of the church, but there is definitely no place for conciliating a wrong doer at the expense of what is right. Considering a person a Gentile or a publican is no ground for persecution, however, for God seeks the salvation of all such. On this occasion, Jesus repeated the charge formerly given to Peter and the disciples, that authority to bind and loose belongs to the church. No reference is made to justify confining this right to a special apostolate; rather the church or the congregation is seen to have the authority to decide upon the inclusiveness and exclusiveness of its fellowship. In addition to the principle of confessing Christ (Matt. 16), it appears that there is also here taught the fact that God respects the principle of congregational government. Wherever "two or three are gathered together in my name, there am I in the midst of them." The assumption appears obvious that any one believer in Christ should find it possible to get along agreeably with other believers in Christ.

Peter raised an interesting question on the subject of forgiveness. How many times, he asked, should one forgive his brother? Wanting to be gracious, Peter suggested seven times. Our Lord answered from a much larger heart, "Until seventy times seven." Feeling, evidently, that Peter did not catch the right spirit, Jesus devoted a parable to the subject. The whole answer to Peter's question, this parable taught, would be found in a proper sense of the countless times such a man as Peter needed God's forgiveness.

IX. At the Feast of Tabernacles (John 7-8)

It appears that after Jesus' visit at Capernaum, he came into contact with his brethren from Nazareth. In view of the Feast of Tabernacles, just at hand, these brethren, not yet more than half-believers, urged Jesus to be present and to perform there some of the mighty works which he had done throughout Galilee. Jesus would not be constrained by them. Rather he insisted upon following a higher time schedule than they knew. Had Jesus sought to win Judea first before preaching in the outlying regions of Galilee and Perea, he doubtless would have brought on his own death before these regions could be reached. Going to Jerusalem, Jesus knew, was to precipitate the crucifixion for himself. This must not be done before his ministry has been completed.

In the midst of the Feast week Jesus made his appearance in the Temple. Although the opportunity to seize him had been awaited by Jewish leaders, they lost their nerve, it appears, when Jesus began to speak. The officers who were sent to take him returned to the chief priests and Pharisees excusing their failure with the admission, "Never man spake like this man."

In his discourse Jesus cut beneath the charges of sabbath breaking held against him and showed up the real spirit of his enemies. They failed to understand his doctrine because they had no purpose to do the will of God. They pretended to be the champions of Moses but they did not do the law of Moses. They were, in fact, murderers secretly trying to kill the One who came from the Father. Having thus so perfectly pointed out the heart purpose of his accusers Jesus held them in abeyance until the end of the week. It is evident that the mutlitudes present provided such sentiment in favor of Jesus that the opposition dared not take him. On the last day of the feast Jesus' compassionate appeal to the multitudes reached its peak when he stood and cried, "If any man thirst, let him come unto me, and drink. He that believeth on me, as the scripture hath said, out of his belly (from within him) shall flow rivers of living waters."

Jesus dwelt much upon the analogy of light. Just as in ages past he as the eternal Word was the light which lighted every man coming into the world, so now in his ministry in the flesh his teaching is as light intended to lead men into the kingdom of the Father. An adulterous woman, condemned according to law, had hope if she would but follow the light. On the other hand, religious teachers who resist light bring to themselves darkness and eternal despair. Believing and walking in the light appear to refer to the same things.

Many believed on him at this Feast season. Upon them Jesus urged the necessity of continuing in the light that they may know the freedom of discipleship.

The subject of freedom led to resentment from Jesus' critics and to very frank words from our Lord. Being Abraham's seed is not enough, Jesus said, one must be free from the bondage of sin and the service of the devil. Those who plan murder, and who lie, are not true children of Abraham but of the devil. They do not know God, that is why they do not recognize the Son and the works which he speaks. At the pinnacle of debate, as stones were being prepared to be hurled at him, Jesus stole from their midst.

4. Discussion and Review

1. What considerations led to Jesus' movement into the region of northern Galilee?

2. Relate the account of Jesus' ministry in the region of Tyre and Sidon.

3. Why had Jesus left the Decapolis area some time before (Matt. 8:34)? What did Jesus do upon his return?

4. What other incidents occurred as Jesus returned north along the east coast of Galilee?

5. What is the basic article of the Christian confession as expressed by Peter? How is the church built upon this confession? Upon what else would the church be built according to Jesus' word at Caesarea Philippi?

6. How did the experience on the Mount of Transfiguration demonstrate the relationship of human history to the coming kingdom? What is made evident as to the desirability of life in the coming kingdom?

7. How was the contrast between kingdom glory and present world need emphasized as the Lord and the disciples descended to the valley? What is the means of present help as indicated by the Lord?

8. What prediction did Jesus repeat as they traveled southward, and with what caution?

9. On the final passing visit to Capernaum Jesus took the time to deal quite intimately with the disciples. What were the special incidents and the particular subjects of discussion?

10. In view of the fact that the Feast of Tabernacles was at hand what did Jesus' brethren from Nazareth counsel him to do? Why did Jesus act differently?

11. In view of Jesus' coming to Jerusalem what plans did the Jewish leaders make? Why did they not carry out their plans?

12. Relate briefly the themes of Jesus' discourse at Jerusalem on this occasion. With what responses?

5. Select Memory Passages

Matt. 16:16b, 17-19; 18:3, 12-14, 18-20; John 7:37, 38

6. Character Review

Identify:

Syrophoenician Woman

7. Bibliography

Blaikie, Wm. G. *Bible History.* Chap. XV. New York: Thomas Nelson Co.
   Topics:
   1. Tyre and Sidon, pp. 436, 437.
   2. Caesarea Philippi, pp. 437-438.
   3. The Mount of Transfiguration, pp. 438, 439.
Kuyper, Abraham. *Women of the New Testament.* Grand Rapids: Zondervan.
   "The Woman of Canaan," pp. 50-53.
Morgan, G. C. *Peter and the Church.* New York: Fleming H. Revell. (An interpretation of the Caesarean Philippi passage).

Chapter 31
THE PEREAN MINISTRY

—Part One
—From the Feast of Tabernacles
to the Raising of Lazarus
(29-30 A. D.)

1. Introduction

There remained one more area where Jesus chose to devote himself in a preaching mission, namely, the country east of Jordan, commonly designated Perea. During the six months following, the Lord made three tours into this area. The first tour was marked by widespread evangelism under the delegated ministry of seventy commissioned preachers. The second was characterized by much teaching. The third is marked by comparative loss of popularity; the crowds were forsaking Jesus as the fuller implications of the cost of discipleship were understood.

Between his preaching tours into Perea Jesus visited different points in Judea. It is in this period that Bethany appears to be something of an adopted home.

Remembering that the Greater Galilean Ministry had ended with announcements of Jesus' final ministry in Jerusalem, it will be understood that throughout this six months Perean ministry the cross constantly cast its shadows upon our Lord.

342

2. Reading Assignment

Matthew	Mark	Luke	John
		9:51—10:24	
		10:25-37	
		10:38-42	
			9
			10:1-39
		11:1—17:10	

(Read the Bible first)

3. Study Outline

I. Seventy Apostles Are Sent into Perea (Luke 9:51—10:24)

Following Jesus' visit in Jerusalem at the time of the Feast of Tabernacles, he moved northward into Samaria. Encountering opposition, he moved across the Jordan into the region of Perea where he launched a major preaching tour. Extending the method which he had used in Galilee he now appointed seventy of his disciples to go into the countryside in advance of his coming. The instructions given these "sent ones" was similar to that which had been given the twelve.

The return of the Seventy was with the note of triumph—even the devils were subject to them as they rebuked them in Jesus' name. Associated with this power over the enemy is the remarkable statement of Jesus that he beheld Satan falling as lightning from heaven. Doubtless this is an allusion, thinks Whedon, to the primeval fall of Satan when because of sin he was cast out of heaven. The allusion also reminds us of the picture set forth in the Apocalypse (chapter) 12) of Satan being cast forth to the consternation of those who dwell upon the earth. The predominant idea in the matter is that in Christ there is power over the enemy. This, however, Jesus reminded the Seventy, is only the negative fact. It is cause for much greater rejoicing that their names are written in heaven.

II. A Lawyer Gets His Definition (Luke 10:25-37)

Following this preaching tour, possibly as Jesus and the disciples traveled toward the vicinity of Jerusalem, a lawyer drew from Jesus his classic definition of the meaning of the word neighbor. The parable of The Good Samaritan was Jesus' answer. The lawyer, whose motive was to trap Jesus, not only got his definition, but in Jesus' two-pronged answer he was given to understand that neither the professional priest nor the Levite was a proper specimen of neighborliness. A good Samaritan, Jesus taught him, fulfills the Law more acceptably than a cold hearted Jerusalem religionist.

III.　Jesus' First Visit in Martha's Home　(Luke 10:38-42)

This is the first of three notable scenes in the home of Martha. It serves to reveal the Lord's fellowship in relation to two personality types. Martha did everything for Jesus. It was her home. She invited him. She prepared the food. She served it. All this she doubtless did well, and since a cup of cold water is not to be unrewarded, Martha deserves a trophy. But Mary, who "sat," did more to satisfy Jesus. She entered into his concerns. She shared the knowledge of his passion. Martha was absorbed with her own home. Mary became absorbed in the home of her heavenly Father. Hers was the one "needful" enduring concern.

IV.　A Man Born Blind and the Light of the World　(John 9)

In John 8 we observed Jesus' characterization of his ministry in terms of light. He had come to show the way and to light up the world. This was a man's great opportunity, but if rejected, it was his greatest loss.

In John 9 we learn that a man had been permitted to be born into the world without the faculty of sight, not because he had sinned, nor because his parents had, but that it might be demonstrated that the Creator of eyes had come into the world.

Jesus' procedure is suggestive of the act of original creation. He made clay, anointed the sightless eyes, and gave an order. The pool of Siloam to which he was sent for washing was perhaps half a mile south of the Temple. The blind man obeyed and he came seeing.

The Jews had agreed that anyone who confessed Christ should be put out of the synagogue. In view of this fact it is of interest to note that the blind man's parents, though they acknowledged the miracle, were unwilling to acknowledge Jesus' claims. It is of interest also to observe the twist which the Pharisees sought to give the healed man's faith, admonishing him to give glory to God and not to Jesus. The pluck of the young man, at this, is arousing. Seeking to put common sense into the Pharisees heads, he found himself cast out of the synagogue. But he had little to mourn and much to gain, for the Lord took him in, leading him to full faith in Himself as the Son of God.

The miracle was then interpreted. It was an object lesson of the twofold mission of the Son of God. To those who are lost and want light Jesus has come to show the way of God's kingdom. Those who are blinded, yet who hypocritically claim to see, Jesus has come to unfrock, lest by their influence they lead others in their own way of destruction.

V. **The One Door and the Good Shepherd** (John 10:1-39)

Following the representation of Christ as the world's light, Christ now represents himself in a further twofold symbol combination. Under the first symbol Jesus is a door. He repudiates as false all other ways of getting into the kingdom than by Himself. Anyone claiming to be a shepherd who comes in by another way is apt to be a thief and a destroyer. His voice should not be heeded.

Changing the point of view, Christ is also the good shepherd. His claim is proved by what he is doing, namely **gathering** the sheep. He is giving his life to this end. There is to be one fold, one flock, and one shepherd.

This discourse became the occasion for remarks on the part of those who heard, variously appraising Jesus. Some of the Jews cornered Jesus as he walked in Solomon's porch and desired a forthright statement on his part as to whether he was the Messiah. Jesus did not answer them by a simple declaration but referred them to his works, and left them to draw their own conclusions. Jesus challenged them to find fault with his fulfillment of the role of a good shepherd, but went further and declared that they had not the capacity to judge. They were not his sheep. There was something wrong with them as followers, not with him as leader.

On this occasion again, the Jews took up stones to cast them at him.

VI. **A Lesson on Prayer** (Luke 11:1-13)

Jesus had been praying, and having been overheard by the disciples, deeply impressed them. They wanted Jesus to teach them to pray. The prayer taught them is substantially the same as had been taught them on the Mount in Galilee. In addition to this prayer, Jesus emphasized, by illustration, the principle of importunity. On the other hand, by reference to the father-son relationship, he emphasized the fact that the Heavenly Father loves to answer prayer. Especially, is he pleased to give his children the gift of the Holy Spirit.

VII. Denunciation of Religious Leaders (Luke 11)

Continuing in the Bethany-Jerusalem area after the Feast of Dedication Jesus engaged in a fiery exchange of words with the Pharisees. Christ's critics were almost constantly at his heels questioning him and trying to catch him in their trap. The eleventh chapter of Luke is an arsenal of denunciation. A dumb man had been delivered from a devil. Jesus read in the hearts of his critics their stock explanation of this type of miracle, namely, that the deed had been through Beelzebub the prince of devils. Some clamored, as usual, for a sign.

Jesus answered both of these points as he had before. A house divided, even though it be Satan's can not stand. It was illogical to attribute the casting out of demons to demons. As for a sign, Jesus branded that request as an indication of evil. It was an indication of woeful unbelief that after all Jesus had done they should have to have more proof. The only sign which Jesus would give them was that of Jonah. This generation was like the Ninevites, only much worse.

On another occasion as Jesus was in a Pharisee's house he sat to eat without washing, illiciting, perhaps intentionally, their criticism. Answering, Jesus turned his searchlight upon their unwashed hearts. They tithed to the finest detail but neglected judgment and the love of God. Their religion was vain display, they loved the highest seats and the salutes of people in public. They in reality are dead, Jesus said, and men stumble unawares into their graves.

The lawyers Jesus charged with heartless rigorism. They make of God's law a tyranny, and they will not exert a finger's strength to alleviate human need. They are one with those who have slain the prophets; they fill up the cup of woe resting upon the enemies of God from Abel's generation to their own. Professionally, they hold the key of knowledge, but they will neither enter into that knowl-

edge nor permit others to do so. Five times in this chapter the word
"woe" is applied to these religious leaders.

VIII. Warnings Addressed to the Multitudes (Luke 12)

In Luke 12, Jesus first of all addresses his disciples. The presence of the multitudes, however, meant that what he said would be
heard and interpreted by all types of persons, pro, con, and in-
different.

Having just denounced religious leaders, Jesus now warned against
them, against their hypocrisy, and against their violent purposes. A
louder note of warning is sounded, however. More to be feared than
those who kill the body is he that hath power to cast both soul and body
into hell (gehenna). But God need not be feared if his will is received. To his children he gives constant care and unfailing security, not merely in this life, but also in that which follows.

Replying to a request for help in settling an estate, Jesus warned
against the folly of covetousness and illustrated his point by the
parable of the rich man and his barns.

Turning more directly to his disciples, most of whom were without wealth, he warned against the folly of anxious care, illustrating
the Father's provision for their needs by his care for the birds and
the flowers. God cares for the animal and vegetable kingdoms,
Jesus reasons, certainly he will care for those who make up his
spiritual kingdom.

Going beyond the level of trust for one's needs, Jesus challenged his hearers to be stewards, and assured them that faithful
stewardship would be adequately recognized at the time of accounting with their lord. The wise servant is he who bestows care upon
God's interests.

The chapter closes with an appeal to the judgment of the multitudes. Why can they discern the weather and not righteousness?
Why must they allow themselves to fall into the hands of the judgment. Christ appeals for individual action in keeping with God's
revealed will, even though this may bring separation from relatives and friends in the flesh

From Bethany through Perea, and Return to Bethany

Christ's next movement, it appears, is back toward Perea. On
the way Jesus met various situations, giving help or instruction as
the cases required.

IX. Repentance and Salvation (Luke 13:1-9)

On one occasion reference was made to certain Galileans who were killed by Pilate, and to others upon whom a wall fell, evidently with the implication that these Galileans must have been very wicked people. To this Jesus declared to the haughty dwellers at Jerusalem: ". . . . except ye repent, ye shall all likewise perish."

X. Woman Healed, Ruler Shamed, People Rejoice (Luke 13:11-17)

A woman was healed of an eighteen year infirmity. Being done on the Sabbath day, this was rebuked by the ruler of that particular synagogue. Jesus so soundly pictured this ruler's hypocrisy that he and all other adversaries were ashamed of themselves, and "all the people rejoiced for all the glorious things that were done by him."

XI. Two Kingdom Parables (Luke 13:18-21)

Christ repeated two of the kingdom parables, previously spoken by the sea of Galilee, namely the parable of the mustard seed and the parable of the leaven.

XII. How Many Will Be Saved and Who? (Luke 13:22-30)

As Christ rounded out his tour in Perea and inclined his journey towards Jerusalem again he was met by a thoughtful questioner who asked, "Are there few that be saved?" Jesus replied in terms of the strait gate, declaring that many will be disappointed because of ineligibility. Their ineligibility, however, is a matter of their wickedness. Simply seeing Jesus' miracles and eating his loaves does not make one a child of the kingdom even though he may be in the blood lineage of Abraham. On the other hand, recruits for the kingdom will come from unpedigreed people, and from the four corners of the earth, to join as the sharers of the covenant of God with Abraham, Isaac, and Jacob.

XIII. Herod the Fox Hedges Jesus (Luke 13:31-35)

Herod (Antipas) ruled Perea. He had imprisoned and beheaded John. Superstitiously, he feared that Jesus was John risen from the dead. Very naturally, he was afraid of Jesus. It is noteworthy that the Pharisees were his instrument in attempting to get Jesus out of the country. Jesus covered both Herod's low stealth and the murderous attitude of Jerusalem Pharisees in his answer. The character and the acts of Herod Antipas were not maligned, but truly pictured in the epithet Jesus gave him. It is possible that Jesus did leave Perea within two or three days (Note John 11:6).

XIV. Jesus at a Chief Pharisee's Table (Luke 14:1-24).

Jesus had been invited to sabbath day dinner. A dropsical man was there. Others were there. The statement that "they were watching him" (Jesus) indicates in all probability that the situation was designed to see whether Jesus would repeat his common "offense" of healing on the sabbath. Jesus put the question up to the lawyers and Pharisees as to the lawfulness of healing on the sabbath. They were silent. Jesus, however, did not need their ruling on the matter, for he was Lord of the Sabbath. As such, he gave to a dropsical man what was probably the most restful sabbath he had enjoyed since he lost his health.

The instruction which followed on this occasion was well suited to the crowd. There was a lesson on modest conduct at a marriage feast. There were also instructions as to whom one should invite when making a dinner or a supper.

The discourse closed with an account of a great supper to which some of the invited guests refused to come, for various reasons. In their place there were gathered the poor, the maimed, the blind, and the lame until the table was surrounded with guests. The parable clearly was having its enactment as Jesus sought everywhere to bring people into the fellowship of the Father.

XV. The Cost of Discipleship (Luke 14:25-35)

Just as in the Greater Galilean Ministry Jesus came to the point where he faced his followers with the cost of discipleship, so he does with the multitudes who surround him in Perea. That cost, Jesus said, is a cross. There must be the renunciation of all, including oneself, in favor of Christ's perfect lordship.

This standard calls for a complete readjustment of life's relationships. No one, not even oneself, is henceforth to be loved, except as in Christ. This brings sadness to the heart of anyone who does not know and trust God. Christians, however, always find that when Christ becomes their mutual center of love they are bound together with a tie more satisfying than they have known before.

XVI. Three Parables of the Lost (Luke 15)

Against the murmuring of the Jewish religious leaders who stood by, Jesus delivered three classic parables by which he pictured in contrast the joyful onlooking angels of God in heaven. A lost sheep, a lost coin, and a lost son are facts which indicate emergency. They call for emergency measures. Something of value is involved. No one would fail to understand and only a fool would remain complacent under such circumstances.

The parables embody an impression of the divine attitude toward a sinner. Care for the sinner, perseverence in his restoration from destruction, and satisfaction in having him in the fold stand out in the first parable. The idea of value is outstanding in the second. In both cases repentance is the fact upon which restoration turns. In both cases great rejoicing in heaven is the divine attitude toward the restored one.

The third parable is a much fuller parallel to the process by which a soul is restored to God. The parallel comes very near to being identical. The way of the sinner is seen. The change of his mind corresponds to the repentance of the first two parables and is the point on which restoration turns. The goodness of his father is counted upon in the decision which he made. The son's willingness to take the most lowly place if only he may be in his father's house again is a sure ear-mark that he was a changed boy. The grace and magnanimity of the Father in granting complete restoration is doubtless the greatest fact of the parable. In contrast, the elder brother represents a type of personality in which righteousness has been emptied of love. No character could more aptly depict the attitude of the scribes, Pharisees, and lawyers who constantly murmured against Jesus for eating and drinking with publicans and sinners.

XVII. Two Parables Warning Lovers of Money (Luke 16).

1. The first of these parables is presented on the assumption that earthly stewardship is a temporary matter. A wise steward will see to it that he has a clientele of friends upon whom he can count when that end comes. The steward of this parable affords a lesson, not by his dishonesty, but by his foresightedness.

Mammon is a poor friend when industry in this life must stop. One had better have some treasures laid up in heaven. Such treasures committed to God and his kingdom interests will provide for one a stewardship when the present one is ended. The Pharisees knew that Jesus intended this for them for they were lovers of money. They exalted themselves in the sight of men for the sake of it. They set aside the principles of the law and the prophets in favor of their enactments, which in many cases were a cloak for sin and window dressing for men. Their setting aside of the ordinance of marriage is cited in this connection, possibly as another example of their forsaking of the true God.

2. The parable of the rich man and Lazarus is the picture of a contrast in this life which will be reversed in the life to come. Two facts stand out. A rich man, heedless of a worthy poor man at his doorstep, will be consigned to the anguish of hell in the time to come. On the other hand, a worthy poor man, whom we may assume to be a believer in God, will enjoy the fellowship of Abraham in the time to come.

Certain other observations may be made. The deceased are in a state of consciousness. They experience either blessing or anguish. Those in hell would warn others to stay out. The function of the law and the prophets is to keep men from going to hell, and if they will not heed there is no power that can change their destiny. Lazarus doubtless represents the many from the east, west, north, and south who will by-pass heartless religionists and ultimately sit down with Abraham, Isaac, and Jacob in the kingdom.

XVIII. Care for "Little Ones" (Luke 17:1-10)

The designation, little ones, as Jesus had taught in Galilee, refers to both little children and those who have become "as little children," i. e., to new converts to Christ. To offend such an one, that is, to frustrate his faith, is to incur God's jealous wrath. Great patience should be extended in assisting these little ones. Rebuke must be given if they sin, but a true spirit of forgiveness must be extended if they fail. How necessary such patient care is can be attested by every mission worker.

One's faith may be as small as a mustard seed but if it is alive, it will be mighty.

In serving God, Jesus said, we do only what a servant should do.

Our debt to God is such that we shall never be able to bring profit to him. His goodness keeps us debtors. The religionists of that day had very little sense of their unworthiness. They gave the impression that they were exactly paid up with God.

XIX. The Raising of Lazarus (John 11:1-54)

The Raising of Lazarus was an important climax in Jesus' manifestation of himself. It is the seventh and the climax of the signs recorded by John of which it was said, "these (signs) are written that ye might believe that Jesus is the Christ, the Son of God, and that believing ye might have life through his name."

This miracle was the greatest which Jesus had performed, from several standpoints. It reached to the greatest need. The composure of Jesus through Lazarus' sickness and death is seen in marked contrast to the despair of the sisters and the hopelessness of Lazarus' mourners. From their standpoint a great calamity had taken place. From Jesus' standpoint all that took place had design. Lazarus was sick, so he tarried—humanly this was folly; for Christ it was part of his teaching process. Lazarus died, and was dead four days—humanly this was a case for the undertaker; for Christ it was the pitch black background for the manifestation of his glory. Human need includes the inevitable and the inglorious experience of death—Jesus' lesson in faith must not be less inclusive. No human sorrow, no grief or loss was to be left unmatched in Jesus' demonstration of redemptive power.

The recorded effects of this climax of miracles or signs indicates that all Judea was stirred. But the widespread and deepened faith which the sign produced was more than matched by the jealousy of the leaders at Jerusalem. The Sanhedrin was stirred to action. Jesus was marked for death. Yet, since his hour had not yet come, he withdrew into Ephraim.

4. Discussion and Review

1. Characterize the Lord's three tours into Perea. Where was he between tours?

2. Relate the account of the ministry of the Seventy, indicating the nature of the Lord's orders, the place of their ministry, and the results reported.

3. What constitutes neighborliness and what is it not? Answer from Jesus' interview with a lawyer.

4. Report the points of interest in Jesus' first recorded visit to Martha's home. What is the main point of instruction in this occasion?

5. What did Jesus teach on the subject of "Light" in John 8 and 9? Make a study of the blind man's healing as to the divine purpose and the results.

6. Characterize Jesus as the door and as the good shepherd. Under these figures how did he distinguish himself from the Jewish leaders?

7. Relate Jesus' instruction to the disciples on prayer at this time.

8. In Jesus' dealings with the religious leaders as seen in Luke 11, what did the leaders say was wrong with Jesus, and what did Jesus say was wrong with them?

9. What warnings and admonition were given in Luke 12?

10. What did Jesus say as to the necessity of repentance (Luke 13)?

11. Describe the words exchanged by Jesus and the ruler of the synagogue after the healing of the 18 year case of infirmity (Luke 13).

12. What two kingdom parables were repeated at this time?

13. How many will be saved and who?

14. What do you know about Herod Antipas and what was the correspondence of Jesus with him at this time?

15. Describe the Lord's visit in the chief Pharisee's home (Luke 14).

16. What did Jesus declare to be the cost and standard of discipleship (Luke 14)?

17. Relate the three "Parables of the Lost" and state the central teaching of each. How did they mark out a contrast from the religion of the Jewish leaders (Luke 15)?

18. Relate Jesus' two parables warning lovers of money and state the central idea of each (Luke 16).

19. To whom did Jesus refer by the term "little ones" (Luke 17)? Discuss.

20. What was the divine purpose in the raising of Lazarus? Show that this was accomplished (John 11).

5. Select Memory Passages

Luke 9:62; Luke 10:17; John 10:9, 14-15; Luke 11:13; Luke 14:27; Luke 17:3-4.

6. Character Review

Identify:

Martha	Herod Antipas	Sanhedrin
Mary	Lazarus	

7. Bibliography

Bible Dictionary (Smith-Peloubet's Teacher's Edition). Chicago: John C. Winston Co.
Articles:
1. Shepherd.
2. Sheep.
3. Bethany.
4. Herod (Antipas).
Kuyper, Abraham. *Women of the New Testament.* Grand Rapid: Zondervan. "Martha," pp. 43-45.
Ockenga, H. J. *Have You Met These Women?* Grand Rapids: Zondervan. Chapter VIII—The Woman Who Made a House a Home."

Chapter 32

THE PEREAN MINISTRY

—Part Two
—From the Raising of Lazarus
to the Passion Week
(30 A. D.)

1. Introduction

Forced from the Jerusalem area by the murderous designs of the Jewish leaders, Jesus had gone north into the hills of Ephraim. Thence, he moved to the northeast and joined the caravan traffic of Jews from Galilee who that week were wending their way to the Passover at Jerusalem. In this company there was no want of interest as questions of every type were put to Jesus.

2. Reading Assignment

Matthew	Mark	Luke	John
			11:1-54
		17:11-19	
		17:20—18:8	
		18:9-14	
19:3-12	10:2-12		

355

19:13-15	10:13-16	18:15-17	
19:16—20:16	10:17-31	18:18-30	
20:17-19	10:32-34	18:31-34	
20:20-28	10:35-45		
20:29-34	10:46-52	18:35-43	
		19:1-10	
		19:11-28	
26:6-13	14:3-9		11:55—12:11

(Read the Bible first)

3. Study Outline

I. **The Ten Lepers—A Stranger Glorifies God** (Luke 17:11-19)

Jesus had before spoken of the **good** Samaritan. Now he directs us to a **thankful** Samaritan. We are not told who these lepers were, but possibly we may assume that the nine were Jews while the tenth was a Samaritan (stranger). Nine consumed Christ's grace selfishly; only one thought more of the Giver than of the gift. This pattern of response was typical of the results which Jesus was receiving in his mission among men.

II. **The Kingdom—The Time and Nature of Its Coming** (Luke 17:20-37)

The Pharisees, as all curious folk, were primarily concerned about "when" the kingdom of God would come. Jesus' answer to their question had to do primarily with the spiritual conditions which would characterize the time of his coming. It is not essentially an external thing but a matter of spirit and relationship. As Jesus had said, it is by way of a new birth that the kingdom must be entered. We enter God's kingdom by becoming his spiritual children.

The time of Christ's coming may be discerned not by visible evidence but by certain conditions—conditions in the world such as existed in the days of Noah and in the days of Lot. By this we may understand that God's time-table in dealing with the race follows a moral pattern. When evil is ready to be judged an age ends, and those who are spiritually qualified enter upon a new age.

III. **Two Parables on Prayer** (Luke 18:1-14)

1. Jesus challenged those with him to importunate prayer and illustrated his point by the parable of the unjust judge. Prayer should be continuous. It is the opposite of fainting. The parable seeks to emphasize the willingness of our heavenly Father to hear and answer prayer. Yet, Jesus remarks, there may be very little answered prayer on earth when the Son of man comes because faith may be very rare.

2. The second parable is directed to a special class who prayed, but without grace. They made of prayer an occasion to vaunt themselves before God. The parable teaches a double truth: that those who count upon their own merit to be justified will not be justified, while those who penitently confess their sins and seek mercy will be justified by God.

IV. **The Moral Law and the Law of Divorce** (Matthew 19:3-12; Mark 10:2-12)

A Pharisee tried to trap Jesus into committing himself with a blanket statement either for or against divorce. Jesus saw through the shallow questioner. He answered him first on the basis of the eternal moral law which is inherent in the nature of things according to creation. Of course God did not intend that a husband and wife should be divorced. On the other hand, Jesus sustained the law of divorce as God's expedient for people who had set aside the law of their own being. If people forsake the principle of love, then divorce may be a necessity. This was neither setting divorce up as an ideal, nor was it repudiating the Mosaic provision for divorce.

Jesus' explanation left no great comfort for divorce seekers. They are hard hearted, he said. Moreover, they are forbidden to put away a companion except on one ground, namely that of fornication, which is in itself a violation of moral law. Still further, one who does put away his wife and marries another, Jesus said, is an adulterer; and anyone who marries the divorced wife is also an adulterer. Thus the whole influence of Jesus was calculated to discourage divorce and to sustain the marriage bond.

V. **Christ Receives Little Children** (Matt. 19:13-15; Mark 10:13-16; Luke 18:15-17)

Just as marital troubles were attributed to hardness of heart, so, also, Jesus rebuked adults for their hard-hearted attitude toward children. Jesus did not permit the impression that children were a bother to him. In fact he clearly implied that they were eligible to the kingdom while it was the adults who were not eligible. Little children naturally have the attitude which all must have in order to enter the kingdom. Of course all, little babes and older ones, enter the kingdom by God's grace.

VI. Cases Bearing on Stewardship (Matt. 19:16—20:16; Mark 10:17-31; Luke 18:18-30)

To this subject Jesus again applied the principle of spiritual devotion as against a legalistic basis in living. The rich young ruler knew that he had a need which must be met if he was to qualify for the eternal kingdom. Yet, measuring himself, he seemed unable to diagnose his need. He thought he had been keeping the law, but Jesus, testing him, proved that he had not. Love for money, not love for God and others, was the ruling consideration of his life.

In relation to this case Jesus made the statement that it is easier for a camel to go through the eye of a needle than for a rich man to enter into the kingdom of God. While this seemed to be an insuperable standard yet Jesus did not fail to say **how** a rich man might enter the kingdom. "With God" all things are possible. On this basis a rich man makes all that he has a matter of stewardship. Had the rich young man let Jesus order his financial matters, he might have been made steward of even more than what he was asked to give to the poor on this occasion. Thus the call to discipleship is a call to potential wealth—a hundredfold in this life (with persecutions) and in the world to come eternal life.

The parable of the householder illustrates the fact that what God desires most is not a carefully measured service for reward, but a glad service which leaves reward as a matter of God's grace. Thus in this case also, God's standard of stewardship is seen to be spiritual rather than legalistic.

VII. Jesus Foretells His Death and Resurrection

After Peter's confession in Galilee (Matt. 16:21-28) Jesus had clearly announced his death and resurrection. Again after descent from the mount of transfiguration (Matt. 17:22-23) he made the same announcement. Now a third time, so far as the record is concerned, he repeats the announcement. As the caravan moves to Jerusalem for the purpose of observing the Passover, Jesus expresses his consciousness of the fact that he is the victim to be offered at this Passover—the Lamb of God slain from the foundation of the world. The important difference between his sacrifice and other sacrifices, however, would be that after three days he would rise again (Mark 10:34).

VIII. **How Kingdom Positions Are Determined** (Matt. 20:20-28; Mark 10:35-45)

For reasons which some feel were carnal James and John wanted places near Jesus in the kingdom. Since Jesus did not rebuke this request perhaps we should not. Is it not possible that these disciples may have desired to be near Christ because of their love for him?

Jesus, however, stated that the matter would be handled by the Father. The Father's decisions will be made on a twofold consideration, at least. First, partaking of Christ's cup, or suffering with Christ, appears to be the disciples' side of the matter. Secondly, the Father's plan is the basic consideration; the best interests of the Father's kingdom and not mere personal desire must determine what position each shall have. The practical consideration with which Jesus closed this lesson was that each should seek to minister, that is, to fill a place of need. This is one's true greatness.

IX. **Miracles at Jericho** (Luke 19:1-10; 18:35-43; Matt. 20:29-34; Mark 10:46-52)

Ordinarily the caravan of worshipers would not have stopped for fellowship at Jericho. Much less would such worshipers have stopped to lodge with a publican. Jesus did both, to the amazement and disapproval of others. In doing so Jesus left another example for Christian workers to go to the socially outcast. Yet Zacchaeus, though a social outcast, was really a man of intelligence. He was more than alert to know and to do the will of God. Such a spirit was Jesus' greatest prize. On another occasion he had said, "the Father seeketh such to worship him." As on that occasion, Jesus now also brought salvation to a sinner and to his people.

As Jesus left Jericho, two blind men, casting aside all propriety, called after him as though their last hope was in him. Many re-

buked them, but Jesus did not. He healed them both, and the
people of this ill-reputed city glorified God.

X. The Parable of the Pounds—Making Good for Christ (Luke 19:11-28)

This parable was given to correct the supposition that Christ's
kingdom was immediately to be set up. It indicates that a time of
testing for kingdom responsibility is to come first. The parable
seems well related to the earlier instruction of Jesus regarding
kingdom positions. The test reveals four types of attitude toward
responsibility:

1. Some hated the Lordship of Christ and rebelled as enemies.
2. One had increased his possessions tenfold.
3. One had increased his possessions fivefold.
4. One had made no increase, because of slothfulness.

Each type made its own future. The rebels were destroyed.
The man of greatest achievement was given corresponding kingdom
responsibility. The man of less achievement was given correspond-
ingly less kingdom responsibility. The man who, though not in
spirit a professed rebel, was heartless, had all responsibility taken
from him. The extra responsibility of the slothful servant was
given to the man who showed the greatest power of achievement.
Thus we have here important principles for testing the service of
our lives. Also we are assured not merely of a reward, but of a
future place for the exercise of our sovereignty under God in the
world to come.

XI. The Victor at Bethany—Anointed and Despised (Matt. 26:6-13; Mark 14:3-9; John 11:55—12:11)

On the Saturday before Passion week (John 12:1), as the caravan
of Jews was pouring into the Jerusalem area to observe the Passover, Jesus made his way to Bethany. Upon his arrival a supper
was made for him at the house of Simon the leper (who was doubtless now- healed). Mary, Martha, Lazarus (whom Jesus had before
raised from the dead), and many more, were there.

This occasion portrays two contrasting climaxes of sentiment.
Simon the leper opened up his home to give Jesus a feast; Lazarus
sat at meat with Jesus; Mary anointed Jesus with costly ointment
of spikenard and wiped his feet with her hair. The house was filled

with the fragrance of her lavish deed. In contrast, Judas, with some others concurring, criticized Mary for what they regarded as extravagance. On the pretext of concern for the poor, Judas rested his case for what in reality amounted to despising Jesus. Jesus was not worthy of the anointing—such was the real meaning of the sentiment represented by Judas.

Jesus related Mary's act to his death and burial. Mary's devoted anointing of Jesus was in view of his supreme sacrifice for the sins of the world; it would be tied up as a precious memorial with the good news of salvation, and the whole world would be inspired by her sentiment.

4. Discussion and Review

1. Why did Jesus leave the Jerusalem area after the raising of Lazarus? Trace his whereabouts until he again returned to Bethany.

2. What pattern of response is seen in the healing of the ten lepers? How does the response to Christ's feeding of the 5000 compare, for example?

3. How did Jesus answer the inquiry of the Pharisees as to the time of the coming of God's kingdom?

4. Give the principal idea in Jesus' two parables on prayer.

5. What did Jesus say of the morality of divorce as related to its legality?

6. Discuss Jesus' attitude toward children as contrasted with a very common adult attitude.

7. Is it possible for a rich man to enter the kingdom of God? If so, how?

8. What fact is taught by the parable of the householder?

9. Trace Jesus' announcements of his death and resurrection.

10. How are kingdom positions determined—by whom and upon what considerations?

11. Why did Jesus lodge at Jericho? What did he accomplish and what did the people do when he left?

12. What is taught by the parable of the pounds?

13. Depict the contrast of sentiments represented in the house of Simon the leper on the Saturday preceding Passion week.

14. How does history evaluate Mary and Judas respectively?

5. Select Memory Passages

Matt. 19:14; Luke 18:28-30; Matt. 20:25-28; Luke 19:10; Luke 19:26

6. Character Review

Identify:

The ten lepers   Simon the leper   Zacchaeus   Judas Iscariot

7. Bibliography

Bible Dictionary (Smith-Peloubet's Teacher's Edition or some other). Chicago: John C. Winston Co.
Articles:
1. The Law of Divorce.
2. The Pound.
Blaikie, Wm. G. *Bible History*. Chap. XV. New York: Thomas Nelson Co.
Topic: His (Jesus') Imagery in the South, p. 441.
Free, Joseph P. *Archaeology and Bible History*. Wheaton: Van Kampen, 1950.
Topics:
1. Zacchaeus the Tax-collector: Archaeological Light, pp. 294, 295.
2. Archaeological Light on the Apparent Contradiction concerning the Healing of Blind Bartimaeus (Luke 18:35), p. 295.
Kuyper, Abraham. *Women of the New Testament*. Grand Rapids: Zondervan.
1. "Salome," pp. 28-30.
2. "Mary of Bethany," pp. 40-42.
Sangster, Margaret E. *The Women of the Bible*. Chapt. XXXVII, "The Sisters of Bethany." New York: The Christian Herald.

Chapter 33

THE PASSION WEEK

—Sunday, Monday, Tuesday
(April 2, 3, 4; 30 A. D.)

1. Introduction

Up until the very last week of his ministry Jesus continually avoided too much publicity of his Messiahship, the evident reason being that this would have hastened a precipitation of opposition in advance of his ministry. The idea of a political Messiah was common, but Jesus resisted this idea consistently, taking in its stead a course which pointed to rejection rather than coronation in Jerusalem. It was time now, however, for him to permit the zeal of his followers to express itself, and to provide a public proclamation of his Messiahship. Ever since his climactic sign of raising Lazarus from the dead, Jesus' favor with the people would have yielded to him a unanimous electoral poll. The Phariseees were utterly dismayed as the "whole world" went after him (John 12:17-19).

Jesus knew that the expression of such popular favor would incite the Jerusalem leaders to their worst means. But the time for his death was now at hand; so he permitted the people to express their reception of his claims publicly and made plans to march into Jerusalem as the anointed Son of David, even though doing so set off the death trap of the Jewish leaders.

2. Reading Assignment

Matthew	Mark	Luke	John
21:1-11	11:1-11	19:29-44	12:12-19
21:18, 19a	11:12-14		
21:12-17	11:15-19	19:45-48	
21:19b-22	11:20-26		
21:28-32			
21:33-46	12:1-12	20:9-19	
22:1-14			
22:15-40	12:13-34	20:20-40	
22:41-46	12:35-37	20:41-44	

(Read the Bible first)

3. Study Outline
(Sunday)

I. **Christ's Triumphal Entry Into Jerusalem** (Matt. 21:1-11; Mark 11:1-11; Luke 19:29-44; John 12:12-19)

Leaving Bethany where Jesus had been given the supper in the house of Simon the leper, Jesus and his party moved toward Jerusalem. Jesus' entry was a unique combination of salutary kingliness and humility. He commandeered the beast, a lowly ass, which was to bear him in the triumphal procession. This procedure had two unique features. First it was a supernatural manifestation of knowledge on Jesus' part. Secondly, it was in fulfillment of Old Testament scriptures (See Isa. 62:11; Zech. 9:9).

Luke records the request of the offended Pharisees to Jesus for the rebuke of the enthusiastic multitude, and the memorable reply of Jesus, "I tell you, if these shall hold their place, the stones will cry out." He also pictures Jesus weeping over the city of Jerusalem in lamentation because of the desolation which was before her at the hands of her enemies.

Mark tells us that after Jesus went to the temple and had

"looked round about upon all things" he left Jerusalem and went to Bethany for the night.

(Monday)
II. The Morning Walk to Jerusalem (Matt. 21:18-19; Mark 11:12-14)

On the way back to the temple Monday morning Jesus again turned aside to the fig tree. One might suppose that he did so because he was hungry for food, but this is hardly the case since it was not the season for figs. It was the season, however, for the tiny green figs to come out of the bark along with the leaves. The fact that Jesus found "nothing but leaves" meant that there was no prospect of fruit, so he cursed it and it withered away. Though no special meaning is assigned to this event, it easily suggests what is elsewhere symbolically set forth, namely, that Jesus the Son of God was disappointed by the barrenness of his people. He clearly intimated that they were doomed to a curse.

III. The Second Cleansing of the Temple (Matt. 21:12-17; Mark 11:15-19; Luke 19:45-48)

It will be recalled that when Jesus left the temple the night before he "looked round about upon all things" (Mark 11:11). We are not told what he saw, but as he entered the temple on Monday morning he appears to have had his mind made up about one thing —the temple needed a cleansing. Upon entering the temple he proceeded to rid it of money changers and merchants. It is of interest to note that Jesus cleansed the temple at the beginning (John 2:13-17) and then again at the close of his ministry, both occasions being at Passover feasts.

To the embarrassment which this caused the Pharisees, the children who were present added a chorus of "Hosanna to the Son of David." The chief priests were frank to offer their rebuke, asking Jesus to quiet the children, and seeking for an opportunity to destroy the children's hero.

At the end of Monday Jesus again went to Bethany for the night.

(Tuesday)
IV. The Morning Walk to Jerusalem (Matt. 21:20-22; Mark 11:20-25)

Returning to the temple on the customary Bethany-Jerusalem

road the disciples observed with astonishment that the fig tree which Jesus had cursed the morning before was withered away. Jesus made of the matter a lesson in faith, assuring the disciples that if they would but have faith they might command the removal of mountains. Jesus offered the reminder, however, that an unforgiving spirit would prevent the flow of God's mercies.

V. **The Challenge of Christ's Authority** (Matt. 21:23-27; Mark 11:27-33; Luke 20:1-8)

As Jesus entered the temple that Tuesday morning there was before him one of the fullest days of his ministry. Jesus had left the chief priests and elders somewhat dazed the night before, but they came back on Tuesday to challenge his authority for what he had done.

Had Jesus declared, simply, what was true, namely that he came forth from the Father, the cry of blasphemy would immediately have been raised. Instead, Jesus put the burden of this question right back upon the inquirers, asking them to state the source of the authority of John the Baptist. John was credited highly by the Jews. Yet John introduced and completely endorsed Jesus as the Messiah. Thus Jesus most shrewdly escaped the trap of his questioners and at the same time left them with the truth to be thought through.

VI. **Three Parables of Warning** (Matt. 21:28—22:14; Mark 12:1-12; Luke 20:9-19)

Parables are a form of symbolism commonly employed to tactfully teach what might be offensive if taught directly. David was led to see his sin and to decide against it through Nathan's parable of the poor man and his lamb. Sometimes parables are interpreted and applied and sometimes they are left to be pondered in the minds of those for whom they are intended.

In these parables the lessons are obvious. In the first Jesus declares the emptiness of pretense without true service and places above it his preference for true service even though it comes from one who has been rebellious. In the second parable Jesus pictured a parallel to Israel's infamous record of insulting and killing her prophets, including the Son of God. Jesus had now gone far enough that the Pharisees caught his meaning. They would have taken him on the spot, except for the fact that the multitudes might have turned upon them.

In the third parable Jesus set forth the kingdom of God in terms of a high privilege to which God is calling all men. To attend the marriage of God's son is to mingle in the very highest level of fellowship. To turn lightly away from it to one's farm, or to his merchandise, or to mistreat the messenger bringing the invitation is an indignity and an offense. This failure to embrace the invitation became the occasion for offering a place at the feast to all men until the seats were filled. Doubtless this is a picture of the transition from the special call of God to Israel to his call to the Gentiles. The third parable includes, also, an important lesson regarding the qualification of participants at the feast. Though they may be from among the good and bad, high and low, they must have on the required wedding garment. Thus the universality of the provision of God's grace is not allowed to destroy the standard of righteousness in the kingdom.

VII. A Barrage of Enemy Questions (Matt. 22:15-40; Mark 12:13-34; 20:20-40)

Though Jesus unmistakably unmasked his enemies through the word pictures which he had given, they came back for more. Three questions were put to him, intended to trap him in his speech.

The Pharisees took counsel to frame up the first trap. Although ordinarily they were at odds with the Herodians, they joined them now in the laying of their trap. After approaching Jesus with flattery calculated to make him speak out rashly they broached the question as to whether it was lawful to pay tribute to Caesar. Before Jesus answered their question he rebuked them for the hypocritical wickedness of their motives. His object lesson from the coin and his memorable statement enjoining appropriate tribute to both God and Caesar caused even his enemies to marvel.

Next the Sadducees laid their trap. As might be expected it dealt with the resurrection. Briefly, they wanted to know whose wife a woman would be in the resurrection who had had seven successive husbands in the present life. Jesus promptly disposed of their question by declaring the error of the assumption upon which it rested. Sexuality, Jesus affirmed, is not a part of the resurrected order. But Jesus went farther, affirming to these skeptical unbelievers in a resurrection the fact that the God of Abraham, Isaac, and

Jaocb is not a God of the dead but of the living. Again his listeners heard his answer with rapt astonishment at his wisdom.

Then the Pharisees returned for their inning with the question as to which is the greatest commandment. Jesus so satisfied his inquirers on this question that he nearly won them. They were silenced and asked no more questions.

VIII. **Christ's Final Unanswerable Question** (Matt. 22:41-46; Mark 12:35-37; Luke 20:41-44)

Although the Jewish scholars claimed to be authorities in interpreting the Scriptures Jesus raised a consideration which they apparently had never had up before. It was concerning David's reference to the Messiah (Psa. 110:1). The following considerations were lifted out:

1. The Christ, according to Scriptures, was to be the Son of David.

2. David called this foretold Son his Lord.

3. Question: How could the Christ be both son and Lord of David?

The question raised was and still is unanswerable to those Jews who have rejected Jesus as the Christ. Jesus as the incarnate Son of God, however, fits David's prophecy perfectly. Being unwilling to admit the claims of Jesus, the Jewish leaders remained silent rather than involve themselves with a more difficult burden of explanation. Jesus' case was completed.

4. Discussion and Review

1. Why did Jesus not publicly announce his Messiahship at an earlier time?

2. Describe the course of events on Sunday of Passion week.

3. Relate what took place as Jesus and the disciples returned to the temple on Monday morning.

4. Describe what took place at the temple on Monday.

5. Relate the conversation of Jesus and the disciples on their way to the temple on Tuesday morning.

6. What question did Jesus face from the chief priests and elders as he returned to the temple? How was it related to what he did the day before? How did he dispose of the question?

7. Relate and pointedly state the lesson in each of the parables which Jesus gave.

8. What three questions were put to Jesus by the Pharisees, Herodians, and Sadducees? How did Jesus reply in each case?

9. What is your answer to the final question which Jesus put to the assembly of Pharisees?

5. Select Memory Passages

Matt. 21:22; 22:32; 22:37-40

6. Bibliography

Bible Dictionary (Smith-Peloubet Teachers' Edition or some other). Chicago: John C. Winston Co.
Articles:
1. Fig Tree.
2. Feast of Passover.

Chapter 34

THE PASSION WEEK

—Tuesday Concluded

1. Introduction

Jesus had reasoned with his enemies to the limit. His reasoning was unanswerable and it left them with no recourse for rebuttal. Parables, questions, and answers now gave place to a dramatic direct pronouncement of judgment from the Lord upon the Jerusalem leaders. While the conversation on Tuesday up to this point was on a give and take level between Jesus and the leaders, now Jesus only is heard. He addresses the multitudes and the disciples. While the Pharisees, Sadducees, and Herodians were doubtless well represented in the assembly, they apparently withdrew from the limelight in which they were seen earlier in the day. Jesus' discourse now was in the nature of a public warning against them and of a public pronouncement of the woes that rested upon them. The blasts of the Lord were indeed terrific.

2. Reading Assignment

Matthew	Mark	Luke	John
23	12:38-40	20:45-47	
	12:41-44	21:1-4	
			12:20-36
			12:37-50
24, 25	13	21:5-38	
26:1-5, 14-16	14:1, 2, 10, 11	22:1-6	

(Read the Bible first)

3. Study Outline

I. **Seven Woes Against the Scribes and Pharisees** (Matt. 23; Mark 12:38-40; Luke 20:45-47)

Against those who sat in Moses' seat but did not fulfill his law, who bound heavy burdens upon others but lifted no burdens, whose works were for show, who loved salutations, who were known as rabbis, as fathers, and as masters but who were not known as servants —against these Jesus uttered seven woes.

In their fulness these woes approximated all the accumulated blood-guiltiness from Abel to Zachariah, Jesus said. Jerusalem might have inherited all of the accumulated blessing. As Jesus contemplated this, his indignation turned to lamentation, and he cried out, "O Jerusalem, Jerusalem, which killeth the prophets, and stoneth them that are sent unto her, how often would I have gathered thy children together, even as a hen gathereth her chickens under her wings, and ye would not! Behold your house is left unto you desolate. For I say unto you, Ye shall not see me henceforth, till ye shall say, Blessed is he that cometh in the name of the Lord."

II. **Christ the Judge of Benevolences** (Matt. 12:41-44; Luke 21:1-4)

What Christ did after delivering this terrific utterance is nearly amusing. While it is not in good taste for us to watch other people give their offerings, it is God's prerogative, and we may be sure that he always observes this act.

His lesson in comparing the amount of the widow's gift in relation to the gifts of others is simply the application of the same principle which he had so often stressed. It is the heart motive and not external acts alone that gives value to a person's life. Thus in this incident Jesus drew forth a fitting object lesson to exemplify the simplicity and wholesome devotion so utterly wanting in the Jerusalem leaders.

III. **Seeking Gentiles and Rejecting Jews** (John 12:20-50)

The coming of certain seeking Greeks to Jerusalem was significant at this Passover season when the Jews came to a climax in their rejection of Jesus. Arriving, they inquired of Philip, who, with the assistance of Andrew, brought them into touch with Jesus.

The seeking Greeks drew from Jesus' soul utterances which revealed both the depths and the extent of his passion. They reminded him of the great harvest which would follow his sacrifice, that like a corn of wheat he should die, but that in consequence many should receive life. The cross would lead many to believe, and the Father would be glorified. So significant was the glory which Jesus referred to that a voice from heaven certified the reality of it.

Three specific things were about to be accomplished. First, the world was about to be judged, that is, it was going to be deeded to its proper possessor. Secondly, Satan who had gained possession of it because of sin, was to be cast out. By a lie maligning God's character he had at the dawn of history usurped the place of confidence in men's minds. The cross would be a drawing point, bringing men into the faith and fold of the Father.

Christ's coming and his being lifted up are further spoken of in terms of light. Those who behold the Son, and receive him, receive the Father. Those who reject him are condemned, not by the Son, but by the truth which they hear but reject. To know the Father as revealed by Christ is to face one's highest point of opportunity. How that opportunity is met determines a man's eternal destiny.

IV. Olivet Discourse—Characteristics of the Age up to Its End
   (Matt. 24, 25; Mark 13; Luke 21:5-38)

Leaving the temple for the last time, Jesus with his disciples walked along a slope leading to the top of Mount Olivet. From this ascent the buildings of the temple site were brought into full view and occasioned the admiring remarks of the disciples. Jesus was in no mood to appreciate their remarks for he had too full a sense of the lamentable fate which awaited the temple. He frankly replied that when God's judgment had been spent not one stone would be left upon another.

As Jesus sat, the disciples drew him out further with the twofold question, "When shall these things be? and what shall be the sign of thy coming, and of the end of the world?" The discourse which followed gives a window-picture of the age ahead together with related spiritual instruction.

Outline of the Olivet Discourse

I. Warning against False Christs (Matt. 24:4, 5, 23-28)

II. What Will Take Place before "the End of the World" (Age) Matt.
24:6-14, 15-28; Mk. 13:7-23; Luke 21:9-24)
1. Wars, Rumors of Wars (Christ's Note: "The end is not yet.")
2. International and Inter-kingdom Conflicts
3. Earthquakes
4. Famines
("These things" are but the beginning of travail.)
5. Tribulations, Martyrdom, Hatred from All Nations
(Consequences):
Many will stumble.
Christians will betray one another.
Hatred will arise.
False prophets will lead many astray.
Love of many will wax cold.
Those who endure to the end will be saved.
6. Worldwide Preaching of the Gospel
To all nations
As a witness
7. "The End" (of gospel preaching and of tribulation)

The above events are the fulfillment of the "abomination of
desolation" (Matt. 24:15-28) spoken of by Daniel, including the destruction of Jerusalem, 70 A. D., but continuing to the end of the
age.

III. Post-Tribulation Events (Matt. 24:29-30; Mk. 13:24; Lk. 21:25)
1. The Shaking of the Heavens
2. The Coming of the Son of Man
With power
With great glory
3. Trumpet Sound—Angels Gather the Elect
From the uttermost part of earth
To the uttermost part of heaven

IV. Additional Instruction Regarding the Signs of the End (Matt.
24:32-44; Mark 17:28-37; Luke 21:29-35)
1. As in the case of the full-leafed fig tree, we may discern
that the end is at hand when "all these things" (under I and
II above) have been "accomplished."

2. Two things will pass away (this generation and heaven and earth); one will not (God's word).

3. The Father alone knows the exact day and hour.

4. The end will come about in a manner similar to the end of the antediluvian age. The elect will be gathered for final salvation; the wicked will be given over to judgment.

5. Believers are advised to be ready at all times (Matt. 24:42-44; Mark 13:33-37; Luke 21:34-36)

V. Four Lessons Showing in What Preparedness for Christ's Coming Consists (Matt. 24:45—25:46)

1. The faithful and wise servant is he who feeds God's household. Negatively, it is not he who delights to think of the Lord's coming as remote and who therefore becomes unruly and self-indulgent (Matt. 24:45-51).

2. It means to wait for Christ's coming providently (Matt. 25:1-13).

3. It means to be a faithful steward for Christ during the interval of his absence (Matt. 25:14-30).

4. It means to have a record of faithfully ministering to the needs of God's children. Specifically, it means ministering to the hungry, to the thirsty, to strangers, to the naked, to the sick, and to those in prison.

V. Jesus Announces the Exact Time of His Crucifixion—Conspirators Plan for It (Matt. 26:1-5, 14-16; Mark 14:1, 2, 10, 11; Luke 22:1-6)

At the close of the Tuesday discourses Jesus, addressing the disciples, told them specifically that he would be crucified according to the Passover schedule; this would be "after two days." The Jewish leaders had stopped reasoning because they could not match Jesus' wisdom. But they had one means of opposition left; they could kill him. Accordingly, they withdrew, apparently, from the audience of Jesus, and convened to plan the step which their hearts contemplated.

It was perhaps Tuesday afternoon or evening that they met. They agreed upon the policy of waiting until after the feast season when the crowds would have left the city, but at this point Judas Iscariot contacted the council with an offer to deliver Jesus to them. The council avidly accepted and agreed to pay him thirty pieces of silver. He was to deliver Christ when there was opportunity to do so with the least interference to the multitudes.

Up to this time Judas had shown wrong motives. He was mercenary. Jesus had rebuked him. Doubtless he was offended. Moreover, tremendous pressure from the Jerusalem leaders was upon Jesus' followers. Under these circumstances Satan entered into Judas for the purpose of executing the betrayal.

On Tuesday night Jesus and the disciples lodged in the Mount of Olives. It is possible that he ministered in the temple the following day (Luke 21:37-38), although there is no record of that day (Wednesday) whatsoever.

4. Discussion and Review

1. What turning point in Jesus' teaching is seen at the point in Tuesday's ministry with which this block of Scripture begins?

2. List the specific sins for which the seven woes of Matthew 23 are pronounced.

3. By what principle of measurement did Jesus estimate the temple givers?

4. Indicate the depth and extent of Christ's passion as revealed on the occasion of the visiting Greeks. (The Greeks may be regarded as representative of all Gentiles.)

5. What is it that limits the number of those who are effectively drawn to Christ according to Jesus' use of the analogy of light (John 12:30-50)?

6. Show from the Olivet Discourse what will take place before the end of the age.

7. Show what will take place after the present age of tribulation ends.

8. What is the lesson of the fig tree?

9. Name two things destined to pass away and one which will abide.

10. Is the exact time of the end known? If so, by whom?

11. What may we learn about the end of this age from Noah's day?

12. Indicate from four lessons in the Olivet Discourse what Jesus meant by preparedness for his coming.

13. What is significant as to the time table of Jesus' crucifixion?

14. From what is recorded and what may be read back of the record indicate what the conspirators were doing from Tuesday night until Thursday night.

5. Select Memory Passages

Matthew 23:37-39; John 12:31, 32; Matthew 24:14, 35, 37-42

6. Bibliography

Bible Dictionary (Smith-Peloubet Teacher's Edition or some other). Chicago: John C. Winston Co.
    Articles:
    1. Alms.
    2. Mount of Olives.
Sangster, Margaret E. *The Women of the Bible.* Chapter XXXVIII, "The Widow with the Two Mites." New York: The Christian Herald.

Chapter 35

THE PASSION WEEK

—Thursday

1. Introduction

The block of Scripture for this chapter portrays the withdrawal of Jesus and the twelve disciples from the multitudes for a final evening of fellowship just before the day when satanically inspired human rulers would nail him upon a criminal's cross. Jesus was perfectly poised with a sense of mission from the Father, and with a sense of the perfect outworking of the Father's time schedule for his ministry. His thoughts were far above the level of the human agents which were about to take his life. He had come to do for the world what the paschal lamb did for believing Israelites when God delivered them from the death angel in Egypt. He had come to be lifted up so that he might do for the whole world what the raised serpent did for the bitten and death-marked Israelites in the wilderness.

But before performing this all availing redemptive act, Jesus took the greatest pains to establish the fellowship which had been begun in the lives of his disciples. These men bore a significant relationship to the world which God gave his Son to save. He wished to vouchsafe to them two important symbolic memorials. He wished to plant within their hearts words which would sustain them when the dark hour of his death would leave them orphans. He wished furthermore to intercede for them and for those who would believe in times to come, who would be his witnesses, and who would hold forth the light of his word to the nations of the world. These were the tremendous concerns which occupied our Lord that night.

377

2. Reading Assignment

	Matthew	Mark	Luke	John
Preparation	26:17-19	14:12-16	22:7-13	
The Eating	26:20	14:17	22:14-18	
Contention			22:24-30	
An Object Lesson				13:1-20
The Betrayer Identified— Dismissed	26:21-25	14:18-21	22:21-23	13:21-35
Christ's Prediction: Peter's Denial The Dispersion of the Twelve	26:21-35	14:27-31	22:21-38	13:36-38
The Lord's Supper Instituted	26:26-29	14:22-25	22:19-20	
Christ's Farewell Discourse to the Eleven				14-16
Christ's Intercessory Prayer				17
Gethsemane	26:30; 36-46	14:26, 32-42	22:39-46	18:1

(Read the Bible first)

3. Study Outline

I. Preparations for the Last Supper

The "Last Supper" is an appropriate name for the occasion related here. It was the end of the Passover as a typical ordinance—the type had led to its fulfillment. It was also the last supper of fellowship with his disciples in the earthly ministry of the Lord.

The Passover was instituted as a celebration of the exemption from death which came to all obedient persons on the night when God slew the first born of all families in Egypt. That event which occurred on the 14th of Nisan was celebrated as one of the three feasts which every Israelite was required to observe at Jerusalem each year. The hasty flight of Israel from Egypt which followed the slaying of the first born had made it necessary for them to take unleavened bread with them. To signify this the memorial observance required the use of unleavened bread on the 14th of the month Nisan and for seven days thereafter. Other preparations for the

Passover, including the selection of the perfect paschal lamb, were to begin on the 10th of Nisan. The lamb had to be eaten in some house in Jerusalem. It is of interest to note that present day Jews do not eat the paschal lamb at their annual passover, although they do observe the period of unleavened bread.

Peter and John were the two disciples ordered to make the preparations. The Lord's orders to them were marked with the same authority and supernatural knowledge as was manifest on certain earlier occasions, such as when Peter was ordered to get tax money from a fish's mouth, and such as when an ass was commandeered for the Lord's kingly entrance into Jerusalem.

II. The Eating of the Passover

The supper began on a specified hour, which we may note to be just forty-eight hours after Jesus' announcement on Tuesday night (Matt. 26:2). Now as they sat down to eat, Jesus expressed the fact that he had greatly desired the occasion and coupled with this the announcement that it would be their last Passover until the time of the future kingdom of God.

The Passover was a full meal. It was as they were eating it that Jesus arose and distributed the bread and wine which were to memorialize his broken body and his shed blood. It is evident that this memorial was not to be a meal (Note I Cor. 11).

III. Contention—The Question of Kingdom Positions

It is one of the regrettable memories of that occasion that what Jesus had looked forward to with such eagerness was made the occasion of personal strife by the disciples. This strife Jesus recognized not as being unusual, but rather the common thing among men (the Gentiles). But Jesus must have felt deeply the failure of the disciples to rise above the common level. This point of contention had arisen at different times before and it is probable that it may have arisen on this occasion in connection with the order of seating in relation to Jesus at the Supper. It was something against which he took particular pains to set an unforgetable memorial in their minds at the close of the Supper by his act of washing their feet.

IV. An Object Lesson in Humble Service

Jesus' washing of the disciples feet on this occasion was not only an expression of our Lord's condescension and service. It showed that. But it was intended as an example. They were to remember this act of menial service of their Lord to themselves, and they were to practice the same humble service to one another. That Jesus waited to give this object lesson at this time doubtless shows that he wanted it to have an abiding impression. He had taught the truth many times before, but knew that it needed final emphasis. Who does not know from the history of Christendom how important this object lesson from our Lord's was, and is?

V. The Betrayer Identified (Matt. 26:21-25; Mark 14:18-21; 22:21-23; 13:21-35)

The saddest feature of this last Passover was the existence among the disciples of a betrayer. The contention of the eleven was pardonable; they are to be credited with a high esteem for the Lord. Jesus' announcement that one of their number should betray him was a shock to all of them, except Judas. Although he had already planned the betrayal, he hypocritically bluffed his way before the other disciples. But Jesus revealed that he knew all about the plot. He gave the sign which pointed out the guilty one, and dismissed him from the assembly.

VI. Christ's Prediction of Peter's Denial and of the Scattering of the Disciples (Matt. 26:21-35; Mk. 14:27-31; Luke 22:21-38; John 13:36-38)

Judas was not the only one of the disciples influenced by Satan in this crisis. The best of the rest of the twelve were tested to the breaking point. Jesus warned them that Satan would sift them like wheat. They would be scattered without a leader; Christ's purpose to accept the cross instead of resisting the enemy would be an offense to them. Peter, in particular, lacked the grace to win a moral victory on such grounds, and as Jesus predicted, he would deny his Lord three times before the second cock-crowing. Had Jesus not prayed for him his faith would have completely failed.

VII. The Lord's Supper Instituted (Matt. 26:26-29; Mark 14:27-31; Luke 22:21-38; John 13:36-38)

The Lord at this point instituted a new memorial. The passover itself was a memorial of the ancient sacrifice of a lamb as a substitute for the death of the firstborn of each household. The new memorial was established to celebrate a greater substitutionary sacrifice which Christ was about to make. When this would be observed in later times it would point in two directions, to the Christ of sacrifice and atonement, and to the Christ of glory. Thus there is embodied in this memorial the perfect basis for full orbed faith, hope, and love. The simplicity of the memorial is its distinction. The reality of the facts represented is certified by the resurrection of Jesus and by his present power in the world through the Gospel.

VIII. Christ's Farewell Discourse to the Eleven (John 14-16)

Matthew, Mark, and Luke left to John the task of relating the major discourse of that upper-room fellowship. Apart from John's record, all that is said about what took place further that night is that they sang a hymn and went out to Gethsemane (Matt. 26:30; Mark 14:26).

Part of this discourse may have been given on the way to Gethsemane. What Jesus said in these chapters made the difference between despair and radiant hope. There was no longer any place for our Lord on earth; his disciples were to be scattered. Against this fact he spoke with certainty of a permanent place which he would prepare for their future eternal home. He himself was the way to this home—he would prepare it and he would come again for the disciples; they would be where he is to be. He spoke of the interval with certain comfort also. He would send another Comforter, the Holy Spirit. By faith and obedience they would continue to be related to him, related as vitally as the vine to the branches. Furthermore, because of this relationship they would be fruitful. They would have love for one another and this would glorify the Father. The Holy Spirit, their Comforter, would henceforth be their teacher, teaching them particularly of Christ. In relation to the world he would convict men of sin, of righteousness, and of judgment. The disciples would henceforth have tribulation in the world, but in Christ they would nevertheless have peace. They were therefore to be of good cheer because of Christ's victory over the world.

IX. Christ's Intercessory Prayer (John 17)

Christ had unbosomed his heart to his disciples; now he does so to the heavenly Father. The first eight verses of this prayer are concerned with the complete accomplishment of the divine purpose, namely, the manifestation of divine glory to the world through the Son.   Although the cross was still ahead Christ anticipated the completion of that ordeal.   He had delivered the word of the Father; the disciples had received it, and by this fact belonged to Christ.   It is remarkable that Christ regarded the success of his mission as having been secured, even though the planting of the word had so far been in the lives of only a handful of men.

The remainder of the prayer is devoted to this handful of men whom Christ delighted to refer to as "mine," and "thine" (the Father's). He prays for their keeping, for their unity, for their joyfulness, for their sanctification, and for the fulfillment of their mission in the world.

While the prayer does not directly include the world, it does include all in the world who will believe through the testimony of the early believers. Thus, Christ here offers a prayer which reaches to the household of faith from the early disciples to the twentieth century believers scattered in hundreds of denominations and in many lands.

X.   **Gethsemane** (Matt. 26:30, 36-46; Mark 14:26; 32-42; Luke 22:39-
46; John 18:1)

According to past custom Jesus went to a special place of prayer (proseuche) in the garden of Gethsemane. On this occasion a tenseness gripped the situation. Christ knew what Judas had planned. In keeping with it, apparently, he commanded his disciples to watch while he retired to pray. One group he left near the entrance of the garden; Peter, James, and John were stationed somewhat nearer his place of prayer.

While slumber claimed the disciples, Christ faced the agony of the cup of suffering which was before him. Three times he sought the support of the disciples but found them asleep. His soul was tempted, more severely than we can know, to bypass the ordeal of Calvary. He might have done so by calling a legion of angels to destroy his enemies; had that course been followed there would have been no way of salvation opened up for a lost race. He took a firm grip upon himself and fully yielded to the Father's plan of love saying, ". . . not my will but thine, be done." Immediately, an angel from heaven sustained him and he followed his purpose without wavering even though the agony brought great sweat-drops of blood. Thus Christ made good the words of his prayer, ". . . . I sanctify myself."

4. Discussion and Review

1. What did the Passover memorialize?

2. What was its typical significance?

3. Evaluate the motives which made the disciples contentious on this occasion.

4. By what object did Jesus deal with the disciples in relation to their concern. State the meaning of this lesson.

5. How did Judas' attitude differ from that of the eleven? How was Satan able to enter him? Why did he not enter others?

6. Show that the Lord's Supper as instituted by Christ embodies a basis for full orbed faith. What fact certifies the reality of the truths embodied?

7. What were the leading ideas of Christ's farewell discourse? What was it calculated to accomplish?

8. For whom and for what did Jesus pray in his intercessory prayer?

5. Bibliography

Bible Dictionary (Smith-Peloubet Teacher's Edition or some other). Chicago: John C. Winston Co.
    Articles:
    1. Lord's Supper.
    2. Gethsemane.

Chapter 36

THE PASSION WEEK

---

1. Introduction

The Gethsemane agony of Thursday night was followed during the early morning hours by the appearance of a "multitude" from the office of the chief priest. Jesus was betrayed to this crowd by Judas, arrested by the Jewish authorities, and arraigned before Annas and the Sanhedrin council. All of this took place before daybreak Friday morning. At daybreak Jesus appeared in a day session before the Sanhedrin. Then he was sent to Pilate for official conviction. Pilate had him appear before Herod Antipas, but Herod returned him for final trial to Pilate. Pilate, under pressure of the Jews gave the order for the crucifixion of Jesus.

After mocking Jesus for a time, the Roman soldiers led him forth to be crucified at about the third hour (9 A. M. Friday). He remained on the cross about 6 hours and was removed for burial the same day. According to the traditional view his body was in the grave part of Friday, all of Saturday, and came forth from the grave early Sunday.

2. Reading Assignment

	Matthew	Mark	Luke	John
Arrest and Betrayal	26:47-56	14:43-52	22:47-53	18:2-12
Jesus' Night Trial by Jewish Authorities	26:57-75	14:53-72	22:54-65	18:13-27
The Morning Counsel of the Jewish Authorities	27:1	15:1a	22:66-71	
The Trial before Pilate	27:2, 11-14	15:1b-5	23:1-5	18:28-38
The Trial before Herod			23:6-12	
The Trial Concluded under Pilate	27:15-30	15:6-19	23:13-25	18:39—19:16
Judas' Suicide	27:3-10			
The Crucifixion	27:31-56	15:20-41	23:26-49	19:17-30
The Burial	27:57-61	15:42-47	23:50-56a	19:31-42
The Watch	27:62-66		23:56b	

(Read the Bible first)

3. Study Outline

I. **The Arrest and Betrayal of Jesus** (Matt. 26:47-56; Mark 14:43-52; Luke 22:47-53; 18:2-12)

The tension which now developed was indeed a revealer of the souls of men. Judas carried his deceitful purposes through to the fullest degree of hypocrisy, prostituting the holy kiss to serve as the token of betrayal to the enemy. Peter's fighting instinct went into operation, and led him to cut off the ear of the high priest's servant Malchus. But Jesus had perfect poise, which he manifested by surrendering. He knew from the Scriptures the pattern which events, under God, would take. The plan was that Judas should be free to do what he would; the Jewish leaders were free to do what they would. The disciples forsook Jesus and fled when it became evident that Jesus permitted no assistance against the course pursued by his enemies. God, though all powerful, was letting the powers of darkness prove their real character. In reality what each did in that hour was in the form of self-judgment. They seemed to be judging Jesus, but in reality they were being marked for judgment by their own deeds. At the same time, unwittingly, they were holding up before men, upon the cross, the spotless Son of God whose love would draw all believing souls to the fold of the Father.

II. **The Night Trial of Jesus by the Jewish Authorities** (Matt. 26:57-75; Mark 14:73-72; Luke 22:54-65; John 18:13-27)

Jesus was first led to Annas the aged, retired high priest, and the father-in-law of Caiaphas who was now high priest (John 18:13-24.) The full body of the Sanhedrin was evidently gathering as Annas conducted what appears to be a preliminary hearing of Jesus. He was out of his place in doing so, not being any longer in authority. He was out of order in his procedure, furthermore, by asking Jesus to testify concerning himself—his disciples and his teachings. When Jesus objected to this illicit procedure he was struck by a bystander. Jesus simply repeated his insistence that the burden of producing testimony rested with his accusers.

Eventually the Sanhedrin gathered, although we are not sure that the attendance was full. It is doubtful whether Nicodemus and Joseph of Arimathaea and persons of their attitude were summoned. The meeting was invalid in a number of respects. In the first place, the Sanhedrin had no authority to try criminals. The time of the meeting, which was at night, was illegal. The trial was out of order, furthermore, because there was no indictment and no warrant for the arrest. When he came before the Sanhedrin there was no charge against him nor were there any witnesses against him. Actually this high court performed the double role of being at the same time both prosecutor and judge. As prosecutors they bribed witnesses to testify against Jesus; the witnesses were neither true to Jesus' utterances nor were they consistent among themselves. Jesus himself was placed in the position of having to testify regarding himself as to whether he was the Messiah. To answer negatively would have been to deny the truth. To answer positively was to incur for himself from his prejudiced judges the charge of blasphemy. When Jesus answered positively, the court ended with condemnation and mockery.

III. **The Morning Session of the Council** (Matt. 27:1; Mk. 15:1a; Lk. 22:66-71)

Since a night session of the Sanhedrin was illegal, the court met the following morning. According to Matthew, the minds of those calling the session were made up—the council was for the purpose of condemning Jesus to death. It would be necessary, however, that the evidence for guilt should be again produced. Accordingly,

Jesus was given the straightforward question concerning his claims. Had Jesus withheld the truth of his Messiahship and of his identity as the Son of God, it is conceivable that there might have been no conviction and that he might have averted their condemnation. But he stated the truth—and that was taken as blasphemy. Jesus of Nazareth died because he claimed to be the Son of God.

IV. The Trial before Pilate (Matt. 27:2, 11-14; 15:1b-5; 23:1-5; 18:28-38)

Recall that the charge upon which the Sanhedrin had concluded to condemn Jesus to death was blasphemy—he claimed to be the Son of God. Now such a charge would not greatly impress a civil ruler such as Pilate. They must therefore exert pressure to bring about a death sentence in some other way. From John 18:28-32 it appears that the Jews had sent Jesus to Pilate asking for his execution merely upon their own recommendation. When asked for their accusation, they replied, in substance, "He is an evil doer. Would we have sent him to you if he were not? Our law says he should die." Asked for specific charges, however, they brought three, neither of which was the charge of blasphemy. First, they said, he perverted the nation. Secondly, they said, he forbad paying tribute to Caesar. Thirdly, he claimed to be a king. The first was too vague to impress Pilate. The second was a lie. The third was a misinterpretation of Jesus claims of kingship; he clearly stated that his kingdom was spiritual and not of this world. Pilate saw no basis of incrimination in the charges brought.

V. The Trial before Herod (Luke 23:6-12)

Herod (Antipas), tetrarch of Galilee and Peraea, was in Jerusalem at this time. Since Jesus was actually a Galilean, Pilate appears to have seen, in this fact, an opportunity of making him responsible for Jesus' trial. Herod had been curious to see Jesus and was eager for the occasion now afforded. A more unworthy ruler to try the case of Jesus could not be imagined. He it was who had beheaded John the Baptist for rebuking his illicit marriage. Jesus had called him a fox. Herod expected to see a miracle or to be otherwise entertained. Jesus was of course well aware of the unworthy man before whom he stood and though he was asked many questions he did not accord him the satisfaction of a word in answer. Nor did the many accusations of the chief priests and scribes bring forth a word. The fact is that Jesus' silence was the very speech needed to rebuke their vanity.

The trial ended in mockery as the disappointed curiosity seekers robed Jesus in royal attire and sent him back to Pilate. In spite of Herod's flippancy he returned a favorable report for Jesus.

VI. The Trial Concluded under Pilate (Matt. 27:15-30; Mk. 15:6-19; Lk. 23:13-25; John 18:39—19:16

Pilate had now to make the final decision regarding Jesus. The weak spot in the situation was the fact that Pilate's office in the eyes of Rome depended upon his successful handling of the peoples of his procuratorship. Should the Jews complain to Rome it might not go well with him; plenty of grounds for complaint existed and Pilate could not afford to add to the dissatisfaction. Pilate knew that Jesus was brought to him out of sheer envy. His wife had had a dream about Jesus and warned Pilate to have nothing to do with him. He tried in vain to free Jesus as against Barabbas, but the Jews wanted Jesus to be executed. Finally, his resources for appeasement exhausted, he gave Jesus up to be executed. Superficially, he washed his hands of Jesus' blood.

More significant than the chief priests realized was the final appeal of Pilate, "Shall I crucify your king?" They went to the full length of self condemnation in answering, "We have no king but Caesar." In one statement they renounced the very hope of the true Jewish faith and embraced the rule of the earthly captor who would in a few years utterly destroy their city.

VII. The End of the Betrayer (Matt. 27:3-10; Acts 1:18b)

We should pause in the narrative of our Lord's last hours to observe the pitiful roles of two of the twelve disciples.

Judas, after having kept the bag for the disciples for over three years, after a miserly complaint at the devotion of Mary, after letting Satan put the idea of betrayal into his heart, after actually becoming possessed by Satan, after hypocritically kissing his Lord for thirty pieces of silver, finally saw the end to which he had brought his Lord. Smitten with remorse, he flung at the feet of the Sanhedrin the cursed money, and went out and hanged himself. How far from the blessed fellowship of his Lord had the seed of covetousness which he nourished in his heart taken him! If the heart tolerates sin there is no predicting how sordid the end of a life may be. "Keep thy heart with all diligence," says the Proverbs, "for out of it are the issues of life."

VIII.　**The Testing of Peter** (Matt. 26:58, 69-75; Mark 14:54, 66-72; Lk. 22:54-62; John 18:15, 25-27)

There was some similarity between Peter and Judas. Both needed discipline and rebuke. On an earlier occasion when Peter would have spared Jesus from death by the cross, Jesus had literally attributed Peter's idea to Satan. In the garden Jesus had to rebuke Peter's untempered and all but murderous means of dealing with his Lord's persecutor. Peter was beaten when he had to give up self assertive means and exercise moral means. Doubtless he reacted in semi-resentment as he fled from the scene in Gethsemane. His zeal was not all gone but it was at low ebb. While John went into the court room Peter stayed out, though not entirely away from the court room. He is seen with the servants at the fire, then again at the door of the court room, drawn back and forth from an interest in Jesus on the one hand and a disposition to blend with the typical Jewish crowd on the other. The fact that he had cut off Malchus' ear could have gotten him into plenty of trouble. Before the cock crew the second time he had denied his Lord thrice. He remembered the Lord's prediction of the night before. His heart was deeply moved. He wept bitterly.

Peter differed from Judas. Peter's zeal was for his Lord; Judas' zeal was for himself. Peter was amenable to discipline and responded with the greater fruits of righteousness. His faith did not fail. Judas contracted his soul away. He sold himself to Satan and would have sold away his Lord. He got his wages. For the forfeiture of Jesus' fellowship he received thirty pieces of silver, an ignominious death, and then he went to his place. Peter's faith endured to an inheritance incorruptible, undefiled, and unfading.

IX.　**The Crucifixion** (Matt. 27:31-56; Mark 15:20-41; Luke 23:26-49; John 19:17-30)

The march from the place of trial to the place of crucifixion is known as the **Via Dolorosa** (the doleful way). The place of crucifixion was Golgotha's hill, just outside the city. According to custom Jesus would have been required to bear his cross to the place of crucifixion. The soldiers for some reason impressed one Simon of Cyrene for this service instead.

The procession which included a vast multitude of people, was marked by weeping women. Jesus turned their weeping from himself as the object of pity to themselves, declaring that existence for those who remained in the land would become unbearable, that persecutions were only beginning to break. Thus Jesus' cross was but the beginning of many crosses which those who professed his name would have to bear.

The order of crucifixion events, as recorded by the four Gospel writers, is as follows:

1. Arrival at the Scene of Crucifixion. Time: "The third hour" (9 A. M.). Place: Golgotha.

2. Upon arrival, wine and gall were offered Jesus, probably by the considerate women of Jerusalem who wanted by it to deaden his pain (Edersheim). Jesus refused it.

3. The three crosses were erected, the cross of Jesus being between those of the two thieves.

4. The soldiers cast lots for Jesus' garments.

5. The soldiers "sat and watched." The "people stood beholding."

6. Pilate's superscription was disputed by the Jews but sustained by Pilate.

7. Jesus' prayer for forgiveness, "Father forgive them for they know not what they do" (First of seven recorded sayings of Jesus from the cross).

8. Taunts of passersby (including chief priests, scribes, and elders, and the robbers on the cross):

    (1) "Thou that destroyest the temple, and buildest it in three days, save thyself."

    (2) ". . . . if thou art the Son of God, come down from the cross."

    (3) "He saved others, himself he cannot save."

    (4) "He is king of Israel; let him come down from the Cross, and we will believe on him."

    (5) "He trusted in God; let him deliver him now, if he desireth him."

9. The salvation of the believing robber. (Second saying of Jesus): "This day shalt thou be with me in paradise."

10. Mary is committed to the care of John. (Third saying of Jesus): "Woman behold thy Son!" "Behold thy mother!"

11. Three hour darkness begins (6th to the 9th hours, 12 noon to 3 P. M.).

12. Jesus' cry of desolation (Fourth saying of Jesus): "My God, my God, why hast thou forsaken me?"

13. Jesus calls for drink (Fifth saying): " I thirst."

14. Jesus declares his task accomplished (Sixth saying): "It is finished."

15. Jesus' cry of committal (Seventh saying): "Father, into thy hands I commend my spirit."

16. Jesus "gave up the ghost."

17. Six supernatural events attending the death and resurrection of Jesus:

(1) The veil of the temple was rent in twain from top to bottom.

(2) The earth quaked.

(3) The rocks were rent.

(4) Tombs were opened.

(5) Many bodies of the saints were raised.

(6) Many resurrected saints were seen in Jerusalem after Jesus' resurrection.

18. Declaration of the centurion: "Truly this was the Son of God" (Matthew). "Certainly, this was a righteous man" (Luke).

19. Reaction of the multitude: ". . . . returned smiting their breasts" (Luke).

20. Request of the Jews to Pilate that the bodies be removed before the sabbath (before sundown)

21. Disposal of the Bodies:

(1) The legs of the robbers were broken.

(2) Jesus being dead, his legs were not broken.

(3) A soldier pierced Jesus' side with his sword, letting out blood and water.

22.   Joseph of Arimathaea, a rich man, and Nicodemus, both members of the Sanhedrin, joined in burying Jesus in Joseph's new tomb, tenderly wrapping it in myrrh and aloes.   The faithful women followed the body, with wistful eyes, to its burial.   They then returned home and prepared spices and ointments to be brought to the tomb after the sabbath.

23.   Second   request   of   the   Jews: that   Christ's   body   be guarded.

24.   The Watch:
   (1)   They sealed the stone.
   (2)   They set watchmen.

X.   The Restless Sabbath

We may easily imagine the restlessness common to all in Jerusalem on that Sabbath following the day of crucifixion.   None were so restless, we may be sure, as those religious leaders who crucified the Lord of Creation.   Their minds were haunted with the fear of Jesus' resurrection.   Their pygmy attempt to keep Jesus in the tomb is interesting.   They might prevent the stealing of his body by men but they could not prevent the power of the Spirit of God from opening the tomb and raising to life that dead form.   Unconsciously, in this careful guarding of the body against its removal by the disciples, the enemies were nullifying the very claim which they later made, which was that this was what had happened.

For the loved ones and friends, and for the disciples, the loneliness of this day may well be imagined.   They were doubtless dazed. We find no trace in their words or actions of the thought that Christ would arise from the grave.   That the women, who were most attached to him, expected his body to remain in the tomb, is indicated by the fact that they prepared to come with embalming spices on the third day.   What it was which caused these doubters on the first day of the week and during the subsequent forty days to completely reverse the course of that Sabbath's gloom, is an unanswerable question for those who deny the resurrection.

4.   Discussion and Review

1. Shakespeare spoke of the world as a stage in which every man must play his part.   Show the truth of this in the arrest and be-

trayal of Jesus. Why did each play the part that he did? What was God's part?

2. Describe the night trial of Jesus and discuss its legality.

3. Relate what took place at the morning session of the council. What was the charge agreed upon?

4. Why did the council not file the charge agreed upon when they brought Jesus to Pilate? What charges did they bring?

5. With what interest did Herod interview Jesus? What did Jesus say to Herod? How did Herod respond?

6. What considerations caused Pilate to be reluctant about a decision concerning Christ? What considerations prevailed? How did he finally rest the case? Who was responsible?

7. Show from the Scriptures the degrees by which Judas fell.

8. Compare and contrast Peter and Judas in the roles which he played during passion week.

9. Describe the Via Dolorosa.

10. Relate from memory the order of events at the hill of crucifixion from the time of arrival to the death of Jesus.

11. Indicate six supernatural events which attended the death and resurrection of Jesus.

12. By way of reaction to the crucifixion of Christ what expressions are on record from the centurion and from the gazing multitudes?

13. What disposition was made of the three bodies and why? How was Christ's death distinctive?

14. Relate the details of Jesus' burial as to who was in charge of it, the place, and those who observed it.

15. What consideration led to the safeguarding of the tomb? How did these precautions emphasize the genuineness of the resurrection?

16. What state of mind prevailed in Jerusalem on the sabbath between the crucifixion and the resurrection?

5. Select Memory Passages

Luke 23:28-31. The seven sayings uttered by Jesus from the cross.

6. Character Review

Identify:

Annas	Herod Antipas	Pilate
Caiaphas	Malchus	Barabbas

7. Bibliography

Bible Dictionary (Smith-Peloubet or some other). Chicago: John C. Winston Co.
Articles:
1. Crucifixion.
2. Crown of Thorns.
3. Burial (Sepulchres).

Chappell, Clouis G. *Faces About the Cross,* Grand Rapids: Baker's Book Store
Free, Joseph P. *Archaeology and Bible History.* Chapt. XXVI, Topic: The Trial and Crucifixion of Christ.   Wheaton: Van Kampen Press, 1950.
Kuyper, Abraham. *Women of the New Testament.* Grand Rapids: Zondervan. "Caiaphas' Maid-Servant," pp. 66-68.
"Pilate's Wife, pp. 54-57.
Sangster, Margaret E. *The Women of the Bible.* Chapt. XXXIX, "The Wife of Pilate." New York: The Christian Herald.
Sangster, Margaret E. *The Women of the Bible.* Chapt. XL, "The Women at the Cross." New York: The Christian Herald.
Stalker, James. *The Atonement.* Cincinnati: Jennings and Graham.

Chapter 37

THE FORTY DAYS

—From the Resurrection to the Ascension
(April 9—May 18, 30 A. D.)

1. Introduction

What took place on Easter Sunday morning and during the following weeks was characterized by such glory on the Lord's part and such excitement on the part of his followers that the formulation of complete records was hardly thought of. Accordingly, at first reading, the four Gospel accounts of the resurrection of Jesus give one the impression of confusion and of contradiction. Let us not overlook the significance of this. It clearly proves that the authors did not invent the accounts. Had they designed the resurrection story there would be signs of copying, collusion, and of harmonization.

First impressions invariably call for fuller study. The impatient or the prejudiced critic hastens to construe all variations among witnesses as contradictions. If courts of law were equally rash, justice would vanish from the land. The faithful jurist must first gather and study the facts of testimony. Facts reported from different persons, must be weighed with due allowances for differences of view point, of time, and place. The jurist seeks for a hypothesis which best serves all facts. If the facts can possibly be accounted for by one or more plausible suppositions there is no proof of contradiction, to say the least. If, as in the case of what took place Easter morning, the witnesses all point to the same essential fact, and if in the variations of their accounts there is no necessary contradiction, we have all that is needed to establish the case for the resurrection of Jesus.

395

2. Reading Assignment

	Matthew	Mark	Luke	John
The Appearances of Jesus on Easter Sunday 30 A.D. (Five appearances)	28:1-15	16:1-14	23:56b—24:43	20:1-25
Sixth Appearance to Thomas and the other disciples on the second Sunday night				20:24-31
Seventh Appearance—to Seven disciples by the Sea of Galilee				21
Eighth Appearance—on the mountain of Galilee (See I Cor. 15:6)	28:16-20	16:15-18		
Ninth Appearance—to James the brother of Jesus (I Cor. 15:7)				
Tenth Appearance—at Jerusalem and Bethany. Ascension from Olivet (Acts 1:1-12)		16:19, 20	24:44-53	

(Read the Bible first)

3. Study Outline

I. What Took Place Easter Sunday

1. The Coming of the Women (Mark 16:1; Luke 23:56) to the Sepulchre.

Time:

(1) ". . . . in the end of the Sabbath as it began to dawn toward the first day of the week (Matt. 28:1)

(2) "Very early in the morning, at the rising of the sun, or as the sun **was about** to rise (Mark 16:2)

(3) "Very early in the morning" (Luke 24:1)

(4) "Early, while it was yet dark" (John 20:1)

Who came:

(1) Mary Magdalene (Matt. 28:1; John 20:1)

(2) Mary the mother of James and John (Matt. 28:1; Luke 24:10; Mark 15:40)

(3) Salome, the wife of Zebedee and mother of James and John (compare Matt. 27:56; Mark 15:40)

(4)   Joanna, the wife of Chuza, Herod's steward (compare Luke 24:10, 8:3)

(5)   Others (Luke 24:1, 10)

Why they came:

(1)   To see the sepulchre (Matt. 28:1)

(2)   To embalm or complete the embalming of Jesus Body (Mark 16:1; Luke 24:1)

Their problem:

On their way they were wondering who would roll the stone away from the sepulchre for them (Mark 16:3).

2.   A Great Earthquake.   An earthquake followed by darkness had accompanied the crucifixion; an earthquake followed by light attended the resurrection of Jesus.

3.   The Angel of the Lord Served the Women (Matt. 28:2-4). The angel did not need to roll away the stone to let Jesus out but to give the women access to the empty tomb, and to declare the truth of the resurrection to them.   The same angel struck the keepers with fear.

4.   Mary Magdalene, it appears, ran to the city, about a half mile away, to tell the disciples that Jesus' body had been stolen. Her mistake probably indicates that she left before the encounter with the heavenly messenger (John 20:2).

5.   The other women entered and, possibly after their perusal of the empty tomb, were confronted by an angel or young man (Matt. 28:5; Mark 16:5).   Luke speaks of two men (24:4).

6.   The Angel's Message and Charge to the Women (Matt. 28:7; Mark 16:7).

(1)   The crucified one is risen.

(2)   Tell the disciples and Peter.

(3)   He will keep his appointment in Galilee (Lk. 24:6, 7). The words "as he said" (Matt. 26:6) were calculated to bring the disciples to their senses, causing them to realize that the resurrection should have been expected.

The women went to the city immediately.   We do not know exactly when they reported to the disciples.

7. Mary Magdalene had found Peter and John and returned to the sepulchre perhaps by another way so that she did not learn at the time of the angel's message. John and Peter ran ahead of her, John arriving first, but Peter entering the sepulchre first. They found the sepulchre empty (John 20:2-9). John notes that the napkin of the Lord's head was neatly rolled up, which he probably understood to mean that the body had not been stolen.

8. Peter and John left the sepulchre, returning to the city, and leaving Mary Magdalene at the sepulchre (John 20:10).

9. As Mary Magdalene wept the two angels of the tomb appeared to her, to whom she complained that someone had taken away her Lord (John 20:14-18). At this point the Lord (whom Mary took to be the gardener) appeared and manifested himself to her. Mark tells us that this was Christ's "first" appearance to anyone (16:9).

10. Mary Magdalene told the disciples that she had met the Lord; they inclined to disbelieve her (John 20:18; Mark 16:10, 11).

11. Jesus met with the rest of the women (after meeting with Mary Magdalene) (Matt. 28:9, 10).

12. The Report of the Watchmen to the Sanhedrin (Matt. 28:11-15). Note that the watchmen reported what had happened but that the Sanhedrin perverted the truth and paid a bribe to induce the soldiers to circulate a lie. Consider the inconsistency of the lie. The watchmen were made the only witnesses of what was alleged to have taken place while they were asleep.

13. The Meeting with Cleopas and his Companion (Luke 24:13-32). One of the touching incidents of Easter Sunday was Christ's conversation incognito with the two disciples on the road to Emmaus. After teaching them and eating with them their eyes were opened. They then promptly made their way to the company of the eleven and others assembled at Jerusalem, where they added their report of a meeting with Christ to the other reports.

14. Jesus' Meeting with Peter (Luke 24:33-35; I Cor. 15:5). Very little is recorded about this meeting. Reference is made to it at the meeting of Easter Sunday evening.

15. The Easter Sunday Night Meeting (Mark 16:14; Luke 24:36-43; John 20:19-25). The place of this meeting is not known but there are good reasons for supposing that it was the home of Mary the mother of John Mark. Thomas was absent. They met behind closed doors for fear of the Jews. Doubtless the subject of conversa-

tion centered in the appearances of the Lord to Mary Magdalene, to the other women, to Peter, to Cleopas and his companion. The evidence of the resurrection must have been marvelous against the background of the sufferings of the Friday before. The Lord impressed upon them the fact of his corporeality. He was not only the Son of God in spirit form, but he was as they had known him, the Son of man. He was still, yes more than ever, a member of the human order. The nail prints in his hands and the sword scar in his side were the evidence.

Five times Jesus had now appeared. Still the disciples could not take it all in. They disbelieved for joy which means not a wicked unbelief but a lack of capacity to accept, in the sense of comprehending, what had taken place.

II.   Other Appearances

1. The Second Sunday Night (John 20:24-31). There is no indication that Jesus ordered the assembly to regather this second Sunday evening, and so far as we know there was no promise that Jesus would meet with them. But they were together, Thomas and all. Doubtless during the week the lie of the watchers had gained currency and the hatred of the Jerusalem leaders against the Lord and his followers grew more fiendish and more desperate. The door of their room, again, was shut. Jesus appeared as he had the week before and duplicated the manifestations of his corporeality. Thomas now confessed, with personal faith, "My Lord and my God."

2. The Meeting by the Sea of Galilee (John 21). Rather naturally, seven of the eleven disciples made their way to their seaside home in Galilee. It was farther from hostile Jerusalem, and they could fish there. Also, they had an appointment with the Lord in Galilee and while we do not know the date, it actually took place rather late in the forty-day period.

On this occasion Peter had taken the lead to go fishing. Luck was against them, a fisherman might say, for they fished all night without success. But their failure was well calculated to finally wean them from the business. Then also against the background of their failure Jesus demonstrated, as he had before, that he is the master fisherman.

The breakfast scene on shore must have been a wonderful experience of fellowship. It covered with tender love the failures and the denial on that night when all forsook him and fled. What a wonder that Jesus still counted upon Peter. Jesus needed a care-taker for his sheep. He impressed this upon Peter. As something of a compensation for this threefold denial, Peter now was led to make a threefold affirmation of love. In this he would make good by a spirit-filled ministry and finally by receiving the martyr's crown.

3.   On the Mountain of Galilee (Matt. 28:16-20; Mark 16:15-18; I Cor. 15:6). This is doubtless the appointed meeting which Jesus had emphasized. We do not know the name of the mountain. Over five hundred assembled, which indicates that in Galilee there was less fear of being identified with the crucified one than there was at Jerusalem. The five hundred were "brethren" and it was upon their shoulders that he placed the task of going forth in his name to make disciples and to teach all nations. The central fact in this commission is the promise of the continued personal presence of the all powerful Christ with those who carry out his commission.

4.   The Appearance to James, the Brother of Jesus (I Cor. 15:7). The single reference which we have of this appearance comes from Paul and not directly from a Gospel account. It is possible that James was an unbeliever until this time since he was not among the believers at any earlier time. He now became one of the apostles and the leading officer in the church at Jerusalem.

5.   Christ's Final Appearance and Ascension (Mark 16:19, 20; Luke 24:44-53; Acts 1:1-12). Back in Jerusalem, at the close of the forty-day period, Jesus again appeared to the disciples. He opened their minds to the Scriptures, particularly regarding his sufferings, death, and resurrection on the third day. He restated the great commission for the evangelization of the world by a cam-paign of witnessing. While in the earlier account of the commission given on the mountain of Galilee Jesus stressed the fact that all power had been given him and that he would be with the apostles, on this occasion he stressed the enduement of power which was to come upon the church. His followers were to tarry in Jerusalem until they were clothed with that power.

Then Jesus led the company forth to Bethany where he as-cended up into the clouds of heaven. Luke gives the graphic picture of this last scene in the first chapter of the Acts. The final state-ment of the future task of the church is made with the clearest out-line—after the enduement the campaign of witnesses was to proceed from Jerusalem, to Judea, to Samaria, and unto the uttermost parts of the earth.

As Jesus ascended from Mount Olivet it appears that the disciple's eyes were unable to cease gazing into the space from which the last outline of his form was seen. Had not the two men in white apparel broken that gaze it might have developed into a fixed hopelessness. But the heavenly messengers made of the **disappearance** of Jesus a memorial to the disciples of the fact of his **reappearance.** He would come back through those same clouds "in like manner."

4. Discussion and Review

1. Of what significance is the apparently confused reports of the Gospel writers relating the account of the resurrection? How should these reports be interpreted?

2. Give a resume of what took place on Easter Sunday morning. During the rest of the day. Enumerate the Lord's five appearances of the day.

3. Describe the meeting on the second Sunday evening. What distinguished this meeting?

4. Relate the account of the meeting by the Sea of Galilee. What was the substance of Jesus' impression upon the disciples as they were together here?

5. Describe the meeting on the mountain of Galilee. Who were present? What commission did Jesus give?

6. What, apparently, was the significance of Jesus' meeting with his brother James?

7. Relate fully the account of Jesus' final appearance.

8. Compare Luke's account of the Great Commission with that of Matthew. What does each emphasize regarding power?

9. What is the essential content of the witness to be borne to the nations? (Compare Luke 24:44-48 with Matt. 24:14.)

10. What might have become the fixed attitude of the gazing disciples had not the heavenly messengers affirmed a new hope?

11. Relate in order the account of the ten appearances of Jesus after his resurrection.

12. Evaluate these accounts as evidence. Do they satisfy your mind?

5. Select Memory Passages

Matt. 28:18-20; Luke 24:44-49; Acts 1:11

6. Character Review

Identify:

Mary Magdalene   Salome   James the brother of
Mary the mother of   Cleopas   Jesus
    James

7. Bibliography

Boardman, George Dave. *Epiphanies of the Risen Lord*. New York: Appleton.
International Standard Bible Encyclopedia. Article on Easter, by H. Porter.
    Grand Rapids: Wm. B. Eerdman.
Kuyper, Abraham. *Women of the New Testament*. Grand Rapids: Zondervan.
    1. "Mary Magdalene," pp. 34-36.
    2. "Mary, the Mother of the Apostle," pp. 37-39.
    3. "Sapphira," pp. 69-72.
Ockenga, H. J. *Have You Met These Women?* Grand Rapids: Zondervan.
    Chapter IX—"The Woman Who Could Not Forget."
Sangster, Margaret E. *The Women of the Bible*. Chapt. XLI, "Mary in the
    Garden." New York: The Christian Herald.

PART NINE

APOSTOLIC WITNESSES IN A WORLD MISSION

Chapter 38

WITNESSING IN JERUSALEM

(30-35 A. D.)

---

1. Reading Assignment

Luke 1:1-4; 24:36-53; Acts 1-7

(Read the Bible first)

---

2. Study Outline

I. Introduction—Transition (Acts 1)

The continuation of the work of Christ after his ascension is the theme of a second book by the author of the third Gospel account. The last chapter of the Gospel by Luke is overlapped by the first chapter of Acts. In the Gospel account Luke tells of "all that Jesus began to do and to teach until the day in which he was taken up" (Acts 1:1; Luke 24). That account closed with the announcement of a campaign of witnessing, and with strict orders to the disciples to remain in Jerusalem until an enduement of power for witnessing was received. In the first chapter of the Acts that final commission and the future program and hope of the followers of Christ are set forth in still clearer relief. In 1:8 are the Lord's words announcing the growing geographical areas of the campaign of witnessing. In fulfillment, the historical outline of the book falls into three general sections which are:

I. Witnessing in Jerusalem (chapters 1-7)

405

II.   Witnessing in Judea and Samaria (chapters 8-12)
III. Witnessing in the Gentile World (chapters 13-28)

It is obvious in this first chapter that the thinking of the disciples was still on a circumscribed level. They thought in terms of starting where Zedekiah ended, of a kingdom of Israelitish proportions. Our Lord never reckoned with them on this scale, and he now finally engaged them in the matter of importance which was immediately before them. The kingdom called for by the Abrahamic covenant, (Gen. 12:1-3), and by the Davidic covenant (Isa. 7; Luke 1:30-33) was to be universal. Such a kingdom called for a program of information and of spiritual regeneration not only in Israel but among all nations of the earth. Though Jesus emphasized this program, nothing is more evident than the fact that those followers would never, upon their own account, have carried it out. They needed a baptism of power by the Holy Spirit. Beyond this, their very chief, Peter, needed a special vision before he would even consent to a campaign which crossed the Jew-Gentile racial wall.

Though limited in their comprehension of the Lord's plan, and though impotent to effectively declare the gospel against the world's unbelief, they were united in tarrying according to their Lord's command. Their tarrying was characterized, not by bickering, nor by selfish concerns but by prayer and supplication, and by a spirit of unity. They were united under Christ and they would in due time be unified by the new leadership of the Holy Spirit.

Those returning from Olivet included the eleven disciples, certain women, Christ's brethren, and others to the number of one hundred and twenty persons.

The choice of Matthias has sometimes been criticized as out of divine order. There is nothing in Luke's account to warrant this objection. On the contrary we note that the procedure was reasonable. A true witness was chosen. The choice was made in the right spirit. They acknowledged their need for divine guidance and accepted the lot as God's decision. After the choice they waited in one accord and in one place.

II. The Promised Power Realized (Acts 2:1-40)

On the day of Pentecost the Father's promise of power was fulfilled. This was the feast of first-fruits of the wheat harvest, just fifty days after the Passover at which Jesus the true paschal lamb

AREAS of the OLD TESTAMENT WORLD REPRESENTED at PENTECOST in 30 A.D.

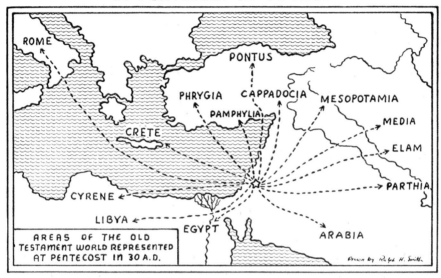

ROME

PONTUS

PHRYGIA CAPPADOCIA MESOPOTAMIA

PAMPHYLIA

CRETE

MEDIA

ELAM

PARTHIA

CYRENE

LIBYA

EGYPT

ARABIA

AREAS OF THE OLD TESTAMENT WORLD REPRESENTED AT PENTECOST IN 30 A.D.

Drawn by Ralph H. Smith

had been slain for the sins of the world. In relation to the original calendar of sacred events it corresponded to the time of the giving of the law on Mount Sinai.

The coming of the Spirit's enduement was sudden. A sound from heaven and the appearance of cloven tongues upon the disciples attended the Spirit's descent. All were filled with the Holy Ghost. They spoke with other tongues as the Spirit gave them utterance so that the devout Jews, gathered in from various nations, understood them, each in his own language. Those present were amazed. But some doubted and mocked, attributing the phenomena of the Spirit to drunkenness.

Peter, now under the Spirit's anointing, was on his feet with a prompt reply to the unworthy insinuations which were made. The sermon (2:14-40) which he delivered remains a classic. He quickly disposed of the charge of drunkenness and identified what had taken place as the fulfillment of the prophecy of Joel. It was the pouring out of God's spirit which was promised for all flesh (all peoples of the world). "The last days" or Joel's prophecy, according to Peter's sermon, are the period of time between that Pentecost and the coming of the "great and notable day of the Lord." Results attending the outpouring are the gift of prophecy, visions, and dreams. It is described as a day of the universal opportunity of salvation: ". . . . Whosoever shall call upon the name of the Lord shall be saved."

Peter's sermon was, in effect, an indictment: Ye . . . . have taken, crucified, and slain Jesus of Nazareth, a man approved of God, being delivered of God, and whom God raised up. He showed that this was in fulfillment of Psalm 16, and that this fulfillment (of Jesus' resurrection) was attested by his witnesses.

The result of Peter's sermon (2:37) was inevitable. Such facts pricked the hearts of the guilty Jews who stood by. When they saw their plight and called for help, Peter had the answer (2:38). His answer contained a command, which was to repent and be baptized for the remission of sins, and a promise, which was the gift of the Holy Ghost. This gracious word was for all who receive God's call. Observe the two calls of this sermon (2:21 and 2:39). About 3000 responded and were baptized that day.

In the days which followed (2:42-47) we see these Spirit-filled disciples, not hidden away in the secret place with doors shut, but in the temple and going from house to house, "in the apostles' doctrine and fellowship, in breaking of bread, and in prayers." Note the prevailing sentiment: fear on the part of all, and on the part of believers, a communal spirit, gladness, singleness of heart, praise to God, and favor with the people. Every day their number grew. One wonders where the Sanhedrin members were. Is it not probable that some of them were among those who repented and were received into Christian fellowship. On the other hand we may suppose that those who still resisted would become increasingly hostile. That this official body continued to function we shall fully realize in the chapters of Acts which follow.

III. Peter's Second Sermon (Acts 3)

Peter preached a second sermon on the occasion of a marvelous healing near the temple gate at the hour of prayer (3:1-11). As the spectators marvelled at the healing and tended to attribute it to Peter and John, Peter arose to speak. His sermon is much the same as that of chapter two, except for a different putting of the message. In the Pentecost sermon Peter had charged, in effect: "Ye have taken, crucified, and slain Jesus . . . . Whom God raised up." "In this sermon (3:12-26) he emphasizes God's sovereign power stating in effect: "God (of Abraham, Isaac, Jacob, and the fathers) has glorified Jesus . . . . whom ye crucified." God had let wicked men do their worst and had overruled their ignorance. Peter urged conversion from sin to Christ in view of the time when he would return to accomplish the restitution of all things.

IV. Opposition and a Second Enduement (4:1-37; 5:17-42)

The twofold reaction to Peter's second sermon is pictured in chapter 4. Many believed (about 5000). But the temple leaders, among whom it appears the Sadducees now prevailed, were "grieved," the sensitive spot being the resurrection. Why anyone should be grieved about this is hard for us to understand.

Peter and John were arrested, jailed, and held for trial the next day. On the one hand were the principal prosecutors of Jesus, Annas and Caiaphas, and their relatives. On the other were Peter and John. There was no charge, only the question, "By what power, and by what name have ye done this?" Peter reversed the situation and in addition to his testimony he turned prosecutor. His answer was not hard to give. It was the name of Jesus of Nazareth. Then as though they might not be familiar with him, Peter boldly added: "whom ye crucified," "whom God raised," the rejected stone of prophecy, and the one indispensible to salvation (4:1-12).

The disposition which was made of this situation (4:13-22) follows the pattern common to those who do not know what to do because they are unwilling to do right. They realized that in the trial of the apostles the trial of Jesus was in reality again before them. The healed man was evidence that Jesus lived and the people commonly understood such evidence. Therefore the Jewish leaders were afraid, not of God, but of losing the people.

They attempted to settle the matter by a threat, but they received from Peter and John an unequivocal rebuff. Christ had ordained his apostles as witnesses and they would not be countermanded. Nevertheless, as the apostles returned to their company, they realized that a serious impasse existed between themselves as Jesus' followers and those men who were in charge of the temple.

The remainder of Acts 4 relates what the apostles did under the Sanhedrin's threat. After reporting to the company of believers, they went to prayer "with one accord." Observe the prayer. It is an appeal to the God of creation and to the God of sovereign power (Psalm 2). It is a petition, not for relief from persecution, but for boldness to speak, for God's healing hand, and for signs and wonders to continue in Jesus' name. God heard them and they were again filled with the Holy Ghost, as at Pentecost.

The result of the new enduement was greater boldness and more marvelous deeds (5:12-16). These in turn again provoked more persecution (5:17-42). The council again arrested the apostles, jailed them, and called them up for trial the following day. The fact that God freed them from prison and that they were commanded by him to preach in the temple, did not cause the Jewish leaders to realize their presumption in calling them up for trial.

Against the apostles they charged, in effect:

1. You have violated our command.
2. You have filled Jerusalem with your doctrine.
3. You intend to bring Christ's blood upon us.

The apostles counter-charged:

1. You have commanded us against God's command.
2. We are witnesses that
   (1) You slew Jesus.
   (2) God raised and exalted Jesus.
   (3) Jesus has become a prince and savior.

The clash became so great that the council planned to kill the apostles. Their heat was cooled by the better advice of Gamaliel. The disciples were not freed unconditionally, however. Before being let go they were scourged and again commanded not to speak in the name of Jesus. The apostles left as moral victors, glad for the honor of suffering for Christ, and they continued to teach and preach daily in the temple and from house to house.

V. **Problems in the Apostolic Fellowship** (Acts 2:42-47; 4:32-37; 6:1-6)
Several notices indicate the blessedness of the fellowship in the

church of early apostolic days. Believers were of one accord. No man said that what he possessed was his own. Each gladly gave what he had to meet need where it arose or placed the means to do so in the apostles' hands. These Christians were happy, even though persecuted. Praise to God was common. They had favor with the people, and they were a growing company.

Problems arose, however. Ananias and Sapphira counterfeited this apostolic grace and were slain of the Lord (Acts 5:1-11).

The apostles tended to be over-burdened with the reception and distribution of goods. Some were neglected and their murmur was a discordant element in the fellowship of the church. To cope with this situation the people were instructed to appoint from their midst those who could "serve tables." These would properly care for their poor on the one hand, and would on the other hand release the apostles for the ministry of prayer and the word.

Observe the procedure in the organization of this committee. Standards were given—the people were to nominate men "of honest report, full of the Holy Ghost and wisdom." The apostles made the appointments, prayed, and laid hands upon the appointees.

Observe that two of the seven chosen for this work, Stephen and Philip, developed into effective spiritual leaders. It is probable that in this incident we have the rise of the office of deacon.

The wisdom with which this case was handled is noteworthy. The complaint arose from Grecian (Hellenistic Jews). The procedure placed the authority and the responsibility for action back upon the people themselves. Relief is usually best cared for when in local hands.

VI. Triumph for the Christians at Jerusalem (6:7)

It is clear that in none of the trials of the apostles were the Jewish leaders successful in fastening any charge against the accused. They were beaten and embarrassed. The believers grew in favor and in numbers. Whereas the main opposition seems to have come from the Sadducees in chapters 2-5, we now are told that many priests (who were usually Sadducees) "were obedient to the faith."

VII. Stephen the First Christian Martyr (Acts 6:8—7:60)

It appears that peace might have settled down upon Jerusalem. But such was not to be the case. As long as there was a Spirit-filled witness for Jesus there would be no peace in the hearts of those who crucified him. The personnel of antagonism differed. Stephen was now the spokesman, and opposition came from leaders of synagogues where Hellenistic Jews worshiped.

Stephen was full of faith and power. He did signs and wonders. By this wisdom he so worsted his disputants that they had no way of resistance left but to suborn false witnesses against him. It is evident that Saul of Tarsus, the young seminarian from the college of Gamaliel, was a leading disputant whose pride on this occasion was wounded.

The charge of the false witnesses was that of blasphemy, blasphemy against Moses, God, Jerusalem, and the law. Against their black lies the face of Stephen shone like that of an angel as he recounted the history of God's gracious providence with the nation Israel, and charged them with continual resistance of the Holy Ghost, the prophets, and God's word.

Unable to dispute Stephen, and being cut to the heart with conviction, they did the thing which impenitents are prone to do, that is, destroy the messenger of the truth. They had no wisdom to resist him so they gnashed him with their teeth. They had no power to reason so they substituted noise for reason. They could not bear the truth so they stopped their ears. Finally they assaulted him, cast him out of the city, and stoned him.

Against their animosity Stephen maintained a heavenly composure. He was full of the Holy Ghost. He looked steadfastly into heaven seeing the glory of God and Jesus standing on the right hand of God. As he knelt in prayer, with stones raining upon him, he uttered two significant petitions. For himself he prayed, "Lord Jesus, receive my spirit." For his persecutors he prayed, "Lord, lay not this sin to their charge."

One is struck with the similarity of the martyrdom of Stephen and the crucifixion of Jesus. Both were charged with blasphemy. Both stressed the importance of spirit in worship as against a building and a place. Both stirred up the antagonism of the Pharisees. Both were convicted by false witnesses. Both were put to death illegally by the Sanhedrin. Both committed their spirits to God in death. Both prayed for the forgiveness of those who slew them.

3. Discussion and Review

1. Show that the Acts is the continuation of the Gospel by Luke.

2. Show the difference between the circumscribed viewpoint of the disciples and the plan of Christ.

3. Describe the tarrying company.

4. Describe the Spirit's coming on the day of Pentecost. How did bystanders regard it? How did Peter interpret it?

5. What are the vital points of Peter's sermon on the day of Pentecost? What were the immediate results?

6. Describe the fellowship of the believers during the post-Pentecostal days.

7. Relate the incident which led to Peter's second sermon.

8. Discuss the thesis of this sermon.

9. What was the twofold reaction to Peter's second sermon?

10. Relate the course which Jewish opposition took in chapters four and five.

11. What were some problems which arose in the early apostolic fellowship and how were they resolved?

12. Reviewing the trials of chapters four and five and considering 6:7, what progress had the early church made?

13. Trace the rise of new opposition.

14. Compare the martyrdom of Stephen with the crucifixion of Jesus.

15. Trace the history of witnessing through chapters 2-7.

4. Select Memory Passages

Acts 1:8, 11; 2:38, 39; 4:12, 32, 33

5. Character Review

Identify:

Matthias	Philip	Joses	Ananias
Stephen	Saul of Tarsus	(Barnabas)	Sapphira

6. Bibliography

Bible Dictionary (Smith-Peloubet or some other). Chicago: John C. Winston Co.
  Articles:
  1. Pentecost.
  2. Deacon.
Blaikie, Wm. G. *Bible History*. Topic: Stephen. New York: Thomas Nelson. Pp. 454, 455.
Free, Joseph P. *Archaeology and Bible History*. Chapt. XXVII, "The Beginning of the Church." Wheaton: Van Kampen, 1950.
  Topics:
  1. Archaeological Evidence of Jews in Many Countries in the New Testament Period, pp. 305, 306.

2. Archaeological Light on the Gate Beautiful (Acts 3), p. 307.
3. Archaeological Light on the Name Sapphira (Acts 5:1), p. 509.
4. Archaeological Light on the Synagogue of the Libertines (Acts 6:9), p. 310.

Gordon, A. J. *The Ministry of the Spirit.* New York: Fleming H. Revell.
Greenfield, John. *Power from on High.* Warsaw, Indiana.
Huffman, J. A. *The Holy Spirit.* Marion, Ind.: The Standard Press.
Kuyper, Abraham. *The Work of the Holy Spirit.* New York: Funk and Wagnals.
Miller, Basil. *The Holy Spirit.* Kansas City, Mo.: Beacon Hill Press.
Morgan, G. Campbell. *The Acts of the Apostles.* New York: Fleming H. Revell Co. Pp. 7-194. An expository treatment of Acts 1-7.
Morgan, G. C. *The Spirit of God.* New York: Fleming H. Revell.
Simpson, A. B. *The Holy Spirit, or Power from on High.* New York: Christian Alliance Pub. Co.
Torrey, R. A. *Baptism with the Holy Spirit.* New York: Fleming H. Revell.

Chapter 39

WITNESSING IN SAMARIA AND JUDEA

(36-44 A. D.)

1. Reading Assignment
2. Study Outline:
   I. Introduction—Transition
   II. The Ministry of Philip
   III. Conversion of Saul of Tarsus
   IV. Peter's Sea-coast Ministries

V. Barnabas the Instrument of Unification
VI. Persecution at Jerusalem
VII. Epistle of James
3. Discussion and Review
4. Character Review
5. Bibliography

1.   Reading Assignment

Acts 8-12
(Read the Bible first)

2.   Study Outline

I.   Introduction—Transition (Acts 8:1-4)

The martyrdom of Stephen was an incident, under God, which proved to be pregnant with change and growth for the church. The persecution which this incident touched off "scattered abroad" the Christians "throughout the regions of Judea and Samaria" and "they went everywhere preaching the word." How fully this corresponded to our Lord's plan of advance we may see by referring to Acts 1:8.

Notwithstanding this dispersion, the apostles remained in Jerusalem, continuing with their ministry there. Had the propagation of the gospel been left to them it never would have been extended. But the program of Acts 1:8 is a program of the Holy Ghost, not of any particular human leaders. The apostles, of course, continued to labor under the Holy Ghost in Jerusalem.

In another respect also, not yet revealed at this point, the incident of Stephen's martyrdom yielded results. Stephen had prayed for Saul, and while Saul was not immediately converted, it is remarkable to note how the sermon of Stephen became the thesis for Paul's later dissertations in his epistle regarding the spiritual and universal nature of true worship.

415

CILICIA

Tarsus•

Seleucia
•Antioch

CYPRUS

SYRIA

The
GREAT
(MEDITERRANEAN)

SEA

PHOENICIA
(Phenice)

•Damascus

GALILEE

SYRIAN

DESSERT

•Caesarea

SAMARIA

Joppa•

•Azotus

Gaza• Jerusalem

JUDAEA

IDUMAEA

ARABIA

JERUSALEM
and
Beyond

Memorable Places
in the early
Apostolic History
of ACTS 8-12

II. The Ministry of Philip (8:5-40)

The mantle of Stephen fell upon his fellow deacon, Philip, leading him into "a (not **the**) city of Samaria." He preached Christ, cast out evil spirits, and healed the sick. The people responded "with one accord," and "there was great joy in that city." We are reminded of our Lord's earlier ministry, perhaps in this very village (John 4), and of his remark that the harvest was then ready.

It is of interest to note that under Philip's ministry the people were led to believe and to be baptized, and that they were taught "concerning the kingdom of God, and the name of Jesus Christ," but that they were not led to receive the Holy Ghost until the apostles Peter and John came and laid their hand upon them for this purpose.

The case of Simon is a study. Under Philip's ministry, after his followers were won to Christ, he himself became, to all appearances, a believer; he was baptized, he continued with Philip and wondered at the signs and wonders done. In relation to the ministry of Peter and John, however, it was proved that his believing was of a spurious sort. He wanted to buy the power of the Holy Spirit, which implied that he was not only still self-centered but that he conceived of divine power as something for a man to **use**. Peter told him his heart was not right, that he was wicked, that he was in the gall of bitterness, that he was in the bond of iniquity, and that he needed to repent because of the thought of his heart. Presumably, Simon was forgiven and found favor with God.

After this incident Peter and John preached the gospel in other Samaritan villages. Philip was led, unexpectedly, to leave Samaria. We know little of the further history of the Samaritan Christians.

Humanly speaking, it might have been reasoned that Philip should have settled down as a permanent leader of the Samaritans among whom he had such success. The Spirit of God led differently. A eunuch of Ethiopia, traveling homeward from Jerusalem via Gaza, was his next subject. This eunuch, who was the treasurer to Candace, queen of Ethiopia, had probably been attending a festival at Jerusalem. The eunuch was probably a Jewish proselyte and may have come to Jerusalem for the very purpose of investigating the reported coming of the servant of the Lord described in Isaiah 53. He was going away unsatisfied. He rode along reading this chapter but did not understand. It was Philip's joy to witness to him of Christ

Jesus, to lead him to believe, and to baptize him. Philip was caught away as they emerged from the baptismal waters.

We have the brief record in 8:40 that Philip proceeded up the sea coast and preached in all the cities from Azotus to Caesarea.

III. The Conversion of Saul of Tarsus (9:1-31)

According to generally received chronologies Stephen was martyred about 34 A. D. Saul's purge continued for about a year later, when he was converted, about 35 A. D. It was according to the providence of God, no doubt, that he was permitted for a certain length of time to scatter the Christians. A note by Luke indicates that in the dispersion of this year the messengers of the word went as far north as Phenice, the isle of Cyprus, and Antioch in Syria.

Saul was a native of Tarsus in Cilicia. He had been educated by Gamaliel at Jerusalem and was evidently a valuable man to the administration there. He had received a warrant from the chief priest to the Damascus authorities authorizing him to arrest and bring to Jerusalem any of the Christian "way." But as he journeyed to Damascus the Lord Jesus Christ arrested him. The stunning light and the voice of Jesus from heaven broke his resistance. He had "breathed out threatenings and slaughter." Now he responded, "trembling and astonished." He was ordered to go to Damascus where further instruction would be given him. In a vision he saw the man who would instruct him.

Simultaneously, God spoke to Ananias in a vision and sent him to minister to Saul at the house of Judas in the street Straight. The revelation to Ananias was that this persecutor was now a chosen vessel for the carrying out of his campaign of witnessing. He would bear the gospel to Gentiles, to kings, and to the children of Israel, and he would undergo great suffering doing so. When they met, Ananias addressed the persecutor as brother Saul. By this ministry Saul's eyes were opened, he was filled with the Holy Ghost, was baptized, and then "took meat."

Although facts are wanting at some points, Saul's life during the next eight or nine years may be outlined as follows:

1. Immediately after his conversion Paul preached Christ, proving him to be the Son of God, the very Christ (Acts 9:19-22).

2. He went into Arabia, remaining for three years, then returning to Damascus (Gal. 1:16-19).

3. After further preaching at Damascus, he was opposed by the Jews. In order to save his life his friends let him down from the city wall in a basket (Acts 9:23-25; II Cor. 11:32-33).

4. He spent a fortnight at Jerusalem but encountered similar hostility, apparently from the Hellenistic Jews. In order to spare his life, the brethren secreted him away to Caesarea, from which port he sailed for Tarsus, his native city (Acts 9:26-30).

5. He remained at Tarsus, so far as we know, for a number of years, until Barnabas called for him and brought him to the Antioch fellowship (Acts 11:25-26).

Following the conversion of Saul the churches entered upon a period of liberty, and the dispersed Christians bore fruit wherever they went. Multitudes were added to their number (Acts 9:31). The labors of Philip and Peter made their greater developments under this new era of rest from persecution.

IV. Peter's Sea-Coast Ministries—Another Step of Transition (9:32 —11:18)

Just as Peter and John followed the evangelistic ministry of Philip in Samaria, so Peter did so in the coastal cities also. At Lydda he healed Aeneas, an eight-year palsy case, which resulted in turning the people to the Lord unanimously. Peter was called to Joppa where he raised Tabitha (Dorcas) from death. Everyone in the area learned of it, and many believed. While dwelling at Joppa with Simon the tanner, God providentially arranged for his next step which was to be at Caesarea. This step was more than geographical; it would involve the surmounting of a racial wall in order to carry forth the plan of advance outlined in Acts 1:8.

At Caesarea there lived a Roman centurion. He was not a Jew, not a proselyte, but a Gentile. But he was a Gentile like Enoch, Noah, and Abraham—a godly man. God's description of him indicates that he was a devout man, he feared God, he maintained a God-fearing home, he gave much alms, he prayed to God always and was heard (10:2, 4); he was a just man, of good report among the Jews (10:22); by inference we note that he feared God, worked righteousness, and was accepted of God (10:34, 35), and by inference also, we note that God had cleansed Cornelius (10:15, 28).

By the appearance of the angel of the Lord to Cornelius, and by the well timed vision of the net and the beasts to Peter, both men were given to understand that God himself was bringing them together in the common fellowship of the gospel.

When Peter met with Cornelius and there had been opportunity to match their experiences, Peter uttered a confession which denoted a milestone in gospel advance. He affirmed the following convictions:

1. God is no respecter of persons (i. e. of nationality).

2. God accepts those who fear him, and who work righteousness.

The sermon which followed was a simple declaration of the coming and the mission of Christ in the world. While he was still speaking the Holy Ghost fell upon the Gentile band as he had upon those at Pentecost and in Samaria. While at Pentecost the promise of the Holy Ghost was made on the condition of repentance and baptism, nothing is said about either in this case. Water baptism was administered, on this occasion, after the baptism with the Holy Ghost.

Peter had been convinced that the gospel was to be taken to the Gentiles. But the Jerusalem church was not yet convinced. Upon returning to Jerusalem Peter was placed upon the carpet to explain why he had gone into the home of an uncircumcised man and had eaten with him. After relating the whole account in order, the church was not only convinced, but it glorified God for having thus granted repentance to the Gentiles.

V. Barnabas the Instrument of Church Unification (Acts 11:19-30; 12:24-25)

We have observed the ministries of Philip and Peter in Samaria and in the coastal cities from Azotus to Caesarea. Doubtless such ministries were duplicated by others elsewhere, though not recorded by Luke. It is clearly indicated that those scattered at the death of Stephen went north of Caesarea into Phenice (Phoenicia), to the isle of Cyprus, and to Antioch in Syria, and that a great number believed and turned to the Lord. This included Grecians (Hellenists).

Barnabas, who was a native of Cyprus, was appointed by the Jerusalem brethren to exercise something of a pastoral care over the new Antioch fellowship. He was ideally constituted for such an assignment, being a "good man, full of the Holy Ghost and faith."

He allowed no trace of racial cleavage to blight the faith of these new converts, but "was glad and exhorted them all, that with purpose of heart they would cleave unto the Lord." Barnabas doubtless acted within the purpose of God in seeking Saul at Tarsus and in making him an associate in the Gentile-Jewish church fellowship at Antioch.

The drought, which was revealed through the prophet Agabus, was doubtless a providence of God in disguise. It gave occasion for the Antiochan Christians to confer a benefit upon the mother church at Jerusalem, thus giving development to the mutual bond of fellowship in Christ. That Saul and Barnabas carried the relief gifts to Jerusalem was a means of binding the Jerusalem church not only with Antioch, but also with the Gentile churches which were to be founded by these two men. Thus is seen the hand of the Master Workman, through the Holy Ghost, and by specially chosen instruments, building his Church. Scattering its members did not destroy it. On the contrary God overruled evil for his own ends, so that at the end of a dozen or more years, the fellowship of Christian love spanned Jerusalem, Judea, Samaria, and distant ports to the borders of Asia Minor.

VI. Persecutions at Jerusalem under Herod Agrippa (Acts 12)

The changing fortunes of Jewish life under Roman rule cannot be fully related in this study (see chapter XXIV). A glance at some major changes, however, should receive our attention. Pontius Pilate, after a cruel massacre of Samaritans, had been deposed, and the tetrarchies (Trachonitis and Abilene) had been conferred by Caligula upon Herod Agrippa, the grandson of Herod the Great (d. 4 B. C.). Herod Antipas, had also been banished to Gaul, and the tetrarchies of Galilee and Perea were added to the dominions of Herod Agrippa. When Claudius succeeded Caligula at Rome Herod Agrippa was assigned all of Judea, Samaria, and Idumea, thus unifying under him the former lands of his grandfather who reigned at the birth of Jesus.

Herod Agrippa inherited not only the lands of his grandfather, but also his vanity, and his insatiable thirst for popularity and lordly estate. To please the Jews he put James the apostle to death; and to please them still further he took steps to put Peter to death after Easter. But it was not God's time to elevate Peter. Moreover, alerted by the gravity of the crisis, the church engaged in unceasing prayer. Peter, though hedged by two military bed fellows, bound by chains, and guarded by keepers at the prison door, was freed by God's angel and restored to the praying company of Christians. Only the damsel Rhoda was able to believe that it was Peter, so sure did it seem that Peter's end had come.

But God not only delivered Peter; he also removed Herod Agrippa. God frequently lets such a man vaunt himself and do his worst before measuring his days. Going from Judea to Caesarea, he made an oration and so illicited the admiration of the people as to allow himself to be deified. In a moment God smote him and he died a horrible death, quite similar to that which had killed his grandfather Herod the Great who sought the blood of the infant Jesus.

It is of interest to note that at this time (ca. 44 A. D.) the Christians at Jerusalem were still meeting at the home of Mary, the sister of Barnabas and the mother of John Mark. Also, it appears that James was something of a chief consultant in the Jerusalem fellowship (12:17).

VII. The Epistle of James

The epistle of James was probably written before the half-century mark of the Christian era, during the times when the Church was still commonly regarded as a Jewish institution. Written by the chairman of the Jerusalem congregation, it provided a pattern for righteousness to the widely scattered Christian Jews. The writer fully assumes that true Judaism and the church are identical. The righteousness of the Sermon on the Mount is reflected throughout, a righteousness which constitutes the glorious fruition and not the abolition nor the frustration of God's law as revealed by Moses. Nor does James recognize for a moment that the faith of the Lord Jesus Christ (2:1) is something new; it is rather the faith of Abraham in its latest and best expression. He taught salvation by true faith attested by works (2:18). "This," says Robertson,[1] "is the position of John the Baptist, of Jesus, of Peter, of John, and of Paul himself."

---

[1] A. T. Robertson. *Studies in the New Testament*, p. 115.

3. Discussion and Review

1. Show in what ways the martyrdom of Stephen furthered God's campaign of witnessing.

2. Relate in order the course of Philip's evangelistic travels.

3. Evaluate the religious experience of Simon Magus.

4. What was the distinct contribution of Peter and John to the Samaritan converts?

5. What was Saul doing between the martyrdom of Stephen and his conversion on the way to Damascus?

6. Relate the account of Saul's conversion indicating the unmistakable providence of God by which it was brought about.

7. Indicate the movements of Saul during the eight or nine years following his conversion.

8. Outline the ministries of Peter on the Mediterranean sea coast.

9. Relate the experiences by which Peter was led to minister to the Gentiles. Show how he was convinced.

10. Who was Barnabas? Show how he was God's instrument in producing unity in the growing Church.

11. Who was Herod Agrippa? What was his policy concerning the Jews and how did this affect the Jerusalem Church? Tell how God overruled him.

12. What place did the Lord's brother James fill in the Jerusalem Church? Characterize his epistle.

4. Character Review

Identify:

Philip	Tabitha	John Mark
Simon	Dorcas	James
Gamaliel	Cornelius	(of Jerusalem)
The eunuch	Barnabas	
Aeneas	Herod Agrippa	

5. Bibliography

Blaikie, Wm. G. *Bible History*. New York: Thomas Nelson Co.
   Topics:
   1. The Gospel in Samaria, p. 455.
   2. The Ethiopian Eunuch, pp. 455, 456.

Free, Joseph P. *Archaeology and Bible History.* Chap. XXVIII. Wheaton: Van Kampen Press, 1950.
Topic:
Archaeological Light on Candace, p. 311.
Kuyper, Abraham. *Women of the New Testament.* Grand Rapids: Zondervan.
1. "Mary of Jerusalem," pp. 73-76.
2. "Rhoda," pp. 77-79.
3. "Dorcas, or Tabitha," pp. 80-83.
Morgan, G. Campbell. *The Acts of the Apostles.* New York: Fleming H. Revell Co. Pp. 194-302. An exposition of Acts 8-12.
Sangster, Margaret E. *The Women of the Bible.* Chapt. XVII, "The Raising of Dorcas." New York: The Christian Herald.
Sangster, Margaret E. *The Women of the Bible.* Chapt. XLIII, "A Damsel Named Rhoda." New York: The Christian Herald.

Chapter 40

WITNESSING IN THE GENTILE WORLD

—Paul's First Missionary Journey
(45-48 A. D.)

---

1. Reading Assignment
2. Study Outline:
   I. Introduction—World Preparations
   II. First Christian Missionary Church
   III. The Missionary Party

IV. Course of Paul's First Missionary Journey
3. Discussion and Review
4. Select Memory Passages
5. Character Review
6. Bibliography

---

1. Reading Assignment

Acts 13:1—14:28

(Read the Bible first)

---

2. Study Outline

I. Introduction—World Preparations for Gospel Advance

In the year that Herod Agrippa died (ca. 44 A. D.), Claudius Caesar came to power in Rome. He had just completed an expedition to Britain extending the horizon of the Roman world for new fields of conquest and trade. Little did Claudius realize that in this God was preparing for the extension of his campaign of gospel witnessing, and that in relation to God's purpose, the purpose of Roman imperialism was but child's play. The conversion and preparation of Saul of Tarsus, the vision of Peter at Joppa, the ministry of Barnabas and others in the formation of the first missionary church at Antioch—all of these were God's preparations for the extension of his campaign of witnessing. The Caesars were but puppets, unwittingly, in setting the stage for God's program of advance. The Britains, under God were eventually to be the major successors of the Greeks in providing the language vehicle for the gospel of an eternal kingdom.

425

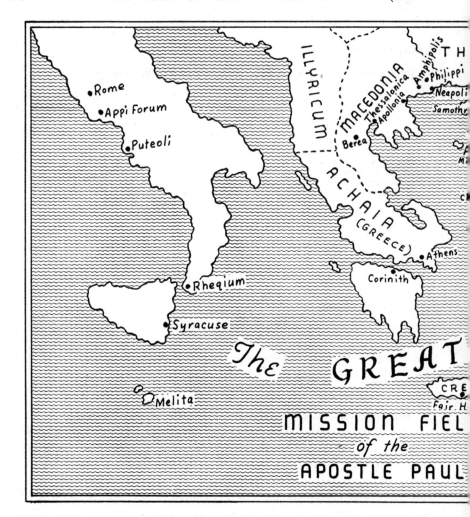

II. The First Christian Missionary Church (Acts 11:26, 27; 13:1-3)

The city of Antioch was ideally situated as a home base for missions, being the center of communication in the eastern part of the Roman empire. Its metropolitan character lent to Christianity an appropriate aspect of world conquest.

It was certainly not the city of Antioch itself which produced the great missionary movement. Its people were a mixture of Greeks and orientals. The city had been founded by Seleucus, one of the

successors of Alexander the Great; it was one of the many cities which he built to satisfy his vanity. It is described by Conybeare and Howson as the city "where under the climate of Syria, and the wealthy patronage of Rome, all that was beautiful in nature and in art had created a sanctuary for a perpetual festival of vice."

It was the ministry, very largely, of Barnabas and Saul, together with one Simon (Niger), Lucius of Cyrene, and Manaen (of the household of Herod the tetraarch) at Antioch, over a period of about a year (ca. 45 A. D.), which begat in the Antioch church a missionary soul. The ministry of "prophets and teachers" is seen to be the source of church missions. Without this preparation, doubtless the church would not have sensed the call of the Holy Spirit (11:26, 27; 13:1-3).

That the followers of Christ were first called Christians at Antioch deserves note. While the name was doubtless given in derision to believers, it served to indicate that the true religion of God was more than a matter of race, and that it could not be contained within a Judaism which disowned Christ or which limited the operation of the gospel to Jewish institutions.

Summarizing, we may say that three factors led to the launching of the mission from Antioch: First, the ministry of prophets and teachers, together with fasting. Secondly, the appointment of missionaries by the Holy Spirit. Thirdly, the separation and ordination of these persons by the church.

It is of interest that nothing is said about financing the enterprise, although we will assume that the apostolic spirit would not have allowed the missionaries to go away empty. It is also of interest that nothing was said as to where the missionaries should go. This is taken care of by the fact that the Holy Ghost sent them forth; on later occasions we observe that he continued to direct the course of the journey.

III. **The Missionary Party** (13:2, 5)

The Holy Ghost named the party, Barnabas and Saul, in this order. Barnabas was the older member and the most responsible member of the group from the standpoint of the Jerusalem church. He had taken the initiative to bring Saul to Antioch. Yet Saul had a more distinct call and in the plan of God was **the** apostle to the west. This was to become more evident.

John Mark was taken along as a minister (attendant). He was not named by the Holy Ghost and the assignment may have been due largely to the desire of Barnabas who was his uncle.

Thus the party was representative. Barnabas was from Cyprus, Saul from Tarsus, and John Mark from Jerusalem. Why, one may well consider, did the Holy Spirit's appointment not include any of the twelve apostles?

IV. **The Course of the First Missionary Journey** (13:4—14:28)

1. **Antioch in Syria** (13:1-3). This is to be distinguished from Antioch in Pisidia. Seleucus, in his vanity, had given this name in honor of his father to not less than sixteen cities.

2. **Seleucus** (13:4). This was the port of departure, no particular ministries being recorded in connection with it.

3. **Salamis** (13:5). They preached the Word of God in the Jewish synagogues. The presence of John as minister is noted here.

4. **Paphos** (13:6-12). After crossing the island they met Sergius Paulus, the deputy of the island, "a prudent man" who called for Barnabas and Saul and asked to hear the word of God from them.

Bar-jesus (Elymas), a Jew but a sorcerer and a false prophet being with the deputy, withstood the missionaries and sought to turn the seeking deputy from the Word. It is of interest that Saul (now called Paul), rather than Barnabas, arose to this challenge. Under the fulness of the Holy Ghost's power, he "set his eyes on him," and rebuked him as a child of the devil. He pronounced a temporary curse of blindness upon him, quite similar to that which he as an opposer of Christ had experienced about twelve years before.

The deputy was led to believe.

5. **Perga** (13:13). After the voyage by sea to Perga, John Mark left them. Catching another ship, he returned to Jerusalem, the home of his mother.

6. **Antioch in Pisidia** (13:14-52). The missionaries went to the synagogue on the Sabbath. According to custom they sat down as auditors in the congregation, after which the rulers of the synagogue invited them to offer whatever word of exhortation they might have for the people. Note that Paul, rather than Barnabas, stood up in response.

Paul's address on this occasion is typical of his sermons as he went from synagogue to synagogue. The dual constituency of the synagogue audience is indicated in his form of address, which is to "men of Israel" (Jews) and "ye that fear God" (Jewish proselytes or Gentiles). Paul rehearsed the history of Israel—God's call, redemption, discipline, and establishment of the nation in Canaan; his deliverances, his establishment of the kingdom first in Saul, but more significantly in David, the ancestor of Jesus the Savior. He carried the account directly up to the Cross, at which point he laid the weight of awful responsibility upon the Jerusalem rulers. But the account ended with the triumph of Jesus in the resurrection and in the commissioned witnesses who are now declaring the "sure mercies of David." In Christ all who believe are forgiven and made heirs of David's heritage.

Many, both of the Jews and of the Gentiles, followed Paul and Barnabas. (Note the order of these names from this point on.) The demand, strongest on the part of the Gentiles, required a meeting on the next Sabbath.

Next Sabbath the whole city turned out. The negative resentment of the Jews on the previous Sabbath (13:42) now turned to envy, contradiction, and blasphemy (13:44-47). The Gentiles were glad. Under such circumstances Paul warned that the opportunity of eternal life would be addressed to the Gentiles. Evidently, this policy was pursued at Antioch until the "word of the Lord was published throughout the whole region."

Just as the Jews had stirred up and influenced Pilate and Herod to raise an official arm against Jesus, and the apostles at Jerusalem, so here they exerted similar pressure to turn the influential people of the community against the missionaries. Paul and Barnabas were expelled from Pisidia, but the dust which they shook from their feet as they crossed the coast line spelled judgment upon those rejectors of eternal life. On the other hand, the disciples left behind were "filled with joy, and with the Holy Ghost."

7. **Iconium** (14:1-7). Crossing over into the province of Lycaonia they went to the synagogue at Iconium. Although Jewish hostility prejudiced some minds against the Word, the missionaries preached here a "long time," "speaking boldly in the Lord" and doing signs and wonders. A multitude both of Jews and Gentiles believed.

As at Antioch, however, great success meant greater envy from unbelieving Jews and when this spirit reached the point of stoning, the missionaries, "ware of it," fled to Lystra and Derbe, and cities of Cilicia.

8. **Lystra** (14:8-20). The healing of a man who had been born with crippled feet set the stage at Lystra for extreme sentiments. First, the natives insisted upon identifying the missionaries as gods, Barnabas as Jupiter and Paul as Mercurius. Greatly chagrined, the apostles did their best to set the natives right and to point them to the only true God. Almost before this sentiment was repulsed the evil leaven of Jewish hostility from Antioch and Iconium influenced

the fickle natives to stone the missionaries. Stoning Paul, they conveyed him to the outside of the city, leaving him for dead. But as the disciples stood about he arose and came back into the city. The next day they went eastward to Derbe, a trek of about twenty miles which was not so bad for a man supposed to have been dead the day before.

9. **Derbe** 14:21-23). The account of this ministry is brief, but significant—they preached the gospel and taught many.

Beyond this, there is something further of significance to be observed. Note on the map the direct distance from Derbe back to Antioch of Syria. The missionaries might have reached Tarsus, Paul's native city the first night, and then, in another day of travel they might have found themselves back in the ideal fellowship of the Antioch Church. Instead, they determined to retrace the steps of their journey against both physical and personal opposition in order to confirm the souls of the disciples, to exhort them to continue in the faith and to arm them for the tribulation involved in entering the kingdom of God. The new groups of believers also needed their own leaders; it belonged to the role of the missionaries to ordain elders among them, and finally after prayer and fasting, to commend them to the Lord in whom they believed.

10. **Return points** (14:21-28). At **Lystra, Iconium,** and at **Antioch in Pisidia** the work of the missionaries was that of establishing the believers in the churches as indicated in the above paragraph.

At **Perga** they preached the Word.

Arriving at **Antioch in Syria** the Christians of the Church were gathered together and told the whole story of the journey, of what God had done through them and of the door which had been opened up to the Gentiles. We can well imagine the great interest and the thrill which the success of God's advancing plan of witnessing gave to their hearts. They stayed at Antioch a "long time," perhaps the larger part of the year 49 A. D.

3. Discussion and Review

1. Point out the concurrence of the Caesars with God's plan of Gospel advance.

2. In what respect was Antioch ideally situated as a missionary base? In what respect was it not qualified?

3. Account for the rise of the name "Christian."

4. What three factors led to the launching of the mission from Antioch? What was the provision for maintaining the mission?

5. Discuss the choice of the party personnel as to who did the choosing, who was chosen, and who was not chosen.

6. Trace the journey relating the experiences and the accomplishments of the missionaries at each point. As a suggestion for class work, let persons be assigned to specific portions of the journey, and let them report in relay.

7. What is indicated of the character of the missionaries in their purpose to retrace their course from Derbe instead of taking the nearest land route home?

8. Trace their return journey. What ministries were performed?

4. Select Memory Passages

Acts 13:2, 3; 14:21-23

5. Character Review

Identify:

Claudius Caesar	John Mark	Sergius Paulus
Barnabas	Bar-jesus	
Saul	Elymas	

6. Bibliography

Conybeare, W. J. and Howson, J. S. *The Life and Epistles of Saint Paul.* London, 1854.

Free, Joseph P. *Archaeology and Bible History.* Chap. XXVII. Wheaton: Van Kampen Press, 1950.
Topics:
1. Archaeological Light and Confirmation Concerning Sergius Paulus (Acts 13), pp. 314, 315.
2. Archaeological Light on the Region between Perga and Antioch; Possible Reason for John Mark's Return (Acts 13:13), pp. 316, 317.
3. Archaeological Confirmation concerning Luke's Indication of the Location of Iconium, Lystra, and Derbe (Acts 14:6), p. 317.
4. Archaeological Light on Zeus and Hermes (Acts 14), p. 318.

Meyer, F. B. *Paul a Servant of Jesus Christ.* New York: Fleming H. Revell.

Morgan, G. Campbell. *The Acts of the Apostles.* New York: Fleming H. Revell Co. Pp. 194-302. An exposition of Acts 8-12.

Ramsey, Sir Wm. *St. Paul the Traveler and the Roman Citizen.* Grand Rapids: Baker Book House. 1949.

Ramsey, W. M. *The Cities of St. Paul.* Part II, "Tarsus." Part III, "Antioch," Grand Rapids: Baker Book House (Reprint).

Robinson, Benjamin W. *The Life of Paul.* Chicago: University of Chicago Press.

Smith, David. *Life and Letters of St. Paul.* Boston: Harper and Harper.

Chapter 41

WITNESSING IN THE GENTILE WORLD

—A Question of Policy at the Jerusalem Council (50 A. D.)

1. Reading Assignment

Acts 15:1-31; Galatians 2
(Read the Bible first)

2. Study Outline

I. Introduction—The Rite of Circumcision

We have already observed the difficulty with which the Jewish Christians were able to recognize Gentile Christians. But we have observed how God by special providences had provided instruction to them. On the day of Pentecost the declaration of God's works in various tongues clearly set forth the fact prophesied by Joel that God's spirit was to be poured out upon all flesh. The conversion of the Samaritans and the gift of the Holy Spirit to them, the vision of Peter and the power of the gospel in the household of Cornelius, the conversion of Gentiles along the western sea coast, in Cyprus, and at Antioch—all of these were God's sign and seal upon the fact that Acts 1:8 was intended by the Lord as referring to an actual gospel ministry to all nations. By the end of the first missionary journey there was little room to question whether or not the gospel was for the Gentiles.

The question which now arose was whether or not Gentile converts must become circumcised as a condition to their acceptance into the Christian Church. This issue was brought up at Antioch by "certain men which came down from Judea," and who taught the brethren: "Except ye be circumcised after the manner of Moses, ye cannot be saved" (15:1).

The rite of circumcision had been ordained of God in his covenant with Abraham (Gen. 17:10). It was a physical operation by which the foreskins of male children were removed. It has been practiced in all ages and among various peoples for both hygienic and religious reasons. Among Abraham's people it was enjoined upon all males the eighth day after birth. It was confirmed by the law of Moses (Lev. 12:3; Joshua 5:2-9). Foreigners who desired to be identified with the Israelites were required to submit to the rite (Gen. 34:14-17, 22; Exod. 12:48).

Though there were other circumcised nations than the Hebrews, it seems evident that the various nations, the Philistines, the Phoenicians, and others, with whom the Jews were in contact, were "uncircumcised," so the word meant about the same, practically, as heathen (Gen. 34:14; Judges 14:3; 15:18; I Sam. 1:20). The "circumcision" came to mean the Jewish nation (Gal. 2:8; Col. 4:11).

Circumcision as a religious rite signified purification. This was, in the case of the Jews, twofold. First, it signified separation from the nations, although as seen above, it was practiced by other nations. Secondly, it was of value, hygienically, in curtailing the development of excessive lust. As to the first, it is clear that God's purpose was to **separate** Israel from the nations. Such separation was important in view of God's purpose of keeping a pure channel for his self-revelation to the world, and for the ushering in of the Messianic kingdom.

In viewing the issue which arose we must not overlook this basis for the Jewish side of the argument. That argument was so strong that it is doubtful whether it ever could have been overcome had God not taken the initiative and had he not himself opened the door to the Gentiles. He had opened that door, and it was obviously apart from the temple, the apostles, and the rites of Judaism that he had done so. What now were men to do about it?

II. The Law of Moses and the Eternal Moral Law

It is evident that in this chapter circumcision stands for the whole law of Moses (vss. 1, 5, 24). As a system the law of Moses consists of the application of the moral law to the Israelitish nation.

As such, it is not a system that is universally appropriate. The Mosaic system was appropriate for that nation during a certain time, in a certain place, and for the accomplishment of particular ends. The law of Moses therefore is not synonymous with the moral law. A failure to properly observe this distinction is serious. The moral law, meaning the revealed will of God, the essence of which is supreme love to God and equal love to man (Matt. 22:37-40), is everywhere applicable and is the basis upon which the judgments of eternity will be made. Its violation called for separation from the Paradise of Eden. Obedience to it is the condition to future participation in the Tree of Life (Rev. 22:14).

The question of salvation, however, involves the assumption that man is guilty of violating God's law, either in the Mosaic expression of it or in another, and that he needs restoration. But restoration to what? The Pharisees said, to the Mosaic system. Jesus had clearly declared in the Sermon on the Mount that he had come, not to destroy, but to fulfill the law of Moses. Yet, if we follow him, we learn that he had in mind the spirit of love. He declared the wine bottles of Judaism worn out, but he did not allow the wine to be lost. As a matter of fact, by the destruction of Jerusalem and the temple, by the dispersion of the Jews as well as by the giving of the Messiah who is the great antitype of Judaism, God had caused the Mosaic system to pass away. But he did not cause true worship to pass away. He had but removed the temporal, which had become formal, in order that faith might lay hold upon the real which is eternal.

To illustrate further, consider the absurdity for the American colonists to have adopted the government of Britain in all of its ramifications. Consider the absurdity of a law against cannibalism in America. Or think of the confusion of trying to apply the governmental system of New York to Hong-Kong. Similarly, the Mosaic system was designed for a certain people, for a certain time, and under given circumstances. To attempt to apply it to the various peoples of the world was never God's intention.

III. How the Issue Was Settled at the Jerusalem Council (15:2, 6)

At Antioch and at Jerusalem alike, there was confusion. An affirmation was set up against fact. The question to be decided was, which of the two should prevail. The dissenting party **affirmed:**

"Except ye be circumcised after the manner of Moses, ye cannot be saved." The **fact** was that God had saved people and filled them with his Spirit apart from circumcision.

Let us note what took place at the council to resolve this dissension.

1. In private council (15:4) Paul and Barnabas related to the Jerusalem brethren all that God had done through them.

2. In the general council (15:6-31) the dissenting party stated its premise and set off much disputation.

3. Peter arose and related the **fact** that the Gentiles had heard and believed and received the Holy Spirit through faith, referring to the household of Cornelius. From this fact he urged the deduction that Jew and Gentile are alike saved by grace, through the Lord Jesus Christ, not by keeping the law of Moses. Peter did not show the lack of validity in grounding salvation upon any other basis but simply let the fact speak. Since God saved Cornelius, the premise affirmed in verses 1 and 5 must be wrong.

4. Barnabas and Paul (who spoke we do not know) buttressed the **fact** presented by Peter with the account of many more cases of salvation among the Gentiles.

5. James, referring to the facts related by Simeon and to the prophecy of Amos, apparently expressed the final thought of the company:

a. Gentile converts are not to be "troubled," which meant that circumcision should not be required as a ground of salvation.

b. Certain moral requirements were to be recognized, namely abstinence from pollutions of idols, from fornication, from things strangled, and from blood.

When this statement was finally formulated into a letter certain other features of interest appear. First, the decision of the council rested not upon a basis of lawlessness or license. It rather rested upon the revealed will of the Holy Ghost. Thus if the church is not to be governed by the law as given to Moses it is nevertheless still amenable to the Holy Spirit who gave the law. It must not be forgotten that the Holy Spirit has laws (see Galatians 5) and that if they are not recognized one may not enter the kingdom of God.

In the second place, this decision was no precedent for the establishment of a conciliar authority in Christendom. The Holy Spirit, not the councils, must guide the church in all current issues. The council is utterly dependent upon divine leadership. If a council is not able to say "It seemed good to the Holy Ghost and to us," it will prove very fallible.

IV. The Letter from the Council

The decision of the council was formulated into a letter and committed to Judas and Silas, trusted men of Jerusalem, who accompanied Paul and Barnabas to Antioch, and delivered it. The fact that the letter was addressed to "the Gentiles in Antioch and Syria, and Cilicia" indicates that it was a circular letter and was doubtless sent or later delivered to the churches of Asia Minor.

The style of the letter is unique. It conveys an apology for the men who had troubled them by presuming to impose a mandate as from the Jerusalem church. The letter disclaimed this mandate. It made no attempt to provide constitution or by-laws for the Gentile churches, but merely affirmed the obligation to moral law. The letter was unofficious, opening with greetings and closing with farewell.

V. Continued Pressure from Judaizers (Gal. 2)

We do not know the exact date of Peter's visit to Antioch recorded in Gal. 2:11 but it was probably sometime after the Jerusalem council. The book of Galatians, written by Paul about 58 A. D., makes evident the fact that the Judaizing party never ceased to be active. Whereas Peter had mingled freely with the Gentiles, going, it would seem, beyond the degree of fraternizing passed upon by the Jerusalem council, he was suddenly brought under pressure from the Judaizing party. As when the cock crew he again became a coward and separated himself from the Gentile Christians. The pressure of the Judaizers was so great that other Jewish Christians as well, including Barnabas, were carried away by dissimulation. Paul openly rebuked Peter, and raised the flag of Christian unity again. This required much courage on Paul's part, but he saved his brethren from their own weakness and won their lasting respect (II Pet. 3:15, 16).

3. Discussion and Review

1. Review the steps by which God had lengthened the cords of gospel witnessing beyond the limits of Judaism.

2. Present the case for the importance of circumcision in the economy of Israel.

3. Discuss the difference between the law of Moses and the moral law.

4. Were Jews saved by their law or by grace (Acts 15:11)?

5. Relate the procedure at the Jerusalem conference.

6. Discuss the validity or the fallacy of the premise affirmed in 15:1.

7. What was the prevailing factor in the contributions made to the council by Peter, Barnabas and Paul, and by James?

8. What was the decision of the conference as stated by James?

9. Did James mean that one could be saved by abstaining from the four sins which he listed? What did he mean?

10. Show that the decision did not arise out of a basis of license to sin.

11. Did the action of this council establish a basis for the finality of conciliary authority?

12. How and to whom was the decision published? Characterize the style of the letter sent out.

13. What is known of the later history of the Judaizing element in Christianity?

14. How did Paul save his brethren from their own weakness?

4. Select Memory Passages

Acts 15:7b-9; 28-29

5. Character Review

Identify:

Judas   Silas   James

6. Bibliography

Morgan, G. Campbell. *The Acts of the Apostles.* New York: Fleming H. Revell Co. Pp. 355-366. An exposition of Acts 15:1-35.

Chapter 42

WITNESSING IN THE GENTILE WORLD

—Paul's Second Missionary Journey
(51-54 A. D.)

1. Reading Assignment

Acts 15:36—18:22
(Read the Bible first)

2. Collateral Reading

I and II Thessalonians

3. Study Outline

I. Introduction—The Importance of the Journey

Paul's second missionary journey was one of the greatest expeditions of its kind in all missionary history. It included central and southeastern Asia Minor, Phrygia, Galatia, Troas, and in Europe the great cities of Philippi, Thessalonica, Berea, Athens, and Corinth. The importance of this journey is artfully described by Stalker in the following paragraph from his "Life of Paul:"

> In his first journey Paul may be said to have been trying his wings; for his course, adventurous as it was, only swept in a limited circle round his native province. In his second journey he performed a far more distant and perilous flight. Indeed, this journey was not only the greatest achieved, but perhaps

439

the most momentous recorded in the annals of the human race. In its issues it far outrivalled the expedition of Alexander the Great, when he carried the arms and civilization of Greece into the heart of Asia, or that of Caesar, when he landed on the shores of Britain, or even the voyage of Columbus when he discovered the New World. Yet when he set out on it he had no idea of the magnitude which it was to assume, or even the direction which it was to take.

II. The Interval between Acts 15:31 and 36

It will be recalled that Judas and Silas accompanied Paul and Barnabas to Antioch for the purpose of reporting the Jerusalem conference. Both were prophets and teachers, and tarried to minister, exhorting and confirming the Antiochan brethren.

After "they were let go in peace from the brethren unto the apostles," Silas was pleased to "abide there still." Paul and Barnabas engaged with many others in preaching and teaching the word, and it evidently intrigued Silas.

It is the belief of some accredited expositors that Peter's visit to Antioch referred to in Gal. 2:11-21 took place at this time. In that event not only Peter but Barnabas betrayed weakness, and there was some ground for believing that he was not sufficiently free from the delimiting viewpoint of Judaism to further be the companion of the apostle to the Gentiles. Nothing is said of this, however, in the account of Luke. The two taught and preached together at Antioch.

III. Personnel of the Second Mission (15:37-40)

The idea to revisit the Christians in Asia Minor was proposed by Paul. Barnabas evidently agreed, yet when it came to laying the plans their divergent tendencies divided their course. Paul, it would seem, was determined to eliminate all weak elements in the party. The mission was everything to him; personalities were nothing in comparison. On the other hand, Barnabas probably felt a personal responsibility for the spiritual development of his nephew, and considering the fact that John Mark became one of the Gospel writers, that was no unimportant concern. The breach upon this difference widened so far that Barnabas and Mark quit the mission and boarded a ship for Cyprus. We hear of them no more in the book of Acts, but later John Mark again became Paul's "fellow-worker" (Col. 4:10).

At this point we can hardly fail to see the significance of the tarrying of Silas at Antioch. Doubtless it was the work of the Holy Ghost to keep him at hand in order to fill the position vacated by Barnabas. It is remarkable that in all of this the confidence of the brethren at Antioch was not unbalanced, and when Paul and Silas started out the church was back of them.

IV.   Course of the Second Missionary Journey

1. **Syria and Cilicia** (15:41). What churches were these? Paul and Barnabas had founded no churches in these provinces in the first journey. This reference doubtless implies some unrecorded history of missionary work conducted by Paul (Saul) during the years before his removal to Antioch at the invitation of Barnabas (11:25, 26).

2. **Lycaonia** (16:1-5). Passing from Cilicia into Lycaonia, Paul and Silas came to Derbe, and then to Lystra. At Lystra, where before, Paul had been stoned and left for dead he found a prized son in the Gospel in the person of Timothy. Humanly considered, the name of Lystra might have carried such an ill omen to Paul as to repel him. In God's service, however, faithful ministry in the bleakest place sometimes yields the choicest fruit.

Timothy was half Jew and half Greek. To overcome the disadvantage of his Greek blood in ministering to the Jews, Paul had him circumcised. Against the possible charge which might come to him as violating the principle of Christian freedom, he bore the letter of the Jerusalem council to the Gentile churches. Timothy with the two streams of blood flowing in his veins became an apt symbol of that unity of Jew and Gentile in Christ which Paul so ably expounded.

3. **Phrygia and Galatia** (16:6). No mention of a visit with the churches in Pisidia is made, except that Timothy was well reported of by the brethren from Iconium. There is every reason to believe, however, that Paul's coverage of the churches was complete. Not only so, but the missionary party traveled north of this area throughout the region of Phrygia and Galatia. This was according to the special direction of the Holy Spirit and against the first plan of Paul which had been to go directly westward into proconsular Asia.

4. **Troas** (16:7-10). Passing into Mysia, their undirected inclination was to go north into Bithynia but again the "Spirit suffered them not." Under his direction their course took them to
Troas, the ancient noted city of Troy.

Paul's Macedonian call was received here in a vision and marked
the divine providence which carried the Lord's campaign of witnessing from Asia to Europe. Paul had no trouble in understanding
such a call. It was all within the main call received on the Damascus
road by which he was appointed God's witness to the Gentiles.

Observe that at Troy the narrator of Acts changes from the
third person to the first, from which we may conclude that Luke,
the writer, joined the missionary party at this point. Luke was a
physician (Col. 4:14) and doubtless ministered to Paul's infirmities
(Gal. 4:13-14).

5. **Philippi** (Acts 16:11-40). After two days of sailing before
a favorable wind, the party consisting now of Paul, Silas, Timothy,
and Luke, reached Philippi. This was a Roman colony or military
outpost, and had very few Jews in it. Paul's stay here centers around
two persons, Lydia of Thyatira who was a seller of purple dyes, and
a divining maiden. Naturally Paul sought out a place of worship.
This turned out to be, not a synagogue but a less formal meeting
place at a spacious spot along a river. A company of women were
accustomed to gather at this place for prayer. The missionaries
spoke to these women. As a consequence Lydia "attended unto the
things which were spoken by Paul"; she and her household were
baptized. Furthermore, she made of her Christian home a hostel
for the missionaries.

Paul's work in Philippi made a target of the work of Satan in
the life of a maid. In delivering the maid Paul unwittingly touched
the purse strings of her master who made merchandise of her satanic
power. Posing as champions of Rome against Jewish innovations,
these masters had Paul and Silas arrested. The magistrate tore off
the clothing of Paul and Silas, had them beaten, and then cast into
prison with special command to the jailor to guard them. To be
very careful, the jailor put them into the inner prison and put
their feet in stocks.

The prayers and songs of praise in the inner prison, an earthquake, and the opening of the prison doors were a strong sermon to
Philippi that night.

The conversion of the Philippian jailor and his house was a brilliant trophy. Together with Lydia there was in their two households the good beginning of a church.

Paul and Silas took full advantage of the act of God by which they were freed. When the magistrates wanted to dispose of the matter by letting the missionaries go and depart "in peace" Paul held them to their responsibility in the matter. When Paul divulged that they were "free Romans" the tables were completely turned. The magistrates were at the missionaries' feet. After a period of rest and refreshment in the house of Lydia, Paul and Silas departed. Luke and Timothy, we gather from a later notice, remained in Philippi.

6. **Thessalonica** (17:1-9). Passing through Amphipolis and Apollonia Paul and Silas went to Thessalonica (modern Salonika) where they entered the Jewish synagogue. As usual they preached, first of all, to the Jews and Jewish proselytes who represented the remnant of faith in an otherwise wicked city.

After three Sabbaths of preaching, a crisis of success (17:4) and of opposition (17:5-9) was reached. The opposition at Philippi had originated with offended business men; at Thessalonica it originated with envious and prejudiced Jewish religious leaders. The difficulty with these Jews was that they, though religious leaders, were not interested in the truth. Their hypocrisy is seen in that while they pretended to be pious they hired lewd fellows to do their dirty work against God's witnesses.

Jason and certain of the brethren gave the magistrates "security" against the charges that the missionaries were anti-Caesar. Paul relieved the situation further by leaving town.

7. **Berea** (17:10-14). Coming to Berea, Paul and Silas went to the Jewish synagogue, as usual. The course of things was similar to what had been experienced at Thessalonica; except that the Bereans were more open minded and more willing to search the Scriptures. Eventually Jewish hostility from Thessalonica caught up with them and stirred up the people. As at Thessalonica, the brethren sent Paul away. Silas and Timothy remained. When Paul arrived at Athens, he sent word to them to come to him with all speed.

8. **Athens** (17:15-34). While Paul waited for them he was not idle. He spoke at the Jewish synagogue on the Sabbath and mingled with the people at the market place. The climax of his ministry here was his famous address at the Areopagus on Mars'

Hill. Athens had been the center of great learning in Greece but in these times, while still a noted university center, it was filled with a rather renegade sort of philosophers (17:17-18). Religiously, the city was idolatrous and philosophically, it was skeptical and agnostic. No great response numerically came of this ministry at Athens. Both the Epicureans and the Stoics ridiculed Paul. Jesus as the Christ of God and the resurrection were ideas requiring too much of a strain upon their minds. However, there were converts, namely, Dionysius the Areopagite, a woman named Damaris, and others.

9. **Corinth** (18:1-17). As Paul came away from Athens, disappointed by its cold intellectualism, he approached Corinth with the purpose to preach to them without any pretense of human wisdom or excellency of speech, but only in the power of the gospel and of the Spirit. Corinth was different from Athens. If not intellectually vain, it was morally corrupt.

The depressing conditions of Corinth were lessened for Paul by the discovery of a Jewish couple, Aquila and Priscilla, who had recently been expelled from Rome by Claudius. Both he and they were tent-makers, and became co-workers in that trade. Paul was noticeably heartened also, by the arrival of Silas and Timothy from Macedonia. They brought good news of the welfare of the churches at Thessalonica and Philippi. It is indicated in 18:5 that their coming released his mind for fuller concentration upon the work of the gospel.

The work at Corinth began in the synagogue where he "reasoned with" and "persuaded" the Jews and Greeks every Sabbath. As usual, the issue came to its crisis, and Paul "shook his raiment" and left. He continued to minister in the house of Justus near the synagogue. There was thus the significant spectacle of two houses of worship, one of Christians and one of non-Christian Jews. Further fuel for the envy of the Jewish leaders came with the conversion of Crispus the chief ruler of the synagogue, the influence of whose conversion and baptism spoke impressively to the whole city. By a special vision God encouraged Paul and assured him of many more potential believers in the city.

A check was placed upon the Jewish pressure group when after they made an insurrection and brought Paul before the Achaian deputy Gallio, he turned upon them driving them from the judgment seat. By this action he practically gave legal status to Christianity as a form of Judaism.

It had doubtless been Sosthenes the new ruler of the Jewish synagogue who had led in the insurrection against Paul. When Gallio drove him away, the Greeks took the incident as an opportunity to express their pent-up anti-Jewish feelings, hence they added to the Jewish leaders' embarrassment a public beating. All of this doubtless created a city-wide sentiment favoring Paul's ministry. He was able to remain for a year and a half in the city.

Paul's earliest letters were written during this stay at Corinth. These were the letters to the Thessalonians. Timothy reported that the Thessalonians were disturbed by a mistaken idea of the return of Christ, which was that his coming was to have been soon. Their anxiety was concerning what would happen to the Christians who had already died—would they be deprived of a part in Christ's glory? The answer to this is found principally in I Thessalonians 4 and 5.

The second letter to the Thessalonians appears to have been written to nullify a forged letter which had dogmatically affirmed that Christ was to come soon. This letter stated two specific developments which would precede his coming, namely, the apostasy of the church and the revealing of the "man of sin."

Both letters are full of encouragement and of admonition to holy living in view of the certain return of Christ.

10. **Ephesus** (18:18-21). Paul stopped but briefly at Ephesus. He reasoned with the Jews in the synagogue, and was entreated to remain longer, but declared his purpose to keep an on-coming feast at Jerusalem. He promised to return, which he did.

Silas and Timothy apparently remained at Corinth or went back to Macedonia. Aquila and Priscilla went with Paul to Ephesus, and remained while Paul went on to Syria.

11. **Caesarea** (18:22). He stopped only long enough to greet the church.

12. **Antioch** (18:22). We are left to imagine what took place on this furlough. There was plenty to report, and there were many friends with whom to share interests.

13. **Jerusalem.** We do not know when Paul fulfilled his purpose of going to Jerusalem at this point, nor do we know any of the facts concerning the visit.

4. Discussion and Review

1. What is Stalker's appraisal of the importance of Paul's second missionary journey?

2. What took place between the Jerusalem council and the second missionary journey?

3. Relate the course of considerations in deciding upon the personnel of the second journey.

4. Proceed according to the suggestion of Review Question number 7 in chapter 40.

5. Give an account of Paul's written correspondence with the Thessalonian church. What were the misapprehensions and what were Paul's explanations?

5. Select Memory Passages

Acts 16:30, 31; 17:22-31; I Thessalonians 4:13-18; 5:14, 15, 16-18, 19, 21, 22, 23.

6. Character Review

Identify:

Timothy	Jason	Gallio
Luke	Aquila	Timothy
Lydia	Priscilla	

7. Bibliography

Free, Joseph P. *Archaeology and Bible History.* Chap. XXVIII. Wheaton: Van Kampen Press, 1950.
Topics:
1. Archaeological Confirmation concerning Luke's Reference to the "Part" (District) of Macedonia (Acts 16:12), p. 320.
2. Archaeological Confirmation of Luke's Reference to the Rulers of Philippi as Magistrates (Praetors) (Acts 16:20), pp. 320, 321.
3. Archaeological Confirmation concerning Thessalonica, Athens, and Corinth (Acts 17-18), pp. 321, 322.
4. Archaeological Light on Paul's Sojourn at Corinth (Acts 18:12), p. 323.

Kuyper, Abraham. *Women of the New Testament.* Grand Rapids: Zondervan.
1. "Lois," pp. 87-89.
2. "Eunice," pp. 90-93.
3. "Lydia," pp. 98-101.
Morgan, G. Campbell. *The Acts of the Apostles.* New York: Fleming H. Revell Co. Pp. 366-434. An exposition of Acts 15:36—18:23.
Sangster, Margaret E. *The Women of the Bible.* Chapt. XLIV, "Lydia, the Hostess." New York: The Christian Herald.
Sangster, Margaret E, *The Women of the Bible.* Chapt. XLV, "A Mother and a Grandmother." New York: The Christian Herald.

Chapter 43

WITNESSING IN THE GENTILE WORLD

—Paul's Third Missionary Journey
(54-57 A. D.)

1. Reading Assignment

Acts 18:23—21:16

2. Collateral Reading

I and II Corinthians; Galatians; Romans
(Read the Bible first)

3. Study Outline

I. Introduction—Farewell to Antioch

Paul's third missionary journey began less auspiciously than had the previous two journeys so far as the departure from Antioch is concerned. We have observed how Jerusalem receded in importance as the home base for Christ's campaign of witnessing, with the development of Antioch of Syria. Now it appears that Paul is more at home in western Asia Minor and Macedonia than in Syria. And

447

from Macedonia he aspires to press farther on, even to Rome (Acts 19:1).

Paul's stay at Antioch, between the second and third journeys, may not have been more than a month or two. His departure now was probably his last farewell to Antioch, although there is an absence of any expressed premonition of the fact. He probably left Antioch alone.

II. The Course of This Four Year Ministry

In this period Paul's main efforts were spent in two places of residence, namely Ephesus and Greece (Corinth). Doubtless there were many unrecorded sallies from these centers. Adhering to Luke's account in the Acts we have the following order of travel:

1. Antioch	11. Trogyllium
2. Galatia and Phrygia	12. Miletus
3. Ephesus (3 years)	13. Coos
4. Macedonia	14. Rhodes
5. Greece (3 months)	15. Patara
6. Macedonia	16. Tyre
7. Troas (7 days)	17. Ptolemais
8. Assos	18. Caesarea
9. Mitylene	19. Jerusalem
10. Chios	

III. Tour Through Phrygia and Galatia (18:23)

Luke's account of Paul's ministry among the Christians of these regions is very brief and there is much to be read behind the lines of 18:23. Paul probably spent the winter in this area. It appears that he suffered ill health and privation during these months (Gal. 4:13-15; II Cor. 12:7). There were many converts (Gal. 4:8). Some were rescued from the beggarly elements of Judaism (Gal. 5:1). Churches were organized (Gal. 1:2). The churches were taught to give in a systematic way (Gal. 6:6-10; I Cor. 16:1, 2). The Galatians were impulsive; they did well for a time but Paul was much distressed as to their fickleness (Gal. 5:7). It is not difficult to see that there was a real need for Paul's best efforts to place these churches upon an abiding basis (Gal. 4:19).

If Paul did spend the winter in this area he may have experienced the suffering mentioned in II Cor. 11:27, "in hunger and thirst, in fastings often, in cold and nakedness." The winter here is bitter and perilous. History records many winter tragedies from deep snow, blizzards, and low temperatures among the shepherds and travelers of these parts.

IV. Paul's Three Year Residence at Ephesus (19:1-41)

1. **John's Disciples Are Led on** (19:1-7). Some followers of John the Baptist were encountered by Paul as he came to Ephesus. Paul led them into a knowledge of Christ Jesus. They were baptized in his name, and the Holy Ghost came upon them by the laying on of Paul's hands. As at Pentecost, they spoke with tongues and prophesied. There were twelve men in all.

Previous to Paul's coming to Ephesus another person, namely Apollos, had come there, and having a similar deficiency was led into a fuller knowledge of Christ by Aquila and Priscilla (18:24-28). There is nothing to indicate any connection between Apollos and these twelve.

2. **Paul's Synagogue Ministry at Ephesus** (19:8). As in other places Paul's first ministries were in the Jewish synagogue until opposition forced him out. In the case of Ephesus this lasted for three months. It was a time spent in trying by disputation and reasoning to lead them into the kingdom of God.

3. **Paul's Ministry in the School of Tyrannus** (Acts 19:9f). Just as in Corinth Paul moved from the synagogue to the house of Justus so now he moved his center of ministry to quarters where there was freedom to teach. Tyrannus is thought by Conybeare to have been a teacher of philosophy or rhetoric.

For two years he conducted a school here. He made his living with his own hands (20:34) as he had done at Corinth, Thessalonica, and elsewhere. His method was characterized by argumentation as well as by instruction. He did not evade the dialectical turn of the Hellenistic mind which called for fact and reason. Yet, of course, his instruction went far deeper than the common vein of Hellenistic dialectics. The gospel brought to men's minds a vast area of truth and of power which lay beyond the horizontal and merely human. Moreover, his instruction was accompanied by miracles of healing and deliverance which brought an answer to the deepest human need.

4. **Unworthy Users of Christ's Name** (19:13-20). Paul's miracles

were out of the class of the deeds of magic which were common to
the orient. This was demonstrated with wholesome results when
seven sons of Sceva, a Jewish chief priest, undertook to cast out an
evil spirit in the name of "Jesus whom Paul preacheth." The evil
spirit knew and feared Jesus and Paul, but discerned that the
Jewish exorcists were without divine power. The result to the
would-be exorcists was an awful boomerang of their undertaking.
They were cast out of the house naked and wounded. We can easily
understand the sobriety which came over other workers of magic
and curious arts. The bonfire of their books, valued at $10,000,
proved that the Word of God probed to the heart of superstition and
"prevailed."

5. **Demetrius the Resentful Business Man** (19:23-41). Similar
to the masters of the spirit-possessed maid at Philippi, Demetrius, an
Ephesian silversmith, stirred up an insurrection against Paul because the gains of his evil business were under-cut by the Word of
God. The market for idols of Diana had greatly died down with
the effect that the sellers and makers were beginning to be without
business. This is the sensitive spot in many a person who is otherwise apparently neither for nor against religion. He is against
whatever affects his pocket. He will fight to keep society in its
rut regardless of where that rut is leading because he wants to
preserve the commercial pattern.

While this mob did not represent high authority, as is seen from
the attitudes of the chiefs of Asia (19:31) and the town clerk
(19:35f), yet the situation was dangerous. It was expedient that
Paul should leave.

We should not suppose that it was merely from expediency,
that Saul left Ephesus. Previously he had given expression to his
forward look—he wanted to pass through Macedonia and Achaia,
and then go to Jerusalem. Beyond this he purposed to go to Rome.
In view of this he had sent Timotheus and Erastus, in advance, into
Macedonia (19:21-22).

6. **Paul's Correspondence with the Corinthians from Ephesus**
(I Corinthians).

Internal evidences indicate that Paul wrote his first epistle to
the Corinthians from Ephesus. Paul had received correspondence
from the church at Corinth relative to various questions (I Cor. 7:1;
8:1; 12:1; and 16:1). Stephanas, Fortunatus, and Achaicus had
come to him from Corinth, probably for the purpose of conferring

on church matters (I Cor. 16:17). The household of Chloe had informed him of the factions which had developed at Corinth. Paul had already written a letter to them on a problem of gross immorality (I Cor. 5:9). He sent Timothy to them to set things in order (I Cor. 4:17; Acts 19:22) in advance of his own coming to them (I Cor. 16:7). Paul had sought to induce Apollos to come with Timothy but Apollos declined to do so; Paul graciously remarked that he would probably do so at some convenient time (I Cor. 16:12).

From Paul's letter it is obvious that the Church at Corinth had fallen into a tangle of spiritual and moral irregularities that called for a strong, yet tactful, disciplinary hand.

The following are the principal subjects with which Paul's letter dealt:

(1) **The Party Spirit**

The church had become carnal, gotten its eyes upon men, and lost its vision of the crucified Christ (1:10-14).

Paul insisted that human leaders were merely the agents to establish them in their faith in Christ (3:1-9).

Paul exemplified the central and fundamental position of Christ by speaking of him as a foundation (3:10:23).

(2) **Immoralities**

Instructions are given against the toleration of fornicators. An incestuous person is singled out and required to be separated from the fellowship of the church (chapter 5).

(3) **Litigation**

Christians had taken their differences to the civil courts for settlement. Paul condemned this vehemently (6:1-8).

(4) **Marriage**

Paul had been asked numerous questions about the proper relationship between man and woman. The letter forbids familiarity in all cases except within the marriage bond (7:1-12). Husband and wife are to honor each other (7:3). If only one member of a union becomes a Christian that member is to seek to win the other (7:16). The life of celibacy is commended as a matter of expediency (7:26), but the instructions of 7:2 are consistent with the general teaching of the scriptures. Widows are advised not to remarry, but they may (7:39-40).

(5) **Meats**

The question of the propriety of eating meats offered to idols arose. Paul considered that since idols are "nothing" there could be nothing defiling about them (8:46). But he begs another consideration. If a weak brother takes offense, the brother taking the liberty should refrain out of love for him (8:13).

(6) The Lord's Supper

This had become a gluttonous feast (11:20-22). The letter gives instructions as to its significance and proper observance (11:23-34).

(7) Spiritual Gifts

One Spirit is the giver of them all (12:4). They are given for edification(12:7). They are given according to the will of the Holy Spirit (12:11). Their working is as the members of a body (12:12-31).

The gift of tongues had been misused. Paul regarded it as a minor gift. Prophecy is a vital gift (chapter 14).

The love chapter is very appropriately given between chapters 12 and 14 which deal with gifts and ministrations.

(8) The Resurrection

Some denied the hope of a resurrection of the body, saying that the believer is risen with Christ in a spiritual manner. Chapter 15 is a masterpiece on this magnificent theme.

(9) Donations for the Jerusalem Church

The church at Jerusalem was destitute and Paul solicited help from the various churches throughout his journey. He appealed to the church at Corinth for a contribution (16:1-3).

V. Paul's Visit to Macedonia (20:1-2)—II Corinthians

Luke takes us directly from Ephesus to Macedonia, omitting a stop over at Troas referred to in II Cor. 2:12. Concerning this visit to Macedonia he tells us rather briefly that he went over those parts and gave them much exhortation.

It appears that after Paul sent his first letter to the Corinthians, he not only sent Timothy to Corinth, but also Titus, and that he possibly sent another letter with Titus. His spirit was now troubled with the thought that his criticisms might have been resented. While at Philippi he was greatly relieved at the coming of the brethren with news that his corrections had been well received (II Cor. 2:12ff). The Second Epistle was written in response.

It is not to be expected that Paul would escape all censure for his disciplinary letter to the Corinthians. In fact there remained a formidable block at Corinth set upon repudiating his authority and influence. It had been charged that he was fickle, insincere, and afraid to speak face to face (II Cor. 10:10). Paul explained that he had tarried in coming to them in order to spare them embarrassment. He hoped that Timothy would have all things set in order when he arrived so that all subsequent dealings might be more pleasant (I Cor. 4:17; Acts 19:22; II Cor. 1:23-24).

Paul approved of the action taken in the case of the incestuous person and favored his restoration (I Cor. 5:1; II Cor. 2:5-11). He rejoiced because the whole church had been led to godly sorrow (II Cor. 7).

Paul's second letter implies that some had challenged his authority as an apostle of the Lord. To this he offered a fourfold basis of evidence:

1. The Corinthian Christians were a great evidence (3:1-6)

2. The purity of his interest was shown by his patience and benevolent labors (3:5, 10, 14).

3. His ministry had been attended by apostolic signs (12:12).

4. The responsibilities of an apostle devolved upon him (11:28).

In Paul's first letter he had solicited financial help for the needy Jerusalem Christians (I Cor. 16:1-3). In the second letter he speaks more fully of the principles and spirit of true Christian giving. He refers to the liberality of the Macedonian churches as an example for emulation (II Cor. 8:1-16). He cites the supreme example of Christ (II Cor. 8:9). He had instructed Titus to communicate this grace of giving to the Corinthian believers (II Cor. 8:6, 16).

VI. **Paul's Visit to Greece—The Roman and Galatian Letters** (Acts 20:2; Romans; Galatians)

Luke tells us nothing about this visit except that Paul abode there about three months. The implication is obvious, however, that something of importance occupied him, else he would have moved on. It is very nearly certain that Paul wrote the letter to the Romans from Corinth at this time. It is possible that his letter to the Galatians was written now, also.

That the Roman letter was written during this three month period is made evident by several observations. The letter appears to have been borne by Phebe of Cenchrea, the port of Corinth (Romans 16:1f). At the time of concluding his letter, Paul was about to start for Jerusalem, after which he expected to go to Rome and Spain (Romans 1:10-13; 15:22ff).

The letter to the Romans is unquestionably Paul's greatest doctrinal masterpiece. In it he rose magestically from the grovelling level of Corinthian factions and personality problems to the universal scope of redemption. His letter began, indeed, upon the low level of humanity's degradation without God, but it arose, stone by stone, by grace, through faith to the level of a walk of fellowship with God in the Spirit. God's universal provision of redemption by justification, sanctification, and by glorification—these are the great strides of the letter.

The letter emphasizes faith as the only basis of acceptance with God, for Jews and Gentiles alike. Yet the letter gives final emphasis to the practical holiness which is the fruit of true faith.

As to the time and place of the Galatian letter, we are not certain. Lightfoot places it in the three-months stay at Corinth (ca. 57 or 58 A. D.). The letter answered to two needs. First, it asserted his claim to apostleship. Against the Judaizers who attempted to make it appear that the Twelve agreed with them against Paul, the Galatian letter answers with facts. Christ had been revealed to him (Gal. 1:15-16). Christ had commissioned him (Gal. 1:16). Peter, James, and John had committed themselves as in agreement with him (Gal. 2:9; cf. Acts 15). The second need which the letter met was a final statement on the relation of faith and law. Faith and not the law was the basis of justification. This was true of the Galatians (Gal. 3:2-3), of Abraham (3:6-9), and of the heathen (3:8). The law had been given on account of transgression (3:19). Its end was to bring men to faith in Christ (3:24, 25).

While this letter thus made it clear that the Mosaic law was temporary and that it was an instrument to bring men to a right relation to God in Christ, it closes with an exaltation of the moral law. The foundation of Christian liberty is love (5:13-14). Obedience to the Spirit is not legalism (5:18), yet there is no risk to righteousness in trusting conduct to the leadership of the Spirit. Its fruit is good (5:22-23).

VII. **Return to Macedonia** (Acts 20:3)

Instead of going directly to Syria, Paul went northward through Macedonia first, evidently to pick up Luke and others who were to accompany him. Observe the reappearance of the pronouns "us" and "we" from hence on to Rome. Passover week was spent at Philippi after which Paul and his companions set their faces toward Jerusalem.

VIII.   Fellowship at Troas (20:6-12)

After five days Troas was reached. The Lord's Supper was observed with the brethren. On the night before Paul left, he preached until midnight, at which time, unhappily, a young man, Eutychus, sitting on the window ledge fell asleep and then fell through the window to the ground. Though apparently dead, Paul restored him. Then, in fond fellowship the company continued breaking bread and talking until daybreak.

IX.   From Troas to Miletus (Acts 20:13-16)

Paul's company went by ship to Assos. Paul preferred, for some reason, to go by foot, and agreed to meet them there. Thence they proceeded to Mitylene, Chios, Samos, Trogyllium, and finally to Miletus. He refrained from stopping at Ephesus because the stop might have made him late in attending the Feast of Pentecost at Jerusalem.

At Miletus the ship stopped long enough to permit Paul to arrange a meeting with the Ephesian elders (bishops). This meeting was one of tender affection combined with a solemn charge. Paul had diligently preached the kingdom of God to them. Now he was to see their face no more. Upon them rested the responsibility to nourish and guard the flock of God. Paul had labored among them without covetousness for three years; other false leaders would arise and like wolves menace the life of the flock. The season of fellowship closed with a scene of prayer upon their knees, and with weeping upon Paul's neck. They accompanied him down to the ship, and one may imagine their affectionate gaze as the ship disappeared out of port.

X.   From Miletus to Tyre (Acts 21:1-3)

Sailing from Miletus they took a straight course for Coos; the following day they made it to Rhodes, and then to Patara. Here they found reservations on a ship which took them to Phenicia. Skirting the north side of Cyprus they went directly to Tyre where they disembarked.

At Tyre they found "disciples." The meeting compares in spirit to the parting at Miletus. Upon leaving, a group, including men, wives, and children, went with them a piece. When out of the city they knelt on the shore and prayed. The ship left and the disciples returned home again.

XI. At Ptolemais and Caesarea (Acts 21:7-14)

Sailing to Ptolemais, they stopped, saluted the brethren, and

stayed with them one day.

Paul's company took its course to Caesarea, where they visited in the home of Philip the evangelist, previously one of the seven deacons at Jerusalem, tarrying there "many days." Philip had four daughters who prophesied. Also, there came to Caesarea one Agabus, a prophet from Judea. He warned Paul of the bonds which awaited him at Jerusalem. Both the companions of Paul and the friends of the city tried to disuade him from going to Jerusalem, but it would have broken his heart to heed them. Considering his cherished purpose of going to Rome and Spain one wonders whether he may not at that time have seen in the prophecy that he would be turned over to the Gentiles (Acts 21:11) the providence by which his goal would be realized. On the other hand, he declared his readiness to die at Jerusalem for the name of the Lord Jesus.

4. Discussion and Review

1. Account for the briefness of Paul's last visit to Antioch.

2. Trace the course of this four year itinerary, noting the element of time.

3. Relate what may be said of Paul's itinerary through Phrygia and Galatia (18:23).

4. How do you account for the presence of followers of John the Baptist at Ephesus? What contribution did Paul make to them?

5. Where did Paul carry on his teaching ministry at Ephesus? Characterize his ministry.

6. Relate the experience of the seven sons of Sceva. What was the effect of their experience in Ephesus?

7. What issue was raised by commercial interests and how did it turn out?

8. Why did Paul leave Ephesus?

9. Give an account of Paul's correspondence with the church at Corinth carried on from Ephesus.

10. Give an account of Paul's correspondence with the church at Corinth carried on from Macedonia (Philippi).

11. Give an account of Paul's correspondence carried on during his three month residence in Greece.

12. Trace Paul's movements and his experiences after he left Greece until he arrived at Jerusalem.

5. Select Memory Passages

I Cor. 2:1-5; I Cor. 13; Romans 5:1-2; Romans 12:1-2; Gal. 5:24; 6:24.

6. Character Review

Identify:

Apollos	Eutychus	Demetrius	Diana
Tyrannus	Sceva	Agabus	Phebe

7. Bibliography

Free, Joseph P. *Archaeology and Bible History.* Chapt. XXVIII. Wheaton: Van Kampen, 1950.
Topics:
1. Archaelogical Light on Paul's Stay at Ephesus (Acts 18:23—21:16), pp 323-325.
2. Paul's Arrest, Trial, Imprisonment at Caesarea, and Voyage to Rome (Acts 21-28), p. 325.
Kuyper, Abraham. *Women of the New Testament.* Grand Rapids: Zondervan.
1. "Mary of Rome," pp. 84-86.
2. "Drusilla," pp. 106-109.
Morgan, G. Campbell. *The Acts of the Apostles.* New York: Fleming H. Revell. pp. 435-482. An exposition of Acts 18:24—21:16.

Chapter 44

WITNESSING IN THE GENTILE WORLD

—At Jerusalem and Caesarea
(58-60 A. D.)

1. Reading Assignment

Acts 21:15—26:32

(Read the Bible first)

2. Study Outline

I. Introduction—A Parallel (Acts 21:12-14)

This lesson finds Paul back again in the scene of his early labors as a Pharisee. He had set his face steadfastly to go to Jerusalem against the continual warning from prophets, prophetesses, and the Holy Spirit that "bonds and afflictions" awaited him there. The pleadings that he refrain from going in the face of this were comparable to the human sympathies by which the disciples had tried to shield Jesus from the cross. Undoubtedly, Paul must have been thinking of that earlier example of unswerving commitment to the program of human redemption. Christ had rebuked Peter sharply for seeking to deter him from faithfully completing His course. Paul turned down his humanistic sympathizers no less abruptly, saying, "What mean ye to weep and break mine heart?" Jesus had come to Jerusalem at the time of the Passover. Paul came at the time of the Feast of Pentecost. In both instances, large crowds represented Judaism and set their seal to the rejection of the Gospel.

458

II. **Paul's Gracious Spirit of Accommodation to the Jews** (Acts 21:15-26)

Coming into Jerusalem in a carriage, Paul's company was gladly received by the brethren. They told the story of God's great work among the Gentiles, and as a token of it presented the gifts which had been accumulated from the churches of Asia Minor, Achaia, and Macedonia. They glorified God together.

Many of the Jews (21:20) who were now assembled at Jerusalem were Pharisees and Zealots who had believed, but were strictly Jewish in their customs. Paul did his utmost, at the suggestion of the Jerusalem brethren, to conform to the customs of these Jews, but as in previous instances conciliation was impossible. Paul had explicitly and consistently maintained that circumcision avails nothing as a means of salvation (Gal. 2:16; 3:11; 5:6; 6:15), but he never taught Jewish Christians to forsake Moses. On the other hand, he had Timothy circumcised, that he might not be offensive to the Jews. He had said, "Was any man called, being circumcised? Let him not become uncircumcised. Hath any been called in uncircumcision? Let him not be circumcised. Circumcision is nothing and uncircumsion is nothing, but the keeping of the commandments of God" (I Cor. 7:18-20).

Paul is sometimes criticized as having made a blunder by assuming a vow. This is argued from the fact that it was while Paul was in the Temple accomplishing the vow that he was apprehended by the persecuting Jews. Upon this it may be remarked:

(1) That Paul showed a good spirit in yielding to the counsel of the Jerusalem elders and their pastor.

(2) The fact that Paul showed this respect for the customs of the Jews undoubtedly had the effect of proving to many Jews that he was not against Moses, although many were too prejudiced to be convinced.

(3) It was clearly understood by Paul and the brethren that this vow was not inconsistent with the decision of the Council of Jerusalem of Acts 15 (21:25).

(4) That Paul was arrested while performing the vow does not mean that he was therefore in error by taking the vow. It doubtless meant the very opposite, for the whole course of affairs was being directed to carry out the divine plan of witnessing to the whole world.

III. **Arrest at Jerusalem**

Among the thousands of Jews celebrating the Feast of Pentecost, those of Asia (21:27) instigated an insurrection against Paul.
One recalls Paul's previous experiences at Lystra, and at Ephesus.
The hatred which had then stirred them to murderous envy now
came again to its boiling point.

The charges made by the instigators were:

1. Paul taught all men everywhere (1) against the people, (2)
   the law, and (3) this place.
2. He brought Greeks into the temple, polluting it.

A typical mob was whipped up. Paul was dragged from the
temple, and the Jews were in the process of beating him when the
Roman centurion came upon the scene.

The centurion assumed from some previous incident that Paul
was a notorious Egyptian gangster leader. His action in putting a
chain upon Paul was therefore in order. He could get no intelligible
charge from the mob so he had Paul taken into the castle. Paul
got the captain's ear, put him at ease as to his identity, and then
received permission to speak to the people.

As Paul arose to address the mob, the scene suddenly became
dramatic with silence. Paul's address was a recital of his life story
featuring against his earlier Phariseeism, his call and commission
from Jesus Christ, and his response as a minister to the Gentiles. A violent outburst from the Jewish mob cut off his speech.
The centurion proceeded to make plans for examining him by thongs
and scourging (possibly the rack). Paul at this point revealed his
Roman citizenship, a fact which made the measures contemplated
illegal. Paul was taken into the castle for the night.

On the day following the chief captain convened the Jewish
Sanhedrin council, set Paul before them, and sought to get an intelligible statement of the charge by them against him. At his first
opportunity Paul declared his sincerity, that he had lived "with
all good conscience before God to this day." Luke's expression,
"earnestly beholding the council," reveals the deep desire of Paul
in behalf of his brethren. If he could only convince them of the
truth of the gospel he would be happy. But the very opposite effect was created. His mouth was stopped at the command of the
high priest.

Paul's reaction to the rude act of the high priest was quick and what he said was all too true. The chief priest was a "whited wall" and God would judge him. Also, Paul described his inconsistency correctly. His apology, upon being informed that he had been speaking of the high priest, was a gracious gesture accompanying the sword thrust of truth which he had dealt his chief accuser.

Paul understood the actual disunity of the council and very tactfully set the members to disputing among themselves. By definitely identifying himself as a Pharisee he won the confidence of at least some of the council. But by introducing the subject of the resurrection, in which the Pharisees believed but the Sadducees did not, he actually set his fellow Pharisees to debating his cause. The chief captain, being unable to stop the confusion, took Paul back into the castle.

During the night following, two lines of development took place. God appeared to Paul assuring him of deliverance at Jerusalem and assuring him that he would yet bear witness at Rome. On the other hand, forty Jews took a vow that they would not eat or drink until they had killed him. Paul must have chuckled when he put these two items of news together. In view of the vision there would not be one dead Jew but forty, unless the forty broke their vow.

Upon learning from Paul's nephew of the plot by the Jews, the chief captain removed Paul to Caesarea during the night. Here his case was turned over to Felix the Roman governor over Judea.

IV. Paul's Two-Year Stay at Caesarea (Acts 23:24—26:32)

From this point we see Paul ministering in a rising scale of society. He had been driven from the homes of men and was unable, henceforth, to go from house to house and from city to city. But he was to go from capital to capital and from ruler to ruler witnessing for Christ. Moreover, as a prisoner, he received the greatest courtesy that could be accorded him. At Caesarea he had freedom to interview relatives, friends, and any who sought him out for counsel. He had complete liberty to witness for Christ.

Hearing before Felix (23:34—24:27). The hearing before Felix was a complete moral victory for Paul. Charges were brought against him by a Jerusalem delegation including the high priest Ananias, the elders, and an orator Tertullus. The general character of these charges is remarkably, indicative of the groundlessness of the accusations. There had been repeated insurrections in Judea which Felix had been very vigorous in suppressing. Josephus reports, "The country was again filled with robbers and imposters who deluded the multitudes. Yet did Felix catch and put to death many of those imposters every day." The lawyer, Tertullus, insinuates that Paul is one of these insurrectionists. It will be recalled that the chief captain's first impression was that Paul was some such criminal (21:38).

Since the charges were not supported by proof Paul simply denied them, and left the burden of proof resting upon the accusers. Paul's main object in speaking was very obviously on a higher level; and he left those present thinking about the subject of the resurrection. The meeting was dismissed with the understanding that it would be resumed when Lysias the chief captain who had arrested Paul could be present to testify.

Felix and his wife later met with Paul concerning faith in Christ Jesus. Paul reasoned with them of "righteousness, temperance, and of judgment" until Felix trembled. He dismissed Paul, promising to hear him again at a "convenient season." Luke, however, tells us that what Felix wanted was money as a payment for release. The last that we hear of Felix he had completely relapsed under the control of greed for money and for the favor of his subjects. To please the Jews, who may have paid him well, he left Paul in bonds when he was obliged to turn his office over to Festus.

Hearing Before Festus (Acts 25-26). Festus came to his position with an unprejudiced mind. But the Jews soon brought pressure upon him. They wanted Paul returned to Jerusalem for trial, the intentions of which we may well infer from the previous plot of the forty. If the forty had not died of starvation they were doubtless still seeking Paul's blood. Festus did not yield to this request, although he did propose it to Paul. The trial under Festus was similar to the one conducted under Felix. No charges were proved. Against the proposal of going to Jerusalem for trial Paul appealed for trial to Caesar. This was Paul's right as a Roman citizen and Festus had no choice as to whether to grant it or not. Yet it left him in embarrassment to send a man to Rome without any charge against him.

Before Herod Agrippa II and Bernice (Acts 26). Just as Pilate had sent Jesus before Herod Antipas who was visiting in Jerusalem, so Festus had Paul appear before Herod Agrippa II who was visiting in Caesarea. Like the former Herod, Agrippa was curious and like him he was a diplomat at pleasing the Jews. Agrippa was living incestuously with Bernice, his older sister at the time, and as they appeared together before Paul it was as though **they** were on trial instead of Paul.

Paul was fully at ease so far as his own status was concerned. Having appealed to Rome, the judicial power of both Festus and Agrippa was cancelled. Yet Agrippa's good will, and if possible, his conversion would help to open the door wider for him at Rome.

Paul's address before these rulers was similar to that made before the mob at Jerusalem, except that here Paul gave a definitely evangelistic turn to his appeal. He was so successful that Agrippa confessed to be almost persuaded to become a Christian. Doubtless the pull of sinful Bernice, and the pull of earthly position tipped the beam against receiving Paul's Christ.

At the end of two years it was clearer than ever that there was no charge against Paul. That he should go to Rome was ridiculous. Yet from the viewpoint of God's providence we are in position to understand that step by step Paul was fulfilling his call to be a **witness for Christ** to the Gentiles.

3. Discussion and Review

1. What parallel do you observe in the ministries of Paul and Jesus as Paul approached Jerusalem at this season?

2. How did Paul strive to accommodate himself to the Jews as he came to the Temple? To what criticisms did he put himself liable?

3. What was the source of the uprising against Paul in the Temple? What charges were made by them?

4. Relate the account of Paul's rescue from the mob. What opportunity did Paul seize from the incident?

5. Relate the proceedings at the council which met next day. What is seen as to Paul's sincerity on this occasion? As to his meekness? As to his tactfulness?

6. Describe the plot laid to take Paul's life and explain how it was averted.

7. In view of Paul's vision (23:11) with what humor could he receive the report of the forty fasting Jews? What do you suppose happened to these men?

8. Indicate the rising scale of society into which Paul's labors now took him.

9. Relate the account of Paul's interviews before Felix. What was the final outcome?

10. Relate the account of Festus' proceedings in Paul's case.

11. Why was Festus interested in having Paul appear before Herod Agrippa II?

12. Indicate how Paul made of the trial before Agrippa an opportunity of bearing witness for Christ.

13. What do we know about the personal lives of Agrippa and Bernice which made Paul's witness a terror to them?

14. What was the opinion of these rulers (Festus and Agrippa) as to Paul's case? Why did they not release him? Why was he sent to Rome?

4. Select Memory Passages

Romans 8:28, 35, 37-39

5. Character Review

Identify:

Felix	Lysias	Bernice
Festus	Herod Agrippa II	Tertullus

6. Bibliography

International Standard Bible Encyclopedia.
   Articles:
   1. Felix.
   2. Festus.
   3. Herod Agrippa II.
Kuyper, Abraham. *Women of the New Testament.* Grand Rapids: Zondervan. "Drusilla," pp. 106-109.
Morgan, G. Campbell. *The Acts of the Apostles.* New York: Fleming H. Revell Co. Pp. 482-528. An exposition of Acts 22:17—26:32.

Chapter 45

WITNESSING IN THE GENTILE WORLD

—From Caesarea to Rome
(60-63 . . . . A. D.)

1. Reading Assignment

Acts 27-28
(Read the Bible first)

2. Collateral Reading

Philemon, Colossians, Ephesians, Titus, I and II Timothy.

3. Study Outline

I. Introduction—Rome and Its Emperor

We enter now upon the last stage of Paul's ministry of witnessing to the Gentiles. Jerusalem, Antioch, and Ephesus have passed as centers of the labors of the apostle to the Gentiles. Rome the capitol of the ancient world is now the center of a new perimeter of witnessing.

Rome is situated on the sacred River Tiber, seventeen miles from the sea coast. At that time its population was probably over two millions, half of whom were free citizens and the rest slaves or foreigners. Of the free citizens the upper levels included a few senators, perhaps 10,000 knights who filled most of the offices, and the troops estimated at about 15,000. The Jewish population of the

465

times is estimated to have been 60,000. Rome was a cosmopolitan city, with all nations and all religions represented.

The larger number of free citizens were idle, content to be fed and entertained at the circus. Most of the responsibilities of work were in the hands of slaves and enterprising foreigners. It was common to find skilled physicians, craftsmen, teachers, and others of professional rank among the slaves. The Greeks were the most common in the trades and the arts. It was in this lower and middle level of society that Christianity first flourished.

Nero had been on the imperial throne for about six years when Paul came to Rome. The fortune of anyone falling into his hands was a great uncertainty. He was now only twenty-two years of age, having begun to reign at the age of 16 years. Burrus, the confidential soldier, and Seneca, the philosopher had guided imperial affairs while Nero was a minor, but their influence gave way as the young ruler became conscious of his independence. His real character was expressed by the murder of his mother and other deeds of shameless violence. Burrus died in 62 A. D. Seneca, without Burrus' support, fell into disrepute and was commanded by Nero to commit suicide (65 A. D.). In 64 A. D. Rome was burned. Though Nero himself is suspected as the doer of this deed, it was charged by him to the Christians, against whom he accordingly instigated a terrible persecution which remained in effect as long as he lived. In 68 A. D. he came to the end of his rope. The senate condemned him to die, and to avert the sentence, he committed suicide.

This, in brief, is the portrait of the ruler to whose judgment Paul had appealed and who doubtless heard his case.

II. Paul's Voyage to Rome (Acts 27:1—28:16)

Paul and other prisoners were placed under the charge of a centurion who commanded Augustus' band and was returning with it to Rome. He was a kind man and especially gracious to Paul. They boarded the freight ship Adramyttium. Paul was accompanied by his friends, Luke and Aristarchus.

Leaving the port at Caesarea, they "touched at **Sidon.**" The winds being contrary, they "sailed under **Cyprus**" (to the right of it), then passed the north of it directly to **Myra** in Lycia. After many days of adverse sailing they came to **Cnidus.** Here the wind made it necessary for them to go either north or south. Going south they passed "under **Crete**" "over against **Salmone**." With great difficulty they managed to come to **Fair Havens**, the port of Lasea in southern Crete.

The season was too late for a continued voyage to be safe procedure, the time being about October 1. Paul advised against the risk. The master of the ship advised going on. The island accommodations were regarded as too limited to accommodate the 276 persons aboard the ship. The decision of the ship's master was followed against the advice of Paul. The intentions were, it appears, to venture to **Phenice** at least. Having put out to sea, the rise of the tempestuous Euroclydon from the northeast suddenly destined them to drive on.

How they kept from being driven into the coast of North Africa, and instead, were able to direct their course in the line of their destination was more than a feat of seamanship. After all was done that anyone knew how to do, they all despaired of hope, except Paul. An angel of God promised him that all persons would be spared though all else would be lost.

On the fourteenth day the shipmen, by sounding, discovered the approach of land. In order not to strike rocks they cast anchor and awaited daylight.

Paul turned out to be the master of ceremonies and procedure. He declared the crisis over and ordered the fourteen-day fast broken. They put out food. Paul thanked God. They "were all of good cheer."

Then they cut loose their anchors, put up the main sail and let her drive, attempting to run it aground at "the place where two seas met." It stuck, but the back end of the ship was broken. They could not return to sea, but they could swim to land.

At an earlier point (Acts 27:30-32) the soldiers had secretly undertaken to engineer an escape for themselves in a life boat, leaving the ship and its occupants to die in the sea. Paul became aware of the plot and frankly warned them that they would not be saved if they proceeded in that manner. Now, again, as all must land, the soldiers "took counsel to kill the prisoners," making sure that none should escape (27:42). The centurion turned aside that counsel because he was unwilling to see Paul killed; he gave orders to swim or otherwise get to land. They did so, and the three points of Paul's prediction were fulfilled: (1) They were wrecked upon an island. (2) The ship was lost. (3) They were all saved. Under God, all 276 owed their lives to Paul.

The island proved to be **Melita** (Malta). The pagans of the island were especially hospitable, building a fire for them against the rain and cold. By miracles, especially by miracles of healing, the power of God was so manifest that the whole island was evangelized. After three months, when the company shipped out for Rome, the natives loaded them with benefits for their voyage.

The voyage was completed on an Alexandrian ship which had wintered on the island. A three day stop was made at **Syracuse**. Then fetching a compass (because of the wind) they came to **Rhegium** where they tarried a day. With a favorable wind they reached **Puteoli** a day later. Here their voyage ended.

Brethren met them at **Puteoli**. We do not know who these brethren were, but an acquaintance was made as Paul ministered to them over one Sabbath. Paul's stay at Puteoli provided time for word of his arrival in Italy to reach the Roman Christians, and to permit them to meet him at **Appii forum.**

Meeting with the Roman brethren at Appii forum Paul "gave thanks and took courage." This was the fulfillment of long anticipation. Doubtless Paul was weary and his chains did not naturally cheer him; but he had every reason to believe that the great purpose of God for his life was being accomplished. He was working under the sovereign plan of God, yet it took the fellowship of brethren to encourage him. Arriving at Rome, the centurion delivered his prisoners to the captain of the guard. Paul was given special quarters. A soldier, chained at his side, kept him.

III. Paul's Two-year Ministry at Rome

Paul proceeded in his ministry at Rome in exactly the same way as had characterized his coming to other centers. He presented the gospel first to the Jews. In this case he had to explain his bonds. There was a similar pattern of response. Paul called the chief Jews together in his house, expounding and testifying to them the kingdom of God, persuading them out of the law and out of the prophets, from morn till night, concerning Jesus. The results were: (1) "Some believed." (2) "Some believed not." With this initial appeal to the Jews, Paul declared that the salvation of God would henceforth be sent to the Gentiles. This is not to be understood as excluding Jews. Rather, during the next two years "he received all that came unto him."

The last two verses of the Acts are a brief but significant record of Paul's two-year ministry at Rome. Note the freedom and the independence with which he ministered. Though a prisoner, he did not accept patronage from Rome for the promotion of the gospel—he dwelt in his own **hired** house. Note the conditions of his work —"no man forbidding him." A simpler, yet more expressive translation, of this expression is "unhindered." What did Luke mean? A prisoner of Rome, chained to a soldier, awaiting trial—and yet unhindered? Yes, **deprived** of many privileges, but unhindered to do the one thing of importance. Yes, unhindered, for it was Paul who said, "I can do all things through Christ which strengtheneth me."

Observe thoughtfully what occupied Paul—preaching and teaching, the specific assignment of the Lord in the Great Commission. Observe also the subject—the kingdom of God and King Christ Jesus. That kingdom which Jesus described as the pearl of great price and which he declared should be preached throughout this age as a witness to all nations was the subject of Paul's ministry to the end of his life. Many rejected it but many entered into it both of Jews and Gentiles. Some were offended because of the teaching and discipline which pertained to that kingdom, but others rejoiced and many of them, as Paul, followed King Lord Jesus at the cost of friends, possessions, and life itself.

IV.   Light upon the Two Years from the Epistles

We have followed Luke to the end of his record. We have further to consider what Paul preached and taught during those years as this is reflected in four letters, the Philippian letter, the Ephesian letter, the Colossian letter, and the letter to Philemon.

The Letter to Philemon. This is a personal letter. Philemon was a member of the church at Colossae and evidently an earnest Christian.

Onesimus was Philemon's slave. He had wronged his master and seems to have run away. Coming in contact with Paul he was converted. He became Paul's helper but Paul considered that he should be returned to his rightful master. The letter was written to secure a kind reception for Onesimus from Philemon. Tychicus,

Paul's co-laborer, was sent with Onesimus. This letter graciously reflects the spirit of Christ in Paul's ministry. It has been a boon to slave emancipation wherever the gospel has been preached.

The letters addressed to the Colossians and the Ephesians were delivered with the letter to Philemon.

The Letter to the Colossians. So far as Luke's record is concerned we know of no visit by Paul to Colossae. Several notices indicate that Paul had not met the Christians there (Col. 1:3-8; 2:1). It was a city of the Lycus valley in Asia, within such radius from Ephesus as to make its evangelization from that center a plausible supposition.

Through Epaphras (1:7; 4:12) Paul had learned of the rise of false teachings at Colossae. Gnosticism with a mixture of Greek and Persian philosophy had undermined the idea of Christ's true deity and his true humanity alike. Jewish Essenism with an enslaving emphasis upon meats, drinks, and holy days, and its neglect of body had exerted a morbid influence upon some. Angel worship had distracted from the true worship of Christ.

The Colossian letter meets these errors by a graphic portrayal of Christ as the very image of the invisible God, the creator of all things, the one in whom dwells all the fulness of the Godhead bodily, and yet the one who indwells believers and is to them the hope of glory. From this sacred union Paul deduces the practical instruction which closes the letter.

The Letter to the Ephesians. It is evident that this was intended as a general letter. The extensive outreach of Paul's ministry at Ephesus would require such a letter. The letter is nearly free from personal details. No special heresy called for the letter and it is free from polemics. Christ is exalted as in the Colossian letter, with special emphasis upon the nature of Christ's relationship to the Church. The letter closes with the figure of the Christian's panoply, drawn very probably from the constant presence before Paul of the soldier to whom he was constantly chained.

The Letter to the Philippians. The statement of Phil. 4:22 indicates the fact that this letter was one of the four written from Rome. Reference to the praetorian guard in 1:13 (R. V.) implies the same.

Epaphroditus had come from Philippi with gifts from the church for Paul (4:10-19). He later became sick, which fact worried the Philippians (2:26-30). Having recovered, he was now returning to the Philippians (2:25) and was to bear the letter to them.

The theme of the letter is on the highest plane. The earnestness of Paul in behalf of the gospel, the humility and consecration enjoined, the zeal for righteousness, and the gracious spirit of the letter combine to reflect the mind of the Lord Jesus Christ. Paul is joyful, and he, though in bonds, admonishes the Philippians to rejoice continually.

V. The Last Years of Paul

There are various Scriptures which point to a continuation of Paul's ministry after the abrupt unexplained ending of Acts 28. It is not certain that he was tried at all; perhaps the absence of a charge eventually led to the dismissal of his case.

When Paul had been in Corinth he expressed the purpose of going to Rome and to Spain (Rom. 15:24); but whether he still planned to go to Spain in view of developments in the subsequent years we do not know. Clement of Rome tells of Paul's trip to the limit of the west. A legend says that he went to Britain. Some have supposed that he was in the far west during the time of Nero's persecution of Christians in Rome in 64 A. D. In his letter to the Philippians (1:26) and to Philemon (22) he spoke of his intentions to come to them soon which was about 62 or 63 A. D.

The Letter to Titus. On his way east Paul left Titus at Crete (Titus 1:5). After a time of labor there he moved northwest. Writing back from Nicopolis Paul expressed a concern for the Cretan Church. He urged the appointment of leaders to shepherd the people and to correct the existing evils. He spoke of sending Artemas or Tychicus to Crete and desired that Titus should come to him at Nicopolis (3:12). Others mentioned as ministering in Crete were Zenas and Apollos (3:13). Thus, the letter to Titus indicates a considerable development in the church of Crete.

The First Letter to Timothy. Paul had left Timothy in charge of the church at Ephesus while he himself went on into Macedonia (I Tim. 1:1-3). He wrote back to offer needed counsel to the young pastor. The letter warns against false teachers, enjoins holy living, and sets forth both negative and positive standards for church leaders.

Paul's Arrest. The burning of Rome in 64 A. D. and the persecution instituted by Nero thereafter marked the beginning of a new but darker day for Christians in the empire. Henceforth, it became a crime to be a Christian. Such a thing as Christians appealing to Caesar was a thing of the past. Christians were hunted down, caught, and, very commonly burned or cast to the lions in the amphitheatre. Under these conditions, it is supposed that Paul was arrested in Macedonia and taken to Rome.

The Second Letter to Timothy. Our sole source of Biblical information of Paul's last imprisonment is found in his second letter from Rome to Timothy. It appears that he had two trials (II Tim. 4:16f). At the first he escaped condemnation and the mouth of the lion. In this narrow escape the Lord had stood with him although no other friends did. Moreover, he would be with him, he believed, and preserve him "unto his heavenly kingdom" (II Tim. 4:18).

Tradition has it that when Paul was brought to his final trial, at which a large number of men attended, he made a bold statement of the gospel, but found no disposition to reason in the crazed mind of Nero. He was beheaded as a Roman citizen on the Ostian Road just outside of Rome. His friends carried his headless corpse to the catacombs (subterranean vaults below Rome).

What shall be Paul's epitaph? We might well select it from his own words: "O death, where is thy sting? O grave, where is thy victory?" "Death is swallowed up in victory."

4. Discussion and Review

1. What were the four successive centers of Paul's ministry?

2. Give a general characterization of the city of Rome at that time.

3. Give a brief sketch of the life of Nero.

4. Who were Paul's companions on the voyage to Rome? Characterize the centurion in charge of the prisoners.

5. Trace the course of the voyage giving an account of incidents that may be noted. It is suggetsed that for class purposes this question be reported on by a number of persons in relay fashion.

6. Give an account of Paul's two-year ministry at Rome as reported by Luke.

7. What epistles did Paul write during this two-year period? Give a brief account of each of these letters. For class purposes this question may be divided up among members of the class, each person reporting on one letter.

8. Trace the probable whereabouts of Paul after the two-year period which Luke's account ends.

9. What epistles did Paul write during the last years of his life?

10. Give an account of each of these letters.

11. What change of attitude toward the Christians developed in the Roman empire after 64 A. D.? What was the result for Paul?

12. Give the traditional account of Paul's death. Suggest an ideal epitaph for him.

5. Select Memory Passages

Eph. 5:1-2; Phil. 3:14-15; Col. 2:9; I Tim. 6:12; II Tim. 2:3, 4; 4:7, 8.

6. Character Review

Identify:

Nero	Aristarchus	Onesimus	Epaproditus	Zenas
Luke	Philemon	Epaphras	Titus	Apollos

7. Bibliography

Free, Joseph P. *Archaeology and the Bible.* Chap. XXIX. Wheaton: Van Kampen, 1950.
   Topic:
   1. Paul's Release from Prison and Further Travels, pp. 326, 327.
   2. Paul's First Epistle to Timothy and His Epistle to Titus, p. 327.
   3. Paul's Last Epistle—II Timothy; the End of His Life, pp. 329-330.
Morgan, G. Campbell. *The Acts of the Apostles.* New York: Fleming H. Revell. Pp. 528-547. An exposition of Acts 27-28.

Chapter 46

ROLL CALL OF MANY WITNESSES

---

1. Reading Assignment

See Introduction

---

2. Study Outline

I. Introduction

The book of Acts is by no means a complete record of the acts of the apostles. At this point we shall examine the records, fragmentary though they be in many cases, of the work done by Paul's associates and by others who labored outside the orbit of the great apostle to the Gentiles.

A word should be said regarding sources. First place is always to be given to the Scriptures. Here we are on solid ground. Beyond the canonical Scriptures, however, there are the apocryphal writings, which though not reliable throughout, are not to be cast aside indiscriminately. Regarding the fabulous elements in these writings Blaikie speaks of martyrdom, saying, "The age was one when martyrdom was regarded with such superstition and idolatrous veneration that anyone who did not die in this way was hardly counted a proper saint." The most trustworthy of ancient writers, Blaikie believes, mention only two Jameses, Peter, and Paul as martyrs among the apostles.

The study of this chapter will make the most of what Biblical sources there are, but it will also make reference to apocryphal and

474

traditional writings. The reader will always make due allowance for the apocryphal character of the latter.

In connection with the lives of Peter and Jude it is desirable that the student should read the two letters of Peter and the letter of Jude.

II. Paul's Companions

The success of Paul's work in uniting the early church was due in no small part to his ability in attracting true friends and of associating with himself trustworthy persons representative of the various churches. When he left Macedonia headed for Jerusalem in 58 A. D. it is of interest to note that besides Luke there was with him a company of seven men. While a prisoner of Caesarea and at Rome he was constantly surrounded by associates. At Rome he made the most of these associates. They assisted in his correspondence, delivered his messages, went on errands and otherwise shared his load. Some of the persons mentioned in his correspondence from Rome included Tychicus, Timothy, Epaphroditus, Epaphras, Onesimus, Luke, Demas, Crescens, Titus, John Mark, Erastus, Trophimus, Eubulus, Pudens, Linus, and Claudia.

Luke was at Rome immediately before Paul's death (II Tim. 4:11) being the only trusted friend to remain with him. Doubtless his skill as a physician meant much to the physical comfort of Paul. Also, he was invaluable as a historian. His accuracy and his capacity for details is seen both in his Gospel and in the Acts.

Timothy had been left at Ephesus when Paul was arrested in Macedonia and taken to Rome. Paul in his second letter appeals pleadingly for him to come to Rome (II Tim. 4). It is probable that he complied with this request, but information is wanting on the question. At one time he was a prisoner (Hebrews 12:23), and according to tradition he suffered martyrdom under Domitian (81-96 A. D.).

Silas (Silvanus), at first a companion of Paul, was later associated with Peter and was the bearer of his letter to the strangers scattered throughout Asia Minor (I Peter 1:2).

John Mark, whom Paul had declined as an associate in his second missionary journey, was reinstated to Paul's confidence, and became his companion (Col. 4:10). In his last days Paul requested Timothy to bring Mark with him to Rome (II Timothy 4:11). Paul's remark, "he is profitable to me for the ministry," in relation to this request, is a very satisfying insight telling us that Mark made good. To come to Paul under the circumstances was no easy test. Later Mark was associated with Peter to whom he is said to have served in the capacity of a historian and an interpreter. As such he was qualified as the writer of the second Gospel. Tradition has it that he later went to Alexandria where he founded a church and finally suffered martyrdom.

III. Labors of the Other Apostles

Much of the history of the Twelve has been left us on no earthly record. What may be found in the Scriptures and tradition, if fragmentary, serves, however, at least to indicate the troubled times which came for the church. It serves also to indicate that these Twelve were witnesses for Christ to the end.

James, the son of Zebedee, was the first of the twelve apostles to suffer martyrdom. He was put to death by Herod Antipas about 44 A. D. (Acts 12:2). Peter narrowly escaped death at the same time.

James, the Lord's brother, who had been the presiding apostle at Jerusalem (Acts 12:17; Acts 15; Gal. 2:9; Acts 21:7ff.) appears to have continued there after Paul's last visit (58 A. D.). As indicated in an earlier study this James was the author of the "Epistle of James" to the twelve tribes scattered abroad (James 1:1), written probably earlier than any other book of the New Testament. Though not one of the Twelve he is called an apostle (Gal. 1:19). The Bible gives no account of his death.

James is sometimes set against Paul theologically, but not properly so. They were in full agreement at the Jerusalem council (Acts 15), and their writings, fairly interpreted, are not contradictory but complementary.

Peter. At the Jerusalem Council Peter stated as a matter of policy that while Paul was called distinctly as an apostle to the uncircumcision, he was called to preach to the circumcision. Nothing is said of Peter in the book of Acts after this council (49 or 50 A. D.), except as we may infer a visit to Antioch between the council and Paul's second missionary journey (Gal. 2). What was the field of Peter's labors during the remaining eighteen years of Paul's labors?

That Peter founded and was a bishop of the Church of Rome,

and that he spent twenty-five years there, as Roman Catholic teachers have contended, is impossible. He may, as tradition asserts, have been martyred at Rome under Nero at about the same time as Paul was martyred (68 A. D.), although this is not at all conclusive. The tradition is in keeping with the Lord's word to Peter that he should die for his Lord (John 21). Apart from his martyrdom at Rome, the papal claims made for Peter in relation to Rome are fiction which a reasonable study of the ministry of Paul will not permit. Paul wrote his Epistle to the Romans about ten years before 68 A. D. Not once does he mention Peter, either in his salutation or in the body of the letter. It is inconceivable that Paul should have made such an omission either purposely or by oversight. Paul would probably never have planned to go to Rome had Peter already founded a church there (note Rom. 15:20).

There is, however, a more positive view to be taken of the matter than a mere denial that Rome was Peter's field of labor. Peter's letters give us clear evidence that his travels were not to the West but to the East. In the salutation of his first letter Peter addresses himself not to people among whom he has labored, but to "strangers." They are peoples, for the most part, among whom Paul had labored —in Pontus, Galatia, Cappadocia, Asia, and Bithynia. The whole tenor of the letters corresponds to the salutation in this respect. The only personal note is a reference to Paul, whom it is implied, they knew well and loved (II Pet. 3:15ff.). This reference in Peter indicates that Peter wrote after Paul's epistles were written. Since all of Paul's general epistles were written by about 63 A. D. it is probable that Peter wrote sometime after that date. Also in this passage there is revealed on the part of Peter a very gracious respect for the ministry of Paul among these strangers. From 58 to 63 A. D. Paul had been away from these "strangers," yet he was greatly concerned about them, particularly, that they should not go back to Judaism but persevere in the faith of Christ. Was it not a cooperation born of the Spirit of God that Peter should have made good his earlier defections (Gal. 2) by getting back of Paul and letting all these churches know that Paul's teaching and emphasis were right, encouraging all "to grow in grace and in the knowledge of our Lord and Savior Jesus Christ" (II Pet. 3:18). In view of the persecutions which descended upon the Christians everywhere after 64 A. D. these letters were a timely fulfillment of Peter's pledge to feed the sheep of God (John 21).

Peter being a stranger to the Christians addressed, did well to make Silvanus (Silas), Paul's co-laborer, whom they knew and trusted, the bearer of his letter (I Pet. 5:12).

The clear meaning of I Peter 5:13 is that Peter and Silas were engaged in gospel labors in Babylon. How long this period of labor was we do not know. One thing is sure, there were at least eighteen years in which Peter cannot reasonably be assumed to have been in the west, and in which James, not Peter, was the leader at Jerusalem. By process of elimination, Peter must have been laboring in the East; that is just where the only source of information available to us locates him. We know, furthermore, from a vast amount of information that the gospel was carried throughout the countries east of Palestine at an early date.[1]

Regarding Peter's death there is, as noted, the tradition that he died at Rome. It is said that he was crucified, by his own request, with his head downward.

Thomas. The last word we hear of Thomas is that he was present with six others at a fish breakfast with the Lord by the sea of Galilee (John 21). From apocryphal sources he is referred to variously as preaching in Parthia (Persia), Edessa, and in India. Doubtless these records, if not fully reliable, represent something of the activity of this apostle in the far East. He is said to have been martyred in India as a sorcerer.

Andrew. Apocryphal writers point to Scythia as the field of Andrew's work. This took him to the shores of the Black Sea, to Byzantium (Constantinople). It is said that he died upon a cross formed like the letter X.

Bartholomew. Apart from the lists of the Twelve there is no reference to this apostle in the New Testament. Tradition gives as his fields of labor "exterior India" (Arabia), Phrygia and Armenia. One source says he was flayed alive, another that he was put in a sack and cast into the sea.

Philip. Tradition assigns him to Phrygia. The apocryphal writers confuse him with Philip the deacon and evangelist. He is said to have been crucified.

---

[1] A scholarly, though readable and fascinating account of the spread of Christianity through the far east is found in the volume by Reverend John Stewart entitled, *The Nestorian Missionary Enterprise*. T. and T. Clark, Edinburgh, Publishers.

Simon. Egypt, Cyrene, Mauritania, and Britain have been assigned by various traditional sources to Simon. He is said to have been crucified in Britain.

Jude (Thaddeus). Tradition connects Jude with Edessa. Jude was the Lord's brother. Domitian is reported to have learned of the fact that relatives of the line of David still survived, which led him to call two sons of Jude for trial. Their humble manners convinced him that they were no threat to his power.

The Epistle of Jude, written possibly as late as 75 A. D., is a letter of warning against fifth column false teachers, libertines, and antinomians and a powerful though brief appeal to Christians to keep themselves in the love of God.

Matthias. This apostle, chosen by the one hundred and twenty in the place of Judas Iscariot, is assigned by some traditional writers to Ethiopia and by others to Cappadocia. One ancient writer says that he died at Sebastopol near the Temple of the Sun.

John. It is recognized that the records of the life of John rest upon better attested grounds than those of the other apostles. Our last notice of John in the Acts is in chapter eight where he and Peter ministered in Samaria following the evangelistic labors of Philip the evangelist. His native abode was in Galilee and he could have worked from that as a home base. There is good authority indicating that he resided at Ephesus for a long time. It was from Ephesus that he was banished to the isle of Patmos by Emperor Domitian. He returned to Ephesus under Emperor Nerva, and his death took place there at a ripe age under Emperor Trojan.

John's writings were left as the work of his ripest years and they constitute a very significant climax to the Bible. Our final chapter will be devoted to them.

3. Discussion and Review

1. Discuss the sources of information drawn upon in this chapter.

2. List Paul's associates in what you consider to be the order of their importance, so far as our knowledge of their work is concerned.

3. Tell what is known of the work of Luke.

4. Tell what is known of the work of Timothy.

5. Tell what is known of the work of Silas.

6. Tell what is known of the work of Mark.

7. What is the Biblical account of the death of James the son of Zebedee?

8. Tell of the work of James the Lord's brother. How were his writings related to Paul's so far as point of view is concerned?

9. Discuss the ministry of Peter after the Jerusalem council. Show where he ministered. Show that he and Paul built together.

10. From tradition and from the Bible what may be said of the ministry of Jude?

11. Indicate the localities to which tradition assigns Thomas, Andrew, Bartholomew, Peter, Simon, Jude, and Matthias.

12. Indicate, geographically, the extent to which Christ's campaign of witnessing had progressed in the first century.

4. Character Review

Identify:

Tychicus	Erastus	Thomas
Timothy	Trophimus	Andrew
Epaphroditus	Eubulus	Bartholomew
Epaphras	Pudens	Philip
Onesimus	Linus	Simon
Luke	Claudia	Jude
Demas	Silas	Thaddeus
Crescens	James	Matthias
Titus	James	John
John Mark	Simon Peter	

5. Bibliography

International Standard Bible Encyclopedia. Accounts may be found of available facts on any Bible character by consulting the appropriate volumes.

Kuyper, Abraham. Women of the New Testament. Grand Rapids: Zondervan. "Euodias and Syntyche," pp. 110-113.

MacCartney, Clarence E. Trials of Great Men. Chap. XIV, "The Trial of Paul." Nashville: Abingdon-Cokesbury, 1946.

Olson, Bessie G. A Man of Purpose. Des Moines: Boone Publishing Co.

Sangster, Margaret E. The Women of the Bible. Chapt. XLVI, "The Honor Roll of St. Paul." New York: The Christian Herald.

Chapter 47

SHADOW GIVES WAY TO REALITY

(65-70 A. D.)

1. Reading Assignment

Book of Hebrews; I Peter 2; Matthew 24; Luke 21

(Read the Bible first)

2. Study Outline

I. Introduction

Just as Jeremiah and Ezekiel lived in the day when Solomon's temple was destroyed and the holy city was razed to the ground, so the book of Hebrews and other New Testament writings bore witness to eternal spiritual realities while the impending hand of destruction was being raised to desolate the city of Jerusalem in 70 A. D. The Lord had spoken specifically of what would take place. Rejecting the Lord of the Temple, Temple worshipers would find their house left unto them desolate (Matt. 23:38) and the destruction of the house would be terrible (Matt. 24:2).

The Lord had couched significant and far reaching truth in the symbolism of the wine bottles (skins). The old container would have to be discarded, but the precious contents would be transferred to new and appropriate vessels.

Paul demonstrated everywhere that the Law and the Prophets had their great fulfillment in Christ, his church, and his kingdom.

481

While the brethren at Jerusalem were slow to see this, they finally came to it.

II.   Thesis of the Book of Hebrews

It is the burden of the Epistle to the Hebrews to fully wean Hebrew Christians from obsolete Judaism on the one hand and to demonstrate eternal spiritual realities on the other hand.   In other words, it draws our focus from shadows or pictures of reality to reality itself.

Who wrote this epistle is, for our present concern, unimportant. It was probably written during the last two or three years prior to the fall of Jerusalem in 70 A. D.   A brief consideration of the contents will make obvious the fact that it was a perfect preparation of the Jewish minded Christians in view of the impending destruction of the holy city.

The opening verses (1-3) in chapter one are a brief epitomy of the whole letter.   The letter does not set aside the past in order to establish the new.   Rather, it sets forth the progressive self-revelation of God through creation, providence, and redemption.

An Epitomy of Special Divine Revelation

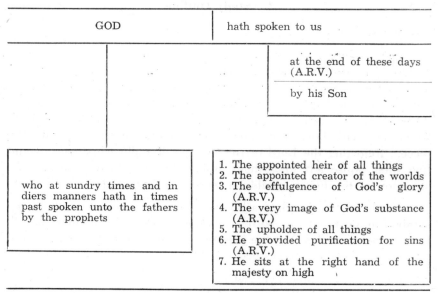

Figure 34

III. The Supremacy of the Son

Having in the three opening verses introduced us to the Son, the letter proceeds, step by step, to portray him in relation to lesser persons and things. The introduction (1:1-3) embodies the fact that the glory of the Son is greater than the glory of the prophets. In 1:4—2:18 the letter represents the incarnate Son as superior to and far more efficacious for the need of man than the angels. In chapters 3-4 the letter reasons of the superiority of the Son over Moses. By way of digression the author warns that Christians should not fail to lose their inheritance in Christ as the Israelites failed to enter into Canaan rest under Moses. In chapters 5-7 is shown the superiority of Christ's priesthood over that of the Levitical priests. Theirs was temporary and typical. Christ's is limitless and real. Like that of Melchizedek, it is not limited by genealogy. It was effective before the choice of the Levites was made. Their function has ceased. Christ is a priest forever.

A New Ministry. In 8:1 to 10:18 the letter leads logically from the fact of an eternal unchanging Priest to a new covenant and higher ministry. There is a different covenant victim, the Son himself, which displaces the ancient Burnt Offering. There is a new blood of sprinkling which is the true cleansing from sin (9:21, 22). In Christ's ascension to heaven there is a new ministry of prayer and intercession. This ministry Jesus demonstrated even while with the disciples (John 17).

The Miniature and the Real Redemptive Pattern. The Old Testament pattern is significantly extended to both personal and universal proportions in 9:24-28. Christ's three appearances are pictured as fulfilling the ministry of the high priest on the Day of Atonement. His atonement on the Cross, corresponding to the sacrifice of a goat upon the brazen altar, has been the one and only sacrifice acceptable to God for sin and it need never be repeated. The second appearance of the Son is at the right hand of the authority on high (1:3) "for us," corresponding to the annual intercessory prayer of the high priest and his application of the blood of the victim before the throne of mercy for the sins of the people. The third appearance of the Son is that which is still future, when he will come back, not to die, but to execute salvation in behalf of all who "look for him," corresponding to the emergence of the high priest from the tabernacle door to pronounce blessing and benediction upon the waiting people.

The Unchanging Way of Faith. Beginning with 10:19, the letter expects us to view all things from the new and larger perspective which has been set forth. Chapter 11 spans all human history and demonstrates by examples that the life of faith has ever been the source and the essence of godly living. This chapter should lift us above a merely dispensational view of grace and righteousness. In 12:1ff. the letter directs us for inspiration to these examples. They testify to us of the fact that faith is the unchanging connection between man and God. Yet, though these witnesses testify to us, they are not the source of our faith. That must be centered in Jesus— he is the author and finisher of our faith. We must look to him without ceasing.

The Holy Life of Faith. Having rightly grounded our faith in the eternal unchanging Son of God, the letter proceeds to an appropriate exhortation to holy living (chapters 12-13). Looking unto Jesus in faith, we are to "follow peace with all men, and holiness (the sanctification, A. R. V.), without which no man shall see the Lord" (12:14).

IV. Peter's Confirmation of Paul's Gospel

The apostle Peter had no different gospel from that of Paul and the Hebrew letter. The second chapter of this first letter, particularly, deserves notice. The Christian, by virtue of being born again, is the member of a spiritual house. He is called to exercise "a holy priesthood" offering up, not animals, but "spiritual sacrifices" acceptable to God by Christ Jesus." What had been said particularly of God's people, when freshly called out of Egypt (Deut. 10:15), Peter now said was the relation of Christians by faith in Christ— they are a chosen generation, a royal priesthood, a peculiar people (people for God's own possession, A. R. V.). Just as God had called the Israelites out of Egypt to be a praise to his name in the world, so Christians are called "to show forth the praises (excellencies)" of the One who called them "out of darkness into this marvelous light."

Thus it is clear that the people of God are such by faith and not by virtue of race nor of dispensation. Peter and Paul both anchor us in the eternal Son of God and join us in fellowship with God's people of all climes and times. God is pictured as Master Architect, and one day his building, composed of spiritual human lives, will be completed and sanctified as an eternal temple of the Lord.

Peter wrote appropriately, also, of the role of Christians in this present world. In contrast to the liberal Jews who resigned themselves to the course of life current in Hellenism, and contrary also to the Jewish Zealots who held out for nothing less than a return of Jewish national autonomy, Peter counseled Christians to recognize their role as being that of "strangers (sojourners, A. R. V.) and pilgrims" (I Pet. 3:11) in the present world order.

V. **The Destruction of Jerusalem in 70 A. D.**

Pilate had asked of the Jews, "Shall I crucify your King?" In their hatred of Christ, they renounced him as their king, and for the sake of expediency professed, "We have no king but Caesar" (John 19:15). The time had now come for those words to be fulfilled. During the thirty-seven years which had passed since they crucified their promised Messiah their necks grew more and more rebellious. Though Christ rose again from the dead, and though he sent the Holy Spirit to plead with their resisting hearts, they clung to their hypocritical leadership at the temple which was called by the name of the Lord, and they did so against all fact and reason.

During the last year of Nero's reign the Jews of Judea galled grievously under the Roman yoke. The Roman governors who succeeded Festus were not inclined to pamper their subjects. Massacres of the people were enacted in various quarters. Revolting against this harshness, the Jews attracted Nero's attention. About the time of Paul's martyrdom Nero sent his ablest general, Vespasian, to quell the revolt. Upon the death of Nero, Vespasian, who had subdued Galilee and now advanced toward Jerusalem, was proclaimed emperor by the army. He returned to Rome, and left the mission against the Jews to be carried out by his son Titus.

It is generally agreed that Christians for the most part had abandoned Jerusalem. Persecution had driven them out. Moreover, they had been warned of the Lord of the fate which was before the city. This means that Jerusalem was occupied largely by such as had spurned the word of the Lord.

Jerusalem was in the hands of the high priest Ananus who represented the Pharisees. Against him were pitted the Zealots, a minority party. The first was the conservative and peace loving party. The Zealots were not only rejectors of the Messiah but they were blind patriots, advocating the strictest and fiercest resistance against Roman rule. In those two parties were represented two Jewish philosophies. The first recognized in the heathen control of the Holy Land the working of God's providence, even though this seemed to contradict his professed choice of the Hebrews as his own people. This philosophy did not set aside all reasonable measures for securing freedom, yet it saw in the domination of the Gentiles something which, in God's permitted degree, was inevitable. The other philosophy was that of an idealism inspired by devotion to absolute freedom and by a zeal which would recognize no sovereignty under God's. The Zealots pressed the theocratic ideal of the Pharisees to its extremest consequences.

The encircling armies of Vespasian and Titus, victorious wherever they had gone, served the purpose, at first, not of unifying the Judean Jews, but of intensifying the clash of their ideologies. In this clash, however, it is only too evident that the blindness described by Isaiah and attributed to them by the Lord and by Paul was upon them. No idealogy, however zealously it is held, makes either sense or virtue if it is held within the general framework of actual rebellion against God.

Titus, instead of hastening to take Jerusalem, retired to Caesarea and waited. He knew that the Jews were destroying themselves with dissension, and that he needed only to wait until they spent their strength to accomplish his purpose. The clash between the Ananus and the Zealot parties became more involved. One John of Giscala, previously the political foe of Josephus in Galilee, professed to ally himself with the party of Ananus, was admitted to its counsels and given important missions; all the while he was secretly conferring with the Zealots. At an appropriate time he cast off his mask and identified himself with the Zealots.

John warned the Zealots that they were certainly destined to defeat by the Ananus party. With this appeal to fear he urged them to seek outside help. Messengers were sent to the Idumeans (Edomites) asking for help. Not inquiring what the issues were, the Idumeans promptly mustered 20,000 troops, ready to be the ally of any Jerusalem faction that would invite them. They had the supposition, evidently, that Jerusalem was in immediate need of defense against their common Roman foe. Arriving at Jerusalem amidst awful rain and storm they found the city shut to them. In the excitement of the storm the Zealots overruled Ananus and threw open the city gates. Villainy usurped supremacy in the holy city. Daylight revealed the slaughter of 8500 persons, whose corpses covered the temple area.

The forces of the Zealots came to be divided under the leadership of John of Giscala and Simon of Gioras who had been the leader of a ruffian band of robbers in Judea. John's faction then also fell into two parts, the dissenting wing following one Eleazar, an ambitious leader who could not bear the bigotry of John. Thus there was the spectacle of three hostile factions of Jerusalem Jews carrying on civil war within the Temple itself. Eleazar was in the Holy of Holies executing an attack upon John in the court immediately below. John, while resisting the attack from above, was trying to attack Simon on the ground below, who in turn was trying to fight both of them. All the while, worshipers from far and near were trying to carry on their sacrifices, doing so at the hazard of their lives. Says Mears, "Madness ruled in the doomed city, and a large part of the work of their enemies was done by the infatuated citizens themselves." Titus himself is reported to have declared that apart from this internal dissension Jerusalem could not have been taken.

The last Passover ever held in Jerusalem was held just as the siege of the city began. Many strangers were gathered in the city. Their worship must have involved a strange intermingling of sentiments as they contemplated God's marvelous deliverance of the nation from Egyptian bondage, and then suffered distraction by the battling factions quartered in the temple. They looked about and saw blood-spattered walls and the dead bodies. They heard the shrieks of the wounded and dying. Looking down over the suburbs of the city they saw the Roman legions.

When Titus finally began operations expediency drove the factions to recognize their common need. Expediency now required what God's good law would have secured. Yet theirs was not a unity to be honored with divine blessing. By a matter of survival of the strongest tyrant their unity had its leadership. The Temple was under control of John the Zealot and the city was under the beastly ruffian Simon of Gioras. Neither of these was a man of faith. The leadership of robber gang leaders, of Zealots, and of assassins had taken the place of ordained men of God.

The siege began at the time of the Passover, April 15, 70 A. D. and continued until August 5 of the same year. It had been the constant policy of Titus to effect the surrender of the city with a minimum loss of life and the least destruction of the city. Nevertheless he operated on a tremendous scale in taking the city. In order to build forts, to fill in approaches, and to build mounds the landscape for twelve miles around was practically stripped of trees. When at last the walls were sufficiently broken down to make access to the Temple possible, Titus attempted in vain to prevent damage to the holy building. But once the soldiers were inside the city walls the confusion of hand to hand fighting removed his control of what took place. It took only a torch thrown into the Holy of Holies by an unidentified soldier to make of the beautiful palatial Temple a roaring furnace.

Describing the scene which followed, Mears writes:
The air was filled with the vehement sorrow of a whole city deploring its doom. The roar of a mighty conflagration and the fierce shouts of the Roman soldiers added to the tumult, which was echoed back from Olivet and from all the neighboring hills. One after another, the various buildings fell in with a crash. In sheer desperation a band of priests mounted the temple-roof and wrenched off the gilded pinnacles, which they flung upon the heads of the soldiers below.

But all serious attempts at defense had been abandoned. The struggle had become a brutal slaughter of helpless victims. No distinction was made between those who resisted and those who surrendered, between soldiers and unarmed citizens, men and women and children, between priests and people. A crowd of citizens who had given ear to the promises of false prophets, that if they would betake themselves to the temple, God would there provide a miraculous deliverance, were cooped up with the combatants to the number of six thousand, and between the burning cloisters and the daggers of the Romans every one of them came to a miserable end. Ten thousand of the garrison also perished on that memorable night. The leader and a few of his men cut their way through and escaped into the upper city.[1]

---

[1] Mears, John W. *From Exile to Overthrow*, p. 457.

VI. Subsequent History of Palestine

1. After the capture of Jerusalem by Titus the tenth Roman legion was left to govern it.

2. In 132 A. D. certain Palestinian Jews revolted under the leadership of Bar Cochba. For three years insurrection gathered momentum until, in 135 A. D., Emperor Hadrian subdued it by force. In an attempt to extract the last roots of Judaism from Palestine, Hadrian rebuilt the city, naming it Aelia Capitolina. He built a pagan temple to Jupiter on the ancient temple site. The city was made into a Roman colony. Hadrian's city continued as such for more than a century and a half.

3. At the beginning of the fourth century Christianity began to make its claim upon the holy city. Emperor Constantine made Christianity the religion of the empire. His mother, Queen Helena, had visited Palestine because she wanted to identify the scenes of Scripture. Identifying what was considered to be the location of Christ's tomb, a church was built about it (ca. 325 A. D.) which still stands and is known as the Church of the Holy Sepulchre. Many other churches were built in Palestine during the next three centuries.

4. With the passing of the Roman empire in the fifth century Palestine was left an easy prey to anyone who cared to occupy it. For thirteen years 615-628 A. D.) the Persians held it.

5. During the next eight years it was taken over and held by by Byzantine kings of the Eastern Roman Empire (628-636 A. D.).

6. From 636 to 1099 A. D. Palestine was under the rule of the Mohammedans. The center of rule at different times was Medina, Damascus, and Bagdad.

7. Moved by the cruelties of the Mohammedan Seljuk Turks toward the Christians of the Holy Land, crusades were organized in their behalf by the Christians of Europe. The crusaders set up the Latin Kingdom of Jerusalem which continued for 89 years (1099-1188 A. D.).

8. After the fall of the Latin Kingdom of Jerusalem, Palestine was again destined to come under the custody of Mohammedans. From 1188 to 1517 A. D. the center of control was Egypt. From 1517 to 1917 Turkey was the source of control.

9. In 1917 the allies of World War I liberated Palestine from the long and ignominious misrule of the Ottoman Turks. General Allenby accomplished this historic feat without the need of firing a

shot in the holy city. Under the Mandate of the Balfour Declaration, administered by Great Britain, the Holy Land was again opened up as the home of the Jews. Jews have returned from all parts of the earth, and numerous colonies have been founded. It is estimated that more than a half million Jews are now in Palestine. Tel Aviv has developed a population of more than 150,000.

10. The logical sequel to what was accomplished since 1917 took place May 14, 1948 when the State of Israel came into being. It is still too early to calculate the extent of the significance of this new state. Certainly it has not yet taken on the proportions, nor the character, of the Messianic kingdom. But just as certainly, we may believe, it is a token of the fact that Palestine belongs to God and that he has a continued purpose for it. The covenant of God, made with Abraham, specifically includes a special eternal destiny for Palestine. Doubtless that purpose is something greater and more glorious than anything known to past history. It remains for us in a final chapter to trace the course of redemption to the final establishment of the New Jerusalem which shall not pass away.

3. Discussion and Review

1. Compare the situation in Jerusalem in 586 B. C. with the situation in 70 A. D.

2. What do you understand by the Lord's figure in Matt. 9:18?

3. Show from a brief analysis of the contents of the book of Hebrews that it was an important preparation of Jewish Christians for the destruction of Jerusalem.

4. Show from Peter's Epistles that he preached the same gospel as did Paul.

5. According to Peter's letter, what is the appropriate relationship of Christians to this present world?

6. Show that the Jerusalem Jews, who had said, "We have no king but Caesar," were finally obliged to "eat their words."

7. What happened to Jewish relations with the Roman government after the rule of Festus?

8. Where were the Jerusalem Christians in 70 A. D.?

9. Characterize the two Jewish parties prevailing in Jerusalem and relate their history during the last year of the city's existence. Describe the last Feast of Passover.

10. Is patriotism always a virtue?

11. Name, identify, and characterize the two men who were in charge of Jerusalem when the siege began. Were they patriots?

12. Give an account of the taking of Jerusalem by Titus.

13. Trace the political fortunes of Jerusalem from 70 A. D. to 1948 A. D.

14. What does the future hold for this city?

4. Select Memory Passages

Hebrews 9:23-28; I Peter 2:9; Matthew 23:37-39; 24:1-2

5. Bibliography

Dale, R. W. *The Jewish Temple and the Christian Church.* London: Hodder and Stoughton.

Mears, John W. *From Exile to Overthrow.* Chap. XXX to end. Philadelphia: Presbyterian Board of Publication.

Morgan, G. Campbell. *Living Messages of the Books of the Bible.* Vol. II. "The Message of Hebrews." New York: Fleming H. Revell Co. Pp. 107-121.

Chapter 48

WRITINGS OF JOHN—
THE CAPSTONE OF SCRIPTURE

(90-100 A. D.)

---

1. Reading Assignment
The Gospel by John; I, II, and III John; The Revelation
(Read the Bible first)

---

2. Study Outline

I. Introduction

Sixty years after Christ's ascension and more than a score of years after the other apostles had died, the apostle John gave to the church his Gospel account, his Epistles, and the book of Revelation. These writings met three distinct needs peculiar to the church at the close of the apostolic century. His **Gospel** account provides a well drawn case calculated to lead a reader of post-apostolic times to faith in Jesus as the Christ, the Son of God. The **Epistles** set forth essential standards for the fellowship of those who believe. The **Revelation** met the immediate need of satisfying those whose expectation of a speedy return of Christ had been disappointed; also, it served the further and more general purpose of connecting the earlier, intermediate, and the final phases of the Creator's redemptive program.

II. John's Gospel Account—The Case for Faith

John's gospel is presented as a case which may be expected, he

492

avers, to lead to a specific result—the Christian faith. He carefully lays the basis for this result by marshaling selected facts regarding Jesus. He gives seven portraits of Jesus at work, which he desig-

THE SEVEN SIGNS

Figure 35

Office	Human Need	Jesus' Command	Physical Result	Spiritual Result
1. Jesus the C R E A- T O R (2:1-12)	"They have no wine,"	"Fill, Draw, Bear."	Perfect wine	"Manifested forth his glory; His disciples believed."
2. Jesus the HEALER (4:43-54)	The nobleman's son near death	"Go thy way, thy son liveth."	Report: "Thy son liveth."	The nobleman and his whole house believed.
3. Jesus the HEALER (5:1-16)	Multitude of blind, halt folks, special 38-year case	"Rise, take up thy bed and walk."	"The man was made whole, took up his bed, and walked."	The Jews sought to kill him; 1. For Sabbath breaking 2. His claim to be God's Son.
4. Jesus the S U S- TAINER (6:1-14)	Food for 5000 men	Make the men sit down.	"They were all filled."	Men said: "This is that prophet." They seek to make him their king.
5. Jesus the SOVER- EIGN (6:15-18)	Storm at sea, Fearful disciples	"It is I, be not afraid."	"Immediate- ly the ship was at land."	"They **willingly** received him into their ship."
6. Jesus the L I G H T OF THE WORLD (9:1-41)	A man born blind	"Go and wash."	"He went . . . . washed . . . . came seeing"	1. The neighbors were curious. 2. Parents disclaimed responsi- bility. 3. Pharisees disbelieved report; regarded Jesus as a sinner. 4. The healed man believed and worshipped.
7. Jesus the HOPE OF LIFE (11:1-57)	Lazarus, a loved one was dead.	"Take away the stone . . . . Laz- arus, come forth . . . . Loose him and let him go."	"He that was dead came forth."	1. Many Jews believed on Him (11:45). 2. Some went to the Pharisees (11:46). 3. Many Jews came to see Laz- arus (12:9). 4. Chief priests plotted his death (12:10). 5. This sign inspired the Tri- umphal Entry (12:17). 6. Pharisees' admission: "Ye prevail nothing . . . . the world is gone after him" (12:19).

SUMMARY

Whoever Jesus was, his works proved him to fulfill the main offices belonging to deity.	Whoever Jesus was, he faced human need with the competence and adequacy, that cause all eyes to be turned toward him for salvation and hope.	Whoever Jesus was, his word had the power of Him who spoke the worlds into being.	Whoever Jesus was, his deeds were of such redemptive character as to constitute him, when the time is at hand, the one who is to "make all things new."	Whoever Jesus was, what he did made observers conscious of "glory," induced many to believe in him, induced the hatred and envy of religious pretenders, and gained for him the unanimous acknowledgement, though not the permanent allegiance of the masses of Judea. Even his enemies acknowledged the reality of the signs which he performed. The important fact is that he established his claims. That he was the Light was made clear to all. What men did about the light threw people into one of two classes, believers or rejectors. Jesus' teaching program accomplished its greatest success in the incident of greatest earthly loss. No event but the Cross could exhibit the exhaustlessness of the divine love. The Cross exhibited man at his worst, but God at his best. Such an exhibition is the most powerful point that a teacher of religion can effect. It is calculated to draw all men to God. Thus Satan's lie regarding God's character was given its full antidote.

nates as signs. "These" he says, "are written that ye might believe that Jesus is the Christ, the Son of God, and that believing ye might have life through his name." The analysis of these signs (see figure 35) discloses a consistent teaching function comparable to that which our analysis of Exodus revealed. In each case the Creator is seen laboring to so reveal himself as to be known and trusted by men.

Besides the portraits of our Lord afforded by these faith-producing signs, John passes on to those who should read, a word portrait of the heart to heart conference of Jesus with his own which took place around the table of the upper room. That discourse was calculated to effectively inspire the faith of believers in their mission for Christ in the world. First, they were fortified against earthly trouble by the assurance that a heavenly home was in preparation for them (chap. 14). Then they were instructed as to the means by which they might produce the fruit of love and thus be true disciples in the world (chap. 15). They were instructed regarding the future teaching ministry of the Holy Spirit in their lives (chap. 16). Finally, in the prayer which John records, there is indicated Christ's concern for the spiritual unity of believers to the end that the world may believe that the Father sent his son into the world, and that the world may know of his love (chap. 17), especially verses 21-23). Thus, from the viewpoint of the signs and of the discourses alike, John gives to the generations who could not see, but must read of Jesus, the facts which serve as the basis of a full orbed Christian faith.

III. The Epistles of John—Who Is a Christian?

John's epistles, as his gospel account, were peculiarly adapted to the times ahead. The question of those times would not only be, "Who is Jesus?" but also, "Who is a Christian?" The epistles are devoted to the answer of this question. Without attempting a minute study of the text, several tests of genuine Christianity may be noted. First is the **test of fellowship** on the part of those who personally witness the presence of Jesus Christ or who have this witness borne to them, and who walk in the light of the truth revealed (I John 1:1-10). **Obedience** to Christ's word is a test (2:1-5). **Love** for others is a test (2:7-11; 4:7-20); love for the world is a negative test (2:15-17). **Confessing Jesus** as the Christ is a test (2:18-28; 4:1-6). **Righteousness** as the habit of life is a test (2:29; 3:7-10). These things are written, John says, for the sake of enabling Christians to know that they are Christians and to realize their privileges as such (1:3; 5:13-15).

In the second letter John continues to draw the line between true and false profession. The hospitable lady addressed is commended for charity extended to believers, but is advised against false teachers who denied Christ and deceitfully took advantage of her Christian hospitality.

In the third letter John also applies tests of genuineness. Three persons are involved. Gaius is commended both for holding the truth and for doing good. Diotrephes is rebuked and judged by the principle: "He that doeth evil hath not seen God" (verse 11). Demetrius is approved because of (1) the esteem of his fellowmen, and (2) because he held the truth.

Thus in the epistles John gives the essential criteria for a genuine and an intelligent church fellowship. Truth and the life of love are to be preeminent in the church, and men belong or do not belong according to these standards.

IV. The Book of Revelation—The Culmination of History

The Bible would be incomplete as the Creator's masterpiece of instruction without the Apocalypse of John. It is the revelation of the ascended Christ to Christians who, during successive generations, must live in an evil world. Christ had given the early Church the substance of this revelation in the Olivet discourse (Matt. 24, 25; Luke 21). In the Apocalypse, however, the veil is further lifted, disclosing the throne of God and the kingly glory of that one for whose kingdom they were praying and serving. Abram's vision of a city with foundations could mean a great deal more, now that there was associated with it one who truly represented the human race. The Son of God was now also the captain of man's salvation (cf. Hebrews 1) and before him all heaven bowed. The city of Abraham now had incorporated in it those redeemed men and women who in human history believed and served God. Yet, its structure in John's time was not completed. The home was being prepared (cf. John 14). The temple was being built (I Pet. 2; Rev. 11:19). Representatives were being gathered from the nations (Acts 15:14; Rom. 11; Matt. 24:14). The king's bride, i. e., the church, was being prepared (Eph. 5). The work of Satan and his followers in the world was in the meantime ripening for final judgment. All of these lines of development are seen to come to a climax, with God's eternal kingdom triumphant.

The book has three distinct divisions. The first (chapter 1) is a portrait of Jesus in the midst of the seven candlesticks (the seven churches) issuing to John a command to write an account of the things seen, past, present, and future. The second part (chapters 2-3) contains messages from Christ to each of seven churches: Ephesus, Smyrna, Pergamos, Thyatira, Sardis, Philadelphia, and Laodicea. The third part (chapters 4-22) gives the panorama, from John's viewpoint, of future historic events. The vision begins with the throne of God whence all human history has its supervision. The unsealing of God's decrees, which is the work of the ascended Christ, issues in a course of history parallel to that previously pictured by the Lord in the Olivet discourse. Conquest, war, famine, death, the persecution of the Church on earth and the appearance of the souls of the martyrs in heaven—these are the issues which follow the opening of the seals.

Human history is seen to culminate, like the culmination of the antediluvian age, in simultaneous divine acts of judgment upon the impenitent and of deliverance for the people of God.

The climax of the present age includes the dissolution of historic institutions. These, in latter times, are seen to be unified under the significant title of Babylon, and are represented by the leadership of a beast and a false prophet. The dissolution of Babylon is followed by the "first resurrection" and the establishment upon earth of the dominion of Christ and his resurrected and tested followers. Christ's dominion, which is described as of 1000 years duration, involves a further testing of the inhabitants of the earth. It is followed by the final judgment of Satan, the resurrection of the remaining dead and their final judgment. The last two chapters are a description of the new heaven and the new earth.

God's Purpose Realized

In the parlance of a sin cursed world, we have come to speak of some things as profane and others as sacred; some things are regarded as earthly and some things as heavenly. Religions of the East have very commonly identified matter with evil. It was not so in the beginning; it will not be so in the end.

In the closing picture of the Revelation, heaven and earth are joined by the New Jerusalem. This is the heavenly city within which is the throne of God and of the Lamb. Yet from it flows a river, on the banks of which are the trees of life bearing fruits each month of the year. Access to the tree of life is provided through the open gates of the city to all nations. Here is pictured the final and perfect integration of heaven and earth.

The purpose of God in the creation of man was that his desire for fellowship might be satisfied. Man was to be the sort of creature that would know God, share his thoughts and purposes, and be as God over the rest of the creation. God communed with man in Eden. In post-Edenic times God "came unto his own" and his own received him not (generally speaking); those who did receive him became his sons. He ordered Israel to make a tabernacle that he might "dwell among them" (Exodus 25:8).

This Tabernacle had its anti-type in the incarnation of the Son of God who became flesh and "dwelt (tabernacled) among us" (John

1:14). But he who thus tabernacled for a short time among men is eternally the Son of Man; he clearly declared that in ascending to the heavens he would prepare a place so that his followers might be with him. In the Father's house, he declared, there are many mansions.

Most consistently, therefore, does the voice from heaven herald the coming to earth of the new Jerusalem, saying, "Behold the tabernacle of God is with men, and he will dwell with them, and they shall be his people, and God himself shall be with them, and be their God."

The End of God's Special Revelation

God himself declared that his special revelation was completed. Begun through the prophets and continued over a period of sixteen centuries it was completed in the unveiling of the Son of God as the redeemer of the world. We are warned of God that his revelation, thus given, is not to be tampered with. The Bible is like a rare work of art. The Artist worked long to bring his design into expression. Finally, he gave it the last touch. Let us, in our ignorance and with our clumsy touch, not presume to improve upon his portrait. So carefully is the Bible picture drawn and so wonderful is its design that it is sheer presumption for man to add to or subtract from it. Let us remember that the portrait of the Artist is for our study. We are not to change it; it is to change us. Those who study it intelligently become aware of its grandeur; for them criticism gives way to admiration, wonder, and worship.

When we say that God's special revelation is complete we do not mean that the Bible says all that might be said, nor that much more knowledge is not in store for God's people. We mean that it is a full unveiling of God and his purposes so far as man's present need and instruction are concerned. In the words of Paul (II Timothy 3:16-17), it is "profitable for doctrine (teaching), for reproof, for correction, for instruction in righteousness: that the man of God may be perfect (complete), throughly furnished unto every good work."

The Word of God and Human Response

Human destiny is determined by what man does about the Word of God. It was so in Eden. It was so regarding the pre-incarnate Word who was the light lighting every man coming into the world. It was so regarding those to whom God sent the prophets. It was so regarding those to whom the Son of God ministered in the flesh. It is so regarding those to whom the gospel is now being given. The Word falls on various kinds of heart soils. In some cases impacted custom forbids the germination of the Word. There is shallowness of purpose in other cases. In many cases there is preoccupation with the world. But from others there is responsiveness, and there are varying degrees of fruitfulness.

The Lord Jesus Christ greatly emphasized the responsibility of those who hear or read his word. The gift of life being for all who believe, destiny depends upon the human response. Our Lord's most celebrated sermon closed with the following picture (Matthew 7:24-27):

> "Therefore whosoever heareth these sayings of mine, and doeth them, I will liken him unto a wise man, which built his house upon a rock: And the rain descended. and the floods came, and the winds blew, and beat upon that house; and it fell not: for it was founded upon a rock. And every one that heareth these sayings of mine, and doeth them not, shall be likened unto a foolish man, which built his house upon the sand: And the rain descended, and the floods came, and the winds blew, and beat upon that house; and it fell: and great was the fall of it."

The Apocalypse repeatedly enjoins this same response, making unmistakable the fact that eternal destiny hinges upon it. To each of the seven churches our Lord closes his message with the admonition: "He that hath an ear, let him hear what the Spirit saith unto the churches." In these letters the appeal, in each case, indicates some particular phase of destiny which depends upon overcoming.

What is meant by overcoming is clear. It does not mean that destiny is dependent upon human self-righteousness. We know from John's epistle (I John 5:1-5) that Christians overcome the world by being born of God, by believing in Jesus as the Son of God, and by their mutual love for one another. We learn also from Revelation 12:11 of those in the Apocalyptic scene who "overcame him (Satan) by the blood of the Lamb, and by the word of their testimony" and who "loved not their lives unto the death." Our ascended Lord, near the close of this last book of Scripture, draws all men with the wooing words:

> "Blessed are they that do his commandments (wash their robes), that they may have right to the tree of life, and may enter in through the gates into the city   .   .   .   .,   .
>
> .   .   .   .
>
> And whosoever will, let him take the water of life freely."

3. Discussion and Review

1. What three distinct needs existed for the continuation of the gospel testimony at the close of the apostolic century? Indicate John's writings which were designed to meet these three needs, respectively.

2. Show from the contents of the Gospel by John how it is designed to lead its readers to believe.

3. Show from the contents of I John what the tests of a genuine Christian are.

4. What bearing did II John have upon the purity of the church in times to come? Of what application is it today?

5. Name three persons of III John who are either approved or disapproved, indicating in each case the reasons.

6. What are the essential tests for church membership according to John's epistles?

7. What would be lacking in our Bibles if the book of Revelation had not been written?

8. What did John see? Tell it in order, as nearly as you can.

9. Show from the last two chapters the fulfillment of the purpose of our Creator-Redeemer God.

10. In what sense may it be said that with this book we have a complete revelation? Complete for what purpose? Does the Bible give you a satisfying basis of faith?

4. Select Memory Passages

John 20:30, 31; I John 1:7; 2:3; 4:1-3; 4:7; 3:10; Rev. 21:7; 22:14

5. Bibliography

Huffman, Jasper A. *The Messianic Hope in the Old and New Testaments.* Chap.
    XVI, "Other Stages in the Messianic Hope." Butler, Ind.: The Higley Press.
Morgan, G. Campbell. *Living Messages of the Books of the Bible.* "The Message
    of Revelation." New York: Fleming H. Revell. Pp. 211-226.
Orr, James. "Revelation of John," The International Standard Bible Encyclopedia.
    Vol. IV. pp. 2582-2587.

SUMMARY

The Biblical Philosophy of History

The Bible begins with God. It continues with what has been predicated of him, that is, with his works. God is the creator, which means that all things owe their existence to him. From highest angels to the smallest cell upon our earth—all is his creation. He caused its existence and it is sustained by him for his purpose. Although he delegated sovereign powers to his creatures, he reigns supremely over all. Nothing, either good or evil, just happens. All power is from him and is accountable to him. Evil is not eternal. While it is temporarily permitted, for reasons not altogether explained to man, it will finally be put away.

Satan, an evil personality whose origin and history are not fully explained to us, has acted the role of the destroyer of God's works; he has been the tempter of man from the dawn of creation. The human family yielded to his lures and has throughout its history been under his dominion. God in his wisdom has not prevented human beings from thus yielding their lives to Satan. Having created man a free being He permitted him the opportunity of exercising his freedom.

God is not represented as having been taken by surprise when the human race turned into a course of sin. On the contrary, the plan of creation also included the provision of redemption. From the "foundation of the world" (Rev. 13:8) the Son of God provided redemptive mercy, even though it was not until after many centuries that he came in the flesh. It was this provision of redemptive mercy which made it possible for God to extend the probation of the human family through the successive generations of history.

The Bible tells a story in three stages. Genesis 1-2 describes a state of harmony in Eden. Genesis 3 to Revelation 20 describes a state of disharmony because of sin together with the application of a program of divine redemption to all who believe. Revelation 21-22 describes a state of harmony under the unrivaled sovereignty of God.

502

The Growth of God's Kingdom

The vital element in human history has been the planting and development of God's kingdom. Whereas the world order was blighted by sin, and was placed under the disciplinary curse of God, redemption has also been operative; in the successive generations of history all who have responded to the Redeemer in faith have come to make up God's kingdom. God's kingdom is not obvious to the world, but it is none the less real. It was more real to men like Daniel than the kingdoms of the Nebuchadnezzars and the Alexanders.

The Word of God in history is not merely a matter of academic interest. It is a powerful force from the Creator himself, creating in free spiritual beings a knowledge of himself and of his will, and providing the incentives calculated to lead all submissive souls into the realm of his blessed dominion. Incidental to this purpose this same Word of God has been the occasion which has ripened impenitent souls in their course of sin. Men like Pharaoh and Judas are, however, not God's product. They are the product of their own choice. They have devoted the very endowments of creation to the destruction of God's kingdom. This being their final choice, eternal damnation must be their final lot.

Although God's kingdom, as a goal in history, has not been obvious to the world, it has been the hope of the faithful in all ages.

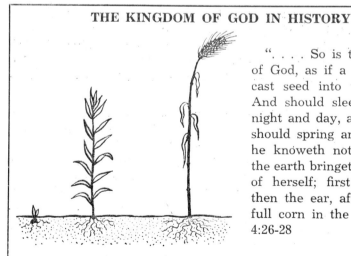

THE KINGDOM OF GOD IN HISTORY

". . . . So is the kingdom of God, as if a man should cast seed into the ground; And should sleep, and rise night and day, and the seed should spring and grow up, he knoweth not how. For the earth bringeth forth fruit of herself; first the blade, then the ear, after that the full corn in the ear." Mark 4:26-28

The very earliest of all prophecies (Genesis 3:15) points to the triumph of man over the Deceiver. Abram was satisfied to be a pilgrim on earth during his lifetime in view of a future time when God's blessing would be realized by all nations of the earth (Genesis 12:1-3), and in view of "a city which hath foundations, whose builder and maker is God" (Hebrews 11:10). Moses was a great leader of the people of Israel under God, but he knew that his leadership was only temporal and that a greater Prophet was to come (Deut. 18:15-18). David was king of Israel but he recognized, in many Psalms, a greater One who was the source of his sovereignty and power. David's important successor was not Solomon, but another whose dominion would never vanish from the earth (II Sam. 7:10-11; Isaiah 7:14; Luke 1:30-33). Daniel, who witnessed the passing of Israel's existence as a free nation was not disheartened; he saw that although the world order would be under the domination of Gentile rulers for many generations beyond his day, there would be a new order beyond the resurrection which he and all the saints of God would share (Daniel 2, 12).

The five centuries following Daniel's day were dark. But in the darkness, hope of the coming Messiah burned continuously as the goal of those who believed. When Jesus was born there was everywhere among those who knew the Scriptures an expectancy that the One foretold was at hand. But many in that generation were disappointed. Although the One who came convinced them by his deeds and words, yet he did not restore the kingdom to Israel. Instead, he died upon a cross. His closest followers, also, were nearly all slain. Yet in spite of this apparent failure, he left his followers with orders pertaining to his kingdom, and he bequeathed to them divine power for a campaign of witnessing to all nations.

The witnesses of Christ were to publish to all peoples the good news of the kingdom in view of the time when the Messiah should manifest himself at the end of the age (Matt. 24:14). Their ministry was interpreted to be an urgent call to reconciliation to God (II Cor. 5:20). Just as John the Baptist and Jesus preached repentance for the remission of sins because the kingdom was at hand, so Christ's witnesses through the present age are to preach reconciliation in view of the king's coming. They are to beseech men, in Christ's stead, saying, "be ye reconciled to God."

Thus while some were disappointed because they wanted the

throne of Zedekiah restored and the Roman yoke thrown off, Jesus had no real set-back to his plans. His procedure was not frustrated by death. He did not change his plans about a kingdom. He was working on schedule all the while. Had the disciples been better pupils they might have learned more about his schedule from what Jesus had taught them. He had clearly said that both evil and good would continue to grow until the end, and that then there would be a harvest. Repeatedly he had pointed to the resurrection, and to the judgment as the events upon which the establishment of his kingdom would rest.

Koheleth, the preacher of the book of Ecclesiastes, set aside all philosophies of life fashioned upon a viewpoint "under the sun." Such philosophies added up only to vanity. Man must plan his life according to a bigger pattern, according to the Creator's pattern. Therefore, Koheleth leaves this timely counsel (12:1-13, 14):

"Remember now thy Creator in the days of thy youth   .   .

.   .   .   .

Let us hear the conclusion of the whole matter: Fear God and keep his commandments: for this is the whole duty of man. For God shall bring every work into judgment, with every secret thing, whether it be good, or whether it be evil."

If by personal experience of redeeming grace we can from our hearts say with the Psalmist, "O how love I thy law," then we give evidence of the divine preparation essential for life in the spiritual climate of God's eternal kingdom.

The Eternal Order

The Bible brings us to the verge of the eternal order, describes that order in only two chapters, and then leaves us to our imagination. God has a way of leading us without overburdening our minds with concern for the future. What we may glean throughout the Scriptures in connection with these final chapters belongs to us, however, and is important to a satisfying philosophy of history as well as to a fully-orbed faith.

Life will not be less real in the eternal order than it is now. It will be more truly real. God's whole creation will then come to its own. The Bible gives no support to the idea that eventually our universe will be snuffed out. Nor does it bear out the pagan notion that materiality will pass away along with evil. Matter is not in itself evil. The heavens and the earth, as the Creator made them, were declared to be very good. The very idea of redemption implies that in the eternal order there will be both terrestrial and celestial orders of being.

The perpetuity of the earth is taught by many scriptures.[1] It is true that there will be cleansing fires of judgment.[2] Malachi describes these fires, saying, "God's wrath shall burn as a furnace, in which all the proud and all that work wickedness shall be as stubble; and the day that cometh shall burn them up;"[3] but at this same time of judgment, Malachi also says, those who fear God's name "shall go forth, and grow up as calves of the stall." This day of God's fiery wrath will not, therefore, destroy the earth nor the righteous who dwell in it.

The eternal perpetuity of men in the flesh is a close corollary to the prospect of a redeemed earth.[4] "It appears clear," concludes David N. Lord,[5] "that the earth is to exist forever under its present great laws; that mankind are to inhabit it and multiply on it in an endless series of generations; and that they are to continue through all their endless successions to cultivate and subsist on its vegetable crops; and thence are to continue in their natural corporeal life."

Our Lord drew out the expectancy of the disciples regarding "many mansions," clearly implying that his redemptive work had to do with vast habitable places which would be prepared for occupation in eternity. Modern astronomy has revealed myriads of worlds although it cannot yet speak of their habitability. But this may well be left to God. If, as seems evident, the human race is to perpetuate itself eternally, God will doubtless have no problem of taking care of the great populations, even though they be more enumerable than the sands of the sea.

Seeking to impress us with the future glory which is to center in this earth, the sainted Thomas M. Chalmers[6] wrote: ". . . . God has never had an opportunity to show man and the universe what a holy race of human beings can be and do. If the propaga-

---

[1] Consider Genesis 8:21, 22; 9:8-13, 16; 17:7, 8; 98:3, 4; Exod. 32:13; II Sam. Romans 8:19-23.

[2] II Peter 3.

[3] Malachi 4:1-3 (ARV).

[4] Consider Genesis 8:21, 22; 9:8-13, 16; 17:7, 8; 48:3, 4; Exod. 32:13; II Sam. 7:10, 16; Luke 1:32, 33; Dan. 4:3, 34; Matt. 5:5; Rom. 4:13.

[5] Lord, David N. Coming and Reign of Christ, pp. 154, 155.

[6] Chalmers, Thomas M. "The Earth the Eternal Seed Plot of the Universe" (ASFPS).

tion of the race is brought to an end at the judgment of the great white throne, then we will never see such a marvelous work of God, a race of men in the flesh dwelling in a renewed earth and utterly apart from sin and unrighteousness. I believe God desires to show this glory to the universe. It will be the true restoration of Eden, the final victory over Satan, when redemption will be fully realized in a holy race.

"Further it is not consonant with the costliness of redemption and with the dignity and majesty of the God-Man, in whom dwells all the fulness of the Godhead bodily that so few should be saved if redemption is not to extend to vast multitudes of men beyond the judgment of the last day. The victory of our Lord over sin and the great Adversary will be far completer if his work of salvation shall embrace countless generations of men through all the ages of eternity. The multitudinous propagation of redeemed men and women in all the future of eternity, born under the (atoning) blood and not owing their uprightness to their own obedience, will contribute tremendously to the fulness of joy in the creatures and to the glory of God."

Dr. S. J. Andrews has left us the following penetrating picture-paragraph of his conception of the ultimate purpose of the universe[1]:

"The universe is what it is because made for Him (Christ); and separated from the divine purpose in Him, its history and destiny cannot be read aright. As seen by science we have only immense masses of matter rolling through space; as seen by the eye of faith, we behold orbs preparing for the habitation of intelligent and spiritual beings made in the likeness of their glorified Lord; orbs into which sin and death can never enter, and from which holy worship, offered in the name of the Son, shall go up forever to the Father of all."

Jonathan Edwards is quoted by Professor James[2] as expressing the following high appraisal of the destiny of a redeemed human being:

"I am bold to say the work in the conversion of one soul, considered together with the source, foundation, and purchase of it, and also the benefit, end, and eternal issue of it is a more glorious work of God than the creation of the whole material universe."

---

[1] Andrews. S. J. *Christianity and Anti-Christianity in Their Final Conflict*, p. 192.

[2] James, William. *Varieties of Religious Experience*, p. 238.

If we multiply this estimation by the countless hosts of redeemed men and women coming into being in endless generations to all eternity, we will form a still vastly greater and nobler conception of the stupendous glory and majesty of the future dominion of our Lord Jesus Christ.

Doubtless if our vision were clearer, we might pierce the eternities and see a perpetually enlarging number of redeemed men and women, getting their beginning on this earth, and then pushing out into the abodes of God's infinite universe. Now our minds and energies are taken up largely with the conflict against evil and with the burdens of the curse. When the earth has been purged, human enterprise will really begin to fulfill its intended purpose. The creatures of earth will groan no more; instead, every one in its way will declare God's glory, and will experience new growth in glory through the ages.

Though our knowledge of eternity is imperfect, enough is revealed to impress us with a sense of the far-reaching significance of the incarnation and the redemptive program of the Son of God. He became the head of a race that will increase, in extent and in glory, in all eternity. Said Isaiah, "Of the **increase** of his government and peace there shall be no end, upon the throne of David, and upon his kingdom, to order it with judgment and with justice from henceforth **even for ever.**" Thus, the hope which Jesus brought to the race corresponds to an eternal purpose. The curtain, at the close of the Bible, is not drawn to terminate human history at the end of the present world order. Rather, the curtain is raised. A redeemed order will embark upon the real beginning of life—life without sin, without a curse—full, and rich, and ever new.

INDEX

Date Due

ERRATA

Page 25, Figure 6—I Peter 2:5 should be II Peter 2:5.

Page 64, map—"Johaz" should be "Jahaz."

Page 73—8th line from top, "ten" should be "nine."

Page 103—Fifth line from top, word "immortality" should be "immorality."

Page 119—Section 2, fourth line, second word should be authorship.

Page 139—Reading Assignment, I Chron. 10 should be I Chron. 1-10.

Page 150—In Reading Assignment, II Kings 1—2:11 should be I Kings 1—2:11.

Page 152—Reference in first column, 6th and 7th lines from bottom (II Sam. 5:24) should be (II Sam. 5:24).

Page 191—In first line, Elisha should be Elijah.

Page 207—In the Reading Assignment, II Kings 8:1-20 should be II Kings 8:16—20:21 and II Chronicles 21:32 should be II Chronicles 21—32.

Page 207—In Collateral Reading add the book of Joel.

Page 213—Second line, word "subscription" should be "inscription."

Page 227—In Reading Assignment add Lamentations.

Page 238—In Reading Assignment, omit I Kings 25.

Page 241—Under caption 5, line 2, the word "time" should be "name."

Page 243—Third line from top, "inquiries" should be "inquirers."

Page 308—In line two from the top, the word "accusation" should be "occasion."

Page 340—Fifth line from top, the word "works" should be "words."

Page 385—In the references under Study Outline, 18:2-12 should be John 18:2-12.

Page 407—In the third line from the bottom, the word "or" should be "of."